WHERE THE FLAMING HELL ARE WE?

Craig Collie is one of Australia's leading writers of military history and author of the critically acclaimed *The Path of Infinite Sorrow, Nagasaki, The Reporter and the Warlords, Code Breakers* and *On Our Doorstep*. He formerly worked as a TV producer–director and was Head of Television Production at SBS.

The Story of Young Australians
and New Zealanders Fighting the Nazis
in Greece and Crete

WHERE THE FLAMING HELL ARE WE?

CRAIG COLLIE

ALLEN&UNWIN
SYDNEY • MELBOURNE • AUCKLAND • LONDON

Allen & Unwin
Cammeraygal Country
83 Alexander Street
Crows Nest NSW 2065
Australia
Phone: (61 2) 8425 0100
Email: info@allenandunwin.com
Web: www.allenandunwin.com

Allen & Unwin acknowledges the Traditional Owners of the Country on which we live and work. We pay our respects to all Aboriginal and Torres Strait Islander Elders, past and present.

A catalogue record for this book is available from the National Library of Australia

ISBN 978 1 76087 919 8

Maps by Mapgraphics
Set in 12.75/16.75 pt Adobe Garamond Pro by Midland Typesetters, Australia
Printed and bound in Australia by the Opus Group

10 9 8 7 6 5 4

The paper in this book is FSC® certified. FSC® promotes environmentally responsible, socially beneficial and economically viable management of the world's forests.

CONTENTS

MAPS

MAPS

'I was out in a little backwater in western Victoria. Never been out of Macarthur. I had an inkling to do better than just be a butcher boy for the rest of my life. I thought this was an opportunity for me to get out. It was just adventure as far as I was concerned, God, King and Country wasn't part of it.'

Vic Hillas, enlisting as an eighteen-year-old in 1939[1]

Part I

PRELUDE

1

BOYS FAR FROM HOME

Down from Newcastle, Bob 'Hooker' Holt was working at a fire station in Sydney when war broke out in 1939. The call went out in November for volunteers, and he hot-footed it to the Marrickville Drill Hall to enlist, giving his age as twenty-one. He was only fifteen but solidly built, so he got away with it. Holt was accepted into the Australian Military Forces 'for service in Australia or abroad'. Like most young men in Australia and New Zealand at the time, he'd never ventured outside his own country. This was an opportunity for excitement and adventure in a world of which he had little knowledge or experience. It wasn't long in coming.

He was soon on his way with the Australian contingent to war in the Middle East. While Holt was on leave in Port Said, a 'guide' attached himself to the fresh-faced, young Australian and showed him around the Egyptian town. They ended up in the overpowering stench of the Arab Quarter where Holt was offered two middle-aged French ladies for a shilling each. Eventually Holt paid off his guide, finding soon after he'd also parted with his wallet and his fountain pen.[1]

About the same time, young New Zealander volunteers were also steaming to the Middle East to join the conflict. Disembarking at Port Tewfik at the bottom of the Suez Canal, Martyn Uren's first impressions of Egypt were equally unfavourable. 'For a place so geographically important,' the newly minted bombardier reported, 'Suez is a singularly filthy and unattractive cess-pool.'[2]

It wasn't a promising start. Uren, an Auckland law clerk, had had no previous contact with Egyptian people but had been primed to expect the worst. If they weren't alert, Kiwis and Aussies were warned by their intelligence officers on the voyage over, Arabs would enter their tents, slit their throats, and steal anything they could sell.[3]

This must have seemed surprising to men on their way to save Egypt from invasion, but this was a country whose people had experienced decades of oppressive British 'protection'. The visiting troops had no knowledge of that, nor any understanding that they weren't there primarily to repel an Italian conquest of Egypt. That was incidental. They were there to prevent the Axis powers, Germany and Italy, getting to Iraq's oilfields, Britain's source of fuel for its war machine. Egypt, the gateway, was de facto occupied by the British, the Suez Canal key to its Middle East strategy. If that was the way it was to be, then Egypt's poor, the vast majority of its people, would grab whatever might be there for the taking.

Marching through villages, the visitors were greeted with a cheery 'Saida [Good day]' by scruffy children skipping alongside. The soldiers waved cheekily at women who averted their gaze and adjusted their veils. Far from habitation, Arab vendors would materialise from nowhere, over a sandhill or out of a wadi (dry riverbed) with oranges and watermelons for sale.[4] Like travellers from another dimension, the young men from the Antipodes had entered a world both exciting and threatening, much of it beyond their understanding.

The Australians and New Zealanders felt besieged by Arabs offering goods for purchase, be they oranges, silks or 'genuine antiquities'. The haggling seemed evidence the hawkers were untrustworthy and out to cheat them. 'In NZ I never used to count my change, here I check over them, double check, then look for the dud coins,' John Westbrook wrote home to Auckland, overlooking that the soldiers tried to pay with Ceylon coins and brass buttons. 'There's hundreds of peddlers and thousands of boot-blacks. If you dare to do as much as look at anything a peddler has, he'll follow you for miles.'[5]

An Australian gunner, Colin Nash, reported in a similar vein. 'Arab boys called *walleds* grin at you from the backs of donkeys,' he wrote. 'Human vultures scrape food in unsanitary gutters or hold out their hand as they see you with diseased eyes.'[6]

The previous generation of Anzacs, en route to Gallipoli, had called Arabs 'wogs'. The new Anzacs revived that term and added 'Gyppos', less clear in its intent.[7] Depending on the attitude of its user, 'Gyppos' could be akin to 'Pommies' or it could convey the same distaste as 'wogs'. Curiously, at some stage the visitors began addressing Arabs as 'George'. Every driver, every boot-black, every hawker was named George. Any disdain was neutralised when Egyptians started calling the soldiers 'George' and it became a sort of shared joke.[8]

To the soldiers, Egypt's cities were bustling and noisy, while a stench pervaded its villages. They were confronted with poverty and misery wherever they went. Bill Thompson recalls the Arab villages consisting of 'mud huts with narrow, dusty lanes running between them. They had no idea of even elementary hygiene. Sanitation or running water was non-existent. They shared their miserable, filthy hovels with pigs, sheep, poultry, goats and rats. The lanes were crawling with dung-beetles,' and yet, 'overall they appeared to be happy and reasonably healthy amid all the filth, and each village produced sufficient crops and fruit from the surrounding fields to meet their food requirements'.[9] For all their disgust, there was often an element of equivocation lurking behind it.

In Egypt, boredom and sickness were the enemy, not the hapless Italians. Any joy from driving them back across the North African desert was lost on plagues of flies, choking dust storms and bouts of dysentery. The desert itself had none of the romantic allure of Foreign Legion stories. Stephanie Lee, a Kiwi nurse, set expectations straight. 'The golden desert people imagine at home is all wrong,' she wrote. 'There is very little of that. The real desert is just bare rocky earth.'[10]

Martyn Uren notes in his diary there is just 'flat featureless desert, dotted everywhere with camel thorn bushes. A more dreary, desolate waste would indeed be hard to imagine.'[11]

But it was the all-enveloping dust storm, called the *khamsin*, that made Egypt especially unbearable. The hot southerly wind blew in from the desert to the military camps near Alexandria and on Cairo's fringe. It lasted two or three days at a time, obscuring the sun and producing a lurid amber fog. All the men could do was wrap a towel around their heads and wait for it to blow through. Yellow dust, fine as flour, got into everything: eyes, noses and throats; stomachs and lungs; wristwatches and the gearboxes and oil sumps of trucks.[12] Even food got covered. Arthur Helm, a signaller from Invercargill, noted after one sandstorm, 'Breakfast was a sorry meal, consisting of porridge and sand, bacon, eggs and sand, tea and sand, and bread and butter and sand.'[13]

The camps were places of transit: Australians on the way to or from driving the Italians back in Libya; New Zealanders standing by in reserve or driving trucks to the front line. Units moved out on such short notice that no one cleaned up before they went. That was left to the next occupants.

So far from home, soldiers would often find themselves sitting in tents with nothing to do. The picture theatre in one camp didn't help, showing inferior movies with frequent breakdowns. Built from old kerosene tins and sacking, it was easy enough to get in for free by tearing holes in the sacking, but management worked that out and closed the cinema for repairs. Incensed at losing their only entertainment in the camp, Australian soldiers burnt the theatre down.[14]

A leave pass to Egypt's two vibrant cities was a more successful answer to soldiers' restlessness, although it introduced new problems. From Britain's far-flung empire, these young men absorbed the exotic surrounds of Cairo in different ways. The more serious took in the classical edifices they'd previously seen only in picture books, the pyramids and the Sphinx. Others enjoyed Cairo's cosmopolitan cafes, the bright, attractive bars, and restaurants with colourful awnings over tables on broad pavements. Or they went to the races at Gezira and Heliopolis.

Still others, not least of all 'Hooker' Holt, let off steam in 'the Berka', the main street of Wagh El Birket, the red-light district. Three- and four-storey buildings ran down one side, working ladies in flimsy gowns parading on upper floor balconies.[15] That was something they didn't see in the cities and towns back home. Across the street were cafes, drinking shops and more brothels.

To manage the incidence of venereal disease, which had been a serious problem in the First World War, the military set up brothels controlled by its Medical Corps, which oversaw regular check-ups of prostitutes by local authorities.[16] Back in their camps, the soldiers were regularly checked too. Although VD was a major health problem with troops in the Middle East, nearly 5 per cent of them ending up infected, it was a considerable improvement on the 14 per cent infection rate of 1914–18.[17]

Alexandria, Egypt's other sprawling modern city, catered for all ranks. For officers, there was a veneer of refinement at Mary's House, a stately Italianate mansion with a long marble-topped bar, attended by white-jacketed stewards.[18] An informal club where a chap could go for a drink in civilised surroundings, it was also a brothel for officers. At the Femina Club, twenty-odd hostesses danced with customers, persuaded them to buy drinks, and kept their ears and eyes open for military intelligence they could sell to interested parties.[19]

The city offered the same cosmopolitan attractions as Cairo and matched its seamy side. 'Sister Street', an alleyway between long rows of tenements, had brothels and low dives, each door and window filled with prostitutes. Ken Clift ventured there with two fellow signallers he'd known from Sydney club rugby, Harry Searl and 'Tiny' Dunbar.

'Harry was the best-looking of the three of us,' Clift recalls, 'and a girl caught his eye. She was Lulu. French-Moorish extraction.' Inside, the three corporals found coffee, cakes and romantic music. 'I was only getting the water off my chest, but it was different for Harry. He was falling in love.'

In the swarming, boisterous street outside, a two-up game would be set up, the working ladies joining in and betting from their balconies. If a girl won, the soldier threw her winnings up to her amid cheers and shouts; if she lost, he went upstairs and recovered his winnings in kind.

Harry Searl was oblivious to all this. According to Clift, 'Lulu was still on the town, but she gave him nude photographs of herself and whenever we came back to camp, she'd be waiting for him.'[20] Or so it seemed to Searl.

In the British high command, Australians and New Zealanders had a reputation from the First World War as hell-raisers, given to rowdy behaviour, drunkenness and a refusal to follow orders. Concerned about this, the Middle East commander-in-chief, General Archibald Wavell, addressed the first Australian contingent on arrival at Suez. Egyptians were apprehensive of Australian behaviour, he said. 'I look to you to show them that their notions of Australians as rough, wild, undisciplined people given to strong drink are incorrect.'[21]

Many of the arriving troops, volunteers and proud of it, resented this sermon. Their feeling was that it should be their own General Blamey to address them on these matters, not some puffed-up Pommie.

Wavell might have found it hard to convince himself that his words of warning had much effect anyway. It started in Palestine where the Australians in 1940 were training for battle in the North African desert. Off duty, they were getting restless and bored with little to do. In March, Colonel George Vasey on Blamey's divisional staff felt compelled to lament, 'Our troops have been behaving on leave as the *Bulletin* and *Smiths* and other papers have illustrated them as behaving for the last twenty-five years.' It made him 'ashamed to wear the uniform'.[22]

Italy joined Germany at war with the Allies in June 1940 and advanced from its colony, Libya, into British-ruled Egypt. By the end of the year, the Italians had been pushed back to the Libyan border by a division from India. Australians relieved the Indians around Bardia, a small coastal town just over the border. On 5 January 1941, Bardia fell in the first major Australian action of the war, and a new issue reared its ugly head.

Looting in North Africa had started before the Australians arrived, by Italians and then by 'natives' (Libyans and Arabs), but the practice was continued by Australians. The provost (military police) unit diary notes on 31 January, 'Considerable amount of looting being carried on by both natives and Australian soldiers', and on 1 February, 'Looting still being carried on mostly by Australian soldiers.'[23] After Bardia, General Iven Mackay, commanding the Australians in Libya, was critical of his unit commanders for allowing soldiers to dress 'in articles of Italian uniform like clowns and not like soldiers'.[24]

Before they'd even gone to Bardia, signaller Ken Clift and his mate 'Blue' Knight-Smith 'borrowed' a Signals truck and took it to Alexandria. They were drinking at the Paradise bar when the air raid sirens howled. The proprietor, staff and customers dashed to the nearest shelter, but the two Australians made a snap decision. They emptied the deserted bar of scotch, gin, advocaat and anything else they could put their hands on, stacked it in the truck and headed back to camp. On the way they stopped off at the Polish regiment's camp and shared the spoils of their night with Poles they had befriended. Clift and Knight-Smith were put on charge for AWL (absent without leave), but there was no proof the abandoned Signals truck had been taken by them.[25]

The night out typified the wilder elements of the Australian and New Zealand forces. Leave in Cairo and Alexandria enabled a release from military discipline, where young men who'd never intended to be soldiers could let their hair down. Aggression, thieving and property damage became recurring problems. Gunner Ralph Nicholson's diary records with no sense of shame: 'Bones, Eric and I went round the streets lassoing wogs. Also swiped a couple of chairs and several trees.'[26] When a cabbie wouldn't take Frank Cox and 'Ned' Kelly back to Amiriya camp, Kelly brandished a .45 revolver and growled, 'It's Amiriya or hell!'[27] One appalled soldier reports personally seeing servicemen not paying the taxi fare, then beating up the driver and overturning his cart, robbing cigarette street vendors of their wares, accosting ordinary women with 'How about a fuck?' and refusing to pay prostitutes for services rendered.[28]

Fights would break out, mostly among the Australians and New Zealanders and often with provosts. 'It was easier to get into a fight than to avoid one,' recalls James Barclay, a Kiwi lieutenant. 'It only took one cross word and you could be in a fight that involved fifty people in no time at all.'[29]

On one occasion, Reg Saunders, a twenty-year-old sergeant who was Aboriginal, and his mate Mick Baxter took a taxi to Alexandria. They sipped cheap beer, watched belly dancers and visited various cafes. Outside a restaurant, four British soldiers asked Baxter, 'Where's your pal from, Digger?'

'Where d'ya bloody well think, mate? That's an Australian uniform, isn't it?'

One of them said to Saunders, 'You're not an Aussie. You're a nigger. Where you from?'

Baxter threw a punch and a fight broke out until the military police arrived and they all scattered.[30]

Australian and New Zealand troops resented being spoken to by British military police, who were generally stricter on minor offences like not saluting, smoking in the street, or drunkenness. 'We tolerated our own provosts,' says one soldier. 'They were bad enough, but we wouldn't have a bar of these Pommie Red Caps. They were bastards.'[31]

Unruly behaviour, particularly in Cairo and Alexandria, was confined to a small but visible minority. The troublemakers had often joined their unit late and had limited training. Some had a criminal record. 'Time and again we arrested the same men or ordered them back to their barracks,' says Max Jones of Provost Corps. 'It got to the point where we knew when we were going to have a busy night just by knowing which units were due on leave.'[32]

Entrenched disdain for Egyptians and the hubris of battle-field success didn't help. What did help ease the problem was the rumour that, after victories at Bardia and Tobruk, the Australians would be moving to a new battle area. Speculation ran within the New Zealand Division that it was going to the Balkans. The men's battledress uniform, for cooler climates, was replaced with pith helmets—did that mean they were going to East Africa instead, to deal with the Italians there?—then re-issued with the battledress.[33]

On 6 March, a New Zealand battalion received orders for sailing the next day to an unstated destination. Three days of torrential rain had turned the dust of the military camp into slush, so they weren't unhappy to be going. At six in the morning, they marched three kilometres laden with gear to a railway siding, then journeyed by train to Alexandria's docks. Embarked on the Royal Navy cruisers, *Orion* and *Ajax*, they were under way shortly after midday, sliding past lines of French warships that had been spirited away from Toulon before the advancing Germans could get them.[34]

This was the beginning of a staggered transfer of Australian and New Zealand fighting men and equipment and English armoured units across the eastern Mediterranean. They didn't know it but they were being sent to stop the German blitzkrieg from rolling into and across Greece. New Zealand units, already in Egypt in reserve, were to go first, followed by Australian units, which were being brought back from the front in Libya.

Planning by Movement Control in Britain's Middle East GHQ was determined by convenience of loading. There was no consultation with Australian or New Zealand commanders, like General Thomas Blamey. Both countries were regarded as no more than colonies whose armies could be deployed as Great Britain saw fit. The piecemeal transfer would take five more weeks, the quickest that the British could make shipping available. Units were still coming across the Mediterranean when the German onslaught began.

Within four days of the first New Zealand battalion's departure, two more Kiwi battalions had left Alexandria for parts unknown, on a cargo ship and two converted passenger ships. Once at sea, each soldier was given a sealed envelope with a message from the commander of the New Zealand contingent, General Bernard Freyberg, explaining to the Kiwi soldiers that they were going to Greece because Germany had vowed to smash the British Empire.[35]

On 14 March, New Zealanders still in Egypt were ordered to be ready to leave on forty-eight hours' notice. The rumoured destination was Greece but nobody knew why. Three days later, an Australian battalion's leave in Alexandria was cut short. On the night before each embarkation, military police stormed through the cafes and other places troops were known to frequent, shouting at the men to return to camp so they could move out in the morning.

Regulars at the Femina Club first heard from its obliging hostesses that one of Australia's three divisions then in the Middle East was going to Greece.[36] Staying in a boarding house, Private Don Stephenson was told by his landlady that he had to go back to camp.

'You're going to Greece today,' she said.[37] Private Vic Solomon wrote in his diary that he worked out where they were going from a 'money-changer coming on board and offering to change our money into Greek currency'.[38]

Three more New Zealand battalions set out, along with the first three from Australia. The English skipper on *Bankura* was surprised to find he was taking Australian infantry as he had expected to be loading three hundred mules for Greece. The ship's holds were fitted out for the mules and there were no facilities for eating or washing by a human cargo. The men slept and cooked on the steel deck. Latrine seats and buckets had been ordered but didn't arrive. The only facilities available on the four-day voyage were three 'squatters'.[39]

Alexandria was the British Mediterranean Fleet's base, its harbour choked with shipping. Destroyers rushed in and out through small craft scuttling in all directions: naval service boats, feluccas and dhows. The transports and their warship escort that made up the convoys to Greece had to thread their way through the maritime melee. Soldiers were stood to attention and bugles blown as they passed each vessel at the anchorage flying the White Ensign. Then they waited in mid-harbour for other components of the convoy to be readied.

On 31 March, troops boarded the Dutch ocean liner *Pennland*. Packed with 2500 Australian soldiers—two battalions and an artillery regiment—when its normal capacity was 1500, the overloaded ship moved into the centre of the harbour and stayed on a buoy until the whole convoy was ready to leave the following afternoon.[40]

Still, they were moving on and soldiers were glad to be looking for excitement somewhere new. An Australian's inspired work captured the mood of many:

Land of flies and sweaty socks.
Sun and sin and sand and rocks;
Streets of sorrow, streets of shame,

Streets for which we have no name;
Harlots, thieves and pestering wogs,
Dust and stink and slinking dogs;
Blistering heat and aching feet,
Gyppo gripes and camel meat;
Clouds of choking dust that blinds,
Droves of flies and shattered minds.
Arabs' heaven, soldiers' hell,
Land of Bastards, fare thee well.[41]

Every day or two from 6 March until 10 April, a convoy set out for Greece from Alexandria's crowded naval base, taking troops and their equipment—trucks, Bren gun carriers, artillery—in requisitioned passenger liners and cargo ships with a warship escort. Some convoys made the journey without incident, the men playing euchre and crown-and-anchor for cigarettes, sleeping on blankets and cooking with primuses on the deck. Others weren't so lucky.

Hellas and the smaller *Marit Maersk*, packed with New Zealanders, set out on a blue, unruffled sea. Early on the second morning, a gale blew up, tossing men and gear about. A water truck in the hold broke loose and crashed against other trucks; the contents of portable toilets sloshed across the deck. The storm and its huge waves continued through the day, the ships eventually sheltering off Crete and anchoring overnight.

By morning the tempest had passed and the battered fleet put into Suda Bay in Crete to disembark two casualties, and for the troops to sort out and dry their belongings. All was calm again that night, as if the storm's fury had only been imagined, and the convoy steamed towards Piraeus, the port for Athens.[42]

The Mediterranean's fickle weather was not a convoy's greatest concern, however. As it approached Greece, it came within range of Italian and German warplanes coming from airfields in southern

Italy and the Italian-occupied Dodecanese islands in the Eastern Aegean Sea. They were tangible reminders that there was a war on.

To the men though, this was an adventure as much as a duty; they had volunteered to be here. The upside of the looser discipline in Australian and New Zealand soldiers that grated with English high command was a willingness to improvise, to sort something out. On many of the ships, troops brought their Vickers machine guns up to the decks, or fetched Bren guns and anti-tank rifles from the trucks below. They were strapped to deck rails as additional anti-aircraft defence.

The Australians on the mule transport *Bankura* mounted Brens on the deck, as well as a Breda machine gun captured in Libya. The ship's captain was unhappy when they fired off a few rounds and had the guns near his cabin removed. As *Bankura* moved into Greek waters, five Italian Caproni bombers attacked. They were eventually driven off by the temporary armaments, but not before they hit a tanker and left it in flames. The chastened skipper asked for the guns to be positioned back near his cabin, but the Italians didn't return.[43]

'Lofty' Fellows, a Kiwi private, remembers an air attack on *Hellas* on the way to Greece. 'All hell broke loose. They dropped torpedoes, and every gun was firing. The destroyers were a marvellous sight, heeling over at a fifty-degree angle as they fired, and the spray flying everywhere. And this went on for about two hours, they kept coming in and getting beaten off, coming in, beaten off, no direct hits, all torpedo attacks. And then it just faded out, and we thought, hello, that's good, they're all going home.

'And then way up in the sky, it seemed to be about twenty thousand feet up, we saw two planes coming, getting closer and closer, our guns were firing at them but they kept sailing along. And then a great big thing that looked like a yellow pig dropped out of each plane, you could see them coming down, they were so big.'

The two bombs fell behind Fellows' ship.[44]

Over time the soldiers' exhilaration would wear thin, along with the convoys' luck. On 1 April, unit advance parties with trucks and Bren gun carriers left Alexandria on *Devis*, *Cingalese Prince* and *Kohistan*. Also in the convoy of eight merchant ships were *Clan Fraser* and *Northern Prince*, carrying ammunition, gunpowder and TNT for Greece's munitions factories and its army. The merchant ships were in various states of repair. Guy Ashfold, an Australian Bren gunner, noted *Kohistan* was 'chipped and rusted in every creaking joint, while many improvisations on the deck left all in doubt as to her sea-worthiness'.[45]

By 4 pm, with all vehicles loaded, the convoy moved out 10 kilometres and anchored until dark. Warned that air attacks had been increasing, the men roped automatic weapons at every vantage point. *Devis* had only three guns and they were there to ward off sea attack, but the added army guns made no difference in the end. On the first afternoon, a German bomber hit the freighter, killing eight Australians on its crowded deck, and wounding five others. The ship itself suffered only minor damage.

Improvised defences were effective on other ships, army gunners on *Kohistan* keeping it undamaged while a destroyer in the escort shot down planes. For the rest, it was something to be endured. 'You just held onto your hat and hoped that it didn't hit you,' says Frank Roy, a driver, 'that's about all you could do. You were like a rat in a trap. Nowhere to go; nowhere to hide.'[46]

The attack enabled Bren gunners on board the ships to develop practical teamwork under pressure, cold comfort perhaps to those on *Devis*. At dawn the next day, all hands assembled on that vessel's deck, the padre's surplice blowing in the wind while 'The Last Post' sounded and eight bodies were lowered into the sea as a destroyer fired a salvo.[47]

It was a sombre reminder that nowhere is safe in a war zone. Indeed, the convoy's misfortune wasn't over. A midday raid by fourteen enemy planes a day later sank the munitions freighter

Northern Prince. The other munitions ship in the convoy, *Clan Fraser*, made it to Piraeus safely.

Crossing the Mediterranean, Australian officers spread out maps in one ship's saloon, studying routes into Yugoslavia and on into Austria. This supreme confidence would soon have a blowtorch applied to it. They were yet to grasp that the German army, the Wehrmacht, was a different proposition from the Italian army they had just sent packing.

The men were meanwhile being coached into seeing Greek people in a different light from Egyptians. The Greeks, Captain 'Bully' Hayes told the unit on board the *Devis*, recovering from its fatal bombing, have a splendid military tradition. They were presently belting the Italians, and had beaten Turks and Persians in the past. 'They don't all run fish and chip shops,' he said, 'but be aware that they put turpentine in their wine, ouzo is best left alone, and their beer is watery stuff like that horse piss from New South Wales.'[48] This battalion had been recruited in Victoria.

Not much of this sunk in, but as troopships moved slowly up the Saronic Gulf, past rocky islets draped with golden flowers and along the Attica coast in the approach to Piraeus, these soldiers from the southern hemisphere, no matter which state of Australia or island of New Zealand they came from, saw something in this coastline that resembled home. For New Zealanders, the first sight of tree-clad hills backed by rugged snow-capped mountains could be North or South Island. Victorians could imagine the Great Ocean Road running along the clifftop. To New South Welshmen, the hard light and grey-green trees, some of them eucalypts, on sheer coastal cliffs were what they imagined would have greeted James Cook nearly two centuries before.

And so on, state by state.

Piraeus was a grimy, bustling port, its foreshore lined with warehouses and shipping offices. Greeks forced out of Asia Minor by the Turks in the 1920s, and refugees from elsewhere in the Balkans, lived in the crowded suburbs behind the port and worked in the local factories. Down on the docks, trucks and Bren carriers that came from Egypt with the advance parties were swung from decks and holds to the quayside, to be taken into Athens for new camouflage, the colours of the North African desert to be painted over with patchy grey-green and brown to blend with the hills and forests of Greece.

A few days later, the infantrymen would arrive, pouring off the temporary troopships onto the bustling dockside and cobblestoned streets, where they sorted through piles of haversacks, personal arms and cooking gear. Some of the gear was put on trucks there to meet them, the rest packed away compactly onto the soldiers' backs or slung over their shoulders.

The Greek flag seemed to fly from every building and fishing shack. Local residents came excitedly from all directions down to the quay to welcome the visitors. An Australian band played 'Waltzing Matilda' and then 'The Woodpecker Song', the tune used for a popular ditty with lyrics reviling Mussolini. The Greeks screamed with delight at the band's choice.[49] The Greek army had driven off an attempted Italian invasion a few months before and patriotic fervour was high.

Germany might have been at war with Britain but it wasn't yet with Greece. Germany's military attaché, dressed like an Englishman in tweeds, wandered around the quayside greeting Australian and New Zealand units as they landed. His English was good enough to fool some officers, who spoke to him freely, mistaking him with his talk about fox hunting for an exiled country gentleman. Mingling with the crowd, his staff made notes of the equipment being unloaded. Of particular interest were the Bren carriers, light armoured vehicles on caterpillar tracks, like an open tank.[50]

The carriers were paraded through Athens' streets, but when they were steered across tram tracks, they slid in unintended directions. Thinking the sharp pivot turns were a display of the drivers' prowess, the crowd cheered and clapped in appreciation. When the carrier drivers worked out the cause of their problem, they carefully skirted the tram tracks.[51]

Over the five-week period of March through to April, each cohort of landed troops was greeted with a grateful enthusiasm that never waned. The streets were lined with crowds holding up blue and white flags and crying out, '*Kaliméra* [Good morning]' in welcome. Children ran alongside chopping the air with their hands in mock execution and shouting, 'Mussolini!' Old men standing on the footpath clapped and called out a more dignified, 'Bravo!' Women threw flowers and offered sweets and cigarettes and small glasses of cool water or wine. The shout went out, '*Niki! Niki stous Afstralous!* [Victory! Victory to the Australians!]', even when they were New Zealanders marching past. The troops noticed a distinctive Greek wave of welcome, palm upwards as if beckoning them in. For the young men from afar, just arrived from the strangeness of Egypt, it was exhilarating. Robert Newbold, an artillery lieutenant, wrote home of the wild, cheering crowds, who 'thought of us as saviours and we felt the same'.[52]

The enemy was certain, but not yet Germany. Greece's impassioned hatred poured onto one man. From time to time, the cheering crowd broke into the current satirical song, '*Koroido* Mussolini [Sucker Mussolini]', two fingers drawn across the throat with each mention of Il Duce's name. It was the tune played by the Australian band at Piraeus, 'The Woodpecker Song', a popular American song of the time. Greeks, however, had co-opted the song in its original form as a 1939 Italian song called '*Reginella Campagnola* [Country Queen]', adding extra bite to the satire, a sentimental Italian song to mock the Italian dictator.[53]

A couple of times, the New Zealanders marching through Athens to their camp passed morose groups of Italian prisoners shuffling in the opposite direction on the other side of the street, a thousand or more in each group, hissed at by the locals. On their way through the city, the Kiwis also passed the German Embassy with two large red swastika banners hanging from the balcony and jack-booted sentries standing in the doorway, taking no more apparent notice of the passing military than they would of a passing ox-cart.

Notwithstanding the public venom injected into the satirical song, a delicate round of charades was in play. Greece was already at war with Italy, having driven Mussolini's attempted invasion back to Albania, but wasn't at war with Germany. Britain and her dominions were at war with both Germany and Italy and the landing of British troops in Greece, ostensibly to assist in keeping the Italians at bay, was in the expectation that Greece would soon be dragged into conflict with the Germans.

_____

Australian and New Zealand infantry were in separate transit camps, the New Zealanders 15 kilometres east of Athens among cypresses and pines on the lower slopes of Mount Hymettus. The Kiwis were driven through green cultivated fields sweeping up to snow-covered hills to get there, reminding them again of home. When they reached the camp, they found tents set up by Cypriot Pioneers, who, along with Palestinians, had been brought in by the British as an army labour force. The new arrivals slept soundly on beds of grass, surrounded by the scent of pine and wild thyme.

Most of the Australians marched to their camp on a hillside at Daphni, among olive trees and little white houses. They had a view down a valley to the Acropolis, towering over the city of Athens. Enjoying the same simple comforts as their compadres from across the Tasman, the Aussies too dwelt on all the little reminders of home.

'We are living in tents. It is something like Warburton [a popular bush camping spot in Victoria] here, only the timber is very much smaller,' wrote thirty-year-old machine-gun sergeant Archie Fletcher to his family in Melbourne. 'Today has been glorious, just like an early spring day at home.'[54]

'I enjoyed my nice clean bed on the grass at Daphni,' adds Sydneysider Jack McCarthy. 'I crawled into it and was soon asleep to the wind in the trees.'[55]

And infantry officer Charlie Green recalls, 'Instead of awaking with eyes, ears and noses full of sand we breathed pure crisp air with the scent of flowers. Flowers! We hadn't seen them since leaving Australia.'[56]

Greeks roamed around the camp at Daphni, friendly and hospitable, in stark contrast to 'the grimy, cadging, thieving mobs of Cairo'. For the soldiers, it was a change to find people delighted that they were there. Children ran about the camp, making friends with these fit, bronzed military men from across the seas. Village women offered to wash, iron and mend clothes for a small fee or for bully beef and biscuits. If they were given two cans of bully beef, one came back as a pie. Beautifully laundered shorts and shirts were returned with little sprigs of lavender between the folds.

The welcome was stirring, but scavenging by Greek people of all ages and the appeal for bully beef, the standard military ration of corned beef, indicated hunger was rife. Archie Fletcher was shocked to see 'respectable-looking old women' wandering around the camp, picking up broken army-issue biscuits the Australians had discarded.[57]

There was another kind of visitor too, to both Daphni and Hymettus, a dapper civilian strolling around the tents with two dachshunds. The German ambassador had unrestricted access. The Greek government, anxious not to provide Germany with an excuse to attack, maintained the fiction that the British military was there to support the battle against Italy, and Germany was happy to play along with the pretence while it too prepared for battle. Each day, the German consul drove through the camps, his staff noting particulars of units as they arrived and left.[58]

Leave for the troops was sometimes slow to come, in which case the Australians took unofficial leave into the nearby village. No steps were taken to prevent it. 'Every second house in Daphni seemed to be a cafe,' says Ken Clift. 'They look the same as an ordinary house and in you toddle and have a drink of wine or beer.'[59] Both were very cheap, the beer malty and not very intoxicating. Officially they weren't allowed to enter civilian homes, but many were invited home by the locals. Clift was offered a hot bath by an elderly couple who lived near the camp.

Once a battalion had settled into the transit camp, its troops were given leave, generally three days. Warned like schoolboys of German fifth columnists, contaminated water and the prevalence of VD, and reminded of the obligation to salute Greek officers, they drew their pay in drachmas and headed into Athens.

The streets there teemed with Australian, New Zealand and British servicemen. They were constantly greeted with shouts of 'Kaliméra [Good morning]', 'Niki! [Victory!]' or 'Afstraloi, kalí týchi [Australians, good luck]'. Charlie Green recalls 'civilians dressed as we used to dress before the war—civilians you could trust, in every way a contrast to the Middle East'.[60]

Chester Wilmot, there to report on the war for ABC radio, saw things no differently. 'We're in a country where you can walk round the streets for hours without being besieged by touts or seedy youths selling dirty postcards,' he wrote.[61] Wrote, but didn't broadcast. Australia's military censors removed any criticism of its allies before a report was allowed to be broadcast.[62]

There was a deeper reason for the Greek admiration of these robust soldiers from the south. Australians and New Zealanders tended to the view that a person's authority had to be earned, and was not just a consequence of rank, however that is gained. Greek society was highly stratified with little interaction between the classes. The hoi polloi respected the visitors for their egalitarian behaviour, their half-hearted salutes and willingness to socialise with people from all walks of life.

From the outset, the soldiers fraternised with ordinary Greek people to a degree that was unimaginable in Egypt. When Bill

Ritchie, a New Zealand driver on leave in Athens, went with a group into a barber shop, the Greeks inside got out of their chairs and offered them to the Kiwis, insisting they get their hair cut first.[63] Shops and restaurants were out to attract trade, displaying signs like 'English spoken', Union Jacks and menus in English with imagined favourites such as 'baconised eggs'.

The people continued their warm welcome on the streets by buying the visitors drinks. In Greek society, alcohol was widespread but consumed in moderation; Greeks rarely got drunk. Although beer wasn't a problem for the troops on leave, because it wasn't too strong, other drinks were unfamiliar and could be damaging: mavrodaphne, a dark purple fortified wine; ouzo, the anise-flavoured spirit; and konjac, a Greek brandy. However, alcoholic indiscretions by the visitors were generally brushed away.

Athenians were constantly looking to assist. Newcastle infantry-man, Jack Smithers, describes a typical interaction in his diary. A civilian offered to show his group around. At a cafe, their guide told them a party of young Greek men on a nearby table were having a final fling before going into the army the next day. Some of the young men came over to the table of Aussies and chattered excit-edly in Greek. 'The guide explained that they were thanking us for coming to Greece to fight for them,' Smithers wrote.[64]

They had some contact with Greek soldiers, but for the most part they were either Evzones—the Royal Guard in short kilt, tasselled slippers and long white stockings—or casualties from the fighting in Albania, some with the toes cut out of their boots to ease the pain of frostbite. There were noticeably few young men in civilian clothes in Athens. The bulk of the Greek army was bogged down in Albania's freezing mountains or guarding the frontier with Bulgaria. Many of the older people wore black armbands for sons lost fighting the Italians. The reading of casualty lists on Athens' street corners was accompanied by women weeping and screaming.

As the campaign progressed, Ken Clift would meet Greek conscripts who 'had a mixture of small arms which must have come out of the Ark, a few ancient trucks, a conglomeration of bandoliers, different sized ammunition, some mules and Christ only knows who fed them. However, they had unbounded faith in Greece and optimism for their future and their ability to drive off the aggressors. God help them, we thought, the poor misguided bastards!'[65] It would prove an ironic observation.

In January 1941, Bulgaria agreed to allow German troops free passage to its border with Greece. A month later, after delays through the freezing winter of 1940–41, the Wehrmacht's Twelfth Army crossed the Danube. There was no doubt Germany was gearing up to attack Greece and extricate Italy, its ally, from the stalemate in Albania. Germany may well have had other strategies in mind too. British troops were being pulled out of North Africa to assist Greece resist the anticipated invasion. When the transfer from Egypt began, two panzer divisions were already stationed near the Bulgarian–Turkish border.

After three or four days in a transit camp, each New Zealand and Australian unit was transported north on a staggered schedule to meet the anticipated invasion on a defensive line determined by British high command. Running roughly north–south, the line stretched about 120 kilometres from Mount Olympus in central Greece along the Vermion Range, a chain of mountains with three gaps, to the Yugoslav border. It was generally known as the Aliakmon Line, even though it did no more than cross the Aliakmon River at one point. The line had no existing fortifications and was little more than a line sketched on a map. New Zealand forces were to be positioned around Olympus Pass and the coast at its southern end, and Australians in the centre around Veria Pass. Greek units already in the region were to cover the northern section.

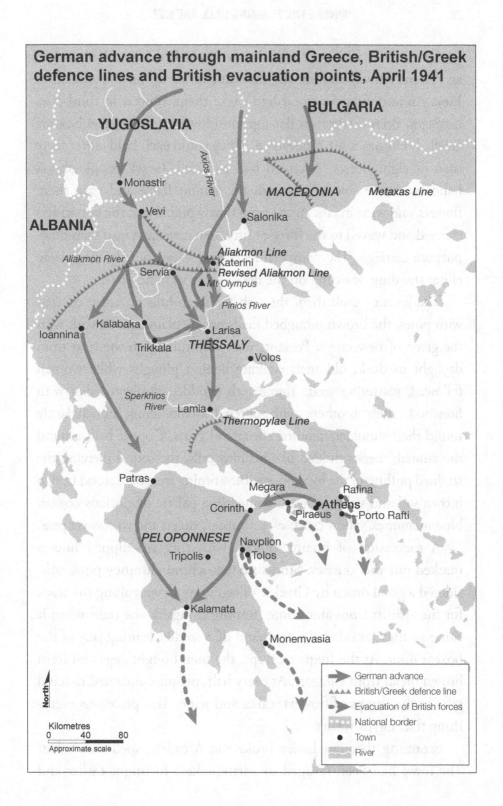

German advance through mainland Greece, British/Greek defence lines and British evacuation points, April 1941

BULGARIA

YUGOSLAVIA

Axios River

● Monastir

MACEDONIA   *Metaxas Line*

ALBANIA   ● Vevi

● Salonika

Aliakmon Line

Aliakmon River   ● Katerini

Servia ●   *Revised Aliakmon Line*

▲ Mt Olympus

Pinios River

Ioannina ●   Kalabaka ●   ● Larisa

Trikkala ●   *THESSALY*

● Volos

Sperkhios River   Lamia ●

Thermopylae Line

Patras ●

Megara   Rafina ●

Corinth ●   **Athens**

Piraeus ●   ● Porto Rafti

PELOPONNESE   Navplion ●

Tripolis ●   ● Tolos

● Kalamata

● Monemvasia

North

Kilometres
0   40   80
Approximate scale

German advance
British/Greek defence line
Evacuation of British forces
National border
● Town
River

On 13 March, New Zealanders were trucked from Hymettus to an Athens railway station, the first unit to set up on the Aliakmon Line. An ancient train stood by to take them: officers in third-class carriages, Bren carriers on flat-tops and lower ranks in steel boxcars labelled 'Hommes 40, Chevaux 8'. They could each hold either forty men or eight horses. A crowd had gathered. Greek people shook hands with the soldiers through the station fence and gave them flowers, and wine in jars. As the train slowly pulled out, the bystanders cheered and waved to the forty or fifty men crammed into each dual-purpose carriage. The compartments were clean but the men were either standing or sitting on the floor. There were no seats.

The journey took them through the steep hills of Attica covered with pines, the brown ploughed fields on the plain a patchwork with the green of new crops. Peasants were seen toiling on the land from daylight to dusk, old men walking behind ploughs while women followed, scattering seed. Young girls prodded donkeys laden with firewood, their brothers with tattered cloaks slung nonchalantly round their shoulders tending sheep and goats. Copper bells around the animals' necks tinkled like bellbird calls, the sound piercing the strained puffing of the locomotive. Blossoming fruit trees stood in rich brown soil and wild flowers bloomed in a palette of glorious colour: blue anemones, yellow crocuses, primroses, violets and wild sweet peas.

A succession of quaint villages with tiny red-topped houses marked out the journey. Storks nested behind chimney pots, considered a good omen by Greeks. Villagers lay in wait along the track for the visitors from afar, some running alongside the train when it came so they could shake the hand of a soldier leaning out of the boxcar door. At the frequent stops, the men bought eggs and fresh brown bread from villagers. At every halt, people continued to hand gifts to the troops of flowers, cakes and wine. This place was everything that Egypt wasn't.

Steaming through Larisa broke the Arcadian spell somewhat. The town had been ravaged by earthquake a fortnight earlier and its streets were littered with debris. Balconies had collapsed, walls cracked and 19,000 of its 24,000 inhabitants had been left homeless. Soon after the disaster, Italian aircraft had pointlessly bombed the devastated town.

From Larisa, the locomotive climbed through rocky gorges in mountainous country as the hues of the setting sun slid in. The snow-capped peak of Olympus towered over them, the black pines on the lower slopes contrasting starkly with the white gleam above. As night fell, the troops found it difficult to find room to stretch out and sleep comfortably. Some were battling with diarrhoea from an over-indulgence in Athenian wine, others had brought something to fortify themselves. The night was cold and there was light snow at dawn as the train rounded Mount Olympus to Katerini on its northern slopes.

Seven kilometres from Greece's east coast, Katerini was at the southern end of the Aliakmon Line. Some eight hundred Kiwis were billeted temporarily in empty houses, barns, the local school and with Greek families. Nothing had been prepared on the line itself—no defences, no placement of troops worked out. After battalion headquarters were set up in a Katerini municipal building, Colonel John Gray and his unit commanders left the town to survey the area allocated to them to defend, figuring out who to put where. They were gone for three days.

Off duty, the soldiers mooched around the town, followed every-where by inquisitive crowds. They were friendly and hospitable but less demonstrative than in Athens. The Kiwis mingled with the civilians, sampling their mavrodaphne, retsina and krasi, communi-cating through a few words of ungrammatical Greek and hand signals. On Sunday, many of the men went to a service in the town's congregational church. The gallery was crowded with townspeople singing heartily in Greek. The New Zealanders on the ground floor listened politely, fascinated by a service they didn't understand.[66]

The colonel and his officers returned and the battalion was packed up and trucked into the hills as far as the vehicles could take them. Their sector was steep, with no roads, just cart tracks still muddy from winter. The troops had to carry haversacks of personal belongings as well as rifles, machine guns and ammunition from the trucks to their designated posts. For some, it was a slippery trek uphill for a few kilometres, exhausting and crippling.

With no prepared defences awaiting them, they carved out the best positions they could on the rocky slopes. Unable to make proper bivouacs on the first night, they slept under blankets, and those who could get to sleep woke in the morning with a light coat of snow on them. They ached with cold, but their enthusiasm wasn't yet dampened. It was still an adventure. They continued to work on preparing their posts. By the third day, the pass far below them was swarming with trucks bringing the other Kiwi battalions to this section of the Aliakmon Line.

Battalions followed in succession, heading north from the transit camps every two or three days. On the way up, one unit passed groups of Greek soldiers on their way back from the Albanian front. Ragged but cheerful, they had donkeys with them, loaded with equipment, and artillery from the 1914–18 war pulled by steam tractors and teams of horses. There were also Greek soldiers travelling in the reverse direction, on their way to reinforce the army in Albania. Dressed in shoddy, drab uniforms, some wore Italian helmets and other bits and pieces of foreign equipment. Some were boys in blue and white Youth Organisation uniforms of short pants, shirt and cap. Marching men were usually led by officers on horseback in dashing uniforms.[67]

As soon as one Kiwi battalion moved out of Katerini to take up its positions on the Aliakmon Line, another arrived. At the central marketplace the men bought fresh vegetables and fruit, bread and eggs. Street stalls sold thin fillets of meat grilled over charcoal braziers. A tin of bully beef could buy several nips of konjac.

The last group to arrive at Katerini was the Maori battalion. Maoris were not precluded from the other battalions but in this one the companies were based on regions, enabling them to keep their tribal connections. Some of the officers were Pakeha (European) but not all, and the second-in-command (2IC), Colonel George Bertrand, was Maori.

The people of Katerini were fascinated by these brown-skinned soldiers. Those with some English were able to ask them where they came from. They were puzzled when they were told they were New Zealanders. The Greeks shook their heads and said, 'But you *mávros* [black], others *áspros* [white].'[68]

When only a few Kiwi contingents remained to move up-country, the Australians started their trek north to the middle section of the Aliakmon Line, around Veria Pass. Some were taken in railway boxcars, some in trucks winding through village after village, rumbling down narrow cobbled streets crowded with waving villagers. As those going by rail headed north, a train came in the reverse direction covered in bushes, like a harvest festival float. At Larisa the railway yards had been extensively bombed, explaining the camouflaged train. Several of the Australian units stopped for a few days outside the ravaged town. It was still suffering periodic tremors. New Zealanders, with their frequent earthquakes at home, barely noticed them, but for the Aussies it was a new and disconcerting experience.

Surrounded by lofty mountains, the Australian units camped in a basin where they were bathed in oppressive heat and mosquitos. It was best escaped by going into the damaged town where wine was sold in a range of places. Bob Holt recalls drinking retsina in a butcher's shop where gallons of ouzo were also being strained through a large cone-shaped canvas. But the abundance of cheap alcohol brought problems and a curfew was soon brought in. The first Holt knew of it was when local police fired at a group of Aussies for being in the street after ten at night. 'When their shots were reciprocated, they took a back seat and didn't bother us again,' he says.[69]

Eventually, much to the relief of local authorities, both Greek and British, the Australians moved on. After being taken further north by truck, they marched into the mountains to reach positions overlooking Veria Pass. One battalion marched to the edge of town to wait for trucks, only to be told they weren't coming until the next day. After a meal in the fields, they marched 25 kilometres in pouring rain to their bivouac site, arriving with feet blistered from their army-issue cotton socks.

At Veria, the troops camped beside a river fed with cold mountain water but they weren't deterred. In the dying afternoon light, naked men bathed in the river, shouting and splashing each other like kids, while Bill Robertson, a company commander looking for a suitable place to set up unit headquarters, stumbled on a tent in the company area. Inside were boxes of Thompson sub-machine guns and ammunition, but no occupant. While Robertson was trying to figure this out, a young English Guards officer arrived, unperturbed by a stranger in his tent. He was with the Special Operations Executive, he explained, helping to arm guerrillas in northern Greece. They chatted for a while and, as Robertson left, the Englishman drew a bottle of whisky from a case of Johnnie Walker and gave it to him.[70]

Specialised units arrived to support the infantry battalions on the Aliakmon Line. They included Australian, New Zealand and British artillery and engineer regiments, and medical and signals corps. Field guns were brought up the roads to the infantry lines by truck and tractor, many having to be manhandled by artillerymen into their final positions in the rocky terrain above key passes. The engineers laid minefields in front of the British positions on roads where the enemy might come, and inserted demolition charges into roads and bridges in case the defenders had to pull back.

Among these groups, and keeping a low profile, was Australia's Special Wireless Section, a radio intercept unit trained initially at home, then on the outskirts of Cairo at an offshoot of Britain's Bletchley Park. Under Captain Ryan, a burly, former chief engineer at Radio 3AW in Melbourne, the unit set itself up in the foothills of Mount Olympus. They were constantly on the move with radio receivers installed in their light trucks, intercepting enemy air-to-ground signals and decrypting the messages with codes the British had uncovered. This was a new type of unit in the Australian army, learning rapidly in the field. At this stage, the section had no intelligence personnel, but Jack Ryan frequently referred to a 'Mr Sandford' who was due to join them. Until this elusive figure appeared, unanalysed decrypts were taken by motorcycle to nearby General Headquarters (GHQ), the nerve centre of the military enterprise in the field.[71]

———

All New Zealand's infantry units were up in their defensive area around Katerini by the end of March. At that time, only half the Australian contingent had reached Veria Pass. While advance parties went up to the pass to determine where the Aussie troops and supporting artillery batteries could best be positioned, Kiwis were busy preparing their defensive positions and mixing with the villagers in whose midst they had been thrust.

One battalion dug in along a six-kilometre front around Ryakia, a picture-postcard rambling hillside village, with uneven cobbled streets winding around stone cottages, cramped wineshops and wooden livestock pens. The village was approached by bullock tracks across several fords. Each day, as evening drew in, goat bells rang out as the herds were driven home. For two weeks the battalion prepared its defences nearby, digging trenches and weapon pits and clearing scrub in the line of machine-gun fire. Some platoons were billeted in the village and learnt rudimentary Greek from their hosts. Others bivouacked in tents.

The newcomers became part of village life. They'd watch peasants bringing sacks of corn in on the backs of donkeys. These subsistence farmers waited at an old stone mill while their grain was ground, paying the miller in corn meal. Locals were treated by the unit's medical officer—his first patient a frightened boy, badly scalded, brought in by his parents. After three days, the soldiers were no longer strangers and the boy came in by himself.

Before long, the troops were giving an evening concert in the churchyard and the locals sang the ubiquitous 'Woodpecker Song'. Padre Spence acquired sixty chocolate cakes from somewhere. The unit's 2IC, Jim Burrows, arranged with the village school-mistress, in stumbling French, for children to come into the school while on holiday. After the youngsters sang several school songs, New Zealand officers handed out cakes. Each child ran home with their unopened gift clutched tightly in a grubby fist.[72]

It was all quite benign, like living in a *National Geographic* article. An air of unreality pervaded the defending forces dug in, or digging in, around quaint Greek mountain villages. In the first week of April 1941, half the Australian force was still making its way north, much of it not yet landed in Greece, and the New Zealanders, already there and having not seen combat in North Africa, had little sense of impending battle.

The German army was waiting across the border in Bulgaria to launch its blitzkrieg on Greece. The defenders had faint awareness of this, knowing they were expecting to face Germans but with no real idea how that would come about.

It had in fact been brewing for months, the outcome of the machinations of geopolitics as Britain tried to build an unlikely 'Balkans front' to turn the tide of war. The British leadership consulted neither the governments of Australia and New Zealand nor their military leaders about what they had in mind, which was a combination of desperation and wishful thinking, dissembling politicians and faint-hearted commanders. On 5 April 1941, the British Expeditionary Force in Greece, mostly Australian and New Zealand combat soldiers, was waiting at the end of a long, weedy path of deceit and self-deceit.

2

MACHINATIONS

Since the late 1920s, Benito Mussolini had dreamt of an Italian Empire centred on the Mediterranean Sea. It would stretch from Gibraltar to the Persian Gulf, north to Austria, Hungary and Romania and south down to east Africa. After accumulating colonial holdings in north and east Africa, he moved into the Balkans in April 1939 with the Italian army annexing Albania. That was easy pickings! A year later, with France teetering under the might of the Wehrmacht, Il Duce opportunistically attacked through the Alps and along the Riviera. The Italian invasion had pushed only a few kilometres into French territory when France capitulated to Germany. Mussolini had to settle for a few crumbs from the spoils of Adolf Hitler's conquest.

South of the Mediterranean, Italy had 215,000 troops in Libya ready to drive the British out of Egypt and seize the Suez Canal.[1] Its garrison was torn in two directions, facing the French in Tunisia and the British in Egypt, but Tunisia ceased to be a threat after the French surrender to Germany. When Mussolini ordered Marshal Rodolfo Graziani to attack Egypt, the marshal protested his Tenth

Army was not yet properly equipped. Mussolini insisted he attack anyway.[2] After stuttering starts, the Italian army advanced along the Mediterranean coast, penetrating 105 kilometres into Egypt to Sidi Barrani. Its units waited in a line of widely spaced, fortified camps there while engineers laid a water pipe and repaired the supply road, broken up by the withdrawing British.

After the fall of France, the Italian press began a campaign against Greece, alleging atrocities on its border with Albania and breaches of its neutrality. Among the claims was that Greeks had brutally murdered a pro-Italian Albanian patriot called Daut Hoxha. In reality, Hoxha was a violent cattle thief beheaded by rival Albanian bandits.[3]

In August 1940, the Greek cruiser-minesweeper *Helle* was torpedoed at anchor with considerable loss of life. The finger of suspicion pointed towards Italy, spoiling for a fight and looking to create an 'incident' to start one. The Greeks, believing their armed forces to be weaker than Italy's, wouldn't take the bait.[4] Their leader, Ioannis Metaxas, a military dictator like Mussolini, asked Britain what help it could provide if Greece was attacked, invoking a 1939 guarantee by Neville Chamberlain. Britain had undertaken to provide armed support to Greece and Romania against aggression by the Axis powers. British military chiefs weren't helpful, advising that until the Italian advance into Egypt was driven back, no force could be spared for Greece.

While Mussolini tried to goad Metaxas into retaliation, General Archibald Wavell, in command of British land forces in the Middle East, planned a counter-attack when the Italians made their next move in Egypt. The ever-cautious Graziani was in no hurry to advance, however. Wavell had to modify his plan, instead ordering a sharp raid on the line of camps around Sidi Barrani.

Mussolini's grand vision of a Mediterranean empire wasn't progressing. Graziani was stalling, Metaxas not responding and Hitler had opposed his planned invasion of Yugoslavia. Hitler was relying on the Balkans for raw materials, particularly Romania's oilfields at Ploesti, and didn't want the region, unstable enough without interference, unsettled further with military conflict. Germany had already intervened to prevent war between Hungary and Romania over disputed territory in Transylvania. He didn't want further spot fires.

On 4 October, the Führer met with Il Duce at Brenner Pass on the border between Italy and Austria. Keen to divert his Italian counterpart from the Balkans, Hitler offered armoured divisions and Stuka dive-bombers to reinforce the Italian army in Libya, but Mussolini saw no immediate need for them.[5]

Three days later, German troops entered Romania to prop up the regime there and guard the Ploesti oilfields. Already smarting at finding himself relegated to junior partner to a leader who came to power eleven years after he did, Mussolini wasn't told this move was coming. 'It's humiliating to remain with our arms folded while others write history,' he complained to his foreign minister, Count Ciano, who was also his son-in-law.[6]

A petulant Mussolini decided two could play that game. He had been planning an invasion of Greece for some time, convinced by his commander-in-chief in Albania that Greece could be taken easily. The Greeks don't like fighting, General Prasca had assured his leader.[7] On 28 October, without notifying his Axis partner and despite the contrary views of his other commanders, Mussolini ordered an immediate confrontation. While forces stood by on Greece's border with Albania, the Italian ambassador in Athens had Metaxas wakened at 3 am with an ultimatum.

For some time, the diplomat Emanuele Grazzi had tried to smooth relations between Italy and Greece with no encouragement from his own government. Now he was given a job to do. Greece was aiding Italy's enemy, the ultimatum stated, by allowing the re-fuelling of British ships and aircraft. The Italian government insisted its troops must have access to unspecified parts of Greece to ensure this didn't continue. A response was required by sunrise.

'I couldn't set my own house in order—much less surrender my country—in three hours,' Ioannis Metaxas is said to have replied. 'The answer is No.'[8]

Before dawn, Italian troops crossed the border into north-western Greece in pouring rain, intending to take the region of Epirus and march on to Athens. The Axis leaders were meeting in Florence that morning with the Vichy head of state, Marshal Petain. As Hitler stepped from the train, Mussolini announced triumphantly, 'Führer, we are on the march!'[9]

In Greece that day there were popular demonstrations of support for Metaxas, the previously unloved dictator. The attack had united monarchists and republicans, the two irreconcilable arms of Greek domestic politics. Political exiles returned to join the fight; Greek men rushed to volunteer; reservists reported without waiting for call-up. Morale was high, in the belief that Greece must fight. Few thought of failure.[10]

The Italians were ill-prepared, with little winter clothing, no maps and no engineer units. Tanks and trucks bogged in the winter mud, Albanian conscripts deserted and the weather was bad enough to prevent air cover for the invaders. They advanced slowly into Greece, securing a bridgehead across the Kalamas River in Greece's far north, but they couldn't break through from there in the bitterly cold winter, with their supply system collapsing.

By 7 November, the Italian offensive had stalled and its troops started falling back. Within a week, the Greeks were attacking on a broad front despite their First World War weapons and ragged clothing. In some places, local civilians pitched into the skirmishes. After another week, the Greeks had crossed back over the Kalamas, driven the dispirited enemy out of most of Epirus and gained a foothold across the border in Albania.

General Alexandros Papagos, commander-in-chief of the Greek army, had concentrated his strength on his right flank, prepared to let his left flank be pushed some way into the Pindus Mountains.

Without tanks, the Greeks had to move stealthily along ridges, but surprise attacks from there breached the Italian positions in several places. The invaders soon found themselves in danger of encirclement and had to bring their advancing troops back hurriedly to avoid being cut off, but by then the key frontier Albanian town of Korçë had been captured by the Greek forces.[11]

Il Duce's Italian Empire had received a serious setback. He replaced General Prasca with General Soddu, at the same time urging Marshal Graziani in North Africa to push further into Egypt. Mussolini wanted to tie up the British so the Middle East force couldn't be moved to Greece, but Graziani continued to hesitate, punctiliously preparing the next leg of his advance.

General Wavell was meanwhile setting up the counter-attack in North Africa with his already stretched resources, but hadn't told Prime Minister Churchill, an amateur military strategist with a history of interfering. When the War Cabinet instructed the military to provide token aid to Greece, the RAF sent a single squadron of Blenheim bombers. To Churchill this was not enough and, without consulting Middle East Command or War Cabinet, he ordered a further four squadrons be sent from Egypt, compounding Wavell's resource shortage.[12] The Blenheims bombed Italian supply lines and Albanian ports, but the squadrons' losses were high and a Greek request for more planes was turned down.

The Greeks were reluctant to allow the RAF to operate from airfields north of Mount Olympus, which would have put them within striking range of Romania's oilfields and risk retaliation from Germany. When the British started flying aircraft from the northern Aegean island of Lemnos, that posed too great a threat to the Führer's invasion of the Soviet Union, then in secret planning. On 4 November, Hitler resolved that the German forces protecting Romania's oilfields would be reinforced during winter to drive a growing British presence out of Greece.[13]

From a cursory look at a map, it should have been obvious to the British that Hitler couldn't ignore their presence on Lemnos. That had probably sealed Greece's fate unwittingly.

———————

By the end of November 1940, there was still no movement by Graziani's force from their fortified camps in Egypt. Wavell told his Western Desert Force commander, General Richard O'Connor, to put the planned raid into action. Spread across 85 kilometres, the Italian camps made too wide a front for O'Connor's liking, so he decided to attack the centre camps first and deal with outlying ones after.[14]

Trucked 140 kilometres from the end of the railway, an Indian division attacked with tank support in the early morning through a gap between the camps. The assault force included a British armoured division, covering any counter-attack from the side or rear. The element of surprise was so decisive that, by the end of the morning, the first fort had been taken along with 2000 prisoners. Some of the Kiwi drivers who'd brought the Indian troops to the battleline joined the fight, the first Anzac soldiers to do battle with the enemy.[15]

By the end of the third day, the remaining Italian defenders were throwing away their weapons and waving shirts in surrender. The raid had captured 38,000 men, along with tanks, guns and vehicles.[16] Dick O'Connor was ready to press on, fortified by his success, but without forewarning him Archie Wavell had already arranged to send the Indian force to Sudan to clear Italian-occupied Ethiopia. The Indians would be replaced by the Australian 6th Division and there would be a hiatus of a few weeks while it got into position.[17] The Italians had withdrawn across the border into Libya.

Australian soldiers began their first combat action of the Second World War at dawn on 3 January 1941, advancing with British tanks across the border to Bardia. By 7 am, the tanks had breached the defensive line, followed by Australian infantry. In three days, Bardia fell. The Australians sustained 456 casualties and the Italians lost 40,000 killed or captured along with 400 guns and 130 tanks.[18] O'Connor immediately sent Australians and armoured vehicles down the Libyan coast towards Tobruk. It was taken two weeks later.

The Middle East Command's structure needed rationalising. It had General Henry Maitland Wilson placed between generals Wavell and O'Connor as a glorified messenger boy, passing on the senior commander's orders to the junior. Wavell relieved Wilson of his role in the Western Desert, putting O'Connor's HQ directly under his own.[19] Wilson was appointed Military Governor of Cyrenaica (eastern Libya) soon after, but that posting would be short-lived.

The Italians were now withdrawing along the coast to Benghazi with its large expatriate Italian community and surrounding cultivation. O'Connor decided to keep pressure on the retreating enemy. The Australians chased them along the coast while the armoured division cut across the desert to block the enemy past Benghazi. The armoured vehicles arrived back on the coast and set up shortly before the leading Italian units appeared. The fleeing enemy was unable to break through, while the Australians rolled into Benghazi behind them.

General O'Connor wanted to drive on to Tripoli, the chief city of western Libya. Its capture would end the Italian occupation of North Africa, open a shipping route through the Mediterranean, and deprive the Axis powers of a port in Libya. On the other hand, there was still a substantial garrison in Tripoli with reinforcements being rushed in. Hitler had been highly critical of Mussolini's strategy in North Africa and had ordered his own Afrika Korps and Luftwaffe to Libya, with a panzer division to follow under General Erwin Rommel.

Badly knocked about from crossing the desert, O'Connor's tanks were withdrawn for maintenance and a refit while Middle East Command considered the problems of a stretched supply line.

Wavell didn't share his field commander's enthusiasm to press on, but in the end it was out of their hands. Churchill had decided on a new priority in the eastern Mediterranean: Greece.

On the wave of the new Mediterranean objective came a succession of manoeuvres, undertakings and machinations by a jumble of British politicians and military commanders. The central figure was the army's Middle East commander-in-chief, General Wavell. Detached and taciturn with little capacity for small talk, he had a reputation as an intellectual general who studied poetry as well as strategy, with a deep attachment to order and tradition. As head of Middle East Command, he was given a wide and unwieldy responsibility—East and North Africa, the Arab states and the eastern Mediterranean—staffed with a conspicuous shortage of talent and seriously under-resourced, including a chronic lack of air support.

Archie Wavell's austerity and self-containment gave him an appearance of calm, but to some he lacked the vigour to wage war. Churchill commented that he would make 'a good chairman of a Tory association', which wasn't meant as a compliment.[20] Wavell was unable to capitalise on his successes in North Africa and his relationship with Churchill deteriorated; a clash between the professional soldier and the amateur strategist. The general's response to his prime minister's meddling was to tell him as little as possible of future plans.

'War is a wasteful, boring muddled affair,' Wavell once said.[21] That might be fair comment, but not reassuring from a military leader.

General Henry Maitland Wilson, Wavell's North Africa commander until his appointment as a military governor, was steadfast and unflappable . . . but not much else. A large, ponderous man with a finely developed sense of duty, 'Jumbo' Wilson stuck to orders without question, a useful quality in a soldier perhaps, but less so in a field commander. A product of Eton and Sandhurst, he was at best a journeyman commander who critics saw as having risen through mediocrity. 'Perhaps the very absence of originality or scintillation enabled him to float upwards unimpeded,' one speculated.[22] His military judgement was limited, seeing no use for tanks,[23] but he had a close professional and personal relationship with his immediate superior officer. Wilson stayed with the Wavells when he was in Cairo.[24]

Sitting above both, the Chief of Imperial General Staff (CIGS), General John Dill, was the professional head of the British army. An Ulsterman, Jack Dill had battled his way to that post, handed to him when Churchill became prime minister. From there, it had been mostly downhill, pilloried for advocating chemical warfare against the Germans if they landed in Britain, and unable to come to grips with Churchill or his meddling. He developed a reputation as unimaginative and obstructive, slow and ineffective. Churchill called him 'Dilly Dally' behind his back, noting 'he strikes me as being very tired, disheartened, and over-impressed with the might of Germany'.[25]

Dill saw it differently. 'I live a very hectic life. Most of it is trying to prevent stupid things being done rather than in doing clever things!' he complained.[26] Pessimism was in his nature.

Despite his misgivings about Dill, Churchill sent him with Anthony Eden to put the new priority into effect. Eden had been Foreign Secretary under Chamberlain, but had resigned in 1938 over the appeasement of Mussolini. He made no protest about the subsequent appeasement of Hitler and would later be dismissed by a political opponent as 'that peculiarly British type, the idealist without conviction'.[27] He returned to his previous portfolio after Churchill became leader.

A self-important, inflexible personality, Eden was an unimpressive public speaker, even at meetings, and sometimes became childishly enraged only to regain his temper within a few minutes.

Many who worked with him remarked that he was 'two men', one charming, erudite and hard-working and the other petty and prone to temper tantrums.[28]

Eden was considered a leader of English fashion. He travelled to Khartoum in khaki shorts and a rose in his buttonhole, wore an Old Etonians' tie to meet the president of Turkey and regularly wore a Homburg hat. He wasn't necessarily a snob, maintaining friendly relations with Opposition MPs and declining to join the gentlemen's clubs frequented by conservative politicians and business leaders.

Calling the shots from London was the master puppeteer. There's no question Winston Churchill was an inspiring wartime leader who could persuade the public that Britain would somehow prevail in this war, but he was also a bully, intruding into military planning with a team of yes-men. Churchill's strength was a two-edged sword. 'His real tyrant is the glittering phrase—so attractive to his mind that awkward facts may have to give way,' noted Robert Menzies, the Australian prime minister, adding that Churchill 'would not actually hear anybody who said No'.[29]

Wavell's problems weren't just above him in the pecking order; they were below as well. Middle East Command's headquarters staff at Grey Pillars, a converted apartment building in a leafy residential part of Cairo, had grown to about a thousand. The officers there habitually took a five-hour siesta in the afternoon, to cope with the rigours of the tropics, and, like good colonials, drank whisky and went to the races or cricket.[30] The approaching Italian army didn't change this routine one jot.

'Cairo is full of left-overs from the Lawrence era—aging imps—living comfortably on his legend,' noted Peter Coats, Wavell's aide-de-camp. 'One of his ex-buddies here is unkindly known as Florence of Arabia.'[31]

The British military across the sea in Athens was, if anything, even more self-indulgent and bumbling. In January 1941, General Thomas Heywood, a monocled, former military attaché at the Paris embassy, took over as head of the British Military Mission, accommodated in the Hotel Grande Bretagne. The hotel also housed the Greek army's headquarters, busy trying to get supplies to its frostbitten troops in the Albanian mountains. To offset staff boredom, Heywood set up an English cocktail bar on the ground floor of the hotel, although the British Club was only a few minutes away. The bar was usually boisterously full before lunch and dinner with the cheerful bonhomie of RAF officers and Mission staff, in full view of Greek GHQ staff dealing with the attempted invasion of their country.[32]

Paddy Leigh Fermor, an English adventurer and jaunty eccentric destined to be played by Dirk Bogarde after the war, was at the Mission briefly. He arrived with no kit, just two suitcases full of cigars and deluxe book editions, did the rounds of parties and sightseeing, and moved on.[33] Captain Michael Forrester of the Queen's Guards was also with the Mission, but he stayed longer, liaising through the king's cousin, Prince Peter, with the Greek GHQ, building an admiration for the Greek army and the Greek people as he did so.[34]

Other groups of English military men were floating about with poorly defined roles. Major Miles Reid led a team from Britain's GHQ Liaison Regiment known as Phantom, its purpose to provide front-line information. It was a team with limited military knowledge and none of them spoke enough Greek to be useful. Blocked by both the British Mission and the Greek army from going to the Albanian front, they settled instead for picking up information at Athens cocktail parties.[35]

The British had never thought to gather practical information about Greece, despite undertaking to come to its aid if it was attacked. Their maps of Greece were out of date and they had no understanding of Greek weaponry, supplied from France and eastern Europe. On the other hand, Germany had invested in Greece's utilities, building its rail system and installing the Athens telephone exchange. Most of the British army's telephone calls went through the exchange, still operated by Germans.

That was the team, and its backing, with which Britain set about to persuade the world that it was in this war with the best of intentions, and to persuade Balkan states that it could hold the German juggernaut at bay.

———

By the end of 1940, Great Britain was near bankruptcy, its currency and gold reserves dwindling. Without American munitions and oil, it would be difficult for Britain to continue the war, so President Franklin Roosevelt was pursuing a Lend-Lease arrangement for anti-Axis countries. Under it, the United States would supply military equipment with payment deferred, settled later as rent for military bases or goods in return. In isolationist America, support for the Lend-Lease Bill was far from assured.

Roosevelt sent Colonel 'Wild Bill' Donovan to advise Churchill that if Lend-Lease was to pass through both houses of Congress, the American public had to be persuaded that Britain's war effort was for fighting Nazism, not preserving the British Empire. That was not well served by stopping Italians seizing the Suez Canal, Britain's sea passage to its colonial possessions, but it might be by challenging German expansion in Europe.[36]

It was something Britain had been shying away from. After the Battle of Britain, its limited firepower was concentrated on protecting the homeland and the Suez Canal. For some time, Britain had been cautious about any substantial commitment to Greece. In 1939, the service chiefs held the view that Greece would 'absorb allied resources which could be used elsewhere'.[37]

Anthony Eden, then Secretary of State for War, was in Cairo soon after Mussolini launched his invasion of Greece. General Wavell told him sending forces to Greece would have no decisive influence on the battle, and would merely divide the meagre British resources and risk failure in both Greece and North Africa.[38] The Italian forces were expected to prevail eventually in Greece, but the Wehrmacht joining the fray was a more fearful proposition. The UK Dominions Office told the Australian government a week later that 'no assistance which we are able at present to make available would materially delay German advance through Greece'.[39]

Churchill saw a way to merge an existing objective with Donovan's advice. Britain's strategy was to protect its Middle East position by denying the Axis control of the eastern Mediterranean. This could be achieved if a 'Balkan front' could be stitched together with Greece, Yugoslavia and Turkey. All three were nominally neutral, unofficially supportive of Britain but economically tied to Germany. All were wary of antagonising the Germans, but a first step had been taken with Greece agreeing to British garrison troops, anti-aircraft guns and equipment being landed on Crete. A naval fuelling facility was to be built at Suda Bay and airfields upgraded at Heraklion and Maleme.

In January, Wavell was ordered by War Cabinet to go to Athens and offer troops, tanks and artillery to Greece for use against the Italians, but the Greeks wanted only aircraft and captured Italian trucks and clothing. Metaxas insisted that if the troops offered were land forces, there needed to be at least ten divisions. Wavell could spare only two or three divisions from his Middle East Command, which was then occupied with driving the Italians back in North Africa. A small British force would only give the Germans a pretext to attack, Metaxas said, and that force wouldn't be able to defend the northern city of Salonika as the British contended.[40]

Wavell maintained a British presence would encourage the Yugoslavs and Turks to resist a German offensive, to which Metaxas replied that its small size would actually discourage them. 'The only obstacle to the Germans coming in today,' he said, 'is Russia.'

Wavell would later write, 'Had the Greeks accepted the offer I should have had to stop my advance at Tobruk. I was relieved when Metaxas refused the assistance.'[41]

Before going to Athens, Wavell had put to Cabinet that the German threat was not real, just part of a 'war of nerves'. The response was a ticking off: 'We expect and require active compliance with our decisions for which we bear full responsibility.'[42] It was not the place of the Middle East commander to challenge political views. An opinion on tactics of the German military might not have been a political view, but the message was clear: Winston Churchill didn't want to be contradicted.

Churchill wasn't able to cut off all doubters. The consensus of his chiefs of staff was that they could do no more than delay German occupation of Greece. That was of no concern to Churchill. The war wasn't going to be won or lost in Greece. It would be won with America's participation, starting with Lend-Lease. The first step on that ladder was taken on 9 February with the US House of Representatives passing the Lend-Lease Bill. The gesture of coming to Greece's aid should ensure its continuing passage through the Senate, whatever the outcome might be in Greece.

The Greeks needed to be persuaded that the British offer was in their interest. After telling them that thirty promised fighter planes couldn't be supplied because of engine failure, Air Chief Marshal Arthur Longmore, the Middle East air chief, found that the US had agreed to supply Tomahawk fighters. Diplomatic pressure by Longmore had the American order rescinded, and Britain found itself able to supply Hurricanes. Greece's dependence on the UK for maintenance and spare parts would allow the British to exert subtle pressure on Greece to accept British troops.[43]

As it happened, German troops were in Romania as neither threat nor war of nerves, but simply to protect the oilfields. When the British moved into striking range of Ploesti, however, Hitler started preparing for confrontation. With the promise of a port outlet on the Aegean Sea when Greece was defeated, Bulgaria joined Romania in signing the Axis's Tripartite Pact. Construction began on bridges strong enough to carry heavy military vehicles across the Danube, from Romania into Bulgaria.

The problem of the gap between what Greece wanted and what Britain could supply eased on 29 January, when Ioannis Metaxas died following a throat operation. He'd been seriously ill with an inflamed pharynx for over six months. With its strongman gone, Greece's government was effectively controlled by the Greek king, George II, who nominated the governor of the Bank of Greece, Alexandros Koryzis, as the new prime minister. Koryzis had neither the strength nor the military know-how of Metaxas but, unlike his predecessor, he favoured accepting the British offer of an expeditionary force. And so did his Anglophile king, a distant cousin of George VI of England.

Encouraged by a possible change in Greek thinking, Churchill wrote to President Inonu of Turkey warning of the German army and air force moving into neighbouring Bulgaria and proposing an Anglo–Turkish alliance. As a sweetener, Churchill offered ten squadrons of British warplanes, although where he was going to find them was anyone's guess. It didn't matter in the end. British planes on Turkish airfields would be within range of Romania's oilfields and would amount to a declaration of war on Germany. Turkey wasn't ready for that, preferring to remain neutral.[44]

In early February, the Australian prime minister, Robert Menzies, visited North Africa on his way to talks in London. On a meet-the-troops visit to Tobruk and Benghazi, he noted in his diary that the Australian soldiers craved home news and were 'boyishly pleased when I pointed out the world significance of the campaign they have been winning'.[45]

He dined several times with his senior commander in the Middle East, Tom Blamey, and in the course of the week-long visit, met with Wavell, Longmore and the Middle East naval commander, Admiral Andrew Cunningham. Menzies discussed the future deployment of the three Australian divisions with Wavell, who said it was 'probably not worthwhile' taking Tripoli, even though that would have driven the Italians out of North Africa. There was no mention of Greece.[46]

Britain's War Office had joined the service chiefs in their pessimism, its intelligence section, MI3, predicting Greece would fall in weeks to a German attack. With Yugoslavia joining the fight, that outcome would only be delayed a few more weeks. This assessment was circulated to the three UK military services and to the Foreign Office, but was no longer being shared with the Australian and New Zealand governments.[47]

Britain and Greece were meanwhile sending out tentative feelers to each other, enquiring by the one what sort of support Britain could give against a German attack, and by the other if British troops would be welcome as soon as the Germans crossed the Danube into Bulgaria. Koryzis now shared his predecessor's concern that an inadequate British force might provoke an attack it couldn't drive back, but he was prepared to talk about possibilities. It was enough for Churchill to canvass options.

Churchill cabled Wavell that it would be bad for Greece to have to make peace with Italy and have German planes operating out of Greek airfields, but 'if Greece with British aid can hold up for some months German advance, chances of Turkish intervention will be favoured'. He followed up a week later, noting that if the Greeks decided to resist German attack, 'we shall have to help them with whatever troops we can get there in time. They will not, I fear, be very numerous.'[48] Hardly a vote of confidence, but Churchill had moved from strategic planning to gesture politics, seeking to curry favour with the American electorate.

Anthony Eden, now UK Foreign Secretary, and General Dill were sent to Cairo to confer with Wavell and pursue a Balkan Pact with Greece, Yugoslavia and Turkey. Eden had been given wide powers 'in all matters diplomatic and military' to make commitments on behalf of the United Kingdom.[49] He saw an opportunity to produce an outcome that would bolster his political ambitions. His first task was to persuade Greece to accept a British force without too many restrictions.

Churchill notified Wavell of the pair's mission. 'Your major effort must now be to aid Greece and/or Turkey,' he wrote. Benghazi was to be secured and Tripoli left for the time being. Wavell replied that he had only New Zealand and Australian divisions to offer Greece, but 'I have already spoken to Menzies about this and he was ready to agree to what I suggest'.[50]

This overstates significantly a conversation Wavell had in very general terms with the Australian leader in Cairo. Wavell had said he hoped the Australian government would give him 'certain latitude as regards use of their troops',[51] without any particular reference to Greece. Menzies would have considered he heard rather than agreed to a broad proposition. So began a stream of misinformation to the two southern dominions.

In Libya, Menzies met General Wilson, recently installed as Military Governor of Cyrenaica. Wilson commented to Menzies that the Australian soldiers had been 'troublesome'.

'Yes,' said Menzies. 'I understand the Italians have found them very troublesome.'

'It's not that. They're not disciplined, you know.' Wilson had seen Aussie soldiers singing 'Waltzing Matilda' around a stolen piano.

'These men haven't spent their lives marching around parade grounds,' Menzies replied curtly. 'They came from all walks of life and they've come over here to do a job and get it over and done with.'

Bob Menzies noted in his diary, 'Wilson seems tall, fat and cunning.'[52]

Menzies' last day in Egypt included a short meeting with Wavell who, the Australian's diary records, 'is clearly contemplating the possibility of a Salonica expedition'.[53] Nothing explicit, it had to be inferred. That was the extent of the briefing the prime minister received on the Greek venture, which the British leadership would pass off as a full explanation with his informed agreement.

Five days later, Australia's most senior commander General Blamey was told by Wavell that an expeditionary force would be sent to Greece under General Wilson. Called Lustre Force, its key components would be the Australian 6th and 7th Divisions, the New Zealand Division, a British armoured brigade and a Polish brigade. A very surprised Blamey said it should be referred to the Australian government, to which Wavell replied that he had already discussed the possibility of the operation with Menzies.[54]

The previous day, Wavell had told General Freyberg that the New Zealand Division was under orders to go to Greece. As with Blamey, the New Zealander's reaction wasn't sought. The Kiwis were to be the advance guard of a force with Australian and British components. They would take up positions on a line Freyberg understood had already been dug along the mountains in Macedonia. Australians would take over the line when they arrived and the New Zealanders would move back in reserve, ready to head north if a threat materialised from that quarter. Freyberg was told that his government had been consulted and had agreed to the venture.[55] There is no record of that being done or of Wavell being told by London it was done.

After Blamey had received similar instructions, the two national commanders met, both disturbed at a venture with such sketchy details. More worrying was that there was little sign of anyone knowing much more. Jumbo Wilson, who was to command Lustre Force, hadn't yet been to Greece, or even told he was commanding, and it appeared that Wavell hadn't ventured much beyond Athens. It was unclear how much input the British Military Mission in Athens had into the plans, but it was known that Cairo had a low opinion of the Mission anyway. There was no evidence of any reconnoitre of the anticipated combat zone.

After a week's delay due to bad flying weather, Eden and Dill finally arrived in Cairo on 19 February to find a cable from Churchill waiting, his boldness flickering. 'Do not consider yourselves obligated to a Greek enterprise if in your hearts you feel it would be only another Norwegian fiasco,' he wrote, referring to an earlier failed attempt to thwart German invasion.[56]

That same day, Wavell's Director of Military Intelligence, Brigadier John Shearer, produced a forthright paper outlining the dangers of a Greek campaign, a view Wavell was also getting from his Joint Planning Staff. Shearer's analysis came back with a hand-written note across the top, enigmatically quoting General Wolfe, the conqueror of Quebec: 'War is an option of difficulties.' Wavell subsequently told Shearer that to let Germany overrun Greece 'would lose the British almost as much prestige as a military defeat'.[57] The general was keeping his personal views to himself, now that he had been put in his place by Churchill.

Another message came from the wavering prime minister the next day. 'The Germans might offer Greece attractive terms to make peace before deciding to attack,' he cabled Eden. 'In that case we couldn't very well blame them, nor should we take such a decision on the part of the Greeks too tragically.'[58] The prime minister had just told War Cabinet that it was unlikely that a large British force could get to Greece before the Germans, the same problem that had plagued the English in Norway.

Eden and Dill conferred with the three commanders-in-chief at Grey Pillars, the Cairo headquarters. Asked for his professional opinion, Wavell told Eden he thought there was every chance of the Allies halting a German advance into Greece, contrary to the advice of his intelligence chief and his planning staff. Eden didn't ask why he'd changed his mind.

Wavell advised proposing to the Greeks that the southern part of the Aliakmon Line be adjusted so it would protect Salonika, vital as a port to supply Yugoslavia and Turkey if the Balkan front was viable. Andrew Cunningham told the gathering that Salonika would need air protection if it was to be used as a naval base, and that was not available. While accepting the venture as politically justified, Cunningham and his RAF counterpart, Arthur Longmore, had serious doubts about its military feasibility.[59]

Immediately after the conference, Eden cabled Churchill that the three commanders agreed that there is 'a fair chance that we can hold a line in Greece', but he doubted that a line could be held covering Salonika as Wavell wanted. The next day, he sent another cable telling Churchill that he thought sending forces to Greece was a 'gamble', but it was better to suffer with the Greeks than to not help them. We might have to play our evacuation card, he added.[60]

Jack Dill commented to Cunningham after the meeting broke up, 'Well, we've taken the decision. I'm not at all sure it's the right one.'[61] Dill had left England with reservations, believing any force sent to Greece would be lost. On his return he told his deputy that he was convinced by the commanders on the spot that sending a force to Greece was the only move that could save the Balkans 'from being devoured piecemeal'.[62]

At 2.30 am on 22 February, Jumbo Wilson was wakened in Tobruk by a telegram from Archie Wavell, telling him to meet him at nearby El Adem airfield at ten. A plane came in from Cairo with Eden, Dill, Wavell and Longmore on their way to Athens with planners and advisors for talks with General Papagos and King George. While the others had coffee in the mess, Wilson was taken aside by Wavell and told that they were on their way to decide if an expeditionary force was to be sent to Greece.

'If it is,' said Wavell, 'you're to command it. I'm very sorry to have to move you again so soon, but you are far and away the best choice for this job.'[63] He gave Wilson a letter confirming the appointment 'with your tactical and strategical knowledge and the prestige of your recent successes'.

'Did Wavell believe that?' asks a Wavell biographer. 'Or did he think the towering bulk of Jumbo Wilson would impress the Greeks?'[64] The architect of the successes in North Africa was, of course, General O'Connor, not Wilson. Wavell, at other times, went out of his way to stress O'Connor's pivotal role in the North African operation.

The British delegation was taken to King George's country residence. English tea with the king was served on a long, polished table. After dinner it became the conference table, with only the main players seated at it, the English politician and military leaders, the Greek king, prime minister and commander-in-chief.

Wavell insisted that, with Libya under control, the troops he could now spare had a good chance of stopping a German drive into Greece. He kept to himself that his staff thought otherwise and that the RAF couldn't provide adequate fighter cover. Eden put figures on the offer, promising 100,000 men, 660 artillery pieces and 142 tanks, more of each than Wavell had available. A Middle East staff officer, Freddie de Guingand, had compiled the figures but they had been inflated by an Eden aide during the flight over.[65] Wavell stayed silent.

Greece already had a defence line, the Metaxas Line. Stretching 155 kilometres across the country's north-east corner, it covered approaches from Bulgaria. It was manned, with twenty-one concrete fortifications dotted along it; unlike the Aliakmon Line, which had no prepared positions of any sort. Dill dismissed the Metaxas Line as 'unsound', although he didn't explain why.

Papagos agreed that forward defence in eastern Macedonia was impractical, if for no other reason than the British were clearly not prepared to place their troops there, and reluctantly accepted he would have to withdraw to the Aliakmon Line favoured by the British. This would mean abandoning Salonika to the enemy and Yugoslavia would be loath to join the battle if its main supply line to the south was undefended. At one point in proceedings, Papagos said the two or three divisions on offer were insufficient for Greece's needs and could be more useful in North Africa, but the British turned a deaf ear to this invitation to pull out of the arrangement, instead pressing the Greeks to accept the token force offered.

With an arrangement agreed in principle, the English believed that the Greek defenders would move back to the Aliakmon Line immediately. That's not how the Greeks saw it. Papagos understood the principle was agreed, but subject to clarification of Yugoslavia's position. Eden had offered to send a staff officer to Belgrade for discussions with the Yugoslav regent, Prince Paul.

Eden reported to Cabinet the outcome of the talks, with Wavell and Dill's advice to send the maximum available military and air support to Greece as soon as possible. At a War Cabinet meeting the next day, Churchill expressed the view that if the Greeks elected to fight the Germans, the British must fight and suffer with them. Anyone with misgivings about that should express them at that meeting.[66]

Robert Menzies was there, the only one to raise any questions, uneasy about the time it would take to ship troops to Greece and get them to defensive positions, whether they would all be adequately equipped and whether, if the expedition failed, the cost would just be equipment. He was assured that no Australian force would be put into battle without all necessary weapons and that all but the wounded should be able to be safely evacuated.

Menzies continued that the venture would only be justified if the Allies could be expected to put up a good fight. If it was a forlorn hope, it was better not undertaken. 'Can I tell Canberra the venture has a substantial chance of success?' he asked.

'In the last resort, this is a question that the Australian Cabinet must assess for themselves on Mr Menzies' advice,' Churchill replied. 'In my opinion, the enterprise is a risk we must under-take.'[67] Churchill was not going to be Menzies' fall guy, but success to Menzies was stopping the German invasion, as indeed it was to the Greeks. To Churchill and Eden, it was persuading Yugoslavia and Turkey to join the war, with Lend-Lease also in their thinking.

Cabinet agreed to provide military aid to Greece, subject to Canberra and Wellington consent. 'No need to anticipate difficulties in either quarter,' cabled Churchill to Eden, jumping the gun. 'Therefore, while being under no illusions we all send you the order "Full steam ahead".'[68]

Combat participants were notified in a more muddled fashion. On 25 February, two days later, the New Zealand government was told for the first time of the proposed Greek expedition. General Freyberg hadn't told them because he'd been led to believe they had been consulted and agreed. The government consented to its force participating on the assumption the general had been consulted, but attached a proviso that the division be fully equipped and supported by a British armoured brigade. Menzies reported to War Cabinet that the Australian government too had now agreed, but reiterated the concerns he'd already raised.

General Wilson was summoned to El Adem airstrip again to meet the party returning from Athens. He spent the best part of the day there, then found they had flown directly to Cairo. Called urgently to Cairo soon after, he was eventually told Lustre Force would go ahead under his command.

Blamey complained to Wavell that the Australians were the largest group in Lustre Force and yet an English general was to command it. The reply was that, although the Australian contingent was only 42,000 men in a force of 126,000, Blamey's concern would be passed on to the British government. Blamey took up the issue with Menzies in England and it was raised in War Cabinet with the same response. It misrepresented the reality. Of Wavell's 84,000 non-Australians, 17,000 were New Zealanders, 14,000 were base units like transport and supply, and 37,300 were units on paper, still in England but theoretically available to reinforce the Middle East, although there was no plan for them to do so. Only 15,000 of them were British army combat troops. The vast majority of combat troops, 59,000 of them, were Australian and New Zealand.[69]

Eden and Dill flew on to Ankara for talks with the Turkish president and prime minister. Unsurprisingly, there was no change in the Turkish position. At the same time, the British ambassador in Belgrade wrote to the Yugoslav regent asking his view on the German threat to Salonika. Prince Paul's reply was sent to Eden the next day through the Yugoslav ambassador in Ankara. In a cranky exchange, the prince's evasive and apologetic message was read out, that Yugoslavia would defend itself against any aggressor and would not allow foreign troops to pass through her territory, but he took no definite position on the issue of Salonika.

General Wilson arrived in Athens on 1 March to take command of Lustre Force, incognito at Greek insistence in civilian clothes as 'Mr Watt'. The subterfuge was to conceal developments between Greece and Britain, but the German Legation wasn't that clueless. Not only was Jumbo Wilson's bulky frame recognisable from photos in the Greek press, but Mr Watt's luggage, delivered to the British Legation where he was staying, was helpfully labelled 'Sir H Maitland Wilson'.[70]

Still in mufti, Wilson conducted his first reconnoitre of the Aliakmon Line with General Heywood of the British Military Mission, flying over northern Greece and along the Vermion Range that comprised the line. They landed at Katerini and drove through the gorges that cut into the line of mountains. These would be key defensive points through which an invader coming from eastern Macedonia would need to pass. The gaps were narrow, apart from one along the coast beside Mount Olympus, but Wilson was satisfied ravines running down to the sea made passage here too difficult for tanks, a judgement that would be tested in due course.

Eden and Dill returned to Athens to find that the Germans were already crossing the Danube into Bulgaria and that General Papagos hadn't yet ordered a withdrawal of Greek forces to the Aliakmon Line. Two days of further meetings between the main players followed as the British and Greeks tried to iron out their disconnect. Dill insisted that the Aliakmon Line was the only sound military option; if there were insufficient Greek troops, they should be withdrawn from Albania.

Contact with the Yugoslav regent wasn't mentioned. It needed Papagos to ask what news had come from Belgrade. While Eden and Dill were in Ankara, he had been asking Heywood constantly what he'd heard but Heywood hadn't let the others know Papagos was waiting on an urgent reply.

The general finally got a reply of sorts. Dill advised they couldn't count on the Yugoslavs and should focus their defence on the Aliakmon Line. In that case, said Papagos, the issue now is that the Germans are in Bulgaria and could attack within ten days, less time than it would take for his troops without motor transport to move from north-eastern Greece to the Vermion Range. It would be better now to hold a line at the Bulgarian frontier, he said, but Dill wouldn't commit Britain's only reserves in the Middle East to an 'unsound plan', dribbling forces forward into battle.[71] As it turned out, that's how the expeditionary force would eventually go into battle on the Aliakmon Line.

The Greeks had political as well as military considerations to weigh up. The Bulgarian government was telling its people Germany had promised Bulgaria could annexe eastern Macedonia. Abandoning the region to the invader would be seen as betrayal by the people of northern Greece. Similarly, the Greek public was still basking in driving out the Italians and would respond badly to withdrawal from Albania.

Official records had not been compared at the end of the February meetings, which were conducted in French. But it was as if they were of two separate meetings. Some of the detail was common to both, but the emphasis in the British record was on immediate withdrawal, in the Greek on Yugoslavia's intentions.

Papagos would not withdraw troops from Albania. His men were exhausted after several months in the front line without relief, and outnumbered. The British would not send a force to Greece unless at least three Greek divisions were available to cover their arrival. The British calculated they had three options: they could accept the Metaxas Line plan they regarded as futile; they could leave the Greeks to their fate, which they considered politically impossible, although Eden had been offered that possibility by Churchill a few days before; or they could defend the Aliakmon Line with a reduced Greek contribution.

Late on the third day, Eden and Dill met with Papagos and King George to hammer out a compromise reflecting the third option. Papagos still believed it more logical to hold a fortified frontier line, the Metaxas, but ordered a partial withdrawal to satisfy the king's need for British aid.

Pressed by Dill on whether he thought they could stop the Germans, Papagos said, 'I don't believe we can defeat them on either line.'

'How can you agree to execute a plan you don't believe in?' Dill persisted, unaware of the irony.

'I accept a solution which isn't the best. Other solutions preclude the British joining Greece. Whatever decision is finally taken, I'll do everything in my power to achieve the result we want.'[72]

By midnight they had an agreed plan. Three Greek divisions would stay on the Metaxas Line. British forces would be despatched as rapidly as shipping allowed to join three other Greek divisions, battle-inexperienced and armed with captured Italian weapons, on the Aliakmon Line.

———

General Blamey sent a letter headed 'Most Secret and Personal' to Menzies in London. He broke down Wavell's force of 126,000 men, with only 15,000 of them British combat troops. In the past, he noted, when British leaders had control of dominion troops, dominion commanders were excluded from all control, planning and policy. 'The plan is what I feared; piecemeal dispatch to Europe,' he added.[73] Menzies didn't reply, later saying he didn't receive the letter.

At the same time, Churchill was telling Eden that War Cabinet was having doubts about the Greek expedition. The chiefs of staff had misgivings too, but didn't feel they could question military advice from 'those on the spot'.[74]

Eden wrote back, 'The hard fact remains that our forces, including Dominion contingents, will be engaged in an operation more hazardous than it seemed a week ago. You will no doubt decide on any communication to be made to the Dominion Governments.'[75]

Churchill could see problems waiting to pounce. He replied that Eden should be careful not to urge Greece into hopeless resistance alone when the Australian and New Zealand governments' further agreement might not eventuate.

Eden responded, 'I need not emphasise to you the effect of our now withdrawing from the agreement actually signed between chief of imperial general staff and Greek commander-in-chief. This seems to me quite unthinkable.'[76] More unthinkable perhaps is that an agreement was signed at all, committing dominion troops to an operation considered more hazardous without consulting either government concerned.

Churchill told Wavell directly that they must be able to tell the Australian and New Zealand governments faithfully that the greater risk was taken because Dill and the Middle East commanders were convinced they had a reasonable fighting chance, not because of a signed agreement. 'A precise military appreciation is indispensable,' he said.[77]

Wavell met with Freyberg and then Blamey, telling them of the changed circumstances and the greater risk involved. A report by Wavell to London, shown to Menzies, said that the two generals showed no signs of wanting to back out. Both would later say they felt they were being informed by their senior commander, not consulted. There was no suggestion their opinion was sought. Freyberg added that he told Wavell he had no illusions about the difficulties and was told the New Zealand government was prepared to go ahead.

The time had passed to back out anyway. Bernard Freyberg left Alexandria that night on the cruiser *York*, along with the first echelon of the New Zealand Division, bound for Greece. Neither the British War Cabinet nor the New Zealand or Australian governments had formally accepted the changed circumstances at that point. The mission was swirling in a mist of contentions, obscuring its rationale. The Balkan front, once the purpose of this venture, was no longer mentioned. Moral obligation was now its justification. The word 'why' had slipped from everyone's vocabulary.

Cabinet met the next day and authorised the Athens agreement, undertaking to communicate that to the dominion governments, who had still not been advised of the new difficulties. At the meeting Menzies said he found himself in agreement with the decision, but while it relied on the judgement of Eden, Dill and the Middle East commanders, all their arguments told against their own advice. The meeting endorsed Churchill's concern that these governments must be able to be told the decision was taken on military advice, not on a commitment by a British minister, and that a military appreciation was indispensable. No appreciation was ever provided.

On 8 March, Blamey cabled Percy Spender, Australia's Minister for the Army, and was given permission to put his views to Australia's cabinet. His detailed appraisal followed two days later. 'Military operation extremely hazardous in view of the disparity between opposing forces in number and training,' he concluded.[78] Unaware of Blamey's views, Menzies was advising that Eden, Dill and Wavell considered the Greece expedition had a good chance of success and that troops could be taken from Libya without endangering the front at Benghazi.

At the same time, the New Zealand cabinet met in Wellington, noting all the possible dangers of the venture with more insight than Eden, Dill and others seemed able to muster, but resolved unanimously that they couldn't 'contemplate the possibility of abandoning the Greeks to their fate, especially after the heroic resistance with which they have met the Italian invader. To do so would destroy the moral basis of our cause.' New Zealand troops, the resolution added 'would be first to approve of the decision now taken'.[79]

The trickle of British forces into positions on the Aliakmon Line had already begun and Freyberg went straight to the line, reporting 'mixed feelings' after meeting the Greek field commanders who said it was impossible to fight in the mountains without mule transport or pack artillery. Already there, the commander of the English armoured brigade, Brigadier Harold Charrington, told him the Greek division with him had 'no possible prospect of fighting usefully as a mobile force'.[80] Another of the divisions had five trucks and the commander's car as motorised transport, otherwise using carts and pack animals.

Early in March, Wavell's chief of staff, Arthur Smith, said to Freddie de Guingand of the Joint Planning Staff (JPS) in Cairo, 'I've heard the JPS is working on a paper for possible evacuation from Greece. Is that true?'

'Yes,' said de Guingand, one of the team working on it.

'The CinC [Wavell] is annoyed with that. It's to stop!'

However, the naval and air representatives on JPS were outside Wavell's command and continued their investigation, as did de Guingand clandestinely.[81]

On 19 March, General Blamey arrived at Piraeus on the cruiser *Gloucester* with his chief of staff Brigadier Syd Rowell and immediately drove north. Blamey found the Greek commanders they met to be defeatist, 'lacking in confidence and not well-informed'. The men, he concluded, would be stubborn fighters in prepared defences, but couldn't fight a well-equipped enemy in a battle that moved around. It was a conclusion British intelligence had also reached but hadn't shared with the Australians.[82]

Tom Blamey was a walking contradiction, truculent and affable, a heavy drinker and womaniser who read serious literature, loved animals and collected wild orchids. Serving as a staff officer in Gallipoli and France, he'd transferred to the Militia after the war and was appointed Victorian Police Commissioner. Blamey's strength lay in strategic planning rather than as a field commander. He gave lucid and precise orders, but was often feuding with fellow officers and pursuing vendettas.

Returning from the Aliakmon Line, convinced his troops were fighting a lost cause, Blamey toured the Peloponnese, the southern region of mainland Greece. Inspecting beaches as they went, his aide-de-camp was told to mark 'convalescent sites' on a Shell road map. Like the JPS, he was already looking ahead at evacuation.

After his discouraging introduction to the Greek campaign, the Australian commander finally arrived at his headquarters, newly set up behind the Aliakmon Line in a village that was a 'collection of wretched hovels and its inhabitants had a bad record of malaria; the houses were infested with vermin and the yards with savage dogs'.[83] Blamey's day hadn't got any better.

Having finally settled on the disposition of their forces, the British and Greek commanders made adjustments to the new reality, waiting for the inevitable, when the ground moved in unexpected directions. First, the Yugoslav regent buckled to Germany's pressure and agreed to a treaty of mutual cooperation. The Yugoslav prime minister, Dragiša Cvetković went to Vienna on 25 March and signed the Tripartite Pact, dashing what little hope remained for the British of a Balkan front.

The British weren't the only ones unhappy with this turn of events. In Belgrade news of the agreement sparked massive anti-German protests. The German ambassador's car was spat at. Prince Paul was ousted in a bloodless coup led by younger officers of the army and air force and replaced with Prince Peter, the seventeen-year-old heir to the throne. Cvetković was replaced as prime minister with an air force general, Dušan Simović.

Both Churchill and Hitler swung into action. Churchill told Eden and Dill, already on their way home, to return to Cairo. He instructed the British ambassador in Belgrade to tell the new Yugoslav government the United Kingdom would recognise it if it denounced its Tripartite agreement, and told the Turkish president this was a renewed opportunity for a Balkan front against the Germans. Brimming with vindication, Churchill wrote to Arthur Fadden, Australia's acting prime minister while Menzies was in Great Britain: 'Thursday's events in Belgrade show the far-reaching effects of this and other measures we have taken on whole Balkan situation. German plans have been upset, and we may cherish renewed hopes of forming a Balkan front with Turkey.'[84]

On the other side, Hitler was far from pleased. His quiet settling of the Balkans had come unstuck, his ambassador's car spat at. The Führer gave immediate orders for an invasion of Yugoslavia 'with unmerciful harshness'. March rains and flooded Bulgarian airfields had delayed the planned German move on Greece, but an attack on both Greece and Yugoslavia was now to take place as soon as practical.

Eden and Dill flew to Athens and found Papagos a changed man, talking of 'a solid and continuing offensive front from the Adriatic to the Black Sea' after 'cleaning up Albania' with the Yugoslavs. But the new regime in Yugoslavia was plagued with indecision. Trying to avoid provoking Germany, it would neither renounce nor implement the Tripartite Pact, hoping instead to replace it. Simović refused to meet Eden, but allowed Dill to meet with Yugoslav high command to present exaggerated troop numbers. Dill came back with no outcome.

Following that, generals Wilson and Papagos crossed the border with staff officers to meet with Yugoslavia's army operations chief, General Radivoje Janković. The discussion began with big plans, the Greeks to hold the German attack at the Metaxas Line, a combined British–Yugoslav force to stop an advance on Salonika through the Doiran-Struma area to where some of Charrington's armoured brigade was deployed, and Yugoslavs and Greeks to attack the Italians in Albania. When Wilson said the British only had one division and an armoured brigade in Greece at that time, Janković remarked that Dill had mentioned four divisions.

The enthusiastic plans devolved into vague undertakings and the parties headed off with nothing concrete achieved, but a disturbing thought had lodged in Jumbo Wilson's mind. Serious doubts were festering about the ability of the Royal Yugoslav Army. The German advance might be able to get rapidly to the Monastir Gap, a short distance from the border with Greece and behind the Aliakmon Line. It had also worried Blamey on his tour of northern Greece, but Wilson was yet to consult him.

The state of play in the eastern Mediterranean was further shaken when General Rommel launched an offensive against the Western Desert Force on 31 March. The British tanks and artillery were depleted and they retreated, abandoning Benghazi to the Afrika Corps. All available military resources were rushed to Tobruk to halt the German advance. On 6 April, a desperate Wavell decided that the second Australian division and the Polish brigade would not go to Greece after all, but would stay in North Africa. An inadequate expeditionary force was to be watered down further. When he told Blamey, the Australian responded that the retention of Libya wasn't vital, but the force in Greece was in grave peril if it wasn't built to sufficient strength.[85] It was all too late.

The hopes of a week before had soured. The waiting resumed, but that wouldn't be for long.

Part II

GREECE

3

TOO LATE, TOO LITTLE

At dawn on 6 April 1941, Hitler's Twelfth Army crossed from Bulgaria into Greece and southern Yugoslavia. One cohort pushed south towards General Dill's 'unsound' Metaxas Line, making little progress against its fortifications. It wasn't until the second night, after a prolonged assault with flame-throwers, that the first of the twenty-one forts was overcome.[1] On another front, the Yugoslav army, underprepared and lacking decisive leadership, offered little resistance to a panzer strike across its southern flank while the Luftwaffe bombed Belgrade. In a three-day blitz the city was pounded into rubble, killing thousands.

Athens was also put under heavy air attack that first day. In Piraeus harbour, congested with shipping, *Clan Fraser* was unloading its cargo of munitions, with 250 tonnes of TNT still in the hold by evening and two barges alongside filled with the explosive. At 10 pm, German bombers headed straight for three ammunition carriers, pinpointed by German legation staff. *Clan Fraser* was hit by three bombs in succession and was soon in flames. At 2 am it exploded, hurling white-hot metal plates into the air and detonating

TNT in the barges, killing a tugboat crew trying to tow them clear. Metal and debris rained down on the harbour, setting fire to ships, small craft and harbourside buildings. Shortly after, the other two ammunition ships blew up. As the sun rose, ships in the harbour and buildings in the dock area were still burning furiously. People in Piraeus, expecting more attacks, had fled to the hills.[2]

The Germans stormed through Yugoslavia to set up additional fronts in Greece. On the second day, a panzer force drove through the thinly defended Doiran Pass on the border, and down the Axios Valley towards the port city of Salonika. Seeing the German tanks coming, a British forward unit sabotaged bridges over the Axios River and withdrew west through the Aliakmon Line. That night New Zealand troops, positioned on the line, watched fires burning in distant Salonika. The next day, black smoke rose from burning oil depots. The enemy was getting nearer and the men bristled with anticipation. By 9 April, Salonika was in German hands.

In four days of fighting, the invaders had only limited success on the Metaxas Line, even with dive-bombers and fighters in support. General Papagos's argument for strengthening the line may have been vindicated, but by then it was too late. Sweeping down to Salonika, the Germans had isolated the Eastern Macedonian Army and its general had capitulated. The German commander, Field Marshal List, refrained from taking Greek soldiers prisoner, impressed by their resolute defence. They were free to return to their homes after surrendering arms and supplies.

While the forces that had taken Salonika were probing the Vermion Range, a third front opened up that would prove decisive. A motorised German force had sped through Yugoslavia around the top of the Vermions, turning south towards Monastir near the border with Greece. The valley beyond, running behind the Aliakmon Line, was more suited to tank and armoured vehicle movement than the hairpin bends and sheer drops on roads through the Vermion passes.

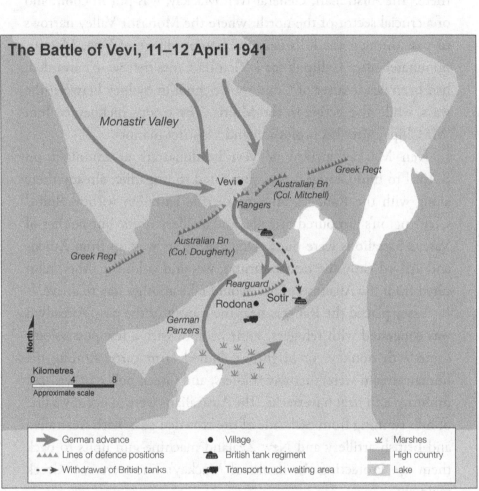

With the Aliakmon Line exposed to attack from the front and rear, General Wilson had to strengthen his defence to the north where it was most vulnerable. He had little option other than weakening the line, already stretched thin, by moving troops north from there. The Australian, General Iven Mackay, was put in command of a crucial sector of the north, where the Monastir Valley narrows to pass through the hills near the border village of Vevi. Mackay, nominated after Gallipoli for a Victoria Cross that wasn't awarded, had been headmaster of Cranbrook School in Sydney between the wars, while also active in the Militia. The troops nicknamed him 'Mr Chips', after his profession and his strict manner.

Iven Mackay arrived at Vevi headquarters at midnight on 8 April to find George Vasey, promoted to brigadier, already there along with the Rangers, an English rifle battalion within 'Rollie' Charrington's armoured brigade, and artillery units, but neither of Vasey's battalions were there. One was on its way up from Athens and arrived early the next morning, wet and cold; the other, relocated from the Aliakmon Line, would take another day to arrive.

Vasey placed the Rangers near the mouth of the pass. Already it was congested with refugees, some on foot with a few possessions, some with donkeys or brightly coloured farm carts. Among the human stream were Yugoslav soldiers, and Greek police in well-cut uniforms and neat haversacks. The Australians were to occupy a line of hills running from each side of the crowded pass, with Australian and British artillery and New Zealand machine-gun units to back them up. Protecting the flanks of Mackay's line were two Greek regiments.

After marching 15 kilometres and climbing up to 1000 metres to their positions overlooking the pass, the first Australians to arrive struggled with cold mountain air gulped into searing lungs. They dug in on the forward slopes as best they could. 'We laid out our groundsheets in the mud and got into bed two together as we had been doing in Libya,' Norm Johnstone, a former Sydney bank teller, wrote home. 'It was miserably cold and wet and our spirits did not improve when we awoke on the morning of the 10th—frozen stiff and covered with the heaviest frost I have ever seen.'[3]

The other Australian battalion had barely put its tents up on the mountainous Aliakmon Line when orders came to move north. Driving without lights through the rain-lashed night, tired drivers squinted at a small light beneath the vehicle ahead to guide them. The men slithered and lurched in the canvas-covered trucks, thrown about with boxes and packs in a fog of cigarette smoke. Finally, after marching 10 kilometres on ground too spongy for trucks, the troops manhandled equipment up a goat track to their designated positions overlooking approaches to the pass.[4]

'It was very near impossible to dig,' says company commander, Bill Robertson. 'It was all stone and rocks. A terrible place.'[5] Instead, they piled stones as a protective wall they called a 'sanger'.

A couple of days before, a British patrol had crossed the border to deserted Monastir, destroyed a bridge over the River Crna and noted German vehicles gathering on its northern bank. The two armies made contact the next day when engineers were demolishing a stone bridge inside Yugoslavia and German motorbikes came down a narrow, winding road ahead of a column of trucks and armoured cars. 'Lofty' King, part of a New Zealand armoured escort, drove forward and opened fire with his Bren gun. The distant column halted and troops jumped out of trucks, replying with mortars and machine guns. These were the SS Leibstandarte, formerly Hitler's bodyguard and now an infantry component of the Wehrmacht's invasion force. The engineers and their escort quickly abandoned the bridge and scuttled with Corporal King back across the border.[6]

By the middle of the day, the invaders had moved to within a few kilometres of the British front line. From their positions on the slopes, the Australians could see a long slow line of tanks, trucks and artillery. Troops were spilling out of the trucks. Cec Chrystal, a lieutenant from Cootamundra, noticed an enemy machine-gun

post being dug in by the railway line and phoned the British artillery to direct fire on them. 'Eventually they got their range and
blew the whole box and dice to blazes,' he says. 'Shortly afterwards,
Jerry opened up his artillery on us and gave us merry hell for a good
many minutes. As his shells hit the snow and burst, huge clouds of
smoke came up and someone asked if it was gas. I yelled "No" and
hoped it wasn't because my respirator was buried somewhere deep
in the snow!'[7]

Peter Cade, bringing ammunition to an artillery post, arrived to
find the position shelled and stretcher-bearers 'carrying out a man
without an arm. There were two killed and two wounded and one
badly rattled. We took the nerve case out up to the artillery OP
[observation post].'[8]

The battle for Greece had begun in earnest. Very few of the
Anzac soldiers there had seen frontline fighting in Libya. For the
rest, it would be their first experience of battle. The individual
soldiers were about to learn how they would handle that first taste
of combat. 'One fellow was just about off his head and I had him in
with me trying to quieten him,' continues Chrystal, holed up in a
headquarters pit. 'Then on top of that Lieutenant Wally Davern was
hit and his sergeant had passed out with shell shock. They brought
Wally up to my hole and Jack Huston and I managed to get his arm
bandaged, and Jack took him to our little hut near the coal village.
I then proceeded to bring the sergeant back to life. He was still
in a bad way, shells were still coming over. Hal [Captain Conkey,
his immediate commander, also from Cootamundra] was still away,
and I was just about going nuts.'[9]

These were not professional soldiers. They had volunteered to be
there out of a sense of adventure or duty, or both. They had been
trained for the flat open spaces of desert warfare and now found
themselves high on rocky slopes, freezing and exhausted. As they
waited for the fighting to begin, they worried whether they'd be
killed or wounded, whether they'd fight or run. Few thought of

being taken prisoner. It's difficult to prepare men for the mental pressure of battle where they are required to kill fellow human beings, difficult to grasp they are facing men intent on killing them by whatever means including deception.

In the evening, troops who had just arrived were scrambling up the side of the pass. While they were digging in, a German patrol infiltrated their lines in the dark and called out in flawless English, 'Stand up, Steve. I can't see you. Where are you, Steve?' Thinking it was a lost British patrol, one of the Aussies stood up and beckoned them, to be met with a hail of machine-gun fire. Some of the Australians were shot, some taken prisoner and marched away.[10]

The British engineers had rigged up explosives that afternoon on the road coming into Vevi, to detonate when an enemy convoy approached. Rangers went on guard at night while the sappers got some sleep. About midnight, a party of seven in Greek uniforms approached and the sentry went forward to explain they couldn't go past. Two of the party fired at point-blank range, killing the sentry. The Rangers searched for the enemy patrol until they heard a motor start in the dark and a vehicle drive off to the north.[11]

During the night it snowed, with fog in the morning. Another soggy day of frostbite and low visibility followed. Hitler's former SS bodyguard unit advanced and was stopped by artillery. A few German tanks came forward, a couple disabled by mines. British tanks, moving into position at the rear, disabled themselves without the aid of mines, six of them losing their metal tracks on the rough terrain. An attempt by the Germans to come around the eastern flank was driven off by the Greek troops there. Under cover of a heavy afternoon snowfall, the enemy moved forward and occupied 'dead' ground on the lower slopes 200 metres away, unsighted by riflemen on top of the slope and too close for the three-inch mortars.

Orders were issued for no man to leave his section after 9 pm, with all movement after that to be fired on. At one point a cultured English voice called out, 'Put down the gun. Put down that gun,

I tell you.' The voice was fired at with machine gun and rifle and it wasn't heard again.[12] That ruse had outlived its usefulness.

After two days of probing, the enemy got serious. It was a day of cold, biting winds with frozen lubricant causing weapons to misfire. The Germans launched a ferocious three-pronged attack on the defensive line, advancing under mortar and machine-gun cover over a wide front. Seeing a forward Australian platoon in difficulty on its right, the Rangers began withdrawing even though only one platoon had been overrun at that stage. The platoon recovered its lost ground, but the Rangers continued withdrawing, drifting back up the pass beyond Australian artillery posts there to cover them.[13]

In the early afternoon, the Germans drove through the vacated mouth of the pass, penetrating the line and threatening to get around behind the Australians. British anti-tank guns were ineffectual against the enemy's heavy-armoured vehicles. Without infantry support, the defending artillery had pulled back, leaving five anti-tank guns behind, stuck in the mud. The German advance was held up for periods by British artillery, Australian rifles and New Zealand machine guns, but over time it moved relentlessly forward as the defenders fell back in stages.

Field gunners reported to Vasey's headquarters that no infantry remained forward of them, but headquarters staff insisted the Rangers were still in position. Vasey ordered the Rangers to hold the advance until dark, only to find they had already moved back behind the Australians, who were still desperately clinging to the hills either side. The Rangers rallied and set up a rearguard across the road back from the pass, but the Vevi defence was unravelling as units prepared to withdraw.

General Mackay had received instructions that morning to withdraw from Vevi in the evening to a new Aliakmon Line, running roughly at right angles to the original line. Defenders pulling back from Vevi were to take up positions on the new line, but German tanks were already driving into the Australian positions, splitting the defence into small groups that fanned out overland as a premature withdrawal gathered momentum. One of the Australian battalions was under fire from all sides. The phone line from its commander, Colonel John Mitchell, to Vasey's headquarters ran through the Rangers area and had gone dead. Two signallers sent to repair the line were not seen again. The SS infantry attacked Mitchell's men in overwhelming numbers, forcing them into chaotic retreat.

By five in the afternoon, George Vasey was phoning Iven Mackay to tell him the situation had become serious, then warning his other battalion commander, Colonel Ivan Dougherty, that the Allied front had lost cohesion on the right and he should prepare to withdraw. 'The roof is leaking' was the coded message in case enemy signallers had tapped their phone cable. Dougherty's men were still holding, but unlikely to survive continued movement of German troops and tanks to their rear. Dougherty ordered Bren carriers and rifles to hold the German advance until dark while the rest of the battalion fell back. Vasey had ordered their transport to be kept well to the rear, out of enemy reach.[14]

Confusion reigned with command communications breaking down. A staged withdrawal was no longer possible and the withdrawal became a flight across rocky terrain, a 12-kilometre race against the SS Leibstandarte and panzers over waterlogged ground between ridges to the relative safety of trucks. Snow was melting, the mud and slush making retreat even more difficult. Bren guns and the useless Boys anti-tank guns were discarded to speed the withdrawal. Some defenders even threw away their rifles as they scrambled for cover. Tanks overran some units, capturing soldiers falling back.

'There were three of us running over the hill,' recalls 'Dasher' Deacon from Sydney. 'A mortar bomb landed between my feet. Luckily for me it sprayed forward, but it killed poor "Buck" Buchannan and Charlie Mynett. My boot was blown off and I wasn't feeling so good. My mates carried me along, but at the rate we were progressing it wouldn't be long before the Hun caught up with us. Private Jack Fitzgerald held me up and wouldn't leave me.'

Luckily, their commander Ivan Dougherty came by in a Bren carrier and gave Deacon and Fitzgerald a lift to the gathering trucks.[15] He was pulling back in a group whose wheeled vehicles had become bogged in marshy ground. 'Except for the carrier,' Dougherty recalls, 'my party threw petrol over the vehicles and their contents and set them on fire.'[16]

For Cec Chrystal, the withdrawal is a memory of confusion and desperation: 'Somehow or other we got to the top and raced over the other side where we found our company sergeant-major, Wym Keast, had been hit in the left leg and arm. We were helping him along when they opened up from the other side where we thought we were safe. We went flat again. Wym let out a yell and we found that he'd been pretty badly hit a second time. Before I knew what had happened, Hal [Conkey] jumped up and grabbed "Keasty", threw him over his shoulder, and we dragged him into a small wadi [ravine] where we were out of view.' Keast was too badly wounded to move further, so Conkey and Chrystal left him there until they could find help. A little further on they found a stretcher-bearer. 'We took a party back, grabbed Wym, and set off carrying him in relays, never daring to stop with Jerry on our heels.'[17] Keast, another Cootamundra boy, survived the war. Conkey was awarded a Military Cross.

Nightfall approached, allowing more time for the Allied infantry and gunners to get away. Lieutenant Sid Diffey collected stragglers and ran into a group with John Mitchell that had been cut off by tanks. They waited in a ravine until dark, then skirted two villages until, at two in the morning, they came across a line of armoured vehicles they assumed were German. Trying to find a way around, they were detected and fired on, then they heard English voices. 'We're Australians!' they yelled.[18]

Sappers meanwhile detonated bridges to delay the pursuing enemy, but they didn't always get it right. 'Immediately afterwards, along came one of our own trucks from the other side,' Norm Johnstone wrote home. 'One second I heard the sound of the racing motor as the truck leaped into space, the next the horrible sickening thud as it crashed into the opposite bank of the river and then dead silence.'[19]

Meanwhile, defenders continued the desperate cross-country trek. A contingent of about seventy, withdrawing late with Major Ken Barham at the rear, moved down the road instead of avoiding it as advised. A small group of Germans on motorcycles caught up with them and, in the exchange of fire, Barham shot one soldier and was himself killed before the Germans rode off. Further down the road, the Australians walked into an enemy position and were disarmed and taken prisoner.[20]

Peter Balfe, a sergeant from Orange, was among the captives who were taken back to crossroads where they buried Barham and were put to work filling a crater in the middle of the road. 'We were soon taken off this job as we proved too much of a hindrance,' he recalls. 'Later we started on our journey to the rear. Back we went, past miles of German transports which were held up nose to tail right through the pass.'[21]

At the other end of the battle zone, a cluster of Aussie and Kiwi drivers waited with their trucks at the rendezvous point. Huddled in the bitter cold around a small fire in a drum, until ordered to put it out in case it attracted an air attack, they turned their truck engines over every hour or so to ensure they would start when needed.[22]

About eleven o'clock, small parties of weary Australians started coming down in the dark from the hills, some without rifles and one or two even without boots. They continued to drift in over several hours. Little was said. Fifty-year-old John Mitchell was among them, physically and mentally exhausted. One by one, the trucks filled and moved smartly off.

Overnight, some of the withdrawing Australians had joined the rearguard, along with British tanks. George Vasey and Ivan Dougherty crept forward before dawn to observe enemy positions at first light. On the plain below, a kilometre away, they saw Germans moving around. A khaki-clad group, more than a hundred men captured during the night, was held in front of the German line. Wearing a white raincoat, Vasey was easily spotted trying to get a better view of the prisoners. He and Dougherty were shot at and slipped away while their artillery returned fire, unaware of the camped prisoners.

Soon after, Germans moved in towards the rearguard, driving a group of captured soldiers in front of them as a human shield. A Vickers machine gun opened up, scattering Germans and their prisoners in all directions.[23] A furious firestorm erupted. Dick Parry, in the midst of it, wrote later in his diary, 'The air becomes one whining, hissing mass of lead at a range of only a few hundred yards and we keep to the bottom of our shallow hole as bullets strike the parapet.'[24]

Someone yelled to withdraw and Private Parry ran 300 metres up a slope under enemy fire. 'I don't know what my thoughts were at this time—probably nil! I start to run but my legs simply refuse to function so I have to walk. Bullets sing and whistle past. They thud on either side of me, but I'm too exhausted to worry,' he writes. 'A bloke in front of me falls and I catch up with him and try to help him. He is shot in the shoulder. He is bleeding badly and blood is spurting out of his boot. I give him a hand and we fall into a wadi, but he dies on the spot.'[25]

The German advance soon drove this defence line back to a second rearguard of British tanks, 20 kilometres further south. In the hurried retreat, one tank had its gun pointing out to one side. Bob Crisp, a tank commander, stared, mesmerised. 'As it thundered down the narrow roadway,' he says, 'the two-pounder muzzle connected with a telegraph pole with a terrific whack. The turret whirled dizzily in a full circle, just in time to hit the next pole. Then it hit a third one before the crew got their crazy world under control.'[26]

The panzers were held up but by the afternoon had moved around swampland to the west. A few got bogged but the rest emerged to use the element of surprise in a sharp battle. With no tank reserve left, Charrington withdrew his armoured force, leaving twenty-one machines broken down and burning. They'd been withdrawn from Libya for maintenance and sent to Greece instead, un-serviced. The British tank force had delayed the German invader by a day at most, but was dangerously depleted.

A week before, with news the Germans had begun the invasion of Greece, the troops in the mountains along the original Aliakmon Line readied themselves to repel the attack. 'We started racing around getting everything ready, but of course the army never does anything right and we are still waiting,' noted one soldier's diary. 'Had a sleep and a chicken for dinner grilled over the fire like a goanna.'[27]

They waited for a week in drizzle while the attack took place at Vevi instead. Under constant low cloud, positions had been dug into frozen ground and were often half-filled with water. Ordered not to start fires with the increasing air threat, the men ate cold rations in freezing conditions. Those taking over from Greek troops relocating further north were given mugs of konjac and ouzo with huge smiles, but no insights or local knowledge.

The lack of a common language between the Greeks and Allies was a constant hindrance. The British army had 3000 Cypriot labourers and drivers in Greece, many speaking both Greek and English, but no one thought to use them as interpreters. As one English officer has noted, 'Our habitual excruciating public-school French, with an interpreter to supply missing words, was inadequate as a medium for military conversations.'[28]

There was also the problem of conveying military needs to civilians. As at Vevi, Greek people headed to the mountains before the Germans arrived. The Australian command was concerned that refugees were choking the road, making military movements difficult, and fixated that 'fifth columnists' might infiltrate the human stream. Ordered to prevent refugees moving through a pass, Ken Hill-Griffith's platoon was told to 'hold them back by sheer physical strength, without violence or the use of weapons'. The only alternative was bluff.

A mayor arriving with his villagers was told to take the coastal road or stay in the village. He replied that they were coming through to shelter in the hills and weren't going to be stopped. The soldiers went through the motions of preparing their weapons, producing a clatter of fixing bayonets and loading rifles amid noisy commands. Then they stood to each side of the road in firing positions, revealing four Bren guns pointing down the road at the crowd. Hill-Griffith stepped forward and told the mayor he would give the order to fire if the crowd moved forward.

There was a brief silence. Then the mayor raised his hat, dropped his head and burst into tears, waving his people back.[29]

After a few days, General Blamey ordered forces still on the original Aliakmon Line back to the revised line, following the Aliakmon River instead of crossing it, to ensure they weren't cut off by the enemy driving down from Vevi. It was a defensive line that Blamey had proposed over two weeks before, and General Papagos even earlier.

Three Australian battalions, some 3000 men, trekked 60 kilometres over rough mountain tracks to the new line. Snow fell heavily and the bitterly cold wind made them shiver despite their exertion. The 'winter' clothes they wore were designed for an Australian winter, not a Greek one. The bottom of Jack Smithers' greatcoat was 'hitting against my legs as though it was made of wood'.[30] Donkeys and troops were heavily laden. The men stumbled in the dark on slippery slopes and were helped up by their mates, their load redistributed.

'With a muttered curse, they clambered to their feet and marched on,' recalls Lieutenant Jack Blamey, a nephew of the general. 'One, who had been off colour for several days, fell from sheer exhaustion. One man took his haversack, another his rifle, another his blanket and we pulled him along, slapping his face all the while to keep him awake.'[31]

Much of the route was ankle-deep in icy slush, with falling snow often obliterating the track. 'One soldier told me he knew we were lost as we twice passed the same pack someone dropped in the snow,' says 'Tom' Selby, leading a medical unit.[32]

Bernie Brearley, a machine-gun sergeant, carried arms, ammunition and personal gear in the moonlight up a hill he thought would never end. 'The track wound up around the mountain, always up, three thousand feet up,' he remembers. 'We staggered on, sweat blinding us, on one side a mountain wall, on the other a sheer drop. About all we could see was the faint outline of the track in the darkness.'[33]

All night, men and donkeys trudged under their loads. Feet stumbled and legs ached. As the sun rose, a group found themselves on top of a pass, below them a silver thread gleaming magically in the dawn light. It was the Aliakmon River. They were in sight of the new line, but they were not yet at the end of the march, making their way down to flat ground for breakfast and to let stragglers catch up. Luck was with one group, stopping at a small village where two old ladies gave them hot milk, boiled eggs and freshly baked bread.[34]

Those further back made camp in cold, wet conditions and moved down to the river at first light. Engineers had rigged a 'flying punt', attached to wire rope and propelled by the river's strong current. The whole day, which happened to be Easter Sunday, was spent ferrying men across the river in the improvised vessel. When they got to the southern bank, troops were surprised to find two men serving tea and chocolate as if they'd turned up at the local sportsground. Father Paddy Youll, a Catholic priest, and Harold Hosier of the Salvos offered tots of Johnnie Walker as well, and Sao biscuits.[35]

The ordeal wasn't over. The men now had to climb out of the river valley up a narrow, rocky track, ankle-deep in snow and mud. A long weary column developed with the stronger men taking turns carrying the heavier loads; the underfed and overloaded donkeys staggering with them. When the animals lost their footing, they had to be unsaddled to get back on their feet and continue up the precipitous, ill-marked track. A small landslide carried away part of the track and some donkeys were lost trying to get around it.

Bill Jenkins had fallen behind his company, assisting his mate 'Troubles', who was struggling with the physical and mental demands of the trek. The pair of them reached the Aliakmon punt at night, just as the engineers were about to sink it believing all troops had crossed. On the other side, Jenkins and Troubles were contemplating the climb when a horseman came down from a group of Greek cavalry.

'*Kalinychta* [good night],' said Jenkins through Troubles' whining.

'What's the matter here?' the horseman replied in good English.

He was an Australian, from Junee where his Greek father had a fish shop. He'd been visiting his family homeland when the war had started and had been called up to the Greek cavalry. The horseman put Troubles and some of Jenkins' gear on his steed and carried them up to a village, while Jenkins got himself up there without the burden of his mate.[36]

On reaching the village, soldiers bathed their feet in a small stream coming off Mount Olympus, the freezing water an anaesthetic for aching feet. Some found their feet frostbitten when they took off their boots; some had lost toenails. After bivouac there, all units had a further final climb to their positions.

Les Cook was with an Australian unit withdrawing by truck. They were one driver short and the men were asked if anyone could drive a 1.5 tonne truck. There was silence. Sitting in a truck back at base camp with a mate from Transport, Cook had been shown the rudiments of driving it and changing gears by double-declutch, but he hadn't ever driven the truck . . . or any vehicle. He hesitantly offered to drive if no one else was able. The eighteen-year-old was not confident driving a truck loaded with men in the dark and without lights, but said he was prepared to give it a go if the passengers were willing to take the risk. Again, silence.

One of the other drivers had to turn the truck around on the narrow mountain road and left it idling with the handbrake on. Cook took over and crawled in low gear in the middle of the convoy, trying to keep the truck in front in dim vision without running into it. It was nerve-racking and draining.

Once off the mountain, the road straightened, the moon came out and Cook grew in confidence, but when approaching a village on a downhill slope, the truck started to get away from him. Heading towards a sharp turn, the young Australian jammed on the brake pedal, declutched and fumbled with the gear lever, missing the lower gear. As his passenger in the front opened the door to jump, Cook managed to slam into the lower gear and slow sufficiently to round the corner. They got to their destination soon after, the men under the canopy in the back oblivious to how close they had come to disaster.

Les Cook switched off the engine, stepped down from the cabin and didn't attempt to drive a vehicle again for fifteen years.[37]

———

With no experience yet of battle in either Greece or North Africa, the New Zealanders had waited for the German army with a mix of naivety and nervousness. Flying low over them on their section of the Aliakmon Line, a Messerschmitt pilot waved at Charlie Upham's platoon, and the Kiwis waved back obligingly. The plane flew on, banked and came back along the same line, this time spraying them with machine-gun fire.

Brian Bassett, a Christchurch lawyer, wrote home that during the day they felt confident and ready to tackle the enemy, but at night 'noises are heard and one cannot help feeling that somehow he has slipped through and he is on us'.[38] Barbed wire was erected. Tins with stones were hung on wire, along with bells taken from goat herds. Richard Kean, at a forward listening post, heard rustles in the undergrowth and a clicking noise like pebbles sliding. The engine driver, also from Christchurch, drew his .45 revolver and discovered two turtles mating.[39] On sentry duty, Murray McColl heard scuffling in the bushes nearby, took his rifle off his shoulder, fixed a bayonet and found a huge rat eating porridge the cook had left soaking for breakfast.[40]

A new element had entered the campaign. The Luftwaffe began attacking from fields around Salonika in formations of often fifty aircraft, bombing and strafing whatever spotter planes could find for them. Sirens, mounted on the leading edge of Stuka wings, produced a piercing scream as the bomber dived, forcing the men below to huddle in their trenches. With only eighty serviceable warplanes at the outset to hold off the 1100 planes of the Luftwaffe and Italy's air force, the Regia Aeronautica, the RAF was in a hopeless position. The constant German air attack was soon operating virtually unchallenged and would have to be endured by troops and civilians alike for the next eight weeks.

While Aussies were trekking across the mountains to their new positions in the foothills of Mount Olympus, some of the Kiwis were trucked to positions alongside, while others stayed where they were. Refugees—women and children with as many of their possessions as they could carry on their backs—swarmed through the defence lines. Some climbed the slopes, where defenders were dug in, to shelter in caves. Greek soldiers from further east shuffled wearily in bare feet along the grassy side of the road, tattered boots in one hand, rifle in the other. A Yugoslav unit came with four new Skoda anti-aircraft guns and set up alongside the New Zealanders. They shot at enemy planes over the next two days until they ran out of ammunition, then pulled out and were never seen again.[41]

The only road from northern Greece, coming down from Vevi, crossed the Aliakmon at Servia. On the afternoon of 13 April, sunlight flashed on the windscreens of a long column of German vehicles, 15 kilometres back from the bridge. Explosives placed in its three steel-trussed spans were detonated and two of the spans dropped into the river.

Motorcycles were the first enemy element to arrive at the demolished bridge. They were shelled and quickly withdrew. The erection of a pontoon bridge failed under constant Bren and cannon fire. Panzers arrived from Vevi with artillery support. In the firefight that followed, the Germans suffered heavy casualties and the river remained uncrossed.

'Hell it was good,' Eric 'Dasher' Davies notes in his diary. 'Stood to all morning and watched our artillery blow the Huns to bits. Should I survive this I'll always remember our first day as front-line troops.'[42] The Wairarapa shepherd's exhilaration wouldn't last long, but he did survive the war.

Overnight, German infantry crossed the river in portable boats and began infiltrating the New Zealand lines. Just before dawn, a sentry challenged footsteps and a voice shouted back, '*Greko! Greko!*' The Kiwi went down and saw a group of about fifty in the gloom, led by a Greek soldier. He waved them through and they crossed a tank trap and then sheltered as a burst of gunfire came from a bigger contingent behind them. New Zealanders nearby returned fire, then the infiltrators brought machine guns and mortars into the crossfire while the higher-positioned defenders used Bren guns and grenades. As visibility improved in the dawn light, German casualties mounted. After a two-hour exchange, the enemy began surrendering in groups with cries of '*Kamerad*' and waving white handkerchiefs. Afterwards, a body in Greek uniform was found among the dead, probably a prisoner used for the deception.[43] The ruse hadn't worked well but the Germans still had a toehold on the Aliakmon's south bank.

Elsewhere on the line, German mountain troops advanced when misty rain rolled in, reducing visibility to a few metres. By the time it cleared, they were moving up deep ravines, out of the firing line. Attacks on Maori battalion positions, firing automatics and shouting, were initially repelled with grenade, Tommy gun and yelling back, but eventually the forward pits were overrun.

Corporal Taituha, a 34-year-old orderly sergeant who had asked to return to combat, sheltered behind a tree and kept shooting so his section could pull back. In the end, the butt of his rifle was blown off and he was so seriously wounded he was left for dead and ignored by the advancing enemy. After the battle moved on, Harry Taituha rose like a ghoul in a zombie movie and wandered aimlessly for a week until he sought medical help in a nearby village and was captured.[44] He was later repatriated by the Germans to New Zealand.

That evening, Jumbo Wilson ordered the whole Anzac defensive line along the slopes of Mount Olympus to begin withdrawing to a new line at Thermopylae, further south. Orders to Maori unit commanders were radioed uncoded in their own language, confident no German signaller could speak Maori.[45] The Kiwis walked along a narrow track in driving rain to meet trucks waiting on the pass road. They could hear Germans somewhere below them on motorcycles. In the pitch black, each man held the bayonet scabbard of the man in front. When anyone slipped, he had to feel with hand and foot to find the scabbard.[46]

Elsewhere, two of the Australian battalions that had trekked to the heights overlooking the Aliakmon got the order to withdraw without even seeing the enemy. The third battalion could not be reached by runner as all tracks were hidden under snow. The unit needed to get rations, however, and a party set out, eventually locating the track. Arriving at the quartermaster's depot, Tom Fairbairn was told his battalion should have withdrawn the evening before. He returned with supplies and the withdrawal order.[47]

The following night, New Zealand gunners and the remaining infantry pulled back under intense German shelling. It was moonless again and groups lost their way over broken rocky spurs and gullies. At 2.30 am, Colonel John Gray arrived quite exhausted and calculated that two of his companies were not yet there. Colonel Howard Kippenberger, commanding the rearguard, held off completing a series of road demolitions so further stragglers could arrive. At 5 am, Kippenberger ordered a bugle blown to warn that engineers were about to set off the last cratering of the road and leave. A faint voice came, 'New Zealand here. Wait for us!' and four stragglers appeared. At 5.30 am, the bugle was blown again and a single voice called out. It took half an hour before a greatcoat-clad private slid down the opposite bank, still carrying his Bren gun and, nearly dead on his feet, struggled onto the truck.[48]

———

After the shattered defenders had withdrawn from Vevi, Allied forces regrouped across central Greece on the new Aliakmon Line as the German invasion drove forward. Concerned that his army faced isolation, General Papagos ordered its withdrawal from Albania, abandoning the gains there. After months in freezing conditions, exhausted and hungry Greek soldiers moved back from frontier mountains to extend the new line west towards the coast. German units, intent on cutting the returning Greeks off, headed for passes through Western Macedonia.

A Greek motorised division blocked the invaders at one pass. To the south, Charrington's light tanks and residue of heavy tanks had withdrawn to the exit from another pass. After a day enduring dive-bombing and strafing from the air, they moved well to the south with only six of the fifty-two heavy tanks that came to Greece still operational. By the time the Germans reached the pass, it was defended by a single inexperienced and poorly led Greek battalion, which lost much of its force to desertion during the brief battle.

Word was coming into General Wilson's headquarters that Greek forces to the west had disintegrated, the Albanian front had collapsed and the men were moving south in groups, some of them unarmed rabble. They were said to have refused to take up positions on the new line and were heading home.

In the heat of battle, rumours are always swirling around the combat zone. Force command, set back from the battlefield, draws some insight from men coming back from the front, but the first to come back are those who have left before the battle is over, sometimes claiming to be the sole survivor of a unit that is actually still fighting. Half the rumours doing those rounds will be untrue, either self-serving or the product of panic. Sometimes they provide useful intelligence, but their reliability can be uncertain.

When Jumbo Wilson heard reports of the Greek army's disintegration, he didn't look for confirmation but immediately ordered the withdrawal of all his defences to the new line at Thermopylae. Accustomed to British troops withdrawing in formation, it doesn't seem to have occurred to Wilson that this Greek 'rabble' might be heading south not to go home but to take up positions on the Aliakmon Line, also to their south.

A British armoured patrol, probing north, had seen no sign of the advancing enemy. This was because, having passed through gaps in the mountain chain, the German army was temporarily impeded by Greek defenders on muddy, winding roads that had turned to quagmire.

Ten days into the German invasion, the British expedition to save Greece from the Nazi juggernaut had been pushed back to central Greece. It was not going well. When the enemy attacked, defenders were still moving into place with too few troops, usually inadequately equipped. Since then, the Allies had pulled back to a succession of short-lived defensive lines with only sporadic exchanges with the advancing Germans. General Wilson had ordered withdrawal to yet another line on the strength of panicked reports from the combat area. On his eastern flank, Greek soldiers coming back from the abandoned Metaxas Line seemed to confirm the rumours about their compatriots to the west but their circumstances were quite different. To the east, they had surrendered their arms and left the battle zone; at the other end, they were withdrawing to a new defensive line. Mesmerised by his western flank, Wilson was distracted from keeping a closer eye on the Aliakmon Line as a whole.

4

THE KNOT TIGHTENS

Brigadier Stan Savige arrived in Greece with the third Australian brigade a week after Germany launched its invasion. Anzac troops on the relocated Aliakmon Line were about to pull south to a new line through Thermopylae. In the belief that the Germans had already pushed through a collapsed Greek defence, Savige's task was to prevent the advancing enemy getting through to cut off the retreating Anzacs.

A butcher's son who left school at twelve, Stan Savige had enlisted in the First World War as a private and been in the rearguard for the evacuation from Gallipoli. He ended the war as a captain. In the Militia between wars, he had a reputation as a pragmatic manager of his men, with an easy-going manner. That would soon be put to the test. He knew his way around the battlefield because he had learnt soldiering the hard way, but he would soon find this campaign unfathomable, sparring with Greeks and seeing nothing of the Germans except in the air.

On 15 April, Savige arrived with two battalions at Kalabaka on the western flank of the Aliakmon Line. Constant German air raids had reduced the town to Wild West lawlessness and thousands of Greek soldiers from the Albanian front, who had been told to assemble in the town, flooded the streets, milling about, hungry. Looting of abandoned shops and homes was widespread. Civilians were stealing food, kerosene and rifles from unguarded army depots. Sporadic rifle fire continued through the night.[1]

Kalabaka sits below the Meteora, towering sandstone pillars rising up to 600 metres. Perched on top were precipitously built Eastern Orthodox monasteries. At night, a light in one was seen blinking on and off, interpreted by the Australians as a fifth columnist signalling. Bren gunfire was directed at the light. British intelligence had concluded that priests were being paid to preach against the Allies, so the connection was readily made . . . but unfounded. The flickering light was actually produced by a curtain blowing in the breeze.[2] In any case, the German front was some 50 kilometres north and the monastery blinked to the south.

That morning, Savige conferred with General Georgios Tsolakoglou, the Western Macedonian Army commander. The Australian was first briefed by Colonel Barter, assigned by the British Military Mission to liaise with the Greeks, and then, with Barter to translate, met Tsolakoglou in a stone residence out from Kalabaka. Finely dressed Greek officers lounged about the village square opposite. A tall man in his fifties with a toothbrush moustache, the general was upstairs sitting on a bare table and eating a boiled egg. He rose when the visitors entered, then sat and returned to his egg. Through Barter, Savige told Tsolakoglou that unarmed Greek soldiers were cluttering the defences and choking the roads. 'Could you assist clearing them from my command area?' he asked.

The general replied, waving his spoon. Barter translated, 'Machine-gun them! They're all deserters.'

'As a British officer, I can't do that,' said the Australian.

Tsolakoglou airily agreed to move the troops outside the defence area and assist the British convoys move in. He said his force was assembling in the mountains to the west. When the Australian commented that his engineers would be placing demolition charges in the road tunnel there, the Greek general, who had engineers already there laying mines, demanded Savige's engineers stay out of *his* area of command. He would not be budged by arguments about 'operational necessity'.

Savige returned to the question of moving the Greek troops with the attack imminent.

'When do you expect it?' asked Tsolakoglou.

'Late this afternoon or early tomorrow morning,' was the glib reply. Savige had no idea when it might happen.

'So soon?' the Englishman translated, unsure if it was mocking or surprised.

Tsolakoglou said he would issue orders immediately and agreed to meet in the evening.[3] With his army reduced to two weakened divisions, he had been placed under the command of General Pitsikas, coming back from Albania, and was due to drive west to Pitsikas's headquarters. Georgios Tsolakoglou was one of several Greek field commanders coming to the view that Greece would have been better to have negotiated an agreement with Germany, as Romania, Hungary and Bulgaria had done. Those countries' towns and villages had not been bombed nor their roads and bridges blown up.

Towards noon, Stan Savige was driven to a bridge on the road into the mountains where a battalion commander, Roy King, had a problem. Some Greek troops were heading west across the bridge into the mountains while others were crossing the bridge in the opposite direction, heading for Kalabaka. Australian soldiers with fixed bayonets were holding angry Greeks at both ends, forcing all of them to move either into or back to the mountains. They had no language in common and were communicating through gestures.

Savige didn't want Greek troops hovering around the Australian front, not having grasped it was also the Greek front. While he discussed the issue with King, what he later described as 'a convoy of magnificent cars and charabancs, filled with Greek officers' drove past on its way to the mountains. Leaning out of a car window, General Tsolakoglou 'waved farewell to me with a broad smile on his face'.[4]

These Australian units had just arrived at the battlefield. In that short time, they had developed differing perceptions of the Greek troops. To Corporal Alan Hackshaw, the Greek army was 'in full retreat' with stragglers blocking the road. 'Some were wounded and most had worn-out or no boots at all. Most had bleeding feet and they could hardly hobble along.'[5] He hadn't seen his countrymen pulling back from Vevi.

'I would have been proud to be killed standing by these soldiers,' says Lieutenant Arthur McRobbie, in the same battalion as Hackshaw. 'They were footsore, hungry and weary, and yet when they heard they were needed, they turned round and went back the way they had come [from Albania], to stand side by side with us and try to hold the onrushing German mass. If that isn't guts, I've never seen it.'[6]

In the evening, Savige received the first of a series of contradictory orders. From Blamey's HQ, he was instructed that his force was to join the general withdrawal the following night, with Charrington's armoured brigade covering. As Savige knew, the British brigade had already passed through Kalabaka, heading south that day. He contacted its commander, but Brigadier Charrington refused to turn back, insisting his tanks were in bad repair and his men exhausted. His two tank units had engaged the enemy just once, and the light tanks were still in good shape.[7]

Blamey had been put in command of the revised Aliakmon Line but Charrington claimed he was authorised to use his own discretion, surprising autonomy for a colonel.[8] In any case, he added, General Wilson had directed the brigade to move back to Thermopylae. Jumbo Wilson had set himself up in a split headquarters, part in central Greece and part in Athens, moving constantly between the two. The Athens staff, who still spent much of their day in the British Club, had already made undertakings to Greek high command without consulting Wilson. Whether Charrington's instructions came from Wilson, one of his headquarters or on his own initiative is unclear.

Harold 'Rollie' Charrington was an odd choice to lead an armoured unit, more like an Evelyn Waugh character than a military commander. Another product of Eton and Sandhurst and an avid bird-watcher, Charrington had written a monograph on the greater virtue of horse over motorised transport in war, and retired soon after.[9] Seven years later, in 1939, he was recalled to the British army and put in charge of troops in armoured vehicles.

In Greece, he ignored orders on at least a couple of occasions, treating a Wilson order to support a Greek counter-attack as a 'suggestion' and doing nothing.[10] In the whole campaign, he issued only one operational order and that was before fighting commenced. His tank commanders had only sketchy second-hand information about the strategy in a rapidly unfolding conflict.[11] While he had dismissed a Greek motorised division as 'just over two thousand untrained and recently enlisted garage hands',[12] he seemed content to let the remnants of his infantry unit, the Rangers, tag along behind his retreating brigade.

The Armoured Brigade trundled along the road towards Larisa. British and Greek vehicles, mules and ox-carts were scarcely able to move, all intermingled and packed two lines deep whenever the road allowed it. Greek soldiers were walking everywhere, 'so tired that they didn't care whether they were run over or not'.[13] To add to the confusion, the main bridge over the Pinios River had been demolished accidentally by New Zealand engineers testing the strength of their charge. The column of humans and vehicles was diverted along a slow, muddy road to an alternative wooden bridge.[14]

German aircraft spent the day dive-bombing and machine-gunning along the length of the road. Losses were surprisingly light, but the Luftwaffe did manage to make a nuisance of itself by destroying the wooden bridge. Only some of the trucks had crossed the river at that stage. Those caught behind unloaded their passengers and drove the long way around to the opposite bank while the men crossed the river on a hastily erected pontoon and waited on the other side to be picked up and continue their retreat.

Driver Tom Wan had brought men up to Kalabaka. Now, he found himself bringing them back without a shot fired at the enemy. 'On our way it was beautiful and peaceful and the people waved and cheered us,' he says. 'Coming back, Trikkala [south of Kalabaka] was a pitiful sight. The place had been twice bombed. With the first bombing, all the casualties were put in the church. The second bombing got the church. We never got any waves or cheers there and I was filled with sadness.'[15]

————

While Jumbo Wilson was plugging the gap he imagined he had in his left flank, he took little notice of the other end of the Aliakmon Line. He had personally inspected the narrow coastal strip past Mount Olympus and concluded tanks couldn't get across its ravines. A high ridge ran down the mountainside there to the sea with only a railway tunnel, or a track deviating over a saddle, for wheeled traffic to get past. Colonel Neil Macky led a New Zealand battalion sent to guard the coastal passage, with an engineer detachment to demolish the tunnel if panzers approached. Macky was an Auckland lawyer, with a Military Cross from the First World War. Nicknamed 'Polly' since boyhood, he was impulsive and inclined to be a law unto himself.

Jim Collingwood, a horse-breaker before the war, was put in charge of a mule corral with several local boys as mule attendants. Mules were hired to carry gear up the slopes. When the defences were in place, a platoon bought a small lamb to roast for Easter Sunday dinner as a reminder of home.[16] The war seemed distant,

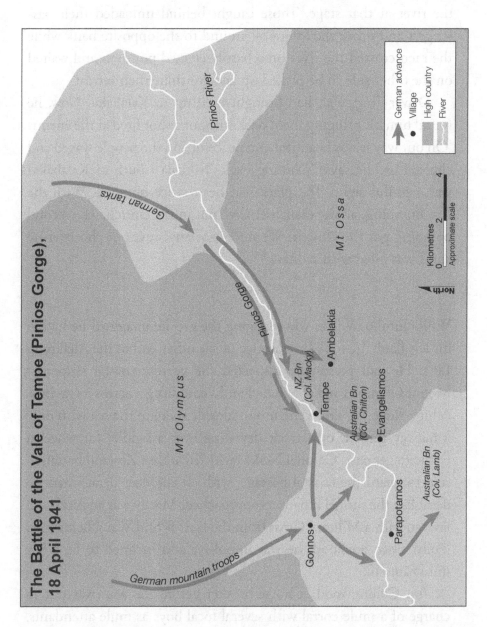

until men stationed up near the saddle saw armoured vehicles gathering on the plain to the north. Macky responded by ordering the engineers to detonate the tunnel and crater the saddle track, but with insufficient explosive and no pneumatic drills, they had to improvise. Gelignite and depth-charges were sealed against the tunnel wall behind sandbags. Although a first detonation had little effect, a second brought down part of the roof. It was estimated it would take six hours to clear. Charges were detonated along the saddle track and mines laid on the slopes.[17]

In the morning, German patrols tried to pinpoint the defences but thick scrub and misty drizzle made their progress difficult and artillery fire eventually drove them back. Home-made grenades, left-over gelignite tied in pairs with an added fuse and detonator, added to the German problems. Anti-tank rifles proved ineffective against tanks trying to force their way over the ridge, but many broke their tracks on boulders anyway. Others pulled back, impeded by the mines and the cratered road.

Late in the day, the German infantry drove back the Kiwi defenders, who were experiencing their first taste of combat. During a night of spasmodic gunfire, defences were infiltrated further and, by morning, New Zealand positions were being surrounded, with prisoners taken. The Germans hadn't eaten for twenty-four hours and demanded food from their captives, later forcing them to help clear the tunnel demolition.

Field-gun ammunition was getting low and near-surrounded platoons were told to come down off the ridge. At 9.40 am, Macky radioed Anzac Corps that their position was precarious. Tanks were approaching the saddle again and the order was given for a general withdrawal with everything destroyed. At 10 am, a signal was sent that the battalion was retiring, then the wireless was wrecked. Macky got a Bren carrier to take him down the road to Pinios Gorge, where he had sent the engineers to set up further demolitions after they had finished at the railway tunnel.[18]

The Germans didn't chase the retreating New Zealanders. Most of their tanks were disabled and their petrol supply was four kilometres back. They spent the rest of the day recovering their tanks, clearing mines and hoisting their flag on an old Turkish fort. It raises a question, in hindsight, of whether Macky's retreat was premature.

On its way to the sea, the Pinios River runs through the Vale of Tempe then the narrow gorge between Mount Olympus and Mount Ossa. Near-vertical walls in the gorge rose above 10-metre-wide tracks blasted out of the rock, the railway running along one side and the road the other. It should have been a natural barrier to an invading army, but the 'impassable' coastal ridge hadn't held the Germans back.

Command attention finally swung across to the Aliakmon Line's eastern flank. Vehicles pulling back to Thermopylae from Vevi and Servia in the centre were converging with those coming down west from Kalabaka, creating a traffic jam stretching back from the Larisa bottleneck. If the Germans broke through on the seaboard, they could block the road before Larisa and isolate the congested forces to the north, some 10,000 men and their equipment.

Disturbed by the reports coming from Macky, Anzac Corps sent Brigadier Cyril Clowes to the Tempe area to make an assessment. Clowes drove through the night, on crowded roads, dodging bomb craters, and on to the seaward end of Pinios Gorge until he found Macky with the scattered remnants of his retreating battalion. Clowes passed on Anzac Corps' orders: the gorge was to be denied to the enemy until 19 April, 'even if it means extinction'.[19] That was three days away, the time it would take to get all the paraphernalia of the British combat force back through Larisa.

The Germans were expected to attack from two directions. Polly Macky's New Zealanders were to stop the enemy coming through the gorge, and two Australian battalions were to deal with troops coming around the other side of Mount Olympus. The Kiwis crossed to the southern side of the river by punt, hand-pulled barge and a railway bridge upriver near the village of Tempe. When the depleted battalion had crossed, Macky ordered demolition of a tunnel, parts of the railway and the railway bridge. The punt was sunk too, delayed by a last-minute crossing of two shepherdesses with a mixed flock of sheep and goats.

Colonel Fred Chilton, commanding the first of the Australian battalions to arrive, set up headquarters that evening in a shepherd's stone hut. A resolute leader, the Sydney lawyer was a careful planner who left nothing to chance. His men arrived during the night, pushing through civilian bullock-carts and donkeys heading south, past burning trucks and improvised graves. They set up next to the New Zealanders, facing the foot of Mount Olympus across the river.

Around midnight, an officer brought in a Greek man suspected of being a fifth columnist. He was strong and shouting incoherently. Chilton said to get him outside and his second-in-command, Paul Cohen, tried to do that, but the man jammed himself in the door-frame. When Cohen raised his revolver to hit him with its handle and knock his grip loose, Chilton thrust out his hand. 'Stop! We don't know for sure,' he said, thinking Cohen was about to shoot the man. Chilton was hit on the wrist, breaking a bone. The Greek was quietened and taken to be guarded in a farmhouse. He took off from there during a Stuka attack.[20]

Amid much toing and froing in the morning, the two Anzac field commanders conferred about defence placements, along with Colonel 'Ike' Parkinson, leading newly arrived New Zealand gunners. Macky proposed that the combined force should come under his command, a suggestion rejected by Chilton, his arm now in a sling.[21] It was resolved with the arrival of the Australian, Brigadier Allen, who had been put in charge of what was now called Allen Force. The colonels were able to agree on defence positions, including for the second Australian battalion in process of arriving.

Across the river, villagers could be seen climbing the Olympus foothills with their belongings strapped to mules and driving flocks in front of them. South of the river, more civilians were heading out of harm's way. The Anzacs started helping themselves to anything that had been left behind. Frank Cox, an Aussie signaller, milked a cow in need of milking and raided a chicken coop, making an eggnog with a dash of rum. 'Best drink I ever had,' he enthused.[22]

Through the morning, German mountain troops could be seen on the hills across the river, having climbed around the mountain with pack mules. Flush with the invasion's success to this point, a group of German soldiers marched to the river, singing and sometimes goosestepping, to be driven back by artillery and machine-gun fire.[23] Later, an attempt to cross the river in rubber boats met the same fate, with most sinking or capsizing under fire. By the afternoon, Very flares were being sent up to tell recce planes circling above where the advancing units had got to. As at Vevi a week before, the feeling of battle about to explode spread through the watching Anzacs, tense and alert.

A tank was seen lurching along the railway line across the river, up to the blocked end of the tunnel. In an exchange of fire, a New Zealand platoon was pushed back, but the tank couldn't get past the engineers' handiwork. Downstream, the panzer force coming along the coast found a place where the Pinios River could be forded. It was tricky, with water coming to just below the turret, but they were able to get to the southern bank and came to a road blockage on that side. An Australian patrol, sent down the riverside, was pinned down near Tempe village by tank gunfire and couldn't get away until dark.

On a ridge overlooking the valley, a troop of thirty men, New Zealand gunners with four Cypriot labourers, came to the village of Ambelakia and arranged to sleep at the school, having set up positions around a nearby windmill. Told by a soldier that the bridge over the Pinios would be blown up at nine o'clock and she shouldn't be scared, the headmaster's ten-year-old daughter, Vassa, ran around the village passing on the message. She spent the rest of the afternoon asking people the time.

At dinner in the headmaster's house, village produce was supplemented from the gunners' provisions. The unit's leader picked up his host's flute and played an aria from *Aida*, then three soldiers took harmonicas from their knapsacks and accompanied him. Wine and tsipouro flowed with singing and dancing.

The teacher said to Vassa's older brother, 'Yiorgos, don't ever forget this night. Tomorrow these young men will die.'

There was a roar and the house shook, with the clock showing nine o'clock. Vassa fainted and was revived by the young commander rubbing 'cologne' on her forehead. One of the soldiers took a silver needle case and a picture of Christ from his pocket and gave them to the little girl.

The troop leader told the village mayor that the village should be evacuated during the night because it would be exposed to crossfire from the valley the next day. Villagers climbed with heavy bundles up the mountain slope, carrying lit candles and oil lamps. Fearing the village might be set on fire, house and stable doors were opened and the animals ran free, horses, mules and goats, dogs and cats.

After dinner, fourteen-year-old Yiorgos and his mates watched the soldiers gathered around the nearby spring of Saint Halkias, shouting and singing in foreign languages, shaving in the moonlight with small portable mirrors, flicking chilly water at each other, all the while laughing as if there was no tomorrow.

Yiorgos's father said to him, 'You! Follow your mother up to the mountain.'[24]

Meanwhile, patrols from the opposing armies were probing both sides of the river below. A German patrol called out from the north bank, in what the Kiwis opposite called 'an accent fondly thought to be Australian', asking what unit they were with. The rude response was in a cartoon German accent.[25] Elsewhere, an Australian patrol was firing at noises across the river. A voice called out in the dark, 'Cut it out, you silly bastards, you're firing on your own men.' The patrol continued firing.[26]

Earlier, Lieutenant Tom Colquhoun led a patrol across the river to assess enemy strength, leaving three of the Australians to guard the punt. While they waited, the three went downriver to investigate a wrecked German plane, with Mick Moss souveniring a Very pistol and Harry Fowler a luminous stop clock. There was a burst of machine-gun fire nearby and Moss and the third soldier, Gilmore, went to check it. Another patrol came near the waiting Fowler, who held fire, uncertain if they were Greek or German. On a new burst of fire, one of this patrol leapt for cover in the dark, almost on top of Fowler who fired off his Tommy gun. A blinding flash followed, hitting the Australian in the shoulder and knocking him into the river. Moss fired the Very pistol, lighting up the area, and the Germans scattered, leaving their dead companion behind.

Harry Fowler's shoulder wound was dressed when he returned. Tom Colquhoun reported that the enemy had occupied two of the villages, was along the north bank in force and was moving west with pack animals.[27] It's possible his patrol's unknown source of gunfire was the Australians patrolling the south bank.

At first light on 18 April, German troops were seen moving along the river. Before long, as the morning mist cleared, large numbers were fanning out, right and left across the Tempe valley. An exchange of fire began. The day became fine and clear, ideal for air attack, but already the anticipated crossfire had built up. The valley filled with the roar of artillery shells, the thud of mortar bombs and the rat-a-tat of machine-gun fire. Enemy troops gathered out of mortar range to cross the river, well to the west and heading towards the main road to Larisa and its bottleneck. Risking premature explosion, Sergeant 'Punchy' Coyle dropped extra charges in the mortar barrel to get more range.[28] Rex Moore, in charge of the Australian Bren carriers, noted in his diary, 'Huns attacked and by 7.30 am we were completely outnumbered. Panic set in and the troops dispersed. Hun tanks making a hullabaloo [from across the river]. NZ gunners were wonderful.'[29]

Polly Macky was already considering pulling back, telling his company commanders that if the battalion was overwhelmed or cut off, small parties should make their way out through the hills, each company on its own initiative.[30] Macky had arranged for transport, but the trucks had been sent south to offload gear and couldn't get back on the crowded road.

The Germans' wide sweep along the river was coordinated with a drive by panzers coming along the gorge, having cleared the road blockage. Supported by artillery across the river, they attacked the New Zealand positions, exposed on the slopes of Mount Ossa, and forced them back. Macky moved his headquarters out of Tempe and up a ridge to one side of Ambelakia.

In time, German troop numbers were greater than Anzac firepower. The enemy crossed upriver on large pontoons each carrying seventy or eighty men. Others waded the river under crossfire, twelve abreast for support against the current with the water up to their chests. Large numbers got across while the dead and wounded floated down the river.[31] Wave after wave of Stukas and a few Junkers bombers attacked ahead of the advancing infantry, along with strafing runs by fighter escorts. A truckload of beer and fruit went sky high.

The panzers moved into vacated Tempe and from there drove back Bren carriers that were preventing enemy infantry clambering across the collapsed railway bridge. German tanks moved out of Tempe in two directions. One group thrust south from the river, breaking up the New Zealand formations. The defence lost cohesion, survivors moving back towards the Australian lines. The gunnery team near Ambelakia, now with no infantry anywhere near them, was in the path of tanks coming around the base of Mount Ossa. Withdrawing up the ridge, Bren carriers held the advancing Germans until mid-afternoon. When the panzers eventually moved forward, a frustrated Allan Lockett rammed the lead tank with his carrier, knocking it off the road.[32]

About midday, Macky's phone went dead. Anti-tank units had taken the breach blocks out of their guns, rendering them inoperable, and gone. Groups of mostly leaderless New Zealand infantry were pulling back through Australian positions. As they stumbled through the Aussies, badly mauled and demoralised, Chilton's 2IC Paul Cohen called out to them, 'Calm down, don't run. The Australians aren't running.' He and Ike Parkinson, the Kiwi artillery commander, tried to rally the retreating mob without success. Many no longer had weapons and they ignored the officers' calls to stand and fight. One New Zealand platoon reported to Chilton, however, asking to be attached to his battalion so they could fight on. They were placed with Bren carriers.[33]

At the same time, more panzers rolled out from Tempe along the river's edge to join with German infantry, by then crossing the river at several points, to attack the Australian positions. The defenders persevered for a while, but by mid-afternoon they too were pulling back amid misunderstandings and contradictory orders.

Gordon Hendry, an Aussie company commander, was about to order a counter-attack with his carriers. His neighbouring commander arrived, telling him both their companies had been ordered to withdraw to a rearguard being set up by Colonel Lamb. Hendry was reluctant, not yet under attack and loath to give up his position without a fight. Nonetheless, he followed orders and moved out on the tail of Allan Murchison's company. Chilton, unaware of the order, concluded the companies had been overrun, but the attacking force had simply moved into the vacated area.[34]

By 5 pm, phone lines to forward units had gone dead. The New Zealand battalion had largely dispersed, the Australian battalions were disintegrating. Light was fading and planes were trying to silence a New Zealand artillery battery before darkness halted the tanks, but the battery stopped the tanks getting to the road to Larisa and withdrew after dark.

At 5.30 pm, 'Tubby' Allen wrote an order to withdraw all of Allen Force, to be delivered to the colonels, Chilton and Parkinson. Pushing through congested roads by carrier, the liaison officer gave the Parkinson order to a gunnery officer, but was wrongly told Chilton's headquarters had been overrun by tanks and looked for him unsuccessfully on the slopes to the south.[35]

The Australian positions came under attack from two directions by tanks and infantry: from the river, and higher to the east where the Germans had driven through the New Zealand positions. In danger of being surrounded, Fred Chilton finally gave the order for remaining units to withdraw, still unaware of Allen's order an hour earlier. The stone house used as his headquarters had barely been vacated when a tank shell demolished it, the last man leaving injured by flying bricks.[36]

'When we got the order to retreat,' recalls Sergeant Edwin Madigan, 'I remember the name of the bloke still, Carl Parrott, we came to a corner of a house, and I said, Carl just have a look. Well, he went white, there was a tank waiting there around the corner. We got into a gully on the near side, so that the tank couldn't depress its gun low enough, and as we scrambled out, the fire was thudding into the far side.'[37]

The retreat became a panicked scramble to get away from the tanks, as Sergeant Don Peirce notes in his diary. 'I ploughed through water up to my waist, nettles, bushes and anything that got in my way,' he wrote. 'I scrambled up precipitous ledges, but all the way kept as low down as possible, because every time I showed myself a shot or two would whistle by.'[38]

Men were jumping into trucks as the sun was setting, but Colonel Lamb stopped the trucks and lined troops and Bren carriers across the road a kilometre back from the collapsed line. Soon after, the first tank came up the road with its lid open, a German officer standing in the turret directing the driver in the twilight. He was riddled with bullets and slumped forward. Five tanks followed close behind; two were knocked out by Kiwi 25-pounders. Turret guns were swinging wildly like cornered beasts and firing in all directions. Jimmy Lamb yelled, 'Keep firing. Fire at the slits. It's getting dark. They can't see where we are.'[39]

Concerned at their sudden vulnerability, and that they might fire at each other in the dark, the tanks turned sharply to get away, running over two privates. Their screams added horror to confusion. Ken Cameron had both legs crushed, but he survived and was later captured. 'Bluey' Dunn's shoulder was smashed but his tin hat and the soft ploughed field saved his head from crushing.[40] The tanks lumbered away and no infantry came to replace them.

Wounded in the shoulder and having difficulty walking, three of Jim Brackenreg's platoon stayed with their leader until nightfall to try to get him out. They heard Germans singing nearby, making camp, but the pain was so bad the lieutenant still couldn't walk. He was given a whistle and told, 'Give us half an hour and blow the whistle. The Germans will come and they'll look after you.' Brackenreg survived the war as a PoW.[41]

The battlefield had eased to a quiet nocturne with scattered voices. It had been a devastating day for young Anzacs so far from home, but when the sun rose, it would be 19 April, the day mandated for the panzer force to be kept at bay. The remaining Australians got into the available trucks, joining some of the New Zealanders heading south.

No tanks got through to the Larisa road that day, but an enemy infantry detachment had crossed the Pinios, made its way around the Australian positions and set up a roadblock north of Larisa. When the Allied convoy reached the block, word drifted back that Larisa was occupied by Germans and traffic accumulated behind halted trucks. There was a concern that the panzers might be following the infantry so trucks and carriers got tangled up with each other turning on the narrow road with marshes either side. Heading across country, many broke down or were irretrievably bogged, all on board grabbing belongings and joining the scattered escapees from the Tempe valley battle already trekking across the Plain of Thessaly to the coast and Volos, down from Larisa.

Martyn Uren had walked to the head of the convoy and found a lieutenant known as 'Daffy', who he'd regarded as a fool, organising the front trucks to go down a track Daffy had seen on a map. Uren was in the group of vehicles that went down the track, 'little more than a wheel run among reeds and mud'. Trucks sometimes got bogged and were pulled out by Bren carriers, but after two hours through the marsh they came to rising ground, then a track around foothills to the main coast road to Volos. 'The sun was just rising as we went up the steep road past the town,' the Kiwi bombardier recalls, 'and as I looked back at the picture painted by its orange glow over the sea, I could scarce believe the events of the night before.'[42]

The morning after the battle, young Yiorgos and his friend Vassilis slipped down from the mountain to Ambelakia. The village hadn't burned and most of the animals had returned to their stables. Dogs and cats were wandering around the streets. That night, village heads and shepherds went to the windmill and buried twenty-seven dead soldiers. Three of the New Zealanders had escaped to the mountains but one was betrayed by a villager. The Germans paraded him in the village in manacles, then executed him.[43] Of the remaining two, one disappeared and probably joined the exodus to the coast. The other hid in an olive grove and was sheltered in another village by a young girl until the war was over.[44]

The withdrawing British force was scattered, its vehicles banked up on the main road, those on foot fanning wearily across the Thessaly Plain towards the coast. Colonel Macky and all his company commanders were missing and on foot, as were Colonel Chilton and several of his senior officers. The first vehicles from the Vale of Tempe had been stopped by the roadblock near Larisa, but eventually someone worked out only a small German detachment was maintaining the block. It was quickly cleared.

Larisa was in ruins from German air attack and the earlier earthquake, not occupied and not worth occupying. Burnt-out and bullet-ridden trucks were heaped alongside the road, fallen masonry littering the streets. Some buildings were still burning. Scattered bodies were covered with sacks, tarpaulins and blankets. Although no living humans could be seen, storks had stayed in their nests. Australian trucks, directed through back streets choked with rubble, passed a coffee shop. 'At one of these, two men sat with drinks between them as if in earnest conversation,' Ed Givney, a lieutenant from Sydney, recalls. Both men were dead, killed by a bomb blast.[45]

Troop transport and armoured vehicles crowded down the main road south to the Thermopylae Line and beyond. At night, over mountainous terrain without lights, it was as nerve-racking for passengers as for drivers. 'During the night, I woke up and peered over the side of the truck. There was nothing there for a couple of thousand feet,' writes gunner Ern Moor. 'Then I wished I had not looked.'[46]

Convoys snaked through mountain passes, trying to reach the cover of trees by dawn when the German planes arrived, bombing and machine-gunning up and down the road. Men leapt out of trucks and scattered across fields. When the planes had gone, the trucks started moving again. Three Greek girls smiled and waved nervously at Michael Kennedy, standing off at a distance while the girls sheltered under a truck filled with mortar bombs, but the truck wasn't hit.[47] On a separate occasion, Stukas attacked a concrete bridge without hitting it, striking instead a truck loaded with three tonnes of explosive. The blast lit up the morning mist and left a lingering smell of explosive. Traffic was jammed for 15 kilometres while engineers organised a labour team to cut a detour and fill the crater blown in the bridge embankment.[48]

Drivers found it difficult to hear approaching aircraft over the truck engine, so they had 'spotters' standing on the running board.

Otherwise, they'd be alerted by workers in the field rushing for cover. 'Over would come the bombers and it would be open up and jump into ditches, anywhere you could go,' recalls Cyril Read, a battalion padre.[49]

Alan Hackshaw, a signaller who had been a truck driver in the Western Australian wheatbelt before the war, has a clear memory of one air attack. 'I saw a few yards ahead three or four blokes in a bit of a hole,' he says. 'There was nothing else and I could hear the scream of the planes getting pretty close so I dived in it with them and snuggled up close. They were trying to hog the best spots themselves but I did all right.'[50]

'I would have to get the boys back into the truck but they didn't want to get back in,' adds the padre. 'They wanted to be on the tailboard and be first off when the next round came.'

To make a bad situation worse, there was only one air force in operation. Kiwi 'Dasher' Davies notes in his diary, 'Many bombs dropped on convoy—hell my nerves are a mess—have never felt so rotten. Bombing too intense so parked up for a few hrs. Hellish number of Nazi planes & not a single RAF.'[51] An Australian artillery officer, Keith Oliphant, wrote in his, 'We reach the stage where we long for night and quietness. All day is a nightmare and the hours of daylight are so long. No British planes are in the sky. What has gone wrong?'[52]

Nothing had gone wrong. There never was, and was never going to be, sufficient aircraft in the Middle East to restrain the Luftwaffe. The predictable outcome added to the general sense of futility.

'Those of us in the back who could manage it were able to get off a few shots as planes flew over,' says Ken Clift. 'It did not do one bit of damage to the planes, but it certainly made us feel better about being shot at.'[53]

Trucks set alight by air attack were pushed off the road by heavy vehicles, so that the side of the road was littered with smashed and burning trucks. Where the road widened, trucks would move two

abreast, often becoming locked. Movement of the column would
have to stop until they could be untangled. Where the narrow road
zigzagged over a pass, the trucks banked up head to tail for hours,
moving a kilometre or two in fits and starts. One truck got stuck
in a bomb crater, blocking a huge British lorry towing a field gun.
In rain and darkness, the driver backed the lorry and gun up the
winding road to a place where trucks following him could get past.[54]
Some drivers fell asleep at the wheel when the column stopped and
didn't see that the vehicle in front had moved off until someone
came from behind and woke them up.

As vehicles shuffled south in their hundreds, the two national
commanders moved around the convoys keeping spirits up and
the stream moving as best it could. Bernard Freyberg, already a VC
from the First World War, stood nonchalantly directing traffic out of
a tangle while a Messerschmitt machine-gunned around him. Iven
Mackay rode up and down the column on the back of a motorbike,
urging drivers to keep on going despite the screaming Stukas. 'They're
notoriously inaccurate,' he assured them.[55] The air attacks continued
remorselessly and unchallenged, preying on the men's nerves, but
doing less damage than might be expected. More trucks were lost in
bogs and through mechanical breakdown than from air attack.

At the other end of the army pecking order was the Maori
driver 'Hori' Martin. When his truck was hit, setting his load of
ammunition on fire, he jumped on the tray and flung ammunition
out. Later, when he was told he could have been blown up, Martin
responded, 'I was too frightened to run away, ay.'[56]

Meanwhile those who had left the battlefield on foot, or had
abandoned trucks and carriers in the marshland on detours from
the main road, were making their way along goat tracks towards the
coast in the hope of finding boats. Changing into civilian clothes
when the opportunity arose, they looked increasingly like the Greek
soldiers they had pitied. They moved in bands of varying sizes, some
just a few weary men, some in large groups, several hundred crossing

the Plain of Thessaly like migratory wildlife. At one stage, Major Paul Cohen was leading a party that had grown to 270, travelling mostly by night to avoid detection from the air.

The trekkers bought food from villagers, who sometimes refused payment for giving up some of their meagre provisions. Trailing behind enemy lines, a few Aussies sheltered in a ditch before sunrise and woke to find themselves beside an airstrip. A German aircrew was nearby, chattering over breakfast beside a bomber. The Australian men kept low in their ditch and slunk away.[57]

Scouring the coast until they could acquire a vessel, be it rowboat or fishing boat, by stealing or hiring, many of the evaders headed to one of the offshore Aegean islands. From there, with advice and assistance from civilians, it was a journey across the Aegean Sea, island-hopping by caïque, a wooden fishing boat rigged with sails. They risked storms, the Luftwaffe and nervous skippers to get to the island of Chios near the Turkish mainland.

Colonel Hughes of the British Military Mission in Turkey and the British vice-consul, Noel Rees, came from Izmir in Turkey to assist evaders arriving in unoccupied Chios to complete their escape.[58] Either a caïque or a cargo steamer was found to take them to Crete or the short voyage to Turkey from where, after brief internment and much red tape, they could move unhindered to Palestine, Egypt or Cyprus, arriving in groups throughout May.

———

By 20 April, Australian and New Zealand infantry and artillery units were setting up defences on the new Thermopylae Line. Along a ridge running east–west across central Greece from the sea to the mountains, the line covered passes in the centre, to be held by the Aussies, and around the coast, secured by the Kiwis. The Sperkhios River ran along the front, mostly through swampy plains. Wilson's headquarters, and those of the Anzac Corps under Blamey, had been pulled back south of the line.

In 480 BC, an earlier invasion force was held back at Thermopylae, a battle between 7000 men led by King Leonidas of Sparta and 150,000 of the Persian Empire of Xerxes I. It lasted three days. Streams from the area's hot springs—Thermopylae means 'Hot Gates'—had been channelled to turn the 100-metre-wide coastal pass into a slippery marsh. A small force of Spartans blocked the invaders on a causeway, wide enough for only a single chariot. There was no other way round for the Persians until a local peasant showed them a hill track used by shepherds and they were able to outflank the defenders.

By 1941 alluvial silt from the Sperkhios had widened the pass to several kilometres. The New Zealanders positioned themselves with sea and mudflats on one side, mountains on the other. The Luftwaffe had been too busy harassing the congested road to the north to molest the troops digging in, but on 20 April that changed. Enemy planes arrived at breakfast time, bombing and strafing the road and defensive areas. The unusual sight of a few RAF Hurricanes was seen briefly over the bay during the morning before disappearing. When one returned shortly after and shot down a Junkers bomber, loud cheering echoed along the foothills and tin hats were thrown in the air as the German plane went into a slow curving dive in thickening smoke.

'It was like a Derby finish,' recalls Ed McAra, a Wellington commercial artist before the war. 'Men leaping in the air, hoarse with excitement as the black shape hit the sea, exploded for a second time and vanished, leaving a blur of flame on the water as the oil burnt out.'[59]

That evening an artillery unit's cook made up a dark green bisque from tins of toheroa shellfish brought from New Zealand, followed by whitebait fritters. The Maori battalion had a quick dip in the warm sulphur creek after which the locality was named. The men renamed it Rotorua after their home town, with its sanitorium and bath-houses.[60]

The Australians, set up on the escarpment overlooking the straight road coming from the north, had Brigadier Vasey to remind them of home. A barrister's son and the product of Melbourne private schools and Duntroon, George Vasey buried an emotional streak under laconic and blunt speech, drinking and swearing a lot, perhaps to cover his patrician origins. Nicknamed 'Bloody George', he had been told by General Mackay that there would be no more withdrawals. This line was to be defended to the bitter end.

Vasey positioned his battalions at the top of the pass. With German armoured vehicles and tanks preparing to advance in the distance, he addressed his troops. 'Here you bloody well are and here you bloody well stay,' he spurred them on. 'And if any bloody German gets between your post and the next, turn your bloody Bren around and shoot him up the arse.'[61]

General Custer couldn't have put it more eloquently.

5

SINKING SHIP

General Wilson had sent Brigadier Savige and Brigadier Charrington (if he wasn't there of his own volition) to shore up the western flank of the revised Aliakmon Line, having heard the Greek army was disintegrating. The Australian and English forces withdrew without firing a shot, leaving Greece's undisintegrated but exhausted army to face the strength of the Wehrmacht alone. Although it had taken a while for the invaders to get past a quagmire and some stubborn Greek resistance, the German army was poised by 18 April to capture Ioannina, where General Pitsikas had his headquarters and where Stan Savige had insisted Greek troops be directed. The Germans were in a position to cut off the Greek army returning from Albania.

A few days before, Ioannis Pitsikas had argued that continuing resistance was futile and destructive, but King George ordered him to fight on, at the same time lobbying the British to assist his family to leave Greece.[1] The government was in freefall. One minister ordered two months paid leave for Greece's soldiers, another approved the same for its public servants. After the king vented his fury on Alexandros Koryzis for not controlling his ministers, the prime minister went home and put a revolver to his head.[2]

Three days later, with the backing of his fellow field commanders, Georgios Tsolakoglou offered his army's capitulation to the German commander, General Jodl. After a formal surrender to Germany was signed in Larisa, Greek officers were allowed to retain their side-arms and the soldiers could return home. Outraged at the exclusion of Italy from the surrender document, Mussolini complained to Hitler, who then overruled his own commander. A re-staging of the surrender three days later in Salonika included an Italian signatory.[3]

Having long lost faith in Britain's ability to halt the German advance, Alexandros Papagos told Jumbo Wilson shortly before Koryzis's suicide that British troops should leave Greece to save it from devastation.[4] General Wavell flew to Athens. At a meeting with the king, Papagos and Wilson, he decided the British Expeditionary Force should be evacuated. The British insisted the Greek army safeguard the exodus, the same army Wilson had persuaded himself had collapsed days before. Unknown to those at the meeting, the army's capitulation was already being offered to the Germans.

At two in the morning on 21 April, Wavell met General Blamey at Anzac headquarters to tell him Tsolakoglou had surrendered and to order the evacuation of British and dominion forces from Greece. Although this had been in the wind for five days at this stage, Wilson had given no indication of it to his Australian field commander. It was the day after George Vasey had given his expletive-laden, 'no further withdrawal' speech to his men.

Both Canberra and Wellington cabled London for assurance that Britain would honour its undertakings to evacuate their troops. Churchill replied that 'safe withdrawal of the men will have precedence over any other consideration except that of honour'[5], while giving different orders to the Middle East commanders. 'You must divide between protecting evacuation [from Greece] and sustaining battle in Libya. But if these clash, which may be avoidable, emphasis must be given to victory in Libya,' he directed. 'Victory in Libya counts first, evacuation of troops from Greece second.'[6] The British force was then being battered by Rommel's counter-attack in Libya, with only the Australian 'rats' holding out in Tobruk. Honour would appear to be an unaffordable luxury in this instance.

A small group in Cairo, only one of them from the army, had been looking at evacuation from Greece since March despite Wavell's objection. Because it could be bad for morale, no one else had given any attention to what would be a highly complex operation under pressure by a rampant enemy. As a result, Middle East Command was woefully underprepared when, a week after the German invasion began, Admiral Turle, the British naval attaché in Athens, advised his commander-in-chief that an evacuation was imminent.[7] Admiral Cunningham sent Admiral Baillie-Grohman to Greece to liaise between Wilson's staff and the Mediterranean Fleet.

Blamey met with Wilson at midnight on the side of the main road south to Athens. They were joined by Sandy Galloway, Wilson's chief of staff, and Tom Baillie-Grohman. Galloway spread out maps and charts on the bonnet of one of their cars to show planned evacuation points.[8] Piraeus, Greece's main port, was out of the question. It was still devastated by the inferno earlier in the month and would be under closest scrutiny by the Luftwaffe. To make air surveillance more difficult, widely scattered locations had been earmarked for the exercise, spread east of Athens and west into the Peloponnese, the peninsula at the southern end of the Greek mainland. Transport ships would arrive with a naval escort an hour after dark so air patrols wouldn't spot the evacuation locations. The ships would then need to be away by 3 am to be within range of Hurricane protection from Crete by daylight.

As movement of troops had to be speedy, the men could take only what was valuable that they could carry: rifles and light arms, gun sights and signal equipment. Everything else had to be destroyed so it couldn't be used by the enemy. Wilson put Blamey in charge of the evacuation of troops while he dealt with the multitude of base, military mission and headquarters personnel in Athens.

Tom Blamey returned to his headquarters at dawn and met with Iven Mackay and his staff officers to pass on the evacuation plans. They were to start immediately, mapping out a staged withdrawal to designated embarkation points. A liaison officer was sent to brief Bernard Freyberg, out on the front line at Thermopylae, for a similar plan to be set up for the New Zealanders.[9]

Two nights later, Wilson told Blamey that Wavell wanted him to take a flying-boat in the morning to Alexandria to impress the urgency of the evacuation on the commander-in-chief of the Mediterranean Fleet. 'For a moment, Blamey seemed about to refuse,' says Baillie-Grohman, 'but Wilson reasoned with him.' There were Australians fighting in North Africa, and Cunningham needed to be properly briefed.[10]

Blamey was to occupy a new position of deputy commander-in-chief, Middle East, to appease the Australian government, which was unhappy with an English general commanding a force of mostly Anzac fighting men. In conveying Wavell's order, Wilson may not have been aware of that; indeed he might have felt the position should have been his, had he known. Political strategy dressed up as military necessity.

Wavell also ordered generals Mackay and Freyberg to Egypt, along with a number of senior officers. General O'Connor and two other British generals had been captured fleeing from Rommel in the Libyan desert and the Middle East commander-in-chief didn't want to provide another propaganda gift to the Germans.

There was room in the Sunderland for twelve men. Eleven of them were indisputable, but the twelfth could have been any of about thirty officers. Blamey resolved that impasse. 'I propose to take my son,' he said. 'He has no special claim other than he is important to me. I know I'll be criticised for it.' Major Tom Blamey was an artilleryman who had been seconded to headquarters staff as a liaison officer. His older brother had been killed in a plane crash in 1933.[11]

The flying-boat left at dawn on 24 April, gone before the Luftwaffe would arrive in force. The following morning another Sunderland left with General Mackay and staff officers from Australia and New Zealand . . . but not the New Zealand Division commander. Freyberg had refused to leave Greece. When told of the order, he responded that he was in the midst of the battle at Thermopylae, attacked by tanks; who would command New Zealand's troops if he left?

'I was told Movement Control [Wilson's staff] would,' he later said. 'I naturally went on with the battle.' Asked to compare his decision with that of Blamey and Mackay, he said simply, 'They went. I refused.'[12]

Theo Stephanides, a British medical officer, went to pick up supplies in Athens. 'To my surprise, I was given all the medical stores I had asked for without any haggling,' he says. 'Something was in the wind.'[13]

He returned to his camp to find everyone gone, even his batman. At Area HQ, lorries were being hurriedly packed. Stores and equipment had been tossed about; officers' suitcases lay with their contents scattered. Distraught civilians wandered around the camp.

Russell Bricknell, a New Zealand gunner stationed north of Athens, recalls, 'The ration store had been burnt by order of the CO [commanding officer] who had lost his head completely. The YMCA had been looted, as well as several wine shops in the vicinity.'[14] A Royal Horse Artillery officer, camped near a New Zealand battalion, took a truck and returned laden with tobacco and cigarettes from an abandoned military canteen. He shared them with his neighbours.[15]

The British were determined to destroy any supply dumps and materials the Germans might use, but the Greeks wanted the supplies for themselves. Greek police at a supply depot tried in vain to stop civilians looting stores. Bullets flew everywhere but mostly in the air. Bricknell adds, 'The Greeks swept through the camp like a plague of locusts. Nothing was sacred. I went later to the latrines but they too had been spirited away.'[16]

Driven through the city to Piraeus, Stephanides found the streets congested with people and British army vehicles. It was obvious the British were pulling out, but the people waved and wished them good fortune. An old woman threw a cluster of carnations into the back of Stephanides' truck. He was taken to a small dock where two Greek steamers were hurriedly taking on troops, British legation staff and residents and, later, two lorries of German prisoners.

Ron Nelson had been taking intercepted enemy messages by motorbike from Jack Ryan's signals unit to Anzac Corps. When the Corps was told of the decision to evacuate, he returned with an order for the unit to close down immediately and get to Piraeus. Blamey wanted valuable personnel and equipment evacuated as soon as possible. In a flurry of activity, the men made a bonfire of secret documents, raced into town to get tins of grapes in syrup, the signals unit's favourite delicacy, and headed for Piraeus.

After sleeping under cover on the way, the radiomen filled their dixies at a well. A stray fox terrier followed them back to their trucks and attached itself to the unit, travelling perched on the petrol tank of the despatch rider's motorbike. Nelson and Micky the foxie led the trucks past burnt-out vehicles, arriving at Piraeus in the middle of an air raid. A ship loaded with ammunition exploded, leaving a consignment of bank notes fluttering in the air.[17]

The wharf was crowded with desperate, jostling civilians, trampling over scattered Turkish and Greek money. In the midst of the confusion, a well-dressed woman called out in refined English, 'Now, I'd like a really nice soldier to take care of my luggage.' Ryan was offered a place for his team on the Greek freighter *Elsie*, going to Egypt. Not much bigger than a harbour ferry, it had no space for the unit trucks that were fitted out for radio intercept work. Wireless equipment, essential stores and a canine mascot were taken with the men and an officer was left with the trucks and their drivers to try to get on a later ship.[18]

On board *Elsie* was a jumble of civilians—women and children, diplomats, British expatriates, political figures—and 107 prisoners of war: German pilots shot down and held in a camp near Athens. They were about to sail when a deputation of Greek officials arrived to insist thirty of the prisoners be released to them. The crowded ship then headed south but only as far as Suda Bay in Crete, not to Egypt.

King George had already left the country the night before. In the evening, after his final broadcast appealing to Greek forces to fight to the end, the royal family flew to Crete by Sunderland. They settled in Knossos at the Villa Ariadne, the home of the English archaeologist Sir Arthur Evans. The party on the flying-boat included Greece's new prime minister, the British ambassador, princes, princesses and Joyce Brittain-Jones, George II's companion, described in many accounts as the king's mistress although both were divorced.

———

While the departure of some of the senior commanders of the British force was being considered, their troops were standing by for the German advance to reach the Thermopylae Line. Cratered roads and the volume of traffic delayed the enemy's column of armoured vehicles, transports and artillery, jammed on the road south from Larisa as the British had been a few days before. But the Germans didn't have constant air attack to unnerve them.

No hint of the evacuation had reached field command. Iven Mackay and Bernard Freyberg, yet to receive their orders, were telling their officers there would be no more withdrawals. Vasey had made his speech. Mackay would later say, 'I didn't dream of evacuation. I thought we'd hang on for about a fortnight and be beaten by weight of numbers.'[19]

Time crawled for the defenders. They demolished the bridge over the Sperkhios. A deserted village provided gardens full of fresh vegetables and they waited.

Kiwis on night patrol, alerted to a possible paratroop attack, had heard that these elite soldiers used whistles and cries to signal between groups. Away in the distance a weird call was heard, answered faintly from a different direction. 'It was a creepy cat-call—sounded like a tomcat in its last agony,' says Noel Bell, an Aucklander on watch. 'It made one's flesh creep and we were certain that we would have parachute troops on our hands at any moment.'

The eerie call was heard again, closer and from a different direction. 'We piquets [forward watch] kept mighty close together, our rifles cocked and ready to open up at the first sign of trouble.' There was no paratroop attack. The next day, one of the New Zealanders thought to ask some Greeks and was told the cries were by a local species of bat.[20]

In the afternoon, two German motorcyclists, a reconnoitre for the panzers, rode up to the demolished bridge. They were quickly driven off, but it was a sign the invasion force was close. A few German vehicles moved up but were sent back by artillery fire. That night, the enemy's trucks could be seen streaming south and spreading along the Sperkhios River, their headlights on. They had no reason to fear attack from above.

The anticipated dawn attack by infantry and tanks didn't happen, with the bridge still disabled and covered by a Bren carrier squad. Instead, the two forces exchanged gunfire intermittently across the river during the day and the Thermopylae Line was pounded from the air. Each evening the men listened to BBC news telling of RAF success against the Luftwaffe in Greece. Greeting the report with bitter laughter, they referred to German planes as 'Berlin Hurricanes'.[21] Jack Millett, a junior transport officer, wrote home that 'several chaps have gone mad with the strain and I sometimes wonder that we are not all the same way'.[22]

That morning, George Vasey was told that the British force was to be evacuated from Greece. It would be a leapfrogging operation, with one unit to form a covering rearguard while another withdrew through it to form a new rearguard further back for the original rearguard to withdraw through. Through this series of moves, all the units would get to their appointed embarkation places on the coast.

Meanwhile, a panic had run through the defending force. An air patrol reported Germans moving down Greece's west coast, threatening to cut off the Anzac line of retreat. Vehicles were said to be streaming out of Ioannina, General Pitsikas's former headquarters. A detachment was sent out to demolish sections of the western road to Athens and block the German forward patrols. When the detachment took up its position, it found the 'Germans' were Greek stragglers from the Albanian front. The German force in western Greece hadn't moved from Ioannina, worn out by their relentless advance.[23]

At dusk, the first of the New Zealand battalions began withdrawing. Told to take only personal gear and limited ammunition, some of the Maori battalion painted rude messages to Hitler on ration boxes they had to leave behind. Before dawn, they hid themselves in olive groves on the way to the coast, with their vehicles camouflaged. Some found a konjac distillery in a nearby abandoned village, the discovery soon becoming known to their commanding officer. Colonel George Dittmer ordered the destruction of all casks at the distillery and any bottles found with his troops. One of Dittmer's staffers was found with a bottle under one arm and a turkey under the other. The colonel ordered the destruction of the former but allowed the latter to be eaten.[24]

Two New Zealand platoons were left under Captain Jock Worsnop to disguise the withdrawal and guard the demolished bridge. When machine-gun fire opened on them, Worsnop ordered Alan McPhail to take a patrol to stop the Germans crossing the river. McPhail couldn't get to the section under fire, so he continued as a one-man patrol with Tommy gun. Getting into position as ten Germans were about to cross, the Christchurch bank officer opened fire, hitting two. The others scuttled back. His fire continued to deter attempts to cross until dark and, with his ammunition running low, he returned to his platoon. The Germans didn't try again until mid-morning the next day.[25]

German heavy artillery had moved slowly down the congested main road, enabling Vasey to withdraw the first of the Australian force before it came under heavy fire. The main body of one of his battalions started leaving in trucks at 8 pm, heading for Megara on the coast west of Athens. Soon after, the first artillery was hooked onto tractors and taken away. The convoy travelled several kilometres without lights, so its departure was shielded from the enemy across the river, then sped up with dimmed lights. The Germans rarely flew at night.

The Luftwaffe would have been satisfied with its daylight success. It had attacked the aerodrome at Athens, forcing undamaged Hurricanes to be moved back to the Peloponnese, but two days later, thirteen of those planes were destroyed on the new airfield and the remainder sent to Crete. No British warplanes stayed on mainland Greece to protect the evacuation of British and dominion troops.

Rearguard troops at Thermopylae were feeling the strain of constant air attack. 'For three hours they gave us everything they had,' recalls Arthur McRobbie, a Perth storeman before the war. 'At this stage, I thought I was finished. My nerves were gone to pieces and I just shook like a leaf, and for the next two hours I fought like hell to get myself into shape. At this time, "Katy" [KT Johnson, a fellow lieutenant] proved a rock of friendship. He helped me no end.'[26]

On the morning of 24 April, dive-bombers attacked the largely abandoned positions of the depleted defence line. Colonel Bill Cremor had moved his guns back a kilometre, but had left the camouflage nets over the pits already located by aerial scouts. Stukas spent two hours attacking the empty gun pits.[27]

That same morning a carrier patrol reported the enemy had repaired the bridge across the Sperkhios overnight. German infantry was advancing under mortar cover towards the rearguard positions, causing severe casualties among the remaining defenders. In the early afternoon, the first two tanks crossed the repaired bridge and continued across the marshy land where Spartans had long ago held back the Persian invasion. Further tanks followed, the front ones stopped by New Zealand artillery fire but able to shield other tanks behind. By late afternoon, nineteen tanks had followed more than fifty motorcycles, advancing on the defences. Twelve of the panzers were destroyed by artillery, but specialist German mountain troops were infiltrating abandoned sections of the surrounding hills.

Other tanks threatened to penetrate Australian defences to the west. Sid Raggett, a gunner, wrote in his diary, 'The pressure is on again and the tanks have broken through—this may be our last stand but we will have a go. Goodbye just in case.'

That attack wasn't able to get through the carrier defence. The enemy became pinned down in scrub country and was still there when night fell. 'Well, I survived to write again, don't know for how long,' was the next entry in Raggett's diary.[28] He survived the war.

Under cover of dark, the remaining guns were disabled and the last of the Thermopylae defenders were taken by Bren carrier back to waiting trucks. Kiwi drivers drove past burning tanks to pick up forward gun crews. Four lorries went too far forward, rounded a bend and found themselves face to face with the enemy's tanks. Jamming on their brakes, the drivers came under intense machine-gun fire and fled into the darkness, leaving the Germans with lorries full of canned pears.[29]

Leading a carrier platoon back in the dark, Ron Sherlock came across a burning German tank, with flames and thick smoke pouring across the road. He told his driver to motor straight through. A platoon truck and another carrier followed. As they emerged from the smoke, they were fired at by New Zealand anti-tank gunners who thought it was an enemy attack under cover of smoke. Sherlock returned fire with his Bren but, with all three vehicles hit, the men leapt out and crawled along a ditch. The altercation finally ceased when the day's password was shouted out from the ditch.[30]

The casualty rate on that last day had been high but the Germans had not been able to progress beyond Thermopylae, giving the withdrawing forces some breathing space in getting to their various embarkation points. Evacuation of the force was about to begin. The Royal Navy's first rescue convoy had left Alexandria on 22 April, reaching the Greek coast two days later. It split into two flotillas, one for Porto Rafti, a small fishing village east of Athens, the other to Navplion to the west on the Peloponnese.

———

While Germans were slowly discovering the Thermopylae positions had been abandoned, truckloads of New Zealand soldiers were making the 250-kilometre journey to Porto Rafti, with side-lights only. Once drivers had put some distance between themselves and the battle front, they turned headlights on and drove at speed. A string of lights wound through the mountains in the hope that the Germans wouldn't start flying at night. Drivers had been told to keep going even if enemy planes appeared. Trucks that broke down were destroyed and pushed off the road, the troops piling into spare trucks. They made their way through the outskirts of a grey and bleak Athens, windows shuttered and streets empty. Martial law had been imposed by the Greek government. Residents knew their army had capitulated, their rulers had fled and the Germans were only days away. General Papagos had resigned but remained in Athens. The retreating convoys had to find shelter in olive groves or pine forests before sunrise when the daily air attacks would start again.

Ken Frater, a Nelson truckie before the war, was sent to pick up a New Zealand platoon. As tired troops emerged from the gloom, the passenger door opened and a voice said, 'Stay where you are, the men are getting in the back. My name is Arthur Wesney.'

There was a slap on the cab roof and, getting into the passenger seat, the man said, 'Right, get going.'

'Are you the All Black?' asked Frater.

'Yes, I am. Now I'd like to get some sleep.'

After he dropped them off at Porto Rafti, Frater went to the back of his truck and found his socks and underwear gone, and his tucker box empty. The men hadn't eaten for twenty-four hours.[31]

At the same time, men and women from base and headquarters units in and around Athens were being taken to Navplion on the coast west of the capital, among them 160 nurses from Australia, New Zealand and Britain. The planners anticipated 5000 gathering in the town, but 7000 or 8000 arrived, mingling in crowded streets with order crumbling. Abandoned vehicles blocked the drifting human stream and had to be moved and disabled.

Bringing instructions from Admiral Baillie-Grohman for the Navplion beachmaster, Lieutenant Anthony Heckstall-Smith was taken to the Hotel Britannique by a local boy. A long, dimly lit dining room was filled with the murmur of soldiers, some sprawled over marble-topped tables with heads couched in arms, others wrapped in dirty blankets on red plush settees or on the stone floor. Faces were grey with dust, eyes swollen and red-rimmed. Some drank straight from bottles, others slept.

'It's good to see you jokers,' said a gaunt New Zealander. 'The navy brought us. The navy takes us away. Is that the idea?'

'Something like that,' said Heckstall-Smith and was offered a swig from a bottle of fiery resinous wine. Told they would probably embark the following night, 24 April, but not before dark because of the Stukas, a chorus of swearing at Stukas broke out.[32]

No one there knew anything about the beachmaster, Commander Clark. He didn't arrive from Athens until the following afternoon, but Tony Heckstall-Smith and his two companions managed to locate the officer in charge of embarking troops there. Colonel Courage had been reassigned from command of Cypriot and Palestinian labourers.

Courage took them by jeep to the beach at Tolos, to be used on the second night of evacuation. Heckstall-Smith questioned whether the water offshore was deep enough for the transfer vessels.

'I'm six foot three [1.9 metres],' replied the Englishman. 'Where I can stand, your craft can float.'

He stripped naked, walked across the sand and waded into the water until only the top of his head was visible. Courage returned to the beach nonchalantly as if he'd illustrated his point on a sheet of paper.[33]

The Germans spent the next morning bombing three cargo ships in Navplion Bay, leaving them burning. The aircraft were too late to spot the influx of Allied soldiers in the town, by then moved out and concealed in olive groves. Townspeople were warned that one of the ships, *Nicholaos Georgios*, was loaded with the high explosive ammonal and, aware of the destruction at Piraeus three weeks earlier, headed for the hills.

In the afternoon, the ship exploded with a blinding flash, a plume of smoke and a wave of turbulence. An eerie silence followed, then the hills sprung to life. Old peasant women clasped their hands in prayer, children chattered like starlings, dogs barked, goats bleated and an Australian soldier exclaimed, 'Well, that's buggered that!'[34]

After dark, soldiers and base workers marched from their shelters through the glass-strewn streets in groups of fifty. They waited in the moonless night in rows on the quay and in the square behind, while six ships anchored in the bay and the troopship *Glenearn*, bombed and damaged on the way, launched its motor barges. By 10 pm, muffled voices and the throb of barge motors could be heard through the darkness by the waiting crowd. *Nicholaos Georgios* glowed red in the bay and a sweeping searchlight picked up a landing barge. The crowd, strangely quiet, started to move towards the jetty.

The corvette *Hyacinth* appeared out of the dark and the beachmaster caught a line and tied it. The captain called out, 'I can take a hundred. Get them to move on.' As the walking wounded boarded, a motor barge pulled alongside and started loading.

The other transport, *Ulster Prince*, came in next. Its captain, suspicious of the depths on the chart supplied and concerned about the fortress islet of Bourtzi at the harbour entrance, was told Commander Clark's orders were to berth. Waiting for the landing craft to move clear, *Ulster Prince* ran aground out from the jetty and swung around, blocking the harbour entrance. *Hyacinth* tried to tow it free but succeeded only in tangling the tow rope in its propellor.[35]

Neither of the escort destroyers could now get around the stranded vessel and Bourtzi to the jetty. The motor barges and some caïques that had arrived were now the only means of boarding the waiting ships. Chugging from the jetty to *Glenearn* and three escort warships, the barges carried the evacuees away from the failed campaign, although not without a last incident.

The nurses were taken by caïque to the destroyer *Voyager*, rising in the swell. An English nurse lost her footing climbing up the webbing draped over *Voyager*'s side and fell between rolling ships. Instinctively, an Australian sailor, Cyril Webb, dived in and held her up until a line was dropped to haul them both to safety. Terrified, relieved and dripping wet, the rescued nurse was wrapped in a dry blanket and given a mug of steaming cocoa, finally welcomed aboard with her comrades.[36]

The convoy was gone by 3.30 am, carrying 6800 to safe haven. *Ulster Prince* couldn't be moved and was left behind, along with about 1000 men unable to be fitted onto the depleted flotilla.

After dark on the same night east of Athens, trucks brought the New Zealand troops to an assembly point just out of Porto Rafti. They were greeted with a confusion of orders. 'Liaison officers bustling, yelling, rushing round in circles, orders and counter-orders from every Tom, Dick and Harry,' one Kiwi describes it.[37] The evacuation ships would be tightly packed and embarkation officers ordered men to discard any surplus gear. In the flurry of orders, radio sets and some rifles were tossed. One soldier smashed all his gramophone records but one, left on a turntable for the Germans to play. It was 'There'll Always be an England'.[38] Most soldiers hung on to their Bren guns and, when the dumping of prized possessions was done, they marched down to the beach in orderly groups.

Two hours later, small boats appeared out of the dark, punctually at 11 pm. Six thousand, mostly New Zealanders, waited on the shore while landing barges pulled up on the beach. Some of the men waded out to smaller boats. Each vessel was filled and moved quietly out to three offshore ships, the converted cargo liner, *Glengyle*, and two navy cruisers.

Once on board, the men took off wet clothes and followed a queue down to the mess deck for a big mug of steaming cocoa, fresh bread with a slice of bully beef and a cheery Royal Navy sailor with a jar.

'Mustard, laddie?'

The troops went to sleep where they could find a spot. Their ships left by 4 am. Their battle for Greece was over.

There were 5750 men taken from Porto Rafti that night. Five hundred left behind were taken down the coast by landing craft to the island of Kea until the next embarkation. When the beach was empty, the beach crew covered all traces of the night's activity, burying abandoned gear and sweeping over footprints.

Patrol planes in the morning would see nothing on the beach, but they saw a large transport sitting in the entrance to Navplion harbour. Bombers came later in the morning and left the stranded *Ulster Prince* wrecked beyond repair.

Four more days of planned evacuation followed. Some of the embarkations went reasonably smoothly, some were disastrous. Like the New Zealanders who had departed mainland Greece a day before them, the bulk of Australian troops were driven through villages where old women offered trays of ouzo and cakes to the passing trucks. John Rogers, the senior intelligence officer in the Australian force, recalls, 'Hundreds, probably thousands, cheered and cheered and rushed us to shake hands. I blush to admit how many times we were kissed. They shouted "Good luck"—"Come back"—"Down with Hitler"—a spontaneous and inspiring demonstration.'[39] A girl threw a card into Rogers' car, her photo on one side and a message in Greek on the other.

As one retreating soldier noted, 'I thought I was pretty tough but tears came to my eyes as this tribute, usually reserved for the victors, was spontaneously rendered to a beaten army.'[40]

Before dawn on 25 April, an ironic Anzac Day, Australian infantry arrived and concealed themselves in olive groves around Megara, their brigade commander, George Vasey, with them. Some 3700 fit troops and 1100 wounded waited in the woods, unobserved by planes patrolling throughout the day. Trucks were to be destroyed, but not burned. Smoke would be seen from the air. Engines were drained of oil, then run until they seized.

General Blamey had left instructions that Australian nurses must be evacuated but Brigadier Large, the chief British medical officer, said it wasn't safe and they couldn't be spared. Rogers and the Australian medico 'Weary' Dunlop disputed this and Large backed off. The nurses were put on trucks and hastened to Megara that night.[41]

The troops emerged from hiding after dark, marched down to Megara's two jetties and waited, orderly and quiet. About 10 pm, three warships and the merchant ship *Thurland Castle* could be detected dimly out in the bay. Anticipation hummed in the standing lines. A second transport, the Dutch ship *Pennland*, had been severely damaged on the way and turned back for Crete. It was bombed again and sunk before it got there.

Some of the troops were taken on board destroyers that could come alongside the jetties. Others were taken by landing barge out to *Thurland Castle* and the cruiser *Coventry*, where they clambered up scrambling nets, hauling with them whatever weapons they had managed to hang on to and their haversacks. On board, the men were given food and cocoa, the officers a whisky as well.

Men earmarked to board *Pennland* had moved down to the harbour to find their ship was no longer coming. They scrambled onto trucks not yet destroyed and were about to start a night drive to the Peloponnese when they were told four more destroyers had arrived. They hurried back to the port to be told the extra ships hadn't come at all. Soon after, that report was corrected and the additional destroyers were at the jetties.[42]

A week before, Sergeant Edwin Madigan had trudged, wounded, from the battle in the Vale of Tempe, ending up in the military hospital near Athens. He was told there that they would probably be prisoners by the morning and thought, 'Bugger that!', so he got himself to the beach at Megara. Seeing black shapes in the bay, he took off his clothes and swam out to them. He had been a lifesaver on Newcastle beaches before the war. When he got near a warship, he called out and a line was thrown down. On board, a voice called out, 'What are you doing here?' It was a fellow lifesaver from Newcastle, now a crewman on the destroyer *Vendetta*.[43]

As it became clear that, without the second troopship, not all those assembled would be able to be taken, a dispute developed between Wilson's chief of staff and Brigadier Vasey, who wanted his troops embarked on the ships before the wounded, arguing there should be a priority for fit soldiers who could continue fighting.

Vasey prevailed in the argument. The convoy left at 3 am for Crete with 5900 on board, including the last eighty nurses, but there hadn't been room for three hundred of the sick and wounded. They were taken in trucks retained for the purpose to new embarkation points further south. As it turned out, they were too late to be able to cross the Corinth Canal into the Peloponnese and most were captured, spending the rest of the war in German hospitals and PoW camps.[44]

Early in the morning after leaving Megara, the naval convoy was subjected to three ineffectual dive-bombing attacks. The skipper of *Vendetta* noted in the ship's diary that the troops on board 'maintained a battery of Bren guns on the fo'c'sle and quarterdeck and appeared to enjoy the air raids, as they said it was the first time they had seen some decent opposition to German aircraft since the beginning of the withdrawal'.[45]

Spreading the Allied evacuation over several departure points carried a significant risk. Access to the Peloponnese was by one bridge only, 40 metres below it the Corinth Canal cutting through the narrow isthmus that joined the Peloponnese to the mainland, turning the peninsula into an island. About 25 metres wide with sides roughly vertical, the canal was not otherwise easily crossed. Movement of British troops south was absolutely dependent on holding the bridge.

A New Zealand brigade with Australian support had formed a temporary rearguard between Thermopylae and Athens to protect the evacuation. The navy decided that the lack of air protection made evacuation from around Athens perilous and proposed the bulk of further embarkation be from the Peloponnese. Rearguard troops were to withdraw there and, when all were across the bridge, destroy it to delay a pursuing enemy. However, if the Germans destroyed or captured the bridge first, the troops would be trapped north of it. It wasn't until Anzac Day that Allied planners thought to have units guarding the bridge as the stream of trucks rolled south over it.

English artillery had been set up to meet dive-bomber attacks. Intelligence indicated the enemy intended to capture the bridge with a parachute attack, but the gun positions weren't moved to meet that threat. When Australian infantry set up on the south side of the canal, Captain Jo Jones crossed back to report to artillery headquarters and found everyone there asleep.[46] He decided to go back in the morning, but the morning was a different day.

At dawn, Junkers bombers came high over the mountains to draw fire from anti-aircraft guns, which were then targeted by dive-bombing Stukas. Messerschmitts sprayed machine-gun fire around the bridge and roads running north and south from it. Many of the anti-aircraft positions were wiped out in half an hour of aerial pounding then, out of the roar of planes and bombs, waves of Junkers 52s came in from the sea and turned into the wind. From about 100 metres altitude, formations of these troop-carriers, three abreast wing-tip to wing-tip, left specks falling behind each plane. Parachutists tumbled out of the outer aircraft, and supplies and ammunition with different-coloured parachutes from centre planes.

Some of the paratroops dropping near defenders were shot in the air, and a few fell into the canal tangled in their harness, but most of the defensive positions were soon overrun. In short time, about a thousand paratroops had landed on both sides of the canal. Watching from the south side, Jo Jones saw 'Allied troops literally caught with their pants down, in their pyjamas, being rounded up by the first wave of the paratroopers'.[47] Twelve gliders, towed by troop-carriers, appeared with engineers aboard. One crashed into a bridge pylon, but enough paratroops landed near the bridge to secure it.

The Allied guards were quickly overwhelmed and the bridge captured intact. German engineers rushed onto it, ripping out fuses and throwing demolition charges to one side. The charges had been attached and primed the day before, but the fuses wouldn't function, disabled either by paratroops or in the crossfire. An English rifleman tried to detonate them from a distance with a direct hit, his first shot missing and drawing machine-gun fire from the opposite bank. He persisted without success until a surprisingly powerful explosion suddenly brought the bridge crashing into the canal below. With it went paratroops running across and a photographer filming the capture.[48] Probably the German officer removing the charges had piled them on the bridge and a chance hit detonated the stack.

Within an hour, the enemy had erected an emergency bridge and crossed to capture Corinth. For the defenders, it was desperation in a hopeless position. Most were killed or taken prisoner, the few who got away joining the exodus south if they were already on the Peloponnese side. As Kiwi defender Fred Woollams' platoon was about to withdraw on the other side, it came under intense fire from a sniper concealed in a tree. 'Some lead sprayed in my direction,' the former Manawatu shepherd recalls, 'my feet unfortunately catching a piece. Then there was a yell from Graham, who had got it in the stomach. Two of his mates considered he was beyond human aid, so they withdrew as ordered.' As they did so, another Kiwi was hit in the back. 'He stumbled up and tried to get away, but the Hun got him again in the same place and position. At this, the remainder of us saw red. As the sniper was invisible, we just sprayed the tree with lead. And there was silence.'[49]

After resisting for most of the morning, remaining defenders around Corinth surrendered, out of ammunition and with no sign of the promised light tanks of Charrington's armoured brigade. They and their field officers had already been captured. Trapped north of the canal, the survivors in Woollams' platoon tried to make their way back to Megara on foot, assisted along the way by Greek shepherds. By the time they got to the port, it was occupied by the enemy. The group stayed on the move for several months trying to negotiate a way out of Greece until they were betrayed to the Greek police and handed over to an Italian occupation force.[50]

On the night following the paratroop attack at Corinth, the Allied evacuation continued on both sides of the canal. There were embarking troops no longer able to get to the Peloponnese and there were those who had already got there. Arthur Pope, a Kiwi driver attached to the field ambulance, was one of the former. Arriving ahead of the invasion force to embark from Rafina, east of Athens, he found an undamaged Humber Snipe among the wrecked vehicles. 'Typical brass hats,' he said to the unit's padre, 'going first and leaving good cars for Jerry.' The pair set about thoroughly wrecking it before a brigadier returned, speechless with fury on seeing his car, left unattended for five minutes.[51]

Pope didn't know this brigadier, but there were only a couple there that day and Harold Charrington was one. After constant withdrawal ahead of the enemy since the initial battle at Vevi, 1200 men from his tank, artillery and infantry units left from Rafina. In all, 3500 New Zealand and English troops embarked at Rafina that night and a further 4720 from Porto Rafti, 25 kilometres to the south.

On the other side of the canal, the embarkation went less smoothly with more serious issues than a vandalised staff car. On the mountain road coming down to Navplion, a line of loaded Greek army mules had been machine-gunned from the air. Over fifty were killed, the wounded bolting or kicking out in terror. One mule smashed in the side of a truck. The stench of dead animals beside the road lingered in the nostrils of passing troops for some time.[52]

The road ahead was jammed with abandoned vehicles. Military police on motorcycles weaved around them, shouting and cursing at drivers to keep moving. On grass verges, trucks were parked under trees. Soldiers alongside sorted hurriedly through their kits, throwing into ditches everything they couldn't carry. Children swarmed among the discarded belongings, picking out items. The wounded, covered with brown blankets, lay on stretchers in the shade of olive trees, the walking wounded resting against the tree trunks.

Greek troops, caked in dust, came by, their uniforms dark with sweat from constant marching. Some still had the will to wave at the passing lorries and shout, '*Nike! Nike!* [Victory!]'.[53] In contrast, among the silent civilians gathered at the outskirts of the devastated town, black-shirted members of Prince Paul's Youth Movement[54] gave passing convoys a mocking fascist salute.[55]

The evacuation fleet had been attacked on its way to Navplion by dive-bombers and *Glenearn*, one of three troop-carriers, was so badly damaged, its engines flooded and the ship listing, that it was ordered back to Crete. After nightfall, the reduced fleet reached Navplion Bay, glowing rosy pink from the still-burning *Ulster Prince*.

A Sunderland flying-boat rode at anchor in the bay and three merchant ships sat in the harbour with supplies that hadn't been cancelled for the retreating army.

Word had come that 3000 were gathered by the beach at Tolos, down the coast from Navplion. Mostly stragglers, unattached from headquarters and base units, and more of the English armoured brigade, they were in a surly mood. Sent speeding after the fleet to recover some of the carrying capacity lost with *Glenearn*, three warships were directed to Tolos. The Australian destroyer *Stuart* was the first to arrive, with six hundred already waiting offshore on a flat-bottomed landing craft. It took those men on board and began a shuttle to the bay where they were transferred to larger ships while the barge returned to the shore to refill. As it approached the beach, a disorderly mob waded out waist-deep in breakers, scuffling to get on board. A stretcher case was tipped into the sea; a wounded man being helped by his mates was pushed under by men following.[56]

Tony Heckstall-Smith was there, wounded in the shoulder by a strafing Messerschmitt during the day. He went forward with a megaphone, 'Let the wounded on first. Stretcher cases and wounded first.' There was a rifle shot in the darkness and a bullet whistled over his head. A large Australian jumped on the ramp and, looking down at the English lieutenant, growled, 'Keep out of it, little man.'

The surging, desperate mob could not be stopped and the barge was soon packed with agitated men. The order was given to pull up the ramp. The barge's engines roared and screamed but the vessel wouldn't budge. It was weighed down on a sandbank. This was not where the naked colonel had waded out a couple of days before.

A voice called out from the motor cabin, 'There are too many on board. You must get some off or we're here for the night.' Heckstall-Smith found an officer in the crowd on board and told him, 'You must get at least a hundred back on shore.'

'I don't think you'll get them to leave.'

'That's your job and I suggest you do it,' he shot back.

The ramp lowered and tired soldiers reluctantly dropped back in the water and waded to shore until the barge was able to drive free of the bank. The craft took four hundred troops out to the waiting destroyer and returned to the beach to reload.[57]

At Navplion around the bay, the wreckage of *Ulster Prince* restricted access by ships to the jetty. Troops were ferried out to two large transports, *Khedive Ismail* and *Slamat*, waiting in the rough sea with scrambling nets hung over the side and slings to hoist stretcher cases. A variety of small boats brought men out from the jetty and a landing barge ferried them from the beach. A loaded whaler capsized and time was lost rescuing troops from the sea.

The heavy-loaded barges had to be pushed off a sandbank into deeper water by soldiers wading waist-deep. On the last load, there was no one to push it out. An officer ordered men to get off and push but they knew that if they got out, there was little chance of getting back on when the vessel was in deeper water.

The officer threatened, 'I'll shoot the first man who doesn't get off the barge!'

The sound of rifle bolts opening and closing could be heard in the crowd and, in the pause that followed with only the sounds of water lapping and the engine idling, the young midshipman who drove the barge said in an English public-school voice, 'It would be better, sir, if you were to get off first and show the men an example.'[58]

Those on the outer edge of the barge got in the water after the officer and pushed it free. Some hung on and clambered aboard, others were left behind.

Because of the ferrying delays, neither troop-carrier was full by 3.30 am when the decision was made for all ships to leave so they could be clear of air attack by sunrise. Captain Lundinga on the Dutch ship *Slamat* didn't acknowledge the signal, possibly under pressure from Australians on board to wait for more of their mates. *Slamat* didn't move for over half an hour until a Royal Navy officer came alongside in a motor boat and gave a direct order to weigh anchor.[59] Finally, at 4.30 am, the convoy departed with 2800 troops evacuated from Navplion, but 1700 were left on shore.

The warships at Tolos had left by 4 am with 2000 troops, including the Tolos beachmaster, an Australian identified only as Major M. On the last ferry run, he told the skipper of the cruiser *Perth* that there were only a few left on the beach and paratroops were closing in. There were actually 1300 still there, although the beachmaster was no longer one of them, and more were coming down from Navplion.

Jumbo Wilson had moved his headquarters to Myloi, around the bay from Navplion. He flew out that night on the flying-boat with fifty-five headquarters staff, leaving Bernard Freyberg as the sole general still in Greece with 20,000 troops yet to be evacuated.

Tom Baillie-Grohman and Sandy Galloway were taken by one of the evacuation destroyers down the coast towards Monemvasia, a port in the south of the Peloponnese to be used for embarkation the following night. They met a flotilla of landing craft lowered from *Glenearn* before it turned back to Crete, clambered down a rope ladder to one of the barges and continued to Monemvasia. After the lighters were beached and camouflaged a kilometre apart, the two senior officers hid themselves and slept.[60]

The rescue convoy from Navplion was still not far from the Greek mainland when the sun rose and the Stukas arrived. Targeting the largest ship, the dive-bombers made two direct hits on *Slamat*, one engulfing the bridge in flames, destroying the wheelhouse and killing the Dutch skipper. Only a few lifeboats could be lowered from the burning ship, veering out of control. The destroyer *Diamond* was soon on the spot, picking up survivors under constant dive-bomber attack and radioing for assistance. *Wryneck* came, collecting troops and ship crew from boats, life-rafts and flotsam.

A few hours later a second air formation arrived, raking machine-gun fire across the crowded decks. Junkers bombers scored direct hits on both destroyers, one hitting a store of torpedoes on *Diamond* and blowing apart its stern. Another holed *Wryneck* in its keel, with a second bomb crashing into its engine room, flooding the ship with sea water. Both ships sank within a few minutes.[61]

After no sighting of or signal from either of the destroyers throughout the following day, another ship was sent to look for them. All *Griffin* was able to find was a life-raft drifting on the Mediterranean with fifty soldiers and sailors from *Wryneck* on board, the sole survivors of the eight hundred rescued from *Slamat* and the two destroyers' crews. Only eight men of those embarked on the Dutch ship lived to tell of its fate.[62]

When news of the loss of the canal crossing reached General Freyberg at his interim headquarters, he sent word to Brigadier Edward Puttick, in command of the rearguard on the other side, to withdraw his force—New Zealand infantry and Australian artillery and engineers—to the beaches at Rafina and Porto Rafti instead of to the now-inaccessible Peloponnese. The last defensive line of the British expeditionary force to Greece pulled out that night in trucks that crawled along winding roads until the order came to switch on headlights.

The convoy sped through empty streets in Athens, its citizens expecting the invasion force at any moment. They were right; the Germans arrived at 9.30 the next morning, too late to catch the British trucks. and promptly hoisted the swastika over the Acropolis.

Just ahead of the invasion force, the retreating units bivouacked in orchards near Porto Rafti. After three weeks of successive withdrawals under constant air attack, many of the troops felt they 'had been pushed around to no good purpose and hadn't even had a good crack at Jerry'.[63] Now with a radical change in the evacuation plan, the men at all levels were tired and nerves were frayed. Howard Kippenberger, a New Zealand battalion commander, was wakened by Bill Strutt, the Australian battery commander. Strutt couldn't find any of the other evacuating units and had concluded they had embarked overnight. 'Your battalion and my guns are the last British troops in Greece,' was his glum assessment.

Kippenberger responded that they'd have to lie low and hope they could embark the next night. He scoured the area and found an abandoned Australian canteen truck with tinned plums and raspberries. Looking further afield, the New Zealander spotted khaki figures through the trees and found Puttick shaving nearby. No one had gone and all were to embark that night.[64]

The New Zealanders moved to defensive positions near a town to cover the road from Athens. As the soldiers marched past houses, townspeople watched from doorways and spilled onto the streets. Some were silent or weeping, crossing themselves, some called out blessings or threw flowers to the men. Women and children ran up with cups of water, carrying rifles while the thirsty troops drank.

Setting up above Porto Rafti beach, they were soon found by the Luftwaffe. Fighters arrived and strafed all the vehicles they could see, setting off a series of explosions in Strutt's ammunition wagon. Random machine-gunning across the surrounding country set a dry field of grain on fire where men were sheltering. The planes attacked the town and a marching column. There were civilian and troop casualties, but the defenders weren't dislodged.

Expecting a ground attack, they could see the dust of a motorised convoy lifting in the distance, but it moved south away from Porto Rafti. Finally, in the mid-afternoon, a column of German trucks, light tanks and motorcycles, were seen going into the town and emerging on the road south away from Porto Rafti. Some of the gunners couldn't resist firing a few shots at the receding column. Motorbikes coming back to investigate came under unexpectedly heavy gun and mortar fire and quickly retreated into the town. German intelligence had reported 'English troops abandoning their vehicles and fleeing on foot towards the coast', but clearly significant artillery defence was in place here. A Stuka assault on the gun positions was ordered. As it was dark before the air attack was ready, it was held over until the morning.[65] By then, it would be too late.

In the late afternoon, troops began destroying vehicles and artillery and sorting through their equipment, preparatory to evacuating. After dark, a cruiser and three destroyers appeared and the men were ferried to them by landing craft and caïque. Brigadier Puttick came on the last caïque. A destroyer was sent up the coast to pick up the last eight hundred of the armoured brigade, including its brigadier. Although no troop-carrier came this time, 4700 men from the two beaches were jammed on warships, the last evacuation from that side of the Corinth Canal. Any stragglers still there were left to their own devices, some managing to find their way to Crete or Egypt.

The Germans had blocked the canal crossing and now occupied Navplion. The only feasible points of escape were the southern Peloponnese ports of Monemvasia and Kalamata. Thousands had already crossed to the peninsula and were mostly streaming towards Kalamata. There were unit formations, stragglers and leaderless British support troops, Greek soldiers and Yugoslavs who had got away from their country's invasion three weeks before, as well as civilian refugees. The Australian battalions under brigadiers Allen and Savige were directed eventually to Kalamata too, many of them after arriving at Megara then Navplion and finding there were no further embarkations at either. They kept being sent further south until there was no further south to be sent to.

New Zealand infantry were scheduled to leave from Monemvasia, along with some Australian detachments that had been sent to the futile defence of the Corinth bridge. Three Kiwi battalions headed towards Tripolis in the centre of the peninsula a full day before the scheduled embarkation. To get there, convoys had to cross rough mountainous country, some of them during daylight hours, climbing 1000 metres on a zigzag road.

It didn't have the nerve-racking uncertainty of mountain driving at night, but instead had the certainty of Luftwaffe attention. From time to time, lookouts shouted, 'Aircraft!', and Messerschmitt 110s dived down with machine guns and cannons blazing, sending men scrambling off trucks to shelter. Some stood up as soon as the plane crossed and were shot at by the rear gunner.

Other battalions travelled by night, but all had concealed themselves around Tripolis by 27 April, ready to move to Monemvasia that night. It was the day after the paratroop attack at Corinth. The enemy air reconnaissance lost sight of the convoys and assumed they were heading towards Kalamata with the human debris of battle. Monemvasia was given little attention.

At midnight, the convoys came into Tripolis and formed into columns radiating out from lead trucks in the town square. Each convoy moved out in staggered starts, driving at speed along narrow, winding hill roads to arrive at the outskirts of Monemvasia and complete camouflage in olive groves before the arrival of the day's air attacks. The New Zealanders settled on the cool grass beneath trees and slept. By tea-time, everyone had washed and shaved for the sea voyage.

Australian infantry, detached to guard an airfield near Corinth, had been ordered to get to Monemvasia overnight and attach to General Freyberg's New Zealanders. In the passenger seat of the lead truck of a dilapidated convoy, company commander Keith Carroll, a Melbourne bank clerk in a previous life, checked maps by torchlight as they went. They were misdirected by a British military policeman at a crossroads, an error Carroll picked up after a few kilometres.

Returning to the crossroads and previously alerted that the enemy was planting English-speaking Germans in British uniforms, Carroll's second-in-command, George Warfe, shot the MP.[66] In the jittery climate, no one seems to have considered it might have been a genuine mistake at night by someone unfamiliar with the area. The summary execution is not mentioned in Carroll's unit diary, however. Warfe would rise to colonel in a distinguished post-war army career.

Carroll reported to Freyberg who instructed the company to cover a small stone bridge on the approach to Monemvasia. The men set up their positions and wandered down to the stream to wash and shave. People from nearby villages brought bread, olives and wine and a few cooked chickens. 'We had nothing to give them and felt ashamed to take their food when we were leaving them to the Germans,' says 'Jo' Gullett, a platoon leader.

In the late afternoon, the Australians saw a uniformed man watching through binoculars from a distant hilltop. Gullett told one of his men, an excellent marksman, to shoot the man, wanting to avoid a burst of fire giving their position away. The man fell back and no one took his place.[67] Friend or foe? In the uncertainty no one knew. You saw something you didn't like; you dealt with it.

When darkness had set in, all troops in the area, Kiwis and Aussies, moved down to the beaches either side of the town's rocky headland. They were placed in predetermined positions in a long line by a New Zealand officer marshalling the embarkation. Two destroyers arrived and a loud-hailer blared out of the dark, 'This is the Royal Navy. If there are any British or Allied troops ashore, announce your formation and the name of your commander. Over.'

Freyberg stepped forward and addressed the night in a surprisingly high-pitched voice. 'We have approximately 1700 all ranks, principally New Zealand infantry with elements of British and Australians. Major-General Freyberg is in command. I am Freyberg.'

'As I am not yet certain of your identity,' said the disembodied voice, 'and must protect His Majesty's ships, I must warn you that all guns of this force are loaded and trained upon you. At the least suggestion of foul play, we shall fire. Is that understood? Acknowledge.'

Freyberg walked over to a launch that came in. After a brief conversation, a naval officer called vessels in to start ferrying troops.[68] A landing craft already filled with the wounded went out first, but came back soon after, still loaded. Only the cruiser *Ajax* had slings to lift stretchers up to the deck and it was still at sea. After midnight, *Ajax* and two more destroyers arrived. The barge full of wounded went out again. This time it came back empty.

Bernard Freyberg and Tom Baillie-Grohman watched from the shore as boats shuttled back and forth between ships and beach. Baillie-Grohman opened his despatch case and took out a bottle of champagne. 'I think the time has come for a drink,' he said. It had been a Luftwaffe-free day, with patrol planes not spotting the troops and trucks concealed among the trees below. The transfer of troops had gone well. The admiral and the general toasted an evacuation exercise that had achieved more than any had expected, despite inevitable hiccups.

'Come on, let's go,' said Baillie-Grohman and the two senior officers got on the last landing craft out to *Ajax*, jumped on the scrambling net and clambered on board, assuming the embarkation at Kalamata had gone equally as smoothly.[69]

6

KALAMATA: DEFIANCE AND FAINT HEARTS

By the day of the Corinth attack, a large Australian force, assembled around the temporary Anzac headquarters at Myloi, was ordered to move on to Kalamata, further south. A column of about six hundred vehicles left at 8 pm and wound with dimmed lights along the mountain roads of the Peloponnese. Wounded men writhed in agony at each jolt as trucks negotiated hairpin bends. At one point, the convoy missed a turn and the column ground to a halt with 10 kilometres of trucks standing by on the narrow snaking road while the lead vehicles backed and turned repeatedly as they carefully swung around.[1]

By evening on 26 April, 15,000 troops had gathered in olive groves around the fishing town, a third of them Australians put under Brigadier 'Tubby' Allen's command. The rest were from various armies, much of them leaderless, disorganised and belligerent. The unattached trickled into Kalamata hoping to slip into embarking units.

In the milling crowd, Major George Smith had come across stragglers from his battalion and said to one of his sergeants, 'I'll put up a piece of paper and, if you see anyone from the battalion, tell them to write their names on it. Where's a good place to pin the paper?'

'Why don't you stick it up your arse!' an eavesdropping English soldier chipped in.

'Oh no, that's no good,' was Smith's unruffled response. 'No one would see it there.'[2]

Roland Griffiths-Marsh was an eighteen-year-old intelligence officer whose unit, broken up in the first battle at Vevi, had since regrouped. He was moving through the town when a young man came out of a house in a narrow street and grabbed his arm, pulling him inside and up the stairs. On a table beside an old man and a woman who spoke passable English were platters of olives, flat-bread and chicken. The Australian said he was sorry they couldn't stop the Germans, which the woman translated. There was an exchange in Greek and she said, 'You will come back. We will be free again.'

Feeling he hadn't earned it, Griffiths-Marsh nibbled at the food out of embarrassed politeness, then ate some chicken when pressed. It was the first proper meal he'd had since leaving Melbourne. When he left, they wrapped their arms around him and wept.[3]

The officer put in charge of the Kalamata evacuation was Leonard Parrington, a 51-year-old brigadier from the British Military Mission, the liaison unit operating out of Athens before the German invasion. He had the men grouped into unit parties of fifty, with each group given a serial number. They were to march in number order to the quay with what weapons, ammunition and personal gear they could carry and would be allocated a ship at a control point there. Parrington demanded 'the highest standard of discipline be observed in accordance with Imperial traditions'.[4] At Allen's insistence, fighting men were to embark before base troops. Armed provosts were ordered to take 'active measures' to prevent troops other than Australians and British filtering onto the ships.[5]

At ten o'clock, lights were seen at sea and the waterfront came to life as groups started shuffling down. Three troop-carriers, the English *City of London* and *Dilwarra* and the Dutch *Costa Rica*, anchored out from the port while two destroyers arrived at the quay to find no one standing by to berth them. The beachmaster, a Royal Navy man, had advised Parrington of the intended embarkation and left organising wharf labour to the army man. Convinced for some reason that the ships wouldn't come, Parrington reportedly told the quay's naval staff they weren't necessary.[6]

Staff had to be chased up and lights rigged. While the ships were berthing, a long line of troops waited in their assigned order on the old stone quay. Tom Burns was there with a British ambulance unit, joining the end of a line of figures in the darkness.

'With the light coming off the water,' he remembers, 'we could see the line and it was up to twenty men deep and 200 yards long, a great packed rectangle of thousands of men. They stood very still, not talking, not smoking; there was an occasional cough, and over the top of the block there played a continual little motion as men rose on their toes to look to the front.'[7]

Passing along two gangways to each destroyer as it came in, the men were packed tightly and shuttled out to the anchored transports. As the queue neared the gangways, the orderly lines began to unravel, with pushing and shoving by some of the troops who were scheduled to embark and anxious that nothing come in the way of it. With the start delayed by Parrington's unreadiness, time was running out. The convoy faced leaving without its full capacity loaded.

Thirty-year-old John Loes, a rural labourer from New South Wales, was at the front of the line and poised to board, when they were halted. Someone shouted, 'Make way, make way,' and brigadiers Allen and Savige strode up.

'Jack Daniel and I are right at the entrance,' Loes says, 'and they said "Make way for two brigadiers". When the two brigadiers walked on, I gave Jack a nudge and said "If it's good enough for two brigadiers, it's good enough for us". And so we marched on as escort and they took us out to the *City of London*.'[8]

A group of Yugoslav soldiers, claiming high priority from Anthony Eden, were not so successful.[9] It would have been cold comfort for them to be told that packing cases with the Yugoslav crown jewels did manage to get on board.[10]

Carrying personal arms, including Bren guns and anti-tank rifles, the men climbed up landing nets hanging over the side of their allocated transports. Some had slipped boxes of ammunition past the scrutineers. Anyone with an automatic weapon was sent to the top deck to join anti-aircraft gunners already there.

Griffiths-Marsh climbed up steel steps below the bridge with a group of battalion mates and found a dozen mattresses laid side by side. The powerfully built Sergeant-Major Watt said, 'This will do us,' and threw his rifle and gear on a mattress. The others did the same.

Soon a sub-lieutenant bounded up and, in an English public-school accent, said, 'I say, chappies, you can't stay there. It's reserved for officers.'

Watt turned to him. 'Get fucked!' he snarled. The young man back-pedalled with mouth agape and disappeared.[11]

The convoy left on time at 3 am with 8650 troops on board but three warships were forced to leave with no evacuees. They had room for up to 3000 more, but they had run out of time. A disorganised and desperate rabble of 7000 were left behind, with nowhere else to go. In charge was a senior officer, Brigadier Parrington, over-whelmed by the task. By the next evening, the rabble had grown to 10,000.

Unarmed and mostly leaderless base troops, including Palestinian and Cypriot drivers and labourers, were swirling into and around Kalamata, along with stray Yugoslav soldiers and Greek civilians, many of them women and children. A group of six hundred RAF ground crew arrived during the day, left behind after all but one of their officers flew out.[12] The only fighting troops in this combustible mix were an 800-strong force from New Zealand and 380 unevacuated Australians. The New Zealanders included a reserve company, transferred from Freyberg's command to Wilson's command in Athens. Not part of the GHQ evacuation plan, they had been left to fend for themselves.

The dawn was greeted with strikes on the harbour and railway station by Junkers 88s. Bombing continued through the day with casualties filling a field hospital set up in the town. In one attack, the sole RAF officer saw a stick of bombs dropped where the destroyers had berthed the night before. Assuming they had time-delayed fuses, and unable to find Parrington or the beachmaster, Group Captain Lee advised a staff officer that destroyers should berth outside the harbour breakwater.[13]

Colonel Renton, an English intelligence officer put in charge of base troops, was told by Parrington that there was no chance of evacuating all the troops that had accumulated at Kalamata. Renton proposed the Palestinians, mostly German Jews, should be embarked first. Their likely fate at the hands of the Nazis was already known, but Parrington wouldn't vary the priority for fighting soldiers, insisted on by Brigadier Allen before departing.[14]

Parrington ordered the wounded in the hospital to be ready to move at nightfall and all troops to parade on the quay. Advised by the beachmaster, Captain Clarke-Hall, that the next embarkation was not until the following night, Parrington had persuaded himself nonetheless that there would be one on both nights. A long wide line was formed again on the quay with the Palestinians near the back. No ships appeared. With a new dawn coming and the Luftwaffe inevitably to follow, a deflated Leonard Parrington ordered the assembled throng to disperse into the surrounding hills for the day.

———

When the withdrawal to evacuate the British force began on 22 April, an English armoured contingent was sent to Patras on the

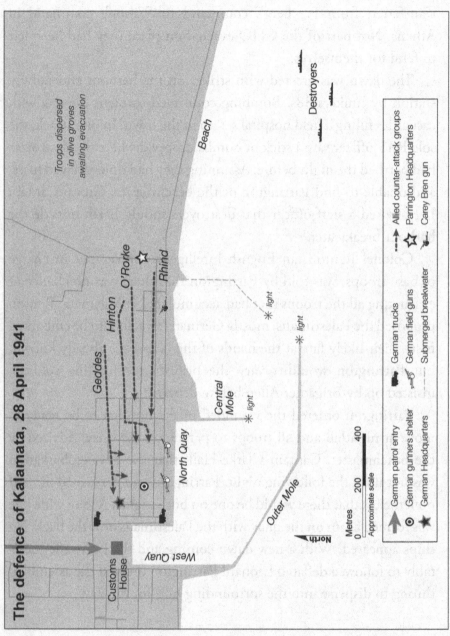

The defence of Kalamata, 28 April 1941

Troops dispersed in olive groves awaiting evacuation

Beach

Destroyers

O'Rorke

Hinton

Rhind

Geddes

Central Mole

North Quay

Outer Mole

West Quay

Customs House

light

light

light

North

Metres
0   200   400

Approximate scale

German patrol entry
German gunners shelter
German Headquarters
German trucks
German field guns
Submerged breakwater
Allied counter-attack groups
Parrington Headquarters
Carey Bren gun

north Peloponnese coast to guard against Germans crossing the gulf there. Historically a cavalry regiment, the Queen's Own Hussars—the queen in question being Charlotte, the wife of George III—now rode light tanks and Bren carriers as part of Britain's Armoured Brigade. On 27 April, the 300-strong detachment moved down to Kalamata to join the evacuation, bringing news that the enemy had taken Patras. It's not clear what resistance the Hussars had offered there, but Parrington sent them 30 kilometres outside Kalamata to beat off enemy patrols. Returning to town for the embarkation that didn't eventuate, they were sent out again the next day.

The non-appearance of the convoy and the troops' dispersal back into the surrounding woods and groves left the men who had drifted to Kalamata with little motivation. The New Zealanders, told by Parrington to cover the embarkation again, waited around in random groups. The RAF group captain, Arthur Lee, took his ground crews to a nearby village where he'd arranged for a fishing boat to take them to Crete. Some of the Palestinians, advised by Renton not to rely on the embarkation plan, followed the RAF men and pleaded to be taken on their boat but Lee said the 10-metre vessel was already dangerously overloaded.[15]

The bulk of the Hussar unit returned in the mid-afternoon reporting no contact with enemy patrols and leaving about a hundred manning the watch. Allied troops were gathering in the fading light at assembly areas on the eastern outskirts of the town, two New Zealand officers waiting further out with drivers and undestroyed trucks to pick up stragglers. By afternoon, their commander, Archie MacDuff, had decided his men should cover the two approach roads to Kalamata, but events overtook that plan.

Soon after the outer watch of Hussars thinned out, a German unit advancing from Patras captured those still manning it, then scooped up the Kiwi drivers further on. Armoured cars and motorised field guns swept unopposed through the north of the town and down to the quay, bringing their new prisoners with them and adding the beachmaster, Clarke-Hall, and his signalman.[16] Drawing up at Customs House on the west side of the quay, the enemy force of about three hundred began probing east along the waterfront, cutting off the waiting evacuees from their embarkation point.

An awareness was growing in the olive groves and assembly areas that an enemy force had arrived. Lorry drivers from the field hospital reported Germans in town and machine-gun fire could be heard. Townspeople and unarmed troops were hurrying away from the quay area. There was no unified response, the men and their officers reacting in different ways. Some took advantage of the low light and limited weapons and made themselves scarce, while others confronted the enemy or organised groups to do so.

Word got through to Brigadier Parrington at his headquarters on the eastern edge of town. At a conference of senior officers, he argued that any attempt to drive the enemy out of Kalamata was doomed to failure. He'd already issued an order to 'Retreat to cover'. Two of the base unit colonels disagreed vehemently and Parrington eventually relented, ordering the New Zealanders to attack.[17]

Private 'Jonah' Jones was among the Kiwis moving back into town at dusk. 'About half a mile from the outskirts Major MacDuff met us and distributed grenades and small-arms ammunition,' he says. 'He was shouting at us to get into it and saying that unless the town was cleared the navy would be unable to take us off.'[18]

MacDuff sent two lieutenants to counter-attack. 'Bob' O'Rorke and Pat Rhind collected about twenty Anzacs and started towards the quay. 'By this time, it was getting fairly dark,' says Rhind, 'and there seemed to be utter confusion in the waterfront area and shots were coming from all directions.' They split into two parallel lines, Rhind's group along the waterfront, O'Rorke's one street in.[19]

Basil Carey, an English tank commander without a tank, had found a Bren gun, gathered a few men and been engaging the intruders from a distance.[20] A group of Australians was sent to join the New Zealanders and a second group pushed along the waterfront. The Germans became disturbed by the numbers of soldiers they now suspected were in and around the town and the signs of a counter-attack developing. They decided that their prisoners, held near Customs House among the lorries and armoured cars, should be marched back out of the town.

Parrington's rescinded order would have been ineffectual anyway. Even while groups were being collected elsewhere to counter-attack, a New Zealand sergeant was already on the move. When told of the order, Jack Hinton said, 'To hell with this! Who's coming with me?', collected a dozen men and led them into the centre of town. A dour, straight-talking public works driver from Greymouth, Hinton hadn't seen any fighting prior to reaching Kalamata but was determined to redress that oversight. Moving towards the waterfront, he went into battle as soon as he saw Germans, rushing at a machine-gun nest firing at him point blank and missing. After wiping out the gun's crew with two hurled grenades, and bayonetting survivors, he moved on to another machine-gun post and a mortar. His crew mopped up with rifle and bayonet, and dealt with intrusions from the side.[21]

With no overall command, fighting was spontaneous and reactive but with little direction. Some men were exhilarated that they were finally coming to grips with the enemy after the frustration of constantly withdrawing under air attack or being held in reserve. A later German report noted there was no initial reaction to their presence, 'then rifle fire began to crackle in the harbour; isolated shots at first, so that nobody bothered, but suddenly it swelled to a hurricane'.[22] Rifle and machine-gun fire stabbed in a darkness broken only by tracer and sudden flares from mortar bombs. Men darted from one cover to the next, taking shots as they went. Men from the evacuees' assembly areas came in from side streets, replacing wounded comrades.

The Germans had two mobile field guns on the quay and soldiers firing from doorways, balconies and rooftops. A runner got through to tell Pat Rhind that O'Rorke's group was pinned by fire from the top of a house. Breaking into an adjoining house, Rhind's crew fired from the rooftop onto the Germans on a nearby roof. A blast of Tommy-gun fire ended that enemy barrage.[23]

Where machine-gun fire was intense, Hinton and his party diverted one block and came in from a different direction, but the sergeant had decided where the pivotal point was. Getting Jonah Jones to provide protection with his Bren gun, he worked his way along the street, darting from doorway to doorway with Jones covering, all the while aiming to get to the first of the two guns on the waterfront. He was within reach of it when a crazy-brave move swept past him.[24]

Doug Patterson had picked up grenades and ammunition and tagged onto Pat Rhind's crew, exchanging fire along the waterfront. 'About a block before the quay,' he recalls, 'a truck without a canopy and full of Kiwis whizzed past me. I saw one chap, a Maori I think, with a Tommy gun and one chap with a Bren gun leaning over the hood. The truck rushed the big gun, the chaps firing as they closed in.'[25]

MacDuff had sent a three-tonne truck into the fray, with Kiwis and Aussies on the running boards and one of his sappers, Bill Gourlick, behind the wheel. The truck was stopped 50 metres from the first gun and the men jumped off, dashing for cover up side streets and opening fire on the gun crew. Caught by surprise, the crew and Germans on the footpath nearby were unable to regain control. When the New Zealanders charged at them with bayonets, the gun crew retreated into two houses, leaving many of their comrades behind, killed or wounded.[26]

When the truck rumbled past, Hinton and his group followed it and joined the skirmish, chasing after the retreating gun crew. Hinton smashed a window of the first house and tossed in a grenade, shouldered open the front door and tossed in another, following with bayonet thrust in front. He repeated the action with the second house, some of his crew following him in through the door.

His companions, along with other groups that had arrived on the scene, were by now engaging Germans scattered around the quayside area. The armed group that had accumulated moved further down the street to where armoured cars were standing, most of their crews upstairs in an adjacent building. Gunners were picked off as they made a run for their vehicles.

Unlike a battle with formed units, many of the men in these ad hoc groups didn't know the men they were fighting alongside, only that they were on the same side. Someone came up with a simple scheme for keeping the groups cohesive. Rhind explains, 'It was dark by this time and the only way we could keep contact was by shouting "Aussie" and "Kiwi" so that we could recognise friend or foe.'[27]

In the melee, Doug Patterson ran into a bricklayer he knew from Invercargill, his home town. It was Jonah Jones. 'I joined up with them,' says Patterson. 'Jones seemed to be enjoying it. I remember him saying that it was the best night he'd had since he left New Zealand.'[28] This from someone from Invercargill!

Jones was returning fire past a telegraph pole at machine guns shooting from the ground floor. 'Bullets were hitting the post and I remember thinking what a rotten shot Jonah was until I saw it was a Jerry on the balcony firing at him,' says Patterson. 'Jonah kept firing at the LMGs [light machine guns] until he was hit in the shoulder and fell across my feet. I looked up and got the Jerry on the balcony. He fell down on the footpath and those on the ground floor seemed to stop firing.'[29]

While Patterson took his mate to the first-aid post, grenades were thrown in ground floor windows and sixty Germans came out with their hands up. One spoke good English and said, 'You'd better look after us because our main party will be here in an hour.' At the RAP (Regimental Aid Post) the boys from Invercargill were revived with brandy. Jones could no longer carry his Bren gun and wanted a captured Mauser so he could rejoin his group, but was talked out of it.[30]

Colonel Geddes, an English base unit officer, had meanwhile taken a contingent to clear the north side of the town, arriving at the German attack force's temporary headquarters. With the building surrounded, Geddes called through an interpreter for the Germans to surrender. A voice shouted from within, 'Fire stopping. Finished,' and a lieutenant came out to negotiate. The building's occupants were running out of ammunition, but more of the attack force was waiting outside Kalamata. Instructed to stall but not surrender, the lieutenant was forced to bring his company commander. According to the German report, 'Australians' threatened to shoot them both unless all encircled in the harbour area laid down their arms.[31]

With that, the quay was retaken and the town cleared. About 120 German prisoners were taken. To celebrate their success, men tried to tip the disabled heavy gun into the sea but it jammed against a tree. German trucks were taken to block the main roads into Kalamata and to carry the wounded to the RAP and the field hospital. Among the casualties was Jack Hinton, finally brought to a stop with severe wounding in the lower abdomen as he pushed on from the quay.

As Clarke-Hall and his signaller were gone, taken out of town with other British prisoners, no one knew where the communications codes for navy ships were, or the radio to use them. A truck was turned around with headlights pointing out to sea. It signalled in Morse code that the waterfront was cleared and they were ready to depart, but no reply came back.[32]

Known jocularly as 'Pig and Whistle', Admiral Henry Pridham-Wippel was in overall command of the convoys extricating the British force from Greece. In order to lift the 7000 waiting at Kalamata in one night, for what was intended to be the navy's last rescue mission, he needed ships that could board the men speedily. Kalamata's quay and breakwater made that possible as warships could berth there, although Parrington's unpreparedness prevented full advantage being taken of it two nights earlier. Warships moved faster across the sea than the converted liners and cargo ships being used as troopships and, if they could dock at a quay, they didn't need small craft to ferry the men to them. Leaving nothing to chance, the admiral sent eight warships to Kalamata for the final night. When he was told there were 1500 Yugoslav refugees as well, he sent three more destroyers.

By 7.30 pm, the convoy was 30 kilometres from Kalamata. Its commander, Captain Philip Bowyer-Smyth, having received no signals from the Kalamata beachmaster and seeing tracer light in the sky, sent the destroyer *Hero* to investigate. Its skipper, Commander Hilary Biggs, saw mortar flashes and could hear gunfire and explosions.

Anchoring east of the town, a light was spotted winking from the shore. Parrington had sent a signaller to the end of the breakwater with a lamp. The message in Morse code was read on *Hero* as 'Boche in harbour British troops to SE of town'. There is conjecture the word in the signal was 'bombs', after Lee's warning, not 'Boche', but Biggs passed it on to Bowyer-Smyth as his signaller read it: 'Harbour occupied by Germans, British troops to south-east of town.'[33]

Biggs sent his first lieutenant ashore with a signalman and armed guard to make contact with Parrington. The beach was reported as now suitable for embarking troops, but not the quay apparently. At 9.30 pm, Biggs ordered a signal to Bowyer-Smyth, 'Troops collecting on beach east of town. All firing ceased in town. Consider evacuation possible from beach.'[34]

While waiting to hear from the destroyer, Bowyer-Smyth, a Royal Navy officer put in charge of the Australian cruiser *Perth*, weighed up his position with puzzling logic. He decided the embarkation would be extremely hazardous with his ships silhouetted against the lit sky if the fleet was attacked from the sea. He was obsessed with the Italian fleet possibly coming from Taranto, twelve hours away, notwithstanding that there was no indication it was actually on its way and that it had barely ventured from the base since its crushing defeat at Cape Matapan a month before. Bowyer-Smyth believed there were enemy submarines about and had depth-charged a 'sub' earlier in the day, although post-war records show there were no submarines in the vicinity that day. He concluded that the number of troops that could be evacuated did not warrant the 'substantial risk to an important force' (the Mediterranean Fleet), even though his superior commander, Admiral Pridham-Wippel, had decided the risk was acceptable.[35]

At 9.30 pm, the same time as Biggs initiated his message that the quay was back under Allied control, Bowyer-Smyth ordered the rescue fleet to turn back and *Hero* to rejoin it. Because of a radio defect, *Hero*'s message didn't get to Bowyer-Smyth on *Perth* for another forty minutes. By then the fleet was 30 kilometres from Kalamata, but the fleet commander refused to change his decision, later claiming the argument for it was unchanged. It was, however, a flawed argument.[36]

Biggs sent two further messages that he was sending boats ashore for troops gathering on the beach and would load as many as possible before departing at 2 am. Two whalers were lowered and came back with defiant, worn-out and hungry troops. Loading was slow as the men had scattered during the fighting and word was just getting around to gather on the beach. Within half an hour, Biggs got the signal to rejoin the convoy and assumed there was a threat he didn't know of. The boats were hoisted under protest from troops already on board and *Hero* steamed out to where *Perth* was imagined to be waiting.[37]

In Crete, Pridham-Wippel saw the radio messages from *Hero* to *Perth* and concluded the latter was near the beach supervising the rescue with Biggs' guidance. At 11.15 pm, a radio message from *Perth* advised that Kalamata was occupied by Germans and the fleet, apart from *Hero*, was withdrawing. By then, the ships were

100 kilometres south of Kalamata. Heading to rendezvous with *Perth*, Biggs read Bowyer-Smyth's signal to Pridham-Wippel and realised he wouldn't meet *Perth*. He returned to the Kalamata beach and resumed embarkation. Scrambling nets and slings were lowered over the side, mess tables used as stretchers for the wounded.

At 1 am, the three destroyers sent belatedly by Pridham-Wippel arrived and anchored 200 metres off the beach. They sent their boats to ferry troops but they only had an hour before they would have to leave.[38] With only the destroyers' whalers working, progress was slow. Men with enough strength left were encouraged to swim out to the ships. Leading Seaman Ward, a torpedo operator on *Hero*, has painful memories of that night. 'The cries of obviously exhausted men, making valiant attempts to swim from the shore, pleading for help, still echos in my ears,' he says.

Voices came from the dark, 'Can you see me?'

'Peering into the inky night blackness, we would, with an effort of untruthful assurance answer "Yes, a few more strokes and you have made it",' Ward confesses. 'A cry, a gurgle and then silence and nothing that we waiting on the ship could do.' Only a few were fished out shivering and half-drowned.[39]

The wounded were taken to the beach from the hospital and the RAP when *Hero* was sighted. With priority for boarding the wounded, the early arrivals were able to get on boats. The later they came, the more they got caught up with desperate men trying to elbow their way towards the boats. A Kiwi, Richard Kean, was one, with two cartons of cigarettes tucked behind his gas mask as he tried to push his way onto a whaler. After several failed attempts, a big navy hand grabbed him by his greatcoat belt and hauled him into the boat, head over heels. He never saw his cigarettes again.[40]

Jonah Jones was taken from the RAP to the edge of town in a truck of walking wounded. Told boats were waiting at the beach, he arrived to find an enormous crowd instead of the few hundred he'd expected. A boat was already filled, but the embarkation officer had delayed its departure, waiting for the truck from the first-aid post. When it arrived, the wounded said, 'Let them go.'[41]

The gesture was overtaken by concerns for the ships' safety as dawn got closer. With the rest of the convoy long gone, the four destroyers working Kalamata beach wouldn't risk delaying their departure, leaving at 2.30 am with only 332 soldiers embarked. More than 8000 were left on the beach. No further whalers came to the shore.

When the rescue ships had gone, Leonard Parrington addressed the senior officers, congratulating them on the spirited action to recover the town. He said the navy would return the next night if holding the town could be guaranteed, but it couldn't take more than six hundred men. That was pure guesswork on his part, but he went on to say they had few weapons, little ammunition and no rations or medical supplies for the wounded. Enemy air attacks would resume in the morning and they knew from German prisoners that there was a large enemy force nearby. That wasn't guesswork.

Parrington said he had already sent a message to the German commander that they would lay down arms at 5.30 am. Any who wanted to escape could do so before that. Surrendering troops were to wait in formation on the beach.

Renton advised against the troops waiting on the beach. 'The beaches will be bombed at daylight,' he said. 'There's no certainty the message will get to the German commander before then. Our prisoners say he's fifty miles away.'[42]

Parrington wouldn't change the order. The beach was dive-bombed in the morning as troops stood there waiting to surrender. There were two hundred casualties.[43] The larger German force arrived during the day and took prisoners, a thousand or more of those left behind escaping into the hills.

Three destroyers were sent to Kalamata that night. Arriving off the beach, the town strangely quiet, boats were sent ashore. They collected only 120 men in the darkness, including Colonel Renton who'd spent the day hiding in a cave. The ships returned the following night, picking up 202 more. They could hear the gunfire of small groups that had decided to fight it out rather than surrender. The navy didn't come again to Kalamata but patrolled the southern coastline for some days looking for stragglers.[44]

So ended a rescue operation that in many ways exceeded expectations, even though it ended on a sour note. In his autobiography, Middle East naval commander Admiral Cunningham describes Bowyer-Smyth's decision to abandon the rescue operation as 'unfortunate',[45] using genteel language befitting his position—or perhaps he didn't want to attract examination of his own decision to tell Anthony Eden what that ambitious politician wanted to hear about sending a force to Greece, instead of giving his own professional opinion. Whatever Cunningham's reason for soft-pedalling, Antipodeans might more vigorously describe Bowyer-Smyth's action as 'gutless'.

Like many who joined the battle and drove off the enemy attack at Kalamata, Doug Patterson was left behind when the destroyers departed. He and a Maori soldier with a badly wounded face found a dinghy, took off their boots and paddled with bits of wood in what they hoped was the direction of Crete. They came near two destroyers in the dark and were nearly run down by one, but men on the other heard their shouts and threw down a rope ladder. The destroyers had spent the night picking up stragglers and took them all to Crete.[46]

The two New Zealanders shared a fate but never exchanged names. It's one of many tales of soldiers left behind on mainland Greece at the end of the evacuation, trying with desperation and mixed success to find a means of crossing the Mediterranean to Crete or Egypt.

A Kiwi driver, 'Shortie' Sutherland, saw the last rescue ship leave Kalamata and joined a party of Aussies. They swam out to a small fishing boat anchored offshore and tried to start the engine with a rope around the flywheel. When that failed, they hoisted its sails and set out for Crete. After six days of carefully rationing a store of water, bread and goats' cheese, they arrived at Canea, the Cretan capital, starving but alive.[47]

Australian infantrymen Stan Wick and Ollie Cooke missed the boat out of Navplion but met others on the run travelling across country and got a rowing boat to the nearby island of Spetsai. There they bought a passage on a large fishing vessel that was going to Crete loaded with British troops, Greeks, Yugoslavs and Athenian prostitutes. Island- and coast-hopping by night and killing and cooking a heifer and goats, they reached Canea on 6 May.[48]

Others moved around the Peloponnese in groups, like the lost tribes of Israel. A band of seventy or eighty headed down the coast in trucks that Australian drivers, who hadn't been told when their brigade was embarking, had decided not to destroy. Captains Woodhill and Vial took a car and followed the truck convoy until the road petered out just as the sun was rising. The group continued on foot along a coastal track until they got to a cove in which a two-masted ketch was moored. Rob Vial stripped and swam out to it. The solid oak vessel was fully equipped with sails, but its diesel engine had been disabled by removing a pipe. A dinghy arrived with another party and was used to bring men out to fix the engine. The others waited on the shore.

Resting on a bunk while the repaired engine was tested, Vial's peace was pierced by the roar of a plane and a row of bullet holes appearing in the wood panel above him. A Messerschmitt was circling the yacht, raking the boat and men swimming for shore with machine-gun fire and leaving the ketch in flames. Ten wounded were helped to shore. Two men drowned, and five killed on board were incinerated in the burning vessel.

Jim Peters, a Melbourne doctor before the war, volunteered to stay with the wounded and those who'd lost heart, while the rest continued down the coast to a village they'd been told had three boats available. Mostly barefoot and thinly clothed, the group spread out and Vial, with feet cut by sharp rocks, dropped behind. At dusk, he got to the village to find many there before him under the command of the English colonel, Geddes. The three boats were unserviceable, but British ships were said to pass by and Geddes had organised watchers and signallers. Coordination of the large party, by then grown to a hundred, proved difficult with small groups deciding what they would do. Seven officers offered to take a shift on watch duty and disappeared in a small boat.

Vial went the next day with a few men to where a boat had been seen in a cave. While they were away, a Greek arrived with a note from a German patrol leader asking if the stragglers intended to surrender or fight on. Geddes sent a message back offering to surrender. Finding the boat gone from the cave, the men returned and met the Greek with Geddes' message. Vial read it and tore it up.

The boat the officers had taken drifted in empty that afternoon. Vial and a Palestinian took a rowing boat out about 10 kilometres until sunset, without sighting a ship. The group resumed its watch that night with an English signaller on the cliffs with a torch. In the early hours, they heard turbines faintly, flashed a message and got a response.

A sleeping Vial was wakened by a soldier. The two rowed until they saw a shadowy shape and called out, 'Are you a British ship?'

'Are you British?' replied a voice in the dark.

'We wouldn't be out in a bloody rowing boat in the middle of the bloody night speaking English if we weren't!'

Then another voice said, 'He's all right. I know him.' It was one of the officers who'd gone in the boat which was left to drift back to shore.

Whalers came ashore and picked up 110 ragged troops, most of them Aussies. The destroyer looked for the group of wounded with Major Peters where they had been left, but was unable to land with dawn approaching. The destroyer took the group of stragglers to Port Said. Peters' group was rescued a day later.[49]

Some were not so lucky. Pat Rhind and four others got in a caïque but couldn't get the engine started. Heading for the hills, they were captured by a German motorcycle patrol.[50]

About 7000 prisoners were taken at Kalamata in addition to those captured in battle and those left behind at other embarkation points. They were taken to unsanitary temporary camps at Corinth and Salonika, transferred by train or marched where railway bridges had been destroyed. There were frequent attempts at escape, some of them successful, some fatal.

Tom Boulter jumped into low scrub unnoticed while being marched to another camp. He lay there until it was dark and, sheltered by Greek people at great risk to themselves, worked his way to Turkey by the end of July. From there the Melbournian went by train to rejoin his battalion.[51]

Charles Downing, another Victorian, was captured sleeping in a shed at Kalamata and taken to the camps at Corinth and Salonika. Herded on to a train to Austria, he jumped into the darkness as the engine slowed to cross a bridge, landing on a blackberry thicket. Helped by Greek villagers, he joined with other escapees and eventually got to Cairo in December by way of Izmir (Smyrna) in Turkey with the assistance of Colonel Hughes, an Australian attached to the RAF and operating from Izmir.[52]

Severely wounded, Jack Hinton survived four years in German PoW camps, his several attempts to escape all ultimately unsuccessful. He was in solitary confinement after one failed attempt when it was gazetted in Britain that he'd been awarded the Victoria Cross for his actions at Kalamata. He was taken from his cell, paraded in front of his fellow prisoners and presented with a replica of the VC by a German general. He was then returned to the cell to see out the rest of his sentence.[53]

Fourteen hundred survivors of the Greek campaign got out of Greece after the scheduled evacuations were over. They included 400 Palestinians and 300 Cypriots who managed to get to the island of Milos, from where they were picked up by the destroyers, *Hotspur* and *Havock*.[54] But despite the futility of the task, the British didn't abandon the enterprise of saving Greece from the Nazis. There was still Crete.

Part III

CRETE

7

WELCOME TO SUDA BAY

The troopship *Costa Rica* arrived in the early afternoon off the north coast of Crete with 2600 evacuees from Kalamata on board. A variety of machine guns and anti-tank rifles had been rigged up on the top deck, already packed with soldiers, and the convoy had driven off two air attacks. After men were drenched from a near miss in the first raid, all but gunners were sent below deck. Four of the gunners played euchre between raids.

A soldier played the grand piano in the saloon of the converted passenger liner and when the klaxon warned of an air attack, he played 'The Wreck of the Nancy Lee' ('The bravest man was Captain Brown, 'cause he played his ukulele as the ship went down.'[1]). In Archie Allan's memory of the saloon, 'gilded mirrors reflected filthy, weary young men and, through the racket, cheers rose and music tinkled'.[2]

The port at Suda Bay was overcrowded. Admiral Pridham-Wippel ordered it cleared and convoys of arriving troopships held offshore temporarily. On *Costa Rica*, the 'All Clear' had just sounded when three bombers glided out of the sun, their engines cut back so their approach wasn't heard. Two bombs dropped a couple of metres from the ship's side, soaking gunners. The vessel shuddered and water started coming in through damaged port-side plates, flooding the engine room.[3] A soldier on another ship in the convoy watched *Costa Rica* as it 'flopped along the water like a wounded duck for a while and then stopped'.[4]

The stricken ship ran two black discs up its foremast. It was slowly sinking. The order was given to abandon ship and the destroyer *Defender* came alongside, rising and falling on a six-metre swell. A hawser between the ships sprung taut, vibrating. Flecks showered from the warship's gunwales as it scraped against the liner's side. All personnel were ordered to muster on deck. Vic Solomon, one of the euchre players, was told to stand by his gun while lifeboats were lowered, 'so I just sat on the rail and had a smoke and waited'.[5] Men lined up in rows and, when the top deck was full, they lined up in darkness below.

'I was down in a passageway and all the lights went out, and there was this big Maori sergeant saying "Don't panic", and so we just went about our normal business,' says Keith Hooper, an Australian infantry sergeant. 'We came on a couple of New Zealanders who had a loaf of bread which they decided to eat, so we joined them.'[6]

Reg Saunders, the Aboriginal sergeant, was also below in the dark. 'For days we had been herded around like sheep, and we reacted, without any question, to orders,' he says. 'When the lights went out, the platoon and section commanders told us to keep still, and that was that. We swapped a few stories, and somebody was talking about football.' When *Defender* was secured alongside, the men were told to leave all arms and personal gear and move on deck in their lines. One turned around, took off his hat with an elaborate sweep, and said to Saunders, 'After you, old chap.'[7]

Some were put on lifeboats, most swung down the side of *Costa Rica* on ropes and jumped onto the rising deck of the destroyer. Movement below was a slow shuffle without panic, each man eventually emerging in the afternoon light. 'Up on deck, we blinked a bit in the harsh sunlight, and looked up at the snow on the mountains of Crete. They reared up out of the sea, quite dramatically,' Saunders recalls.[8]

Defender was filled and replaced by *Hereward*, then *Hero*. All on the sinking troopship were transferred to the three destroyers, although one soldier misjudged the jump and fell into the sea. A lieutenant jumped in, calling for a line, and the two were hauled out before the two hulls came together again.[9]

Eventually the liner had sunk so low the last men could step across to the destroyer. The anti-aircraft gunners were the last to leave, apart from Theo Walker, commander of the main Australian contingent on the ship. He went around to see if everyone was off before he left. Fifteen minutes later, the ship's boiler blew and *Costa Rica* sunk quickly.

All arms and personal gear had been lost but 2600 men had been trans-shipped with no sign of panic in forty-five minutes. The troops disembarked at Suda Bay in the late afternoon. Ray Lawrence, a machine gunner, crossed from *Hereward* to another ship tied up at the wharf to finally get on shore. An air raid siren wailed as he did so and he galloped across the ship, diving for shelter among some crates. When the 'All Clear' sounded, he found the crates were marked, 'Handle with care—HIGH EXPLOSIVE'.[10]

Welcome to Suda Bay!

———

Each day in the last week of April, warships packed with evacuees sailed into Suda Bay. Already cluttered with the masts and funnels of sunken vessels poking above the surface, the harbour filled with ships, small craft darting about and landing barges unloading soldiers. The abandoned cruiser *York* sat half-submerged near the shore after an Italian torpedo attack a month earlier.

Troops were landed at Suda, a small town clustered around a quay with a stone jetty poking into the bay. One of the first arrivals was

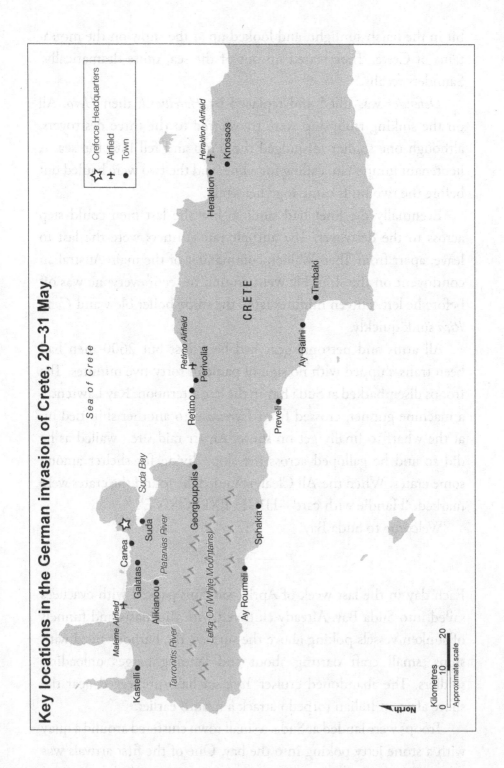

Key locations in the German invasion of Crete, 20–31 May

Legend:
☆ Creforce Headquarters
✝ Airfield
● Town

Labels on map:
Kastelli
Maleme Airfield ✝
Galatas ●
Canea ●
Suda ●
Suda Bay
Alikianou ●
Platanias River
Georgioupolis ●
Tavronitis River
Lefka Ori (White Mountains)
Ay Roumeli ●
Sphakia ●
Preveli ●
Retimo ● / Retimo Airfield ✝
Perivolia ●
Ay Galini ●
Timbaki ●
CRETE
Heraklion ●
Herakion Airfield ✝
Knossos ●
Sea of Crete
☆ (Creforce Headquarters near Canea)

Scale:
Kilometres
0   10   20
Approximate scale

North

the freighter *Elsie* from Athens. Civilians were ferried ashore while soldiers and German prisoners were kept on board overnight, the Germans sweeping and dusting their quarters during the evening. Next morning, the prisoners disembarked, followed by Jack Ryan's Australian radio intercept team with its fox terrier mascot.

The first of the combat troops arrived soon after from Porto Rafti and Megara, climbing down scrambling nets and rope ladders to landing barges. Launches circled around warships disembarking troops, British staff officers yelling out that all arms except rifles and side-arms were to be stacked on the pier. Jimmy Hargest, a New Zealand brigade commander, yelled back at one, 'We'll do no such thing. My men will keep their arms and march off with them.'[11]

Not all did. British provosts on the quay continued to order men to dump their heavy weapons as the evacuees milled around, looking for mates and trying to work out where they were supposed to go. The pile of weapons grew steadily by the dock wall.

The quayside was more chaotic and confused when destroyers landed the men rescued from *Costa Rica*, none of whom had weapons of any sort or much in the way of personal possessions. Don Stephenson from Melbourne was one, arriving with only a pouch of tobacco and a tin of sausages. On Suda jetty, he ran into his brother who he hadn't seen for months. They sat down and 'had a sausage and a smoke'.[12]

At the end of the pier, an officer shouted out, 'New Zealanders to the right, Australians to the left.' The British garrison already in Crete had set up a reception centre with trestle tables in an olive grove. Tea, chocolate and biscuits were served to the arrivals while unit leaders listened to orders barked out, giving bivouac locations for each unit.

Units marched 5 or 10 kilometres, sometimes more, in different directions to destinations vaguely described to junior officers who had no maps and no knowledge of Crete. An Australian staff officer drove around in a Ford utility giving direction assistance from a 1908 map.[13] One battalion was told their camp was 'two miles inland' but after marching for two hours they hadn't found it and were told it was 'another two miles around the next bend'. They didn't find it there either.[14]

For a week, groups were constantly marching along dusty roads with directions they didn't understand to camps that often didn't yet exist. Those that couldn't find their assigned camp location settled, when they'd had enough marching, for somewhere that looked comfortable, preferably in an olive grove with a thick carpet of turf somewhere near a stream. It didn't matter where. Unattached troops wandered around aimlessly until they found some soft ground to sleep on.

After the ordeal of constant withdrawal and evacuation on the Greek mainland, a combination of resignation and relief set in. Having escaped from the sinking *Costa Rica*, Australian Jim Carstairs was making his way to the reception area with other survivors. 'As we did, an air raid started,' he says. 'It was not very close. We were heartily sick of air raids. No one took the slightest notice of it.'[15]

Part of the evacuation had been landed on Crete to allow the fast turnaround of warships, and an order had been placed with Middle East Command in Cairo for tents, clothing and blankets for 30,000 men. Less than half the blankets needed were there when the men landed.

Despite the chilly nights most slept well, fully dressed or sharing blankets. Improvisation was the name of the game. One group built a roofless, stone 'igloo' with bracken and grass flooring, and one greatcoat over four clothed men. Washing in streams when they woke, the soldiers cooked breakfast in cut-down petrol tins, using food cans as plates and eating with utensils fashioned from wood and pieces of wire. Two gunners from Harry Spencer's unit were at a stream when he got there. One said, 'G'day. You got a tooth-brush?' The Blenheim engine-driver had one and all three cleaned their teeth with it.[16] After a week, clothes, towels, cigarettes and soap started arriving at the camps. A truck drove around, 'Annie Lorry' painted on its side, dumping tins of bully beef, biscuits and plum jam, and bags of tea and sugar.

Crete became a huge field hospital, rest centre and transit camp. All the soldiers expected that they would soon be shipped to Egypt. A trickle had already departed. Jack Ryan believed his radio intercept section would be gone in a few days. Some war correspondents who had been on *Elsie* with them had got on a ship to Alexandria on short notice, letting the radiomen have several chickens they were cooking on an improvised spit.[17]

The soldiers settled into a rhythm of sorts while they waited. Days were spent swimming and sunbathing. With a few packs of cards about, euchre, five hundred and bridge filled the men's time. They foraged for food in vineyards, cornfields and vegetable patches, and fished in pools using Mills bombs. Villagers supplied chickens, eggs and oranges, and meals of bread and cheese, sometimes refusing payment. Local women washed and mended the soldiers' clothes, the men spending the day in their underpants while their clothes were laundered.

One New Zealander wrote home that 'all we do is eat oranges and swim. Having a marvellous time. God! I am as fit as a fiddle—a real box of birds.'[18] It was a paradise, but an illusory one. The preparation of Crete for the inevitable invasion had been one of fumbling inaction.

These soldiers had been dumped unceremoniously on a rough-hewn, elongated island, about 260 kilometres long. Rocky outcrops rose to rugged peaks on high, snowy ranges running along Crete's southern coast, the mountainsides scarred by ravines. Watercourses ran over coastal slopes covered with scrub, olive trees, and vineyards terraced with stone banks and walls. Twisting roads, lined with poplars, ran between villages with white-washed houses clustered around a square and an Orthodox church. Along the coastal strip on the north side were fields of rye, barley and oranges, as well as the larger towns, including the capital, Canea, and the most populous, Heraklion.

Greece had allowed Britain to build a naval fuelling station at Suda Bay, upgrade the airfield at Heraklion and build another airfield at Maleme. The Greek army's elite division of 18,000 Cretan soldiers was transferred to the front in Albania with Britain agreeing to take over defence of the island. A few infantry battalions and an anti-aircraft battery arrived from England in November 1940 to form a small garrison, all General Wavell deemed necessary. Instead of the major naval base ordered by Churchill, Wavell merely strengthened the port area. John Pendlebury, an archaeologist long working in Crete, was put in charge of creating a force to replace the division sent to Albania. An eccentric romantic with no military experience whatsoever, Pendlebury had been educated at the prestigious Winchester College, which was apparently considered sufficient to qualify him for the task.[19]

Defence chiefs in London regarded air defence as vital to Crete. If the Germans overran Greece, an air invasion of Crete was thought inevitable. However, by the end of March 1941 there were no permanent fighters on Crete, all available aircraft having been sent to the mainland. When Group Captain George Beamish took command of the RAF in Crete in mid-April, the only aircraft there were antiquated Fleet Air Arm planes to defend the port on Suda Bay.[20]

The army garrison in Crete had six different commanders over six months, starting with Brigadier Ord Tidbury in November 1940. None had the time or the resources to prepare for German invasion. Local supplies were inadequate and there was a shortage of transport, labour and storage. Requests for tools or equipment were regarded by Cairo as a nuisance. No arms arrived, the reserve Cretan division wasn't formed and lethargic British troops enjoyed island life. The commanders were there to administer the small garrison and guard Suda Bay; there was no suggestion from high command they might have to repel an invasion. After six wasted months, the garrison would not have been able to withstand any large-scale attack.

As the Wehrmacht advanced through Greece, there were belated moves to rectify the neglect of Crete. Greece sent 1000 recruits to its police academy on the island and nearly 5000 troops straight from training in the Peloponnese. Only half of them had weapons. In January, the chiefs of staff in London had ordered a Royal Marines unit to Crete to upgrade Suda Bay to a naval base. Called a Mobile Naval Base Defence Organisation (MNBDO), the unit was designed to be deployed quickly as needed, but the deployment of this unit was anything but speedy. Its commander, General Weston, was sent ahead . . . arriving nearly three months later.

Eric Weston produced a plausible outline of an invasion—a German parachute attack supported by a sea landing—and detailed steps needed to be taken to resist it.[21] It was the first comprehensive blueprint for defence of the island, but marines to put it into action would not start arriving until May. For a month, it was not clear if Weston or Brigadier Chappel, the garrison commander, was in charge on Crete. Weston wasn't officially put in command until 26 April, as the first evacuees were arriving. The new arrivals were disorganised and uncertain, and found themselves in a military structure that was no better organised.

Among the evacuating troops in Crete was their commander-in-chief from Greece—General Wilson. Wavell's instruction to Wilson was that Crete was expected to be attacked and was to be denied to the enemy. Troops already there were to defend it until they could be replaced with fresh troops from Egypt. Wilson conferred with Weston about the size and make-up of the force needed. A German seaborne attack couldn't be easily repelled due to the air cover it would bring with it. A combined sea and air invasion seemed very possible and very likely to succeed.

Jumbo Wilson told Archie Wavell, 'I consider that unless all three services are prepared to face the strain of maintaining adequate forces up to strength, the holding of the island is a dangerous commitment.'[22] It was astute advice but not what London wanted to hear.

Bernard Freyberg disembarked at Suda Bay on the morning of 30 April but he had no intention of staying. He would ensure that his two brigades then on Crete joined the third brigade already on its way to Alexandria, then fly to Egypt to meet his wife coming from London. He planned to reintegrate and re-equip the New Zealand Division in Egypt but, as it turned out, only his headquarters staff went on. The two brigades and their commanders remained on the island, as did Freyberg. Wavell neither sent spare staff officers from Cairo nor ordered the return of New Zealand divisional staff.

Defence chiefs in London had questioned whether General Weston, as a garrison commander, was right for the coming battle for Crete. Winston Churchill, concerned that it needed a fighting general, pressed his Chief of Imperial General Staff, General Dill, to appoint Freyberg. Dill dutifully passed on the 'suggestion' to Wavell. 'Would suggest Freyberg to succeed Weston in Crete,' he cabled. 'It only need be temporary command and Freyberg could collect later his scattered flock.'[23]

On the morning he arrived in Crete, Freyberg was called to a meeting at Wilson's headquarters in a large seaside villa near Canea. He came with his chief of staff to find an assortment of people waiting with Wilson on the villa's tiled balcony. General Weston was there, along with the British ambassador to Greece, General Heywood of the British Military Mission, George Beamish of the RAF and Wilson's chief of staff. A staff car brought a tired and drawn Archie Wavell from Maleme airfield, having just flown in from Cairo. This was clearly more than a friendly chat.

While the rest made small talk and Freyberg tried to work out what the meeting was about, Wavell and Wilson had a private conversation to one side. 'I want you to go to Jerusalem and relieve Baghdad,' Wavell said. In Iraq, a coup d'état had installed a new government which was agitating against the British presence there. Wilson had little idea of what was happening outside Greece but his pessimistic assessment in Crete had disqualified him from command there.[24] That may well have been his intention; he had no wish to repeat the experience of Greece.

Wavell next took Freyberg by the arm and told him how well he thought the New Zealanders had done in Greece, particularly in their handling of the withdrawals. In truth, New Zealand's role had been the smaller of the two Anzac partners, but Freyberg was just being softened up before the main strike. Wavell's tone turned formal. 'I want you to take charge of the combined Allied force in Crete,' he said. The Kiwi general was to be commander-in-chief of Creforce, the name given to the new patched-up force.

Freyberg was taken by surprise. He'd assumed Wilson was in Crete to continue his role from Greece. 'I don't see how I can,' the New Zealander murmured. 'I need to get back to Egypt to train and re-equip the division. My government won't agree to the division being split.'

'It is your duty to remain and take on the task,' Wavell insisted solemnly.[25] He offered Freyberg a promotion to lieutenant-general but the New Zealand commander elected to remain a major-general. 'I did not require any inducement to do my duty,' he would later explain.[26]

London-born, Freyberg was two when his family moved to New Zealand. In the First World War, he gained a reputation for reckless bravery, swimming ashore at Gallipoli to light false beacons, and earning a Victoria Cross at the Western Front. Between wars, Freyberg joined the Grenadier Guards and delighted England's artistic and intellectual elite as an uncomplicated man of action.

He became friendly with Churchill, appealing to the politician's infatuation with soldiering. These days we'd call it a 'bromance'. At a country-house weekend, Churchill asked Freyberg to take off his shirt and counted twenty-seven wounds. 'You nearly always get two wounds for every bullet or splinter,' said the man of action, 'because mostly they have to go out as well as in.'[27]

At the outbreak of a new war, Churchill encouraged the New Zealand government to have Freyberg command its expeditionary force. As a professional soldier well regarded by the British military establishment, he was an obvious choice even if he hadn't lived in Wellington since 1913. He was duly appointed. The public reason for Freyberg's commission in Crete was Churchill's admiration for his First World War exploits, but more likely it was to placate the New Zealand and Australian governments over growing concerns about the Greek campaign.

When Wavell finished his discussion with Freyberg, the formal meeting began on the villa balcony. There was only one item on the agenda, the defence of Crete, and not a great deal to discuss at that stage. Wavell advised that an attack was envisaged by five or six thousand airborne troops along with a seaborne attack, the primary objectives thought to be the aerodromes at Heraklion and Maleme. Crete was to be denied to the enemy as an air and submarine base.

Later, Wavell took Freyberg for a private walk in the garden. He told the New Zealander he would receive Ultra reports, intelligence summaries drawn mostly from decrypted German radio signals. The British had begun to penetrate the enemy's Enigma code. Freyberg was not to mention the existence of Ultra to anyone on Crete and never to take action solely on Ultra intelligence. That might alert the enemy that its messages were being read.[28]

Bernard Freyberg moved that afternoon to Creforce head-quarters in an old stone quarry in the hills above Canea. Stone huts were scattered around the quarry floor and staff were quartered in dugouts set into its wall. The location had a panoramic view of the old walled city of Canea and its stone breakwater around a small picturesque harbour full of colourful caïques.

When he got to his new headquarters, Freyberg found Eric Weston had already moved out and taken most of the staff with him. Weston had a reputation for moodiness, so many saw this as an act of sulking, but Weston had staffed his headquarters from his Royal Marines and simply took them back with him. Whatever the reason, Freyberg had only two of his own divisional staff with him on Crete and had to recruit Creforce staff from British, Australian and New Zealand officers already on the island.

There were 42,000 Anzac and British soldiers there, but a third of them were gunners without guns, drivers without vehicles, signallers and engineers without equipment. Of the 17,000 British troops, only 6400 were combatants. The rest were from specialist units, mostly no longer functional. In addition, there were 10,000 poorly armed Greek soldiers, non-Cretan conscripts, and the Cretan gendarmerie. Freyberg had few staff officers, unreliable communications and a shortage of heavy weapons. Many of the units landed on Crete had disintegrated, leaving weary and demoralised soldiers without officers, arms or equipment. The new force commander's task was to fashion this mixed bag into a fighting force capable of holding a well-trained German army at bay.

Identifying the most likely targets for air and sea invasion required neither spies nor Enigma. It had been obvious to the first of the garrison commanders—the aerodromes and the two ports— and nobody since had thought differently, including the Germans. Freyberg planned his defences, putting the New Zealanders, now under Brigadier Puttick, in charge of defending Maleme airfield, still in the late stages of construction. Puttick had been promoted temporarily to general. The Australians under Brigadier Vasey would be responsible for Retimo's small airstrip. Some of the English and an Australian battalion were placed under Brigadier Chappel to cover Heraklion's airfield and port. General Weston was to look after Canea and Suda Bay: the former with the Black Watch, a renowned Scottish regiment already in Crete as part of the British garrison, and the Royal Marines when they arrived; the latter with a collection of composite units and unarmed artillery under Colonel Cremor, the Australian artillery commander.

Grumpily dubbed 'His Majesty's Unarmed Forces in Crete' by its commander, Bill Cremor's force was made up of two composite battalions and 2280 Australian gunners without artillery. The composite formations were patched from specialist units without specialist equipment. Armed as infantry with rushed infantry training, they included the residue of infantry units broken up in battle or by the randomness of evacuation.[29] Reg Burgoyne, an Australian who had fought at the Vale of Tempe, was now part of a composite battalion. 'We were only a depleted battalion,' he says, 'made up of odds and sods. Cooks, clerks, you name it and they were all there. Some could shoot, some couldn't. All we had was out-of-date equipment.'[30]

Within a day, Freyberg was in a position to give Wavell his assessment of the strength of Creforce. The land force, he said, was 'totally inadequate' to meet the anticipated attack, with artillery and transport left in Greece and equipment and ammunition low. It had no hope of holding out the enemy by itself. Fighter aircraft and naval forces were needed to deal with the seaborne attack. If they were not available, the decision to hold Crete should be reviewed.[31]

It was much the same as Wilson's assessment, but Wavell had no back-up plan. Already, Churchill had commented enthusiastically on the imminent airborne attack on Crete. 'It ought to be a fine opportunity for killing parachute troops,' the great orator said. 'The island must be stubbornly defended.'[32] Wavell believed the Germans weren't greatly interested in taking Crete but were using it as cover for an attack on Syria or Cyprus. No one shared his view.

Wavell replied to Freyberg the next day that he thought the War Office's intelligence on the attack's scale was exaggerated. Admiral

Anzac troops gathering at Alexandria's docks to embark for Greece.

Australian troops taken to Greece on *Pennland*, in convoy with *Cameronia*.

TOP: Athens crowds welcome New Zealand troops (viewed from the top of a troop truck).

MIDDLE: Australian Bren carrier arrives at Daphni, near Athens.

BOTTOM: Australian soldiers on leave from Daphni camp join Greek soldiers on leave from Albania at an Athens cafe.

On the outskirts of Athens, New Zealand soldiers watch Italian prisoners from the Albanian front.

Train taking troops north to Katerini in central Greece, in carriages that doubled as horse floats.

Road gang of Greek women in central Greece.

Cargo of TNT explodes in the freighter, *Clan Fraser*, after the Luftwaffe bombed Piraeus, 6 April 1941.

Traffic congestion in a Macedonian village, northern Greece, from British and Greek military and civilian refugees moving in different directions.

Australians above the snowline on the Aliakmon Line.

Australian artillery unit on a mountain road near Ptolemais, northern Greece.

Villagers leave their homes and head
south or into the hills with their
belongings, ahead of the advancing
German invasion force.

Children in the village of Germania, Blamey's 'collection of wretched hovels'.

Greek soldiers moving to a new defensive line.

Australian driver giving biscuits to village women.

Australian infantrymen carried by ferry across the Aliakmon River.

New Zealand soldiers climb the track running up from the Aliakmon River.

TOP: German panzer tank crossing the Pinios River.

MIDDLE: British convoy withdrawing south through central Greece.

BOTTOM: General Tsolakoglou (wearing spectacles) surrenders to the German army at Ioannina, 20 April 1941.

Infantry withdrawing from forward areas during the retreat in Greece.

Australian nurses sheltering in a cemetery from a German air attack on the Peloponnese.

New Zealand gunners camouflaging their positions on the Thermopylae Line.

Troops evacuated from the Greek mainland disembarking at Suda Bay, Crete.

Australians boiling a billy as they settle into preparations for the defence of Crete.

Ships in Suda Bay burning after an air attack.

Two-up school near
the town of Suda.

General Freyberg
(right) confers with
Brigadier Hargest
(centre) and Colonel
Andrew (left).

Paratroops dropping near Suda Bay, 20 May 1941.

German mountain troops boarding a Junkers Ju-52 troop carrier to land at Maleme in Crete.

German mountain troops landing under fire at Maleme airfield.

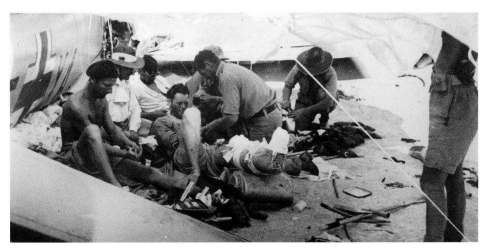

An Australian Regimental Aid Post set up alongside a crashed German plane.

Kiwi soldier at a water well.

Cretan partisans.

New Zealanders awaiting evacuation at Sphakia.

Temporary Creforce HQ in a cave overlooking Sphakia, General Freyberg in centre, Captain Morse on the right, Private Hall (Freyberg's batman) on the left.

Awarded the Victoria Cross in the Greek campaign: Clive Hulme, Charlie Upham and Jack Hinton.

Evacuated from Sphakia, soldiers relax on a destroyer taking them to Egypt.

A wounded soldier (Arthur Midwood of the Maori battalion) disembarks at Alexandria.

Allied prisoners of war being marched back to Canea from Sphakia.

Left behind at Sphakia: Reg Saunders (left); Charlie Jager and Ben Travers (right).

Execution of Cretan civilians by German paratroops, 2 July 1941.

Cunningham would provide naval support, Wavell said, artillery
and other equipment was on the way, and fighter reinforcement was
expected from Britain,[33] a radically different story from what he had
told Wilson a week before. Assurances now with fingers crossed.
In any case, Wavell added, he was unable to evacuate the troops
from Crete as he didn't have the necessary ships. He had the 'naval
support' but not the ships! It was all on a wing and a prayer.

———————

While their commander-in-chief dealt with political and military
leaders demanding a lot and offering only woolly promises in
return, his men were torn between the adventure of a bush camp
and the dawning realisation that they were jetsam left to fight the
campaign's next and last battle. Through the first week of May,
units dispersed along 120 kilometres of northern coastland between
Heraklion and Maleme, preparing defences they hoped might repel
the air and sea invasions when they came. They brought with them
from Greece the bitter taste not only of defeat but also retreat, the
feeling by many that they hadn't had a chance to 'have a go' at the
enemy. A brittle mentality festered in the random force that had
accumulated on Crete.

Weary, sullen and hungry, unattached troops roamed the
countryside armed with rifles, looking for food and making no
attempt to join their units. They camped in the hills and olive
groves and made a nuisance of themselves in the villages. Provosts
tried to round up these stragglers but a shortage of transport made
collecting them difficult.

Soldiers on the loose were wandering around Canea unkempt,
tipsy and singing sentimental or bawdy songs. Most of the townspeople regarded it as high spirits, but civilian authorities were
reporting to brigade headquarters instances of damage to property
and personal injury. The problem was particularly noticeable around
Suda where the unattached were being grouped as composite units or

were still at large. They were Australian, New Zealand and probably British as well, although the Australians managed to attract more attention to themselves. New Zealanders around Maleme didn't get the same reputation, perhaps because they arrived and remained in formed units.

After a few days of poor discipline, a 6 pm curfew was declared in the Suda–Canea area with men not in formed units or under camp control to be treated as deserters. George Vasey conducted field court martials and had two barbed wire enclosures erected for those convicted.[34] Transferred to a Field Punishment Centre near Maleme, they worked on roads, delivered ammunition and, when the German invasion began, would be attached to a nearby battalion. Similarly, when fights broke out involving Australians in cafes in Retimo, Ian Campbell, the commander there, declared the town and surrounding villages out of bounds and had them patrolled by provosts.

Freyberg complained to Wavell, 'There are some ten thousand here without arms and with little or no employment other than getting into trouble with the civilian population.' He wanted them evacuated as soon as possible, along with 14,000 Italians captured in Albania.[35] Both were draining an already depleted food supply. Cairo's slow response, using ships returning empty after landing supplies, managed to evacuate 7000 of the troublesome troops, along with the nurses brought from the mainland, but none of the Italian PoWs.

The Italians had not been unhappy to be taken from a severe winter in Albania's mountains. Nine-year-old Yianni Spyrakis watched a PoW work party shuffle through his village. He still remembers the distant sound of musical instruments growing louder as the column passed. As the tail moved past, he saw one Italian strumming a mandolin and another playing a harmonica.[36]

There was another group the commander would happily have seen off the island. When he was appointed, Freyberg wasn't told the Greek king, prime minister and cabinet and their families were in Crete. He soon persuaded the king that the families should move to Egypt and they left for Cairo with Jumbo Wilson. A week later, Freyberg persuaded the king that he and his government should also go, but the British cabinet overruled that, deciding it created a bad impression internationally for the king and his government to leave the last unoccupied Greek territory.[37]

They stayed but neither was popular with Cretans despite the appointment of a Cretan banker, Emmanouil Tsouderos, as the new prime minister and a Cretan, General Skoulas, as military commander. The Crete Division's commander, General Papastergiou, a mainlander, had returned to Crete with none of his soldiers and was assassinated on a Canea street.[38]

The Allied forces were badly unprepared. Although blankets and shirts were starting to arrive, the picks and shovels, promised for trench-digging, were slow to appear. A shipment of tools had gone to the bottom of Suda Bay. Until some arrived, bayonets and steel helmets were used to dig trenches and weapon pits.

There was widespread unhappiness with the British store staff who had been brought across from Cairo. Despite the imminent invasion, they worked the same hours as they had in Egypt, including a siesta between 1 pm and 5.30 in the afternoon.[39] An old Turkish fort had been converted to a canteen but it was for British troops only. At a depot in an old Venetian storehouse in Canea, John Bellair was told he needed a requisition in triplicate for the items he requested. Bellair asked to see the officer in charge and was told he wasn't available until three o'clock, but the Australian machine gunner could have his items if he paid cash over the counter.[40] It might have been partly a supply problem, orders not filled correctly in Cairo or provisions shipped from Egypt not getting past the Luftwaffe. Of the 27,000 tonnes of munitions that left Egypt over three weeks in May, less than 3000 tonnes landed in Crete.

Many of the young Anzacs were raised in rural areas and had learnt to make do with whatever they had at hand. Kiwi infantry made grenades out of jam tins filled with bits of concrete and gelignite.[41] Having lost all his gear on the *Costa Rica*, Phillip Hurst was issued with a new Tommy gun without webbing. He tied two socks together to carry the ammunition around his neck.[42] Murray McColl had a Vickers machine gun without a tripod. He tied it to the fork of a tree.[43]

The men became skilled scavengers. Those positioned near the airfields cannibalised wrecked planes for Browning machine guns. Jack Ryan and Bill Hill searched the wireless rooms of ships wrecked in Suda Bay and found intact wireless and direction-finder equipment for the Australian radio intercept unit. The truck they'd had in Greece hadn't been evacuated.[44]

To an urgent Freyberg request for guns and ammunition, Middle East Command sent one hundred field guns. Mostly French and Italian, and some without sights, they were unwanted in North Africa where even reserve units already had new 25-pounders. Home-made sights were made from bits of wood and chewing gum, but calibration of the guns over the next few days revealed a worrying number of duds and misfires. Only forty-nine of the shipped guns were usable and not much ammunition came with them.[45]

The French guns had been captured by Italians in North Africa and, along with Italian guns, subsequently captured by the British. The Italian guns had only half the range of the 25-pounders that had been left in Greece. Artillery commander Bill Cremor tossed a coin to see which of his units would get this mixed bag of guns, saying, 'It's a good toss to lose.'[46] Issued with guns supposedly captured at Tobruk, Michael Clarke, leading a gun crew, doubted even that. 'Personally, I rated them as Great War relics,' he comments, 'or maybe some Greek uprising against the Turks last century. One box of shells read "Use by November 1916".'[47]

Provisions were also in erratic supply, with little variation. At first, meals were army food eaten with the makeshift utensils. 'It was amusing to see everyone from the colonel down eating their meals out of an empty milk tin with the aid of a couple of biscuits,' notes Ken Atock, an Australian private.[48] After a few days, the men were getting pay and were able to supplement the army rations of bully beef, 'M and V' (meat stew and vegetables) and hard biscuits. In the villages they bought omelettes at local cafes, and chickens, eggs and honey to take back to the camps. Fruit was cheap and plentiful, the oranges big and sweet.

It was an opportunity for the more adventurous to try new foods: cheese made from sheep and goats' milk, and crusty stone-ground bread. Frank Atkins, a farmhand from Western Australia, had tried snails in Retimo and found them to his liking. He'd seen the hills at night alight with the lanterns of women collecting them. Atkins came across a place swarming with large brown snails and boiled some up in his tin helmet, but this produced a filthy green scum on the surface and the snails tasted dreadful. He learnt later that the villagers fed them first on bran to clean them out.[49]

Cretans had a reputation as being suspicious of strangers and wary of authority, slower to accept outsiders than other Greeks. Despite this, a strong rapport built between the soldiers and Cretan civilians. The Cretans noticed the young Anzacs avoided the class consciousness and snobbery of the English. These men didn't stand on ceremony and helped out when needed. On one occasion, a queue had formed outside a village bakery so a soldier gave the baker a hand. Soon he was putting another batch in the oven and the smell of hot bread drifted out. The queued villagers were served, then each soldier in the group got a loaf of fresh wholemeal bread.[50]

In Crete, a strict delineation between the roles of men and women rubbed against Australian and New Zealand manners of the 1940s, despite similarities in social behaviour. Passing through a village, one of a group of Western Australians took over from a young woman pumping water from a well. The males sitting around were getting agitated, until it was sorted out with the foreigners noting that, in Greece, it was a woman's job to get water from the well.[51]

With a strict moral code in Crete linking a woman's chastity to her family's honour, soldiers' closer contact with Cretan women was mostly limited to Canea's thirty-seven brothels. George Brown, a Kiwi lieutenant, went into Canea with some of his platoon. When they were about to go back, one of the men said, 'Sir, do you mind going back on your own?' Brown asked why and was told, 'Well, the battle will be starting before very long and we want to go to the brothel. We'd hate to be killed without having been to the brothel.'[52] Adolescent fantasy tainted with dread.

What the two cultures had in common was the capacity for making the most of difficult times and for high-spirited enjoyment, the larrikinism of Aussie soldiers and its slightly more reserved form in the Kiwis. The Australians found that, like themselves, many Cretans were mad gamblers. 'Chook' Fowler and Lionel Baker, from a bayside composite unit, ran a nightly two-up school with locals who would bet up to 5000 drachmas (about 25 Australian dollars) on a spin. It was very devil-may-care; Aussies running out of cash would borrow from the Cretans and vice versa.[53]

A nearby tavern had a radio set where the troops could listen to BBC music but, as that was often jazz, they'd switch to German radio for 'real music'. They did, however, enjoy the BBC's occasional sessions of evergreens like 'There's a Tavern in the Town' and 'Roll Out the Barrel' where they would all sing along.[54]

The BBC also provided a news service, but it often didn't ring true and the men found 'Lord Haw Haw' on German radio more entertaining. Lord Haw Haw was William Joyce, an English fascist, born in America and raised in Ireland, who broadcast Nazi propaganda in order to undermine British morale. He referred to Crete as the 'island of doomed men', creating an Anzac determination to prove him wrong. The broadcast would finish with 'Run, Rabbit, Run', an English song used originally to poke fun at the Luftwaffe. The Cretans thought the soldiers' enthusiasm for a broadcast designed to undermine their morale was perverse.[55]

Lord Haw Haw's broadcasts served as an inspiration to an Australian infantryman who had been a Perth journalist before the war. Put on cookhouse fatigues for an unauthorised visit to Retimo, Laurie 'Bouff' Ryan whiled away his punishment time rekindling the frustration, still in vivid memory, of a Greek campaign under constant, unchallenged air attack.[56] The result was 'The Isle of Doom':

> 'Twas just a month ago, not more,
> We sailed to Greece to win the war;
> We marched and groaned beneath our load
> While bombers bombed us off the road.
> They chased us here, they chased us there,
> The blighters chased us everywhere
> And while they dropped their loads of death
> We cursed the bloody RAF.
> Yet the RAF were there in force,
> (They left a few at home of course).
> We saw the entire squad one day
> When a Spitfire spat the other way
> And when we heard the wireless news
> When portly Winston gave his views
> 'The RAF,' he said, 'in Greece
> Is fighting hard to bring us peace'
> And so we scratched our heads and thought
> This smells distinctly like a rort
> For if in Greece the Airforce be
> Then where the flaming hell are we?[57]

Meanwhile back in Greece young German paratroops waited impatiently, many of them teenagers recruited from Hitler Youth and eager for the adventure of battle. It was thought they would go unnoticed, dressed in standard Luftwaffe uniform without their parachute emblem and camped by the sea in captured British tents, but their presence had already been revealed by the paratroop attack on Corinth Canal. Swimming, sunbathing naked and swaggering around their base wearing only tiny shorts, they were noticed anyway. Laird Archer, an American medical worker, noted in his diary, 'They take their improvised showers unsheltered and completely unclothed, regardless of the daughters of the families whose gardens they occupy.'[58]

A parachute invasion of Crete was the brainchild of General Kurt Student. As a young man he had volunteered for flying training at cadet school and became obsessed in the war that followed with warfare from the skies. When Germany re-armed between the wars, he was given oversight of a parachute school where his new enthusiasm grew. Quietly passionate, attracted to the unconventional, and meticulous with detail, he inspired fierce loyalty from his troops, but was less popular with German high command, who didn't share his unshakeable belief in parachute operations. One fellow general commented that 'Student had big ideas but not the faintest idea how to carry them out.'[59]

He found a believer, however, after a successful raid in Holland: his commander-in-chief, Hermann Goering. That was May 1940. Student had waited since then to demonstrate his paratroop division's value on a larger scale and, as the campaign in Greece moved towards completion, his opportunity came. Student proposed an airborne landing on Crete. He and Goering met with Hitler, who was persuaded that a base in Crete would protect Romanian oilfields.[60] Student left the meeting jubilant, unaware the operation would be a cover for the secret preparation for the invasion of Russia, Operation Barbarossa. Wavell had been right about Germany's intention with Crete, but not the detail.

Directive Number 28, issued by Hitler on 25 April, was for 'an operation to occupy the island of Crete as an air base against Britain in the Eastern Mediterranean'.[61] The Führer wanted the attack to take place as quickly as possible under Goering's overall command, with a simultaneous landing from the sea so the operation 'would not be standing on one leg'.[62] The army was to provide reinforcements and an armoured detachment by sea in conjunction with the Italian navy. Goering, aware of Operation Barbarossa, was instructed that the movement of parachute troops should not interfere with it.

Student had over 450 superseded Junkers-52 bombers for the Crete operation, to be used as paratroop carriers, with some rigged to tow gliders. He proposed simultaneous attacks on four objectives: Canea and the three airfields. General Alexander Löhr, who Goering had appointed field commander over Student, preferred a massive assault on Maleme for a bridgehead, followed by the capture of Canea and Suda Bay to land seaborne troops and equipment. The Luftwaffe didn't have enough aircraft to protect troop-carriers in four different places, so Goering's staff came up with a hybrid plan. The attack would be on Maleme and Canea in the morning, then the planes would return in the afternoon to Retimo and Heraklion.[63]

While the British were making inroads into the Luftwaffe's Enigma-encrypted radio messages, those of the German army and navy were still unable to be read. The Ultra reports Wavell had mentioned to Freyberg were summaries drawn from information in Luftwaffe decrypts and speculation by the intelligence officers who wrote them. They were of limited value. The writers, mostly recruited from English universities, had little military experience and the recipients of Ultra in the field didn't know what in the reports was hard intelligence and what was inexpert speculation.[64] As the war progressed, Ultra became a valuable intelligence tool for the Allies but in May 1941 it was very much in its teething stage.

Needing the Australian intercept unit to be nearby, Creforce HQ set it up in empty holiday villas overlooking Canea and its harbour. The villas' gardens, wells and almond grove were a tempting target as air raids increased and the unit prudently moved its wireless sets into a disused concrete tank, roofed it over with timber and camouflaged its aerials.[65] Jack Ryan continued to insist that 'Mr Sandford', the intelligence officer, would arrive any day and on 8 May he did, coming from Alexandria by destroyer.

A lanky extrovert, 25-year-old 'Mic' Sandford was from the Adelaide establishment, the son of a wealthy engineer and conservative parliamentarian. He'd studied law and languages at Oxford and had come straight from a course at a Bletchley Park offshoot near Cairo, bringing with him the German air-ground codes then in operation. A cosmopolitan raconteur, Sandford's fancy ways, nurtured in Oxford and English intelligence circles, were a revelation to the young Australians that made up most of the unit, but he earned their respect with his cryptographic skills and single-minded approach to their use.

General Freyberg was supplied with a steady stream of operational intelligence from lower-grade ciphers, intercepted and decrypted by the Australian unit, and Ultra reports sent from Cairo. High-level German signals in Enigma code were intercepted by the unit and in Cairo, sent to London to be decrypted and interpreted, then sent back as Ultra reports to Cairo. Some, but not all, were sent on to Creforce's commander-in-chief through Lieutenant Sandford.[66]

On 27 April, the Joint Intelligence Committee (JIC) in London had confirmed the anticipated joint attack on Crete, having picked up a coded signal with Hitler's directive. No date for the attack was provided beyond 'imminent' and the 'scale of attack' was JIC guesswork. An Ultra message, sent to Cairo on 6 May and possibly brought to Crete by Sandford, contained the critical information that the attack would be ready by 17 May. There would be parachute landings to seize Maleme, Heraklion and Retimo, as Eric Weston had concluded in April.[67] The seaborne landings would bring further troops and supplies, including 'armoured units'. The JIC had already noted tanks could be landed by sea.

Five elaborating messages over the next six days were evidently not sent to Crete. Instead, a commentary summarising them was sent on 13 May. Parachute landings would be in two sorties, followed by gliders, aircraft landings when airfields were secured and seaborne landings, all on day one.[68] Freyberg had a framework of sorts to plan for, although he had to be careful not to reveal his source to his own strategists.

The air defence of Crete was in a sorry state. The RAF wouldn't station its depleted squadrons permanently on airfields with no repair facilities and no ground cover from air attack, but also made no move to install them. Crete's airfields were useful only as forward landing grounds for fighters. All serviceable Blenheim bombers had been sent back to Egypt, leaving ground staff waiting to be flown back. Six Hurricanes remained at Maleme, along with a couple of Fleet Air Arm's obsolete planes.

Now that the mainland was no longer a battleground, enemy air raids on Crete increased. Stukas were used there for the first time, bombing around the airfields but not the runways, and attacking the shipping and quay at Suda Bay. Crews working on Suda's docks were under constant threat from the air and soon refused to unload ships. Volunteers were sought—engineers and gunners—to unload equipment for themselves, working even during bombing attacks. 'You can dive over the side if the ship you are on is hit by a bomb,' they were told.[69]

The routine air bombing and strafing was called the 'daily hate' by troops on the ground. With a full moon on 13 May, the Luftwaffe began raids at night as well and the soldiers' rattled nerves under constant air attack resumed. As defensive positions were well concealed and batteries instructed not to fire unless under direct attack, much of the assault was at no particular target. Queenslander Lindsay Negus notes in his diary, 'Again we went to our holes in the earth or under olive trees. All our time is spent living around the hills, under or behind a rock.'[70]

'Roy' Coates, a clerk from Auckland, lay flat on his stomach, looking upwards as two Messerschmitts sprayed the area around him. 'I could see it all, what was happening,' he says. 'Bill Somerville, who was next to me, tried to get a slightly better view. He lifted his head a bit more, and I just started to say "Pull your head in", and he suddenly slumped against me. I half turned round and it had just ripped his throat right open. He was dead. I didn't think you could die so quickly.'[71]

'After raids, there was always a rush for the latrines as the fear and terror they engendered seemed to upset our internal workings,' recalls Geoff Ballard of the radio intercept group.[72] Different individuals responded in different ways. For New Zealander Bill Gentry, the monotony of the constant drone of planes flying over the treetops and spraying the area with machine-gun fire produced drowsiness.[73]

Under constant air attack, the island's defences had to be prepared with what resources they had and what restraints they had to endure. Three hundred air staff, left on Crete in a chain of command separate from the army's garrison, saw the turn of events as an island holiday and ignored requests to assist. A bridge across the river at one end of Maleme airfield was thought to be, and turned out to be, a crucial point in defence of the airfield, but the field of fire around it was obstructed by tents and huts occupied by RAF and Fleet Air Arm crew. As well, the RAF officers' mess sat on the proposed defence line. A request by New Zealander Colonel Andrew, in charge of Maleme's defence, for airfield crews to be placed temporarily under his control had to go through their commanders in Egypt and was refused.[74] The tents and huts stayed put, their occupants' comfort not to be disrupted by steps to repel the invasion.

The first contingent of Royal Marines finally arrived in mid-May, 2200 mostly young and inexperienced men to set up the naval base in Suda Bay . . . at least six months too late. The officers arrived with trunks, hat-boxes and mess gear. Essentially a construction and garrison force, it was well equipped but had no training for operations against an invasion force.[75] Bofors anti-aircraft guns were placed around Maleme airfield on a flat patch of sand close to the runway. Without camouflage, they were clearly visible to pilots. Marines' orders came from Canea, not the local army commander, so Les Andrew pointed out their vulnerability through the lines of command and an order to reposition eventually came, too late, on the day of the invasion.[76]

Preparation continued as best it could. Ian Campbell had his men dig dummy trenches along Retimo airstrip. No one occupied the weapons pits or fired at patrol aircraft, so the enemy concluded the only defenders were Greek conscripts. A reconnaissance plane crashed near Retimo after an engine was hit by RAF machine gunners. A charred aerial photo recovered from the wreckage had six suspected defence positions marked in red ink. None was correct but two were close and immediately moved.[77]

Wavell had complained to Churchill about the desperate shortage of tanks across Middle East Command after those sent to Greece failed to last the distance. The military proposed to ship new tanks around the bottom of Africa, but Churchill insisted they be sent through the Mediterranean in a convoy of fast ships. It was one of his more astute decisions. Instead of the disaster the military predicted, the Germans were caught by surprise and only one ship was lost. The convoy landed ninety-nine light cruiser tanks and 180 heavy Matilda tanks at Alexandria.

Churchill suggested one ship go via Crete and offload a dozen or more of its tanks, but accepted the military's argument that this risked losing the entire cargo to air attack. He then proposed taking twelve tanks to Crete after the full cargo had been landed in Egypt, to which Wavell advised he had already arranged to send fifteen cruiser tanks and six Matildas.[78] Not mentioned was that these weren't newly delivered tanks but workshop wrecks, described by tank squad skipper Roy Farran as 'battered ancient hulks which had been hastily patched up'.[79] Without cooling systems for their guns or wireless sets installed, they were in no better shape than the tanks that had failed in Greece.

A freighter with a cargo of light tanks and trucks was attacked by Stukas in Suda Bay, a bomb falling through its after-hatch. The ship filled with water, settling on the shallow seabed. Only tanks in the upper hold and trucks lashed to the decks were salvageable, the rest being underwater. Stripped to the waist and knee-deep in water in the bowels of the ship, the tank crews worked to unload each of their machines, winching them up and onto a barge alongside. Bombs dropped elsewhere in the harbour sent concussion waves thumping into the outside of the ship's hull. Through this nerve-racking experience, twelve cruiser tanks got to dry land.[80]

As the invasion day indicated by Ultra of 17 May approached, the ground defences to meet a mass paratroop drop were in a rough sort of readiness. Artillery was less than ideal but concealed and operational. Few sites had been spotted by enemy air patrols. Six Matilda tanks had been delivered with two hidden at the end of each airfield. Bren carriers had also arrived from Egypt, thirty of them salvaged from another cargo ship sunk in the bay. The men knew the invasion was expected as a parachute attack, but some had difficulty grasping that prospect. 'We thought it was bullshit,' says 'Dasher' Davies, 'we couldn't see how they could land thousands like that.'[81]

Ultra had reported twelve ships assembling at Naples and Sicily for the Crete operation, with successive reports giving intended routes and timings. A sea landing was of particular concern to Freyberg because it could deliver tanks. He felt he had the firepower to deal with parachute troops, but German tanks would tip the scales against him, his six dilapidated Matildas no match for them. To make matters worse, Freyberg believed he knew where the tanks would be landed, but the secrecy needs of Ultra prevented him taking advantage of it.

Three days before the expected invasion, Kiwi strategists began to worry that the outer bank of the Tavronitis River, running past the western end of Maleme airfield, had been left unguarded. It was suggested the Greek regiment at Kastelli Kissamou, a small port 22 kilometres west of Maleme, be brought in closer to cover that side of the river. Freyberg appeared to agree then cancelled the move, explaining there was not enough transport to relocate the Greeks nor time for them to dig in.[82]

The Creforce commander's main concern was not the unguarded river bank, however. Ultra indicated paratroops would be dropped at Kastelli, a strange target as the fishing village had no obvious strategic value. Freyberg inferred they were to cover an amphibious landing of tanks the next day. He didn't want to move troops in from Kastelli, but to strengthen the Greek force already there. Unable to explain that to his staff officers, Freyberg appealed to Wavell and was told London would rather lose Crete than lose Ultra.[83]

The Germans were unaware their high-level secret messages were being read, although imperfectly at that stage. They were equally unaware their aerial invasion of Crete would be armed with their own seriously flawed intelligence. Patrols had failed to spot well-camouflaged defence positions and had drawn little gunfire. An intelligence briefing the day before the attack advised the island was thinly defended by a British garrison of 5000, only four hundred of them at Heraklion and none at Retimo, and that all the troops from mainland Greece had been evacuated to Egypt. It predicted an enthusiastic welcome by the Cretans, mostly republican and unhappy with British soldiers fighting to save the Greek monarchy.[84]

By 16 May, the defenders of Crete were as prepared as circumstances allowed to meet a German invasion force the next day. They knew the attack would be by parachute with a seaborne landing to follow. That day, Ultra reported the attack date had been changed to 19 May. Three days later, a new report referred to the following morning, 20 May, as X-Day. The operation had been delayed until a tanker could bring 5000 tonnes of aviation fuel down the Adriatic Sea to the Germans.[85]

Only General Freyberg knew the day it was thought the enemy now planned to invade. He had impressed on his troops through their commanders that mobility would be key to the coming battle, that they must launch swift counter-attacks to recover any lost ground. They were now armed, although not adequately. The four areas of battle had little communication with each other or with Creforce HQ. Roads were poor, wireless sets few and phone lines easily cut. Each area was largely autonomous, their senior commanders having to make their own decisions as needs arose.

The defenders had endured six weeks of constant unchallenged bombardment from the skies and their nerves were rattled to varying degrees, but they were ready. And they held a significant card in their hand: the enemy didn't know they were there.

8

INVASION FROM ABOVE

They came with guns blazing at what they believed to be a small garrison force. As the sun rose on a clear Mediterranean day, German Junkers 88 bombers attacked gun pits, and Messerschmitt 109s, roaring at treetop height, sprayed olive groves with bullets: the 'daily hate'. Screaming plane engines, machine-gun chatter, the whistle and crump of bombs and the thud of Bofors guns; the attack on this day, 20 May, seemed more intense than usual and concentrated on the strip from Maleme to Suda Bay. After an hour, the attackers headed off, leaving thick, choking dust and an eerie silence. Cordite lingered in the nostrils.

The noise of cooks preparing breakfast resumed and the men, mostly New Zealanders at this end of the defence zone, either got back to their meal or started on one they'd held off. Before many had finished, a second air raid began, shorter but equally as fierce. Men rushed back to their trenches, the ground shuddering under them, and bombs threw more earth in the air. The raiders left after half an hour. Huge clouds of dust reduced visibility to a few metres in many places and eyes and mouths were full of grit.

There wasn't time to get back to breakfast. Coming in under the cover of the air attack's smoke and dust were squads of Junkers troop-carriers towing gliders, about eighty of them. Released as they crossed the coast, they were silent as ghosts after the screeching of warplanes and ordnance. The gliders banked in long slow turns, giant wings swishing as they swooped down to hastily selected landings, kicking up more dust as they slid across the ground. Some crashed onto boulders or olive trees; some bellylanded on the flat mud and dry shingle of the Tavronitis River beside Maleme airfield. A gravel bed 800 metres wide, the 'river' was only a shallow creek running down the middle.

Some gliders were shot down, and others were put under heavy fire by fortified ground defences as they unwittingly landed near them. The German troops who survived poured out of the landed gliders, running to nearby cover. Their job was to disable anti-aircraft gun posts around the airfield and near Canea, but they had little knowledge of the waiting force or where it was placed.

On the other hand, the unwillingness of the Allied gun crews to arm themselves with rifles or machine guns played into enemy hands. Bofors posts between Maleme's airfield and the river were quickly overwhelmed, some before the gun could be disabled. Soon, captured guns were being used against the Allied defenders.

Hot on the heels of the gliders came formations of the three-engined troop-carriers: the airborne invasion that had been anticipated for three weeks. Each carrying eighteen paratroops, the planes came in columns, three abreast to a dropping height of about 100 metres, too low for the anti-aircraft guns that had survived, but an easy target for the Bofors.[1] Several of the transports were shot down on approach, causing the formations to lose cohesion and their drops to be scattered wide of the target areas. One or two planes broke up under gunfire with bodies falling out like sacks of potatoes.[2]

Most of the planes were able to drop troops somewhere over the coastal area in which the gliders had selectively landed. Parachutists spilled out of side doors, tugging on their rip-cords, and the sky filled with colour 'like balloons coming down at the end of a party',[3] white for the troops and colours for officers, supplies and equipment. Thousands of coloured specks, such an extraordinary sight, almost inspirational, it was hard to register fear. To New Zealander Sandy Thomas, the parachutists looked like 'little jerking dolls whose billowy frocks of green, yellow, red and white had somehow blown up and become entangled in the wires that controlled them'.[4] To driver Colin Farley, they were 'white handkerchiefs being let go out of a carriage window'.[5]

There was dead silence for several seconds, then all hell broke loose. Anyone with a gun opened up. Within minutes there was firing up and down the coastal strip, an eruption of chattering machine-gun fire, thudding field guns, and the crackle of rifles. Officers told their men to hold fire until the parachutists were 10 or 15 metres off the ground and aim at their boots, so they'd fall into the gunfire.

Alf Watt, a labourer from Whakatane, says, 'Like everyone I was scared out of my wits, until we started really fighting. Then we were so busy recharging our rifles, we had nothing else to think about.'[6]

Fred Irving, a 22-year-old sawmiller from Southland, didn't think twice about shooting the parachutists: 'They were just there swinging around. They were getting so close they were almost at the end of the rifle so you had to do it and you just did it.'[7]

Some parachutists were shot during their short descent, jerking when they were hit, dangling like old-fashioned fob watches, until they crumpled on hitting the ground, their parachutes a shroud falling softly over them. Bullets tore into billowing chutes, setting them on fire. Some got entangled in treetops. One plane swooped into a group of descending troops and careered to earth festooned with parachutes.[8]

Colonel Friedrich von der Heydte was among those who jumped. Standing at the aircraft door in preparation he could see the town of

Alikianou below him. 'I could see people in the streets staring up at us, others running away and disappearing into doorways,' he recalls. 'I pushed with hands and feet, throwing my arms forward as if trying to catch the black cross on the wing. And then the slipstream caught me and I was swirling through space with the air roaring in my ears. A sudden jerk upon the webbing, a pressure on the chest which knocked the breath out of my lungs, and then—I looked upwards and saw, spread above me, the wide-open, motley hood of my parachute.'[9]

Most of the paratroops carried just a pistol, a knife and a couple of grenades, which they dropped while descending. Rifles and other arms were dropped separately in containers which they had to find on landing. Only a highly trained soldier could drop with a submachine gun strapped to his body and avoid injury on landing. Those men held quick-firing Schmeissers between their legs but the swaying descent prevented aiming their fire. Without the ability to steer, paratroops crashed through village roofs, onto bamboo thickets and telegraph wires, and among vines and olive trees. Those that landed some distance from defenders had maybe ten minutes to find arms and gather to fight as a team.

Some units didn't have that option. One battalion of six hundred men fell directly on New Zealand infantry positions in an area German intelligence had reported as undefended. About four hundred were killed, including the battalion commander and they ceased to exist as a coherent fighting force.[10] Others landed by the Maori battalion headquarters. The Maoris let them land, then rushed at them with war-cries and bayonets. Kiwi officers stopped men running out after paratroops who landed out of gun range, instead sending out organised patrols. The patrols found themselves stepping over bodies as they moved through the olive groves. Parachutes of all colours were draped over the trees, some with a dead soldier swinging in the harness.

The New Zealand troops were joined by Cretan villagers with clubs, knives and old guns, even axes and spades. When asked where they were heading without guns, some women with sticks said, 'We will take them from the Germans.'[11] Michalis Doulakis recalls his uncle clubbing to death a paratroop entangled in a harness.[12] Stamatis Borakis says, 'If you made a hole in his parachute, he'd shoot down to the ground like a stone and get killed. Then you'd grab his gun.'[13] Others waited around wells with seized weapons until the enemy became desperate for water, a trick from the days of uprisings against the Turks.[14]

A former paratroop tells of a figure, dressed in black with a bandanna around the head, leaping from cover and shooting two Germans with a German automatic rifle, then 'sliding away into the bushes like a snake'. Cornered and brought down with a hand grenade, the dying partisan looked about eighteen years old. 'Before he died, he looked deep into my eyes and smiled,' says the German. When they pulled off the bandanna to lie the young man down, half a metre of long black hair tumbled out. 'He' was a young woman.[15]

The cool of the morning turned to sweltering heat as the sun blazed down from the cloudless sky. Paratroops, wearing uniforms designed for northern Europe, sweated profusely, discarding overalls and hacking off their trouser legs with a knife. Conditions were harsh in the New Zealanders' trenches too with water low and limited visibility due to the smoke and dust clogging eyes and throats, but at this early stage they were on top.

Sniping battles broke out in the vineyards and orchards, with light casualties on both sides, but the invaders had already suffered devastating losses in planes shot down and in their parachute drops. The orderly structure and chain of command of the German assault force had broken down, particularly with commanders lost. Only when small pockets of troops were able to assemble and form a front with a conventional pattern of attack could the surviving officers' discipline and leadership come into play. There were only a few who got to that stage and they were mostly in a holding pattern on that first day.

One of the parachute regiments had been ordered by General Student to capture a 'tented encampment' on the coast near Canea. It had been bombed and strafed during the morning air attack but when troops stormed the camp, they found it was a field hospital full of sick and wounded soldiers, not barracks. Tents were burning and riddled with machine-gun fire; some patients and medical staff had been killed, others wounded.[16]

A swastika flag was laid out to prevent further air attack, and staff and patients were herded out of trenches and across the road to the dressing station,[17] many barefoot, some in pyjamas or blue hospital gowns. Some of the serious cases were allowed to stay behind. After the captors shot at a sniper firing from the trees, John Plimmer climbed awkwardly from a slit trench with a wounded arm in a sling. The unarmed doctor was shot and killed by a jumpy German.[18]

Twenty paratroops had corralled about three hundred captives from the hospital area into an open space and made them sit by the roadside with hands on their heads. The guards got increasingly anxious as sounds of gunfire got closer. A British cruiser tank gave them a careful burst of fire before backing off to find water to cool its guns. Realising they were isolated, the captors herded the prisoners into a column and set off slowly through olive groves. They followed the road towards Galatas, expecting to join the main body of their regiment. They never got there.

Marching up the hill, the worried guards were urging their captives on when a hidden Bren carrier opened up on them. The guards took cover while their charges dropped to the ground. Some were hit before the Bren gunners heard them yelling that they were prisoners. 'Not for bloody long,' was the shouted reply. When the Germans tried to shift their position, the gunners abandoned their caution and, in that outburst, several of the captors were killed as they tried to get away.

A padre got to his feet, saying, 'If we have to go out, let these Jerries see we can go out as men. Let's walk.' And a group actually did, getting up and walking with him to safety with one wounded the only casualty. Others crawled on their bellies to the New Zealand positions. By late afternoon, eight hours after the hospital was overrun, one wounded German was the only surviving captor.[19]

The hospital attackers' main force didn't get to Galatas that day. A small town of narrow winding streets, it was perched on a hill five kilometres from Canea. Around it ranged five more hills, named Red, Wheat, Ruin, Pink and Cemetery Hill by the British. The hills provided elevation to fire on the surrounding area. Paratroops had landed in a valley running back from Galatas. Known as Prison Valley, after the Cretan prison there, it was under fire from the hills around.

Colonel Richard Heidrich had made an ad hoc base in the prison, welcomed by its Greek governor, a sympathiser, bowing elegantly and offering his services as interpreter in impeccable German.[20] Heidrich directed his men to occupy the heights around Galatas, beginning with Pink Hill. At the foot of the hill, they brushed aside Greek defenders whose colonel hadn't issued ammunition. It was still held in a store which the Germans then seized.[21] Through the gap created, a fierce attack was launched against the composite unit occupying Pink Hill. Poorly armed themselves, the unit, made up of Kiwi drivers fighting as infantry, fought valiantly. There were high casualties on both sides.

Michael Forrester had been sent by the British Military Mission to liaise with Colonel Kippenberger, who was in command of New Zealand and Greek forces positioned around Galatas, and report back. Instead, he stayed and rallied the demoralised Greek regiment, found more weapons and brought the troops back about midday to the slopes near Galatas where the battered enemy was starting to edge forward.

Brian Bassett, Kippenberger's brigade major, had assigned the Greeks to the Englishman. 'Suddenly Forrester began tootling a tin whistle like the Pied Piper,' he says, 'and the whole motley crowd of them surged down against the Huns yelling and shouting in a mad bayonet charge.' Several hundred Greek soldiers and Cretan civilians, including women and children, charged down the hill behind Forrester. The stunned Germans wavered and broke, heading back to their prison base. This steadied the Greeks who, with composite units, held Pink Hill for the remainder of the day.[22]

Howard Kippenberger, a Christchurch lawyer, saw from his hilltop headquarters that the enemy had landed unopposed up Prison Valley and assembled around the prison. He urged his divisional commander to approve a counter-attack to take the prison and clear the valley, but General Puttick vetoed the plan, keeping troops ready to meet the seaborne attack expected to follow the air drop.

In the late afternoon a report came through, extracted from a prisoner, that the Germans were building a landing strip in Prison Valley. Where in the valley wasn't known, but Puttick reversed his earlier decision and ordered the landing ground destroyed and the prison cleared. The order didn't get through to Kippenberger, however. He first became aware of it when three light tanks reported to him for instructions. With dusk falling and no time for detailed preparation for an attack on an unknown location, Kippenberger cancelled the attack he'd been unsuccessfully advocating all afternoon. As it turned out, no airstrip was being built.[23] Interrogated prisoners don't always tell the truth.

Kippenberger had seen one of his Greek regiments pulling back, although some of those men had rallied under Forrester. Another regiment was out of his line of vision, deep in Prison Valley. He assumed it had disbanded and told Puttick the regiment was now 'only a circle on a map'. The regiment was made up of a thousand men with old Steyr rifles. They had lost most of their officers but, unknown to the New Zealanders, continued fighting the Germans along with armed villagers who had joined in.[24]

Paratroops had landed among the valley's cactus groves and found themselves attacked by Greek soldiers and men, women and children with scythes, shotguns and weapons looted from canisters and dead Germans. Cut off from the rest of the Allied force, the defenders held out on ridges and cottages in Alikianou, the main village at that end of the valley. There were heavy losses on both sides, but the invaders were pinned in their area, their patrols constantly forced back. They ceased to venture up that end of the valley. A composite Kiwi unit, driven from the middle of the valley, reported wrongly that the regiment was 'hopelessly dispersed and disorganised'.[25] They had been unable to spot them, the same problem the Germans were having.

Galatas and Prison Valley were sideshows, however, in the paratroops' attack plan along that coastal strip. The main game there was the airfield at Maleme, whose capture would enable the Germans to fly in supplies and reinforcements. Glider troops had landed on the Tavronitis riverbed and paratroops were in force among the undefended vineyards and olive groves west of the river. Their mortars and machine guns had been dropped nearby to take the airfield.

Les Andrew was a worried man. Responsible for defence around Maleme airfield, he'd had no situation reports from his forward platoons under fire from air-dropped mortars and field guns. With the shortage of radios, communication was by phone but the lines had been cut. He was relying on runners and not much information was coming in. Runners—those that get through—are messengers carrying orders out and bringing requests in from fighting units. They have limited knowledge of how the battle is actually going. Andrew had gone forward earlier to a New Zealand post and found those trenches empty. He feared the worst.

A professional soldier, unlike most of his men, 44-year-old Colonel Andrew was a dour and conscientious disciplinarian. He had earned a Victoria Cross at Passchendaele in the First World War, but that war had instilled an orthodox tactical mentality in him, as

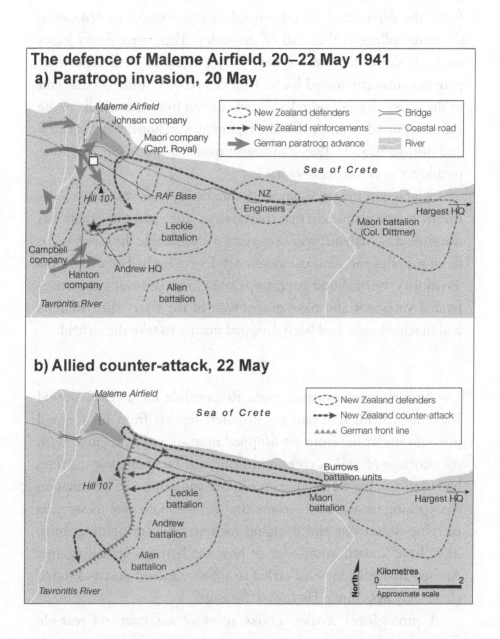

The defence of Maleme Airfield, 20–22 May 1941

a) Paratroop invasion, 20 May

Maleme Airfield
Johnson company
Maori company
(Capt. Royal)

Legend:
- New Zealand defenders
- New Zealand reinforcements
- German paratroop advance
- Bridge
- Coastal road
- River

Sea of Crete

Hill 107
RAF Base
NZ Engineers
Hargest HQ
Maori battalion (Col. Dittmer)
Leckie battalion
Campbell company
Andrew HQ
Hanton company
Allen battalion
Tavronitis River

b) Allied counter-attack, 22 May

Maleme Airfield

Sea of Crete

Legend:
- New Zealand defenders
- New Zealand counter-attack
- German front line

Hill 107
Burrows battalion units
Leckie battalion
Maori battalion
Hargest HQ
Andrew battalion
Allen battalion
Tavronitis River

North

Kilometres
0   1   2
Approximate scale

it had with several of his peers. To them, battles were fought across a line separating two opposing armies, but in the aerial invasion of Crete there was no battle line, the two armies intermingled from the outset. Andrew was having trouble adjusting his thinking.

The New Zealand defenders at Maleme were dug in on a broad hillock they called Hill 107 with an imperfect sight of the airfield and its surrounds. While they had dealt decisively with enemy landing on or near their positions, their low elevation didn't allow them to see over the dense foliage and deep riverbanks blocking their view of the Tavronitis. Dust clouds from the bombing obscured it further. Through the morning they were heavily shelled from across the river.

Within an hour some of the depleted German force had formed small groups that assembled by an iron bridge at the western end of the airstrip. The RAF base had the best view of the bridge but, as they had refused to move, the Kiwis were unable to see Germans dodging between the bridge's stone supports. A small group charged from the bridge into the RAF camp, sweeping up the under-prepared airmen who they used as a screen in pushing forward towards Hill 107. Frank Twigg, an intelligence sergeant from Gisborne, was approached by a party of thirty or forty 'variously uniformed men with hands above their heads, many terror-stricken, all yelling and pleading with us not to shoot, meaning at the enemy, but to let them come on or they would be shot in the back'.[26]

Gordon Dillon, a provost sergeant, was one of the captives. 'When any defences were seen, the Jerries just took one or two of us and pushed us ahead into the defence,' he says. 'The Jerry doing it put a Luger in your back and just pointed. It was easy to understand. They would keep close behind in case of shooting. Some damned good shots picked the three Jerries off.'[27]

Petty Officer Wheaton, an English electrician with Fleet Air Arm, was pushed forward with an RAF man in this manner. The two hostages whispered they should run for it at the first opportunity.

When they approached a crest with New Zealand tin hats poking above a slit trench, Wheaton shouted and made a zigzag dash for the trench, throwing himself in with bullets flying around. The RAF man hesitated. The Kiwis recovered his badly wounded body after driving the enemy away. He'd been shot in the back.[28]

Les Andrew's headquarters was on the rear slope of Hill 107. He had radio contact with his brigade commander, Jimmy Hargest, and reported in the mid-morning that he'd lost contact with some of his units but the battalion was holding its position. Shortly after, he arrived at the headquarters of the adjacent battalion 'very shaken and disturbed' to ask if they could reach one of his companies a kilometre away. He'd lost contact with them and didn't know if they were still actively fighting.[29] A patrol found the missing company and was mistakenly shot at by it, concluding it was still fighting. No one thought to report this to Andrew, by then back at his headquarters.[30]

Andrew's ability to assess the battle was impaired by a wound sustained during the dawn air attack. He dismissed it as 'a wee piece of bomb that stuck in above the temple and when I pulled it out it was bloody hot and I bled a lot'.[31] Nerves on edge from the daily hate over the weeks before wouldn't have helped. Airmen who'd escaped ahead of the charge through their base brought panicked reports of the action there. Lacking word from any troops on the edge of the airfield, Andrew assumed that they too had been overrun. At noon, he radioed Hargest again to report his battalion was under heavy bombardment.

Through the afternoon, Andrew tried desperately to get an understanding of the enemy's progress, persuading himself they had broken through his defences in places. While trying to ignore his head wound, he was jumping to conclusions from the snippets of information he had, trying to decipher a battle dynamic outside his experience: no battle line, just scattered bits of combat.

Glider troops had attacked the western end of the airfield from the riverbed, using the shingle bank as cover. They were held off by the defence Andrew believed to be overrun, but not without casualties. Robin Sinclair, a platoon leader wounded in the neck, tried to ignite a petrol dump alongside a stack of RAF incendiary bombs, but fainted from the loss of blood. Nearby, John Mehaffey flung his helmet over a grenade lobbed into his trench and jumped on it to save the lives of two comrades. Both his feet were blown off and he died soon after, as did his two mates.[32] The Hawkes Bay clerk, twenty-four years old, was recommended for a VC.

Andrew believed the defences between Hill 107 and the river had also disintegrated. Two men guarding the bridge with an anti-tank gun fell back to the camp as German numbers grew on the riverbed. In the attack from the bridge, one was killed, the other captured, but the accuracy of defending riflemen halted the German attempt to take the strategic hill. Andrew allowed a soldier, who pulled back from the battle, to convince him wrongly that the company was lost. Once again, rumours and self-serving stories from the front were determining tactics.

Some of the airmen and gunners who had come back from the airfield were organised into patrols and given captured arms. Marcel Comeau, an English aircraftman, was patrolling with Hess, a German Jew who'd fought for Germany in the First World War and was now with the Palestinian military. They came across a paratroop lying propped up on his Schmeisser. Hess prodded him in the back with his rifle and shouted in German. The machine gun dropped and Hess kicked him flat, the soldier shrieking in agony. His trouser leg was soaked in blood and Hess cut it away to reveal a pulp of flesh and bone. The two did what they could to dress the wound and Hess started chatting to the paratroop while Comeau went looking for water. Returning with radiator water, he found Hess and the German showing family photos to each other. The German showed them how to use the Schmeisser and they left him.[33]

Prior to the invasion, Hargest had passed on to his battalion commanders General Freyberg's order for swift counter-attacks to reclaim any lost ground at airfields. By mid-afternoon, Andrew was reporting to Hargest that his left flank had given way and he needed reinforcements. An hour later, he asked for a counter-attack by Colonel Leckie's battalion nearby, but Hargest replied that it was 'engaged against enemy paratroops in its own area'.[34]

That was not what David Leckie had reported. At midday, he had signalled that his area was 'under complete control' and he could support Andrew if required. Hargest messaged back, 'Will NOT call on you for counter-attacking unless position very serious. So far everything is in hand and reports from other units satisfactory.'[35] Andrew's request should have been the time to make that call.

It was only through political intervention that Jimmy Hargest was there at all. In the First World War, he had been wounded at Gallipoli then served on the Western Front, winning a DSO and bar, but he'd suffered nervous shock under intense shellfire in that war. Short and stocky, the genial Southland farmer with a reddish pudgy face had been elected to the New Zealand parliament in 1931. He occasionally succumbed to post-war shell shock and in 1939 was deemed by the medical board to be unfit for overseas service. Although an Opposition MP, he appealed to the acting prime minister, Peter Fraser, and was confirmed as a senior officer in the New Zealand Expeditionary Force, despite Freyberg arguing against it.[36]

Initially the 49-year-old seemed self-assured, but the day before the air invasion Hargest told intelligence officer Geoffrey Cox, 'I don't know what lies ahead. I only know that it produces in me a sensation I never knew in the last war. It is not fear, it is something quite different, something I can only describe as dread.'[37] A day later, he's in the midst of battle and cracks are appearing.

Growing frustrated with his isolation, and misreading how his units were faring, Les Andrew shopped around in his mind for other solutions. Signalling by semaphore and flares to Leckie had drawn no response. In the morning, Stan Johnson, leading the company at the airfield, had suggested a counter-attack with the two Matilda tanks. Andrew had decided against it then, but by afternoon, when he believed Johnson's company was lost, he had changed his mind and sent the tanks with a small infantry escort to stop the surge from the bridge. Heading for the river instead of the airfield and camp, one tank turned back without firing. The gunner had the wrong ammunition and the tank's turret wouldn't turn.

The other Matilda continued, firing at enemy troops still on the riverbed. It went under the bridge, crushing a mortar crew as it went, and on for a short distance until it got bogged in mud. The crew quickly abandoned it and were captured, putting their infantry support under devastating fire. Only nine of the escort of twenty-six got back; the rest were captured or killed.[38]

Advised by Johnson's runner that the tank attack had failed, Andrew continued to assume that the company had been wiped out. He reported the tanks' failure to Hargest by radio and asked for permission to withdraw from Hill 107 to a ridge to its east where they could still cover the airfield. Hargest's resigned response was, 'Well, if you must, you must'—not a sign of a senior commander in command—but he added that he'd arranged for two companies to move across and reinforce Andrew's defences.[39]

Andrew said later that 'from the gist of the message [from Hargest] I expected the companies almost immediately',[40] although he knew one was from the Maori battalion 12 kilometres away, a three-hour march. He told Syd Hanton, leading the defences on Hill 107, that reinforcements were coming, but not until 9 pm when Hanton's company was to pull back behind the hillock and await an order for a further withdrawal at midnight. The company commander was surprised as 'things were not bad with me'. The enemy's attempt to take Hill 107 had been pushed back.[41]

One of the companies sent by Hargest arrived at dusk and was told to occupy the riverside positions of the company Andrew believed lost. They would be a rearguard for troops withdrawing from Hill 107 while runners were sent to Andrew's other companies to withdraw with them. Only one runner got through. The withdrawal of defenders from Hill 107 was completed and the borrowed unit returned to its sector.

Andrew was worried his losses exposed him to attacks across the river. Believing he was at half his original strength and couldn't withstand renewed ground and air attack the next day, he needed to adjust his positions under cover of dark. In fact, the Germans held only a weak presence on the western edge of the airfield and encroaching below Hill 107, but he didn't know that. Worse still, when Andrew got to the withdrawal point on a nearby ridge, he realised that in the morning it could be fired on from Hill 107. He ordered a full withdrawal, abandoning the airfield altogether.[42]

Andrew's second-in-command, Jim Leggat, went to report to Hargest after midnight that the battalion had left Maleme. Just awake and in pyjamas, Hargest was extremely surprised, having understood Andrew to be falling back only a short distance. The battle had seemed to be under control. Hargest was not well informed but, if he thought Andrew was 'flapping', made no effort to go forward and find out.[43]

While Hargest's first reinforcements had been standing by to repel an attack that didn't come, a Maori company under Captain Rangi Royal tried to find its way to Hill 107 in the dark. Unfamiliar with the route, Royal took the main road and they were twice challenged by paratroops, the second shouting, 'We surrender!', then throwing a grenade. The incensed Maoris charged with bayonets, a few standing back and doing hakas. Twenty-four Germans were killed.

Taking a wrong turn, the group got to a village that wasn't on the way and then to the east end of the airfield before finally getting to Andrew's deserted headquarters. On the way back, Royal came across Andrew and reported what he'd seen at Maleme, the hill unoccupied and evidence defending troops were still fighting there. 'You're damn lucky to be alive,' was Andrew's only comment.[44] Had he turned back, he would have found his 'lost' units were active, with only fifty-seven disorganised Germans at the western end of the airfield, short of food and ammunition. A counter-attack would have dislodged them.

By dusk, with two of Andrew's companies still fighting, the German attack lost momentum. The riverside company had stopped the paratroop charge from the riverbed, although they'd suffered casualties and their ammunition was running low. Their spirit was still strong, however. Tom Campbell, the company commander, took men to battalion headquarters for supplies and found the HQ abandoned. At 3 am, Campbell felt he had little option but to withdraw. Morale fell flat and groups pulled back haphazardly.[45] Some were captured; some were joined by stragglers from the air base. A sergeant-major tossed a grenade among sleeping Germans 'for good luck', but there was no retaliation.

At the end of the day, Stan Johnson's company was also still active, holding the beach and the inland side of the airfield. Badly mauled, their firepower was strong and had forced away two Junkers that had tried to land in the late afternoon. 'The surviving men were in excellent heart in spite of their losses,' says Johnson, a Wellington school teacher. 'They had NOT had enough.'[46] A pre-dawn patrol returned with news that Germans were occupying the battalion headquarters area. With pockets of the enemy around them, Johnson realised they'd soon be the focus of attack from both ground and air. He decided to withdraw.

A unit runner, Jimmy Christian, had got through the German lines by taking off his boots, so a group of about thirty decided to do the same. After the critically wounded had been made comfortable and given food and water, they took off their boots and hung them round their necks, then crept in single file around the sleeping Germans snoring in their foxholes. By dawn, they were out of sight of the enemy. Boots were ordered back on and they made their way through vineyards to a grove, sheltering under the trees during the morning blitz.[47]

By the end of the first day of their airborne invasion, the Germans around Maleme and Canea, far from capturing the airfield and Suda Bay naval station as planned, were just hanging on, anticipating a counter-attack in the morning that would probably finish them off. They didn't know that the defenders had withdrawn from Hill 107 and the airfield; they didn't know how the afternoon attack on Retimo and Heraklion had gone.

Not all aircraft returned to Athens from the morning sortie over Maleme and Canea. Waiting at the airfield for the afternoon attack on Retimo and Heraklion, paratroops were dismayed to see Junkers returning with damaged undercarriages and bullet holes in the wings and fuselage. Dust kicked up by propellors had delayed the morning schedule, compounded in the afternoon by the need to refuel by handpump. When the first planes took off, already later than scheduled, dust clouds caused further delays. Because of the loss of aircraft in the morning, six hundred men were left behind.

In the late afternoon, Dorniers and Messerschmitts attacked blindly around Retimo's small airstrip, the absence of anti-aircraft gunfire seeming to confirm it was undefended. Further east, the town of Heraklion was also bombarded, but the Allied anti-aircraft guns were ordered to stay silent. The pilots concluded they had been destroyed in earlier raids. Aware of the morning attacks, the Retimo commander, Ian Campbell, figured the Germans were now coming his way.

The Australians at Retimo had seen gliders turning towards Maleme in the morning, but there were no gliders this time. Soon after the raid, formations of Junkers 52s came from the sea, turned and flew along the coast, dropping paratroops and weapon canisters either side of the airfield. Drawing unexpected machine-gun fire, the planes quickly lost coordination, coming in loose groups or singly. Several were brought down along the beach, others were raked by gunfire as paratroops jumped. Some of the planes flew away on fire, one trailing entangled parachutists.

Medical orderly Edgar Randolph, a Perth taxi driver in civilian life, watched a plane brought down. 'The front engine caught alight, the fire spread backwards in seconds and the plane nosed down,' he says. 'Four men got out but their 'chutes had no time to spread and they all went in hard.'[48]

Some paratroops drowned in the sea, smothered by their silk canopy; some were impaled in a bamboo thicket. Many floated down near machine-gun posts, dead by the time they hit the ground with a sickening thud. Two canisters, dropped near a weapons pit, were dragged in by Australian gunners. They contained a 4-gallon thermos of coffee and eight dozen hot cakes.

'One parachutist landed almost on top of me and immediately surrendered,' recalls Clive Dieppe. 'He was shaking like a leaf and produced his identity card. He offered me a drink from his water bottle which I duly sipped. It was like warm coffee.'[49] A paratroop taken prisoner at Retimo complained that the defenders should not have shot at them while they were descending. 'You must wait until we have landed and formed into our units,' he insisted.[50]

An hour later, little more than two hours before dusk, the faint hum of distant planes could be heard further down the coast at Heraklion. A bugle sounded and shouts, then troop-carriers came roaring along the shore, popping out parachutists over concealed positions. Guns opened up. Some planes exploded in mid-air; others caught fire as the men jumped. Nine Junkers 52s headed in a line towards the hidden Australians. The first, hit square on the nose, burst into flame and crashed on the shore. Two caught fire, their paratroops jumping with burning parachutes. The tail of another was shot off, the men jumping without enough height for their parachutes to open fully. One plane flew away with a parachutist suspended from the tail. The pilot shook the tail vigorously and threw him into the sea.[51]

'As the paratroopers landed, the earth seemed to absolutely disgorge our men. They appeared from everywhere, shooting and running to pounce on the paratroopers,' former bank teller Norm Johnstone wrote home. 'They had to drop through a hail of machine-gun and rifle fire and many were dead before they landed, some having as many as fifty bullet holes in them.'[52]

Bill Andrews was shooting at Germans without his trousers. He had the only respectable pair in his section and a mate had borrowed them to go into Heraklion just before the attack started. He never got them back, wearing a dead German's pair instead.[53]

Back in Retimo, enough paratroops landed beyond one end of the airstrip to attack Australian machine-gun posts and force their way onto a hill, imaginatively renamed Hill A by the military. Colonel Campbell ordered his two Matilda tanks in to stop the enemy advancing towards the airfield, but their poor performance in Greece continued. One didn't bother using the bridge across a drain and got stuck; the other fired off a few rounds then slid into a ravine. The tank commander emerged from his vehicle in the drain and was shot dead. The two crews were captured and taken away to a vacated olive oil factory the Germans had commandeered. Undaunted, Ian Campbell ordered another counter-attack at dawn to drive the Germans off Hill A.

Paratroops landing west of the airfield had tried to occupy the town of Retimo, but were forced back by well-trained Cretan police into the nearby village of Perivolia. There was a Hill B at that end of the airfield. Driven back from it by Australian and Greek soldiers into the vineyards around Perivolia, the invaders were unable to fight their way out. The Greeks had little training, never having fired their weapons, and during the preliminary bombing they had drifted back from their positions. Australian NCOs, sent out to rally them, brought them back in and steadied them. Air-dropped arms and ammunition were seized by the poorly equipped Greek soldiers and, by evening, they were clearing isolated pockets of Germans.

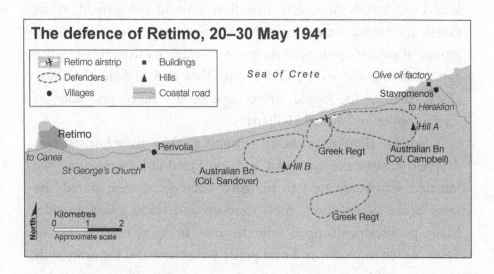

The defence of Retimo, 20–30 May 1941

Legend:
- ✈ Retimo airstrip
- ⬭ Defenders (dashed outline)
- ● Villages
- ■ Buildings
- ▲ Hills
- ▬ Coastal road

Sea of Crete

Olive oil factory
Stavromenos
to Heraklion

Retimo
to Canea
Perivolia
St George's Church ■

Greek Regt

Australian Bn
(Col. Sandover)
▲ Hill B

▲ Hill A

Australian Bn
(Col. Campbell)

Greek Regt

Kilometres
0   1   2
Approximate scale

North

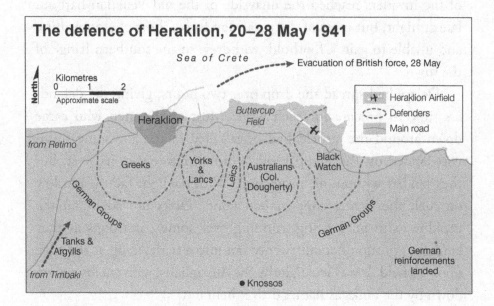

The defence of Heraklion, 20–28 May 1941

Sea of Crete

→ Evacuation of British force, 28 May

Kilometres
0   1   2
Approximate scale

North

Legend:
- ✈ Heraklion Airfield
- ⬭ Defenders (dashed outline)
- ▬ Main road

Heraklion

from Retimo

Buttercup
Field

Greeks

Yorks
&
Lancs

Leics

Australians
(Col.
Dougherty)

Black
Watch

German Groups

German Groups

Tanks &
Argylls

from Timbaki

German
reinforcements
landed

● Knossos

The English garrison commander in Heraklion, Brigadier Brian Chappel, had positioned his garrison force, now strengthened with Ivan Dougherty's Australian battalion, around the airfield, while Greek regiments were assigned to defend the town. Two small groups of paratroops fought their way through its sixteenth-century gates and into the walled Old Town. They had to fight their way along narrow, dog-legged streets against the fierce resistance of Cretan police and armed civilians.

Christos Bantouvas heard shouting that parachutists had dropped outside the Gate of Canea on Heraklion's west side. 'We ran to a warehouse next to the gate where guns were stored,' he says, 'broke down doors, took weapons and stood guard outside. Many paratroops dropped into the area, firing at us. We shot at them as they came down. Local police were there and the army split into groups. Our number increased as people left villages to join us. Women brought food and water and fought along with us.'[54] Some of the invaders reached the quayside of the old Venetian harbour late at night, but most of the paratroop force, short of ammunition and unable to gain a foothold, withdrew to the southern fringe of the town.

Delays had spread the drop over two hours, giving the defenders time to prepare for each wave. Most of the men who came down around the airfield had been killed in the air. Some survivors landed on Buttercup Field, a broad meadow to its west, but they landed without air protection. With daylight fading and low on fuel, the fighter support had gone. Tanks moved in on the meadow with guns firing, running over some paratroops as they landed. A group of about twenty ran into a barley crop at the edge of the airfield. It was set alight by the Australians, with enemy mown down by the tanks as flames drove them out.

The Germans had failed to capture either of the eastern airfields. A night of scattered rifle and machine-gun fire and Very flares followed as they tried to assemble their devastated and dispersed force.

British and Greek losses had been light and they, along with the Cretan irregulars, were able to stock up on captured arms, ammunition and rations. In Retimo, German planes had mistakenly dropped containers with fresh bread, mettwurst, chocolate and cigarettes among the defenders. It capped a bad day for the invaders.

———

On the wall was a large map of Crete with paper flags pinned on it; on a broad table in the centre, three field phones sat beside a tangle of wires, papers and files; to one side, a large ashtray filled with cigarette butts. Plush and spacious under electric chandeliers, Germany's Crete operation had set up its control room in the curtained ballroom of the Hotel Grande Bretagne in Athens. Wehrmacht staff rushed around a room bristling with anxiety. Reports of the invasion's progress were coming in on a weak radio signal and there were signs that all was not going well.

By midnight, it was clear that none of Crete's airfields was in German hands and that the paratroops had suffered heavy casualties. General Student and his staff officers pondered the plans that had gone disturbingly awry. Some urged calling off the invasion but Kurt Student had too much at stake to willingly let it go. Boldness had to be his friend. His best option was Maleme. If they could gain control of that airfield, they could land mountain troops and additional arms and equipment at will. With a reserve of only six hundred paratroops to drop the next day, all would be put into Maleme. Captain Oskar Kleye was ordered to test the water by trying to land a Junkers transport on Maleme airstrip at first light.

At dawn the next morning, Kleye swung a Junkers 52 over Hill 107 and down over the trenches abandoned two hours earlier, touching down on the dirt runway. Shuddering to a dusty halt near the Tavronitis River, out of range of much of the light artillery fire, Kleye took off after a brief stop. He radioed his commander that aircraft could land on the far side with a reasonable chance of success. Student immediately ordered the Luftwaffe to fly mountain troops to Maleme, crash-landing if necessary, as long as reinforcements and supplies got to his beleaguered force.[55]

In the early light, a German patrol had found Hill 107 unoccupied. The paratroops moved onto it and began cautiously advancing along the airstrip, finding the defenders had withdrawn from there also. Red, green and white Very lights beamed through mist above the olive groves, signalling to planes patrolling above for supplies and calling for areas to be attacked. The Germans spent the day expecting a counter-attack they doubted they could hold back, but it didn't happen. Instead, the three New Zealand battalion commanders decided to hold their positions, back from the airfield, while Andrew reorganised his battalion . . . and the enemy consolidated its tenuous position.

Following Kleye's test landing, pilots Koenitz and Steinweg responded to a message that paratroops by the Tavronitis River were nearly out of ammunition and their leader, Brigadier Meindl, would die without hospital treatment. The unauthorised flight landed on the beach west of the river, took on board a half-delirious Meindl and seven other stretcher cases and just managed to take off.[56] Soon after, six more Junkers 52s, sent by Student, crash-landed on the sand with ammunition and supplies.

The New Zealanders remained passive during the morning. Artillery and mortar fire came from the airfield, but Hargest issued no order to counter-attack. No skirmishes confronted paratroops edging along the airfield, merely return of fire and some small arms fire, probably from Cretan civilians.

While the defence dithered, Student's reserve paratroops dropped at each end of the airfield. Unopposed west of the Tavronitis, they moved over the bridge to join their comrades. The last reserves parachuted east of the airfield, assured by German intelligence it was 'free of enemy'. It was anything but. Landing over the Maori battalion, who were preparing for a night attack, many were killed in the air or while undoing their harness. Maori bayonets were fixed and rushed at those who survived. 'Chas' Kelly was forward with an Australian group when the paratroops dropped. He exclaims in his diary, 'The Maori troops down on the left go into a bayonet charge and the noise of their yells and the Germans screaming chills the blood.'[57]

Despite paratroops and supplies landing and Freyberg's instruction for rapid response, General Puttick approved a Hargest proposal to wait until night to counter-attack the airfield. They would have no strafing to deal with then but the attack plan was complicated. Two Kiwi battalions, with three tanks in support, were to re-occupy the airfield and Hill 107 by morning. Two more battalions were to relieve them at different points. The essence of the counter-attack was speed of execution, before dawn brought the Luftwaffe back.

One of the battalions, stationed near Canea, was not to set out until an Australian battalion was brought 30 kilometres by truck to take over guarding the shore against the expected sea landing. Theo Walker, commanding the relieving unit, surveyed their new location with Lindsay Inglis, the commander they were to come under. The third of the New Zealand brigade commanders, along with Hargest and Kippenberger, Inglis was a Timaru lawyer with a reputation as quick-witted, but pugnacious and opinionated. Walker, a Melbourne accountant, was well regarded by his men. He expressed concern at bringing a battalion to unfamiliar territory at night to relieve another battalion going on attack that same night. Inglis, brought straight to Crete from Egypt, replied scornfully that 'a well-trained battalion could carry out such a relief in one hour'.[58]

Soon after, formations of Junkers transports started coming in, circling around Maleme and dropping down on the airfield for little more than a minute at a time while they offloaded men and equipment with engines running. The troops made a dash for shelter under fire as the plane took off in a cloud of dust. At its peak, a plane was landing every few minutes. Not all went smoothly. Coming under fire from New Zealand and Australian batteries using captured Italian field guns, some fully laden planes were shot down before they could land. Others careered along the runway on broken undercarriages with troops jumping from the moving plane. It wasn't, however, a one-sided exchange. Batteries revealing their positions when firing were set upon by dive-bombers and fighters.

When aircraft wreckage piled up on the runway, pilots landed on beaches and in vineyards, while ground crews used captured Bren carriers to drag wrecks to the edge of the field. About twenty planes were shot down, but some 650 mountain troops were landed successfully. By the afternoon, the invaders controlled the airfield perimeter and by evening they occupied villages beyond. Their advance stopped when they got to the defensive line their intelligence had told them wasn't there. They lodged in abandoned houses and dug in behind walls and ditches, two kilometres beyond the airfield they were now defending.

General Freyberg met with his senior commanders at 4 pm. If he thought their plan flawed, he didn't say so, but with his headquarters on the far side of Canea, he had to rely on his field commanders' assessments. Freyberg was concerned at the threat of an enemy flotilla. Consistently mentioned in Ultra reports since he arrived in Crete, it could land fresh troops and equipment on the island, including tanks. That day he was hearing from the Australian sigint (signals intelligence) unit's intelligence officer, Mic Sandford, that they were picking up signal traffic from a naval formation coming their way.[59] Paratroops had put signal lights on landing beaches to guide the flotilla in.

Theo Walker's relieving Australians were ready to move forward by late afternoon, but their trucks and drivers were nowhere to be seen. Eventually they drifted in, one by one, the Cypriot drivers unnerved by Stukas. The convoy set out and was soon spotted by six predatory aircraft. Under attack, it splintered with only two units going ahead. Fighters cruised above straight stretches of the winding road, waiting and watching.

Henry Marshall, the battalion's second-in-command, was in the passenger seat of the lead truck. 'Twice I watched a plane single us out, bank and then turn to machine-gun us along the straight and I told the driver to crank it up,' he says. 'I hoped the battalion was following.'[60] Most of the trucks survived these dashes, only to get confused by the narrow streets of Canea. Vehicles started arriving at the New Zealand positions by sundown, but the last of the trucks were only then beginning the three-hour drive.

A final briefing of the battalion leaders at Hargest's farmhouse headquarters recapped the attack plan, unchanged despite the enemy's reinforcement during the day. Freyberg's staff had arranged with Cairo for the RAF to bomb the airfield at midnight, but that never happened, and units would start moving towards Maleme an hour later. Puttick's chief of staff, sent to the briefing, was disturbed by Jimmy Hargest's exhaustion. 'In my opinion, he was unable to think coherently,' Bill Gentry says. Hargest had no doubts about the plan and seemed unconcerned that troop-carriers had been landing during the day.[61] Jim Burrows, whose battalion was to be relieved by the Australians, has a similar recollection, 'Hargest, while giving orders, was so exhausted that he could not complete one sentence at a time.'[62] The counter-attack, over-planned and delayed too long, was starting to unravel.

By 10.30 pm, Walker was urging the New Zealanders to set out without waiting for all the Australians to arrive. Burrows phoned Inglis and was told they must not leave until they were fully relieved. Like his commander-in-chief, Inglis had his binoculars trained on signs of a new but not unexpected threat. Out at sea to the north, sudden flashes and the thunder of guns had caught their attention. A dull red wavering glow was colouring the distant night sky.

———————

While the operation at Maleme was on a knife's edge, the Germans had made little progress that day in other targeted areas. In Prison

Valley, opposing forces spent much of the second day of the battle bombarding each other. After von der Heydte's men found a gramophone and records in a dugout, dance music had echoed across the valley, blending with the artillery cacophony. In a pause in the firing and the music, a German voice shouted, 'Wait a moment while I change the record.'[63]

In another exchange that day, 'Jim' Weston's platoon had been looking for the reported landing strip in the valley, unaware the patrol had been called off. Weston, a Taranaki farmer, had advanced with his men during the night towards the prison, but by dawn he realised they were on their own in enemy territory. Looking for a place to wait until dark, they found two paratroops with serious injuries from landing on rocky ground. After disarming them, the New Zealanders dressed their wounds. The platoon shared its water with the injured enemy and the paratroops shared their rations. Both were ardent young Nazis who spoke good English and expressed dismay at Rudolf Hess's flight to Scotland eleven days earlier.[64]

The Kiwis moved on, some of them wounded in a later clash and taken prisoner. After the war, they said they'd been treated well because of their treatment of the injured paratroops.[65]

In Retimo, the invasion force went backwards on its second day. The dawn assault on Hill A ordered by Colonel Campbell was driven back initially by the paratroops occupying the summit but, recognising that he had to win this battle in short time or concede high ground, Campbell sent in an increased force three hours later. The task was made easier by German planes bombing their own front line there, killing sixteen just before the Australians attacked. Hill A was retaken, forcing Germans to disperse and hole up in the olive oil factory.

West of the airfield, the Australians cleared groups still scattered around Hill B, capturing their commander, Colonel Sturm, and finding a full set of German operation orders on a dead officer. An Australian officer, Ray Sandover, interrogated Sturm to find out if reinforcements were planned. It proved unpleasant and unproductive. 'He was far older than I was and he couldn't talk English and I could talk German,' says Sandover, who was English-born but went to school in Germany, 'and I had his Operation Order which he didn't like and he'd lost his brush and comb set and he was a very frightened man. And he didn't like me at all!' Sturm didn't seem to like anybody or anything. He told Sandover, 'It was a shit of a plan and a shit of a drop.'[66]

At Heraklion on the second day, the invaders decided to storm the town again on the back of an air attack. Paratroops broke through a gate in the Venetian wall, killing civilians, but got caught up in savage street fighting with Greek soldiers armed with captured guns. Casualties were considerable on both sides. A Greek major and Heraklion's mayor offered to surrender the town, but the timely arrival of English troops put an end to that and, short of ammunition, the Germans later withdrew from the town at night.[67]

Getting back to his own lines there, John Renwick saw dead paratroops hanging on telephone wires in their harnesses. 'The scenes turned my stomach,' the Englishman's diary says, 'to see even enemy with their chests and backs and legs completely blown out or off. Any still alive, by the roadside, wounded and desolate, calling for "*wasser, wasser*".' In some cases, thirst gave way to dysentery from drinking water in irrigation ditches. Renwick went down to the cellar of a ruined tavern where 'in full uniform including jackboots were three Germans hanging from a heavy wooden beam'.[68] Cretans were not going to hand over their island graciously.

———————

Since he arrived early in May, Mic Sandford had been taking Bletchley Park's Ultra reports to Bernard Freyberg, sent via Cairo. As instructed, he would wait in Creforce's quarry headquarters each time until the general had read and destroyed them. Sandford or a runner would also bring messages in lower-grade ciphers intercepted by the Australian sigint unit located above the quarry. During the day on 21 May and into the evening, radio traffic indicated a German flotilla was heading for Crete from mainland Greece.[69] In the afternoon, a runner brought a message that escorted boats had been sighted by an RAF patrol and a British naval force was moving in to intercept it. It was the seaborne invasion that Enigma intercepts had anticipated, and which had been worrying Freyberg.

At about 11.30 pm, a squadron of seven British ships confronted the convoy 30 kilometres out from Canea. Made up of twenty-five requisitioned caïques carrying 2300 mountain troops and two small steamers with guns and ammunition, it had been delayed by a jumpy German admiral. The thinly protected convoy had continued into the night without air cover.[70]

Flares lit up a sky streaked with tracer and pom-pom fire. Destroyers rammed caïques, emptying soldiers and Greek crew into the cold night water. Ships' searchlights swept the dark and an English cruiser opened fire on men in the water clinging to rafts and wreckage.[71] General Freyberg, watching through binoculars above Canea, felt a surge of relief on seeing the burning vessels.

While the seaborne threat appeared to have been averted, the Maleme counter-attack was still in a dilemma, already running late. The Maori battalion had been waiting at the start point for four hours with only two units of the second New Zealand battalion replaced with Australians and standing by. Knowing the sigint unit had picked up the radio traffic of a second convoy, Puttick refused permission for the counter-attack to go ahead with unreplaced units.

Jim Burrows and the Maoris' commander, George Dittmer, decided they should attack with what they had. It was 3.30 am, two and a half hours after the planned starting time. Their men were on edge. For Keith King, a schoolteacher turned platoon leader, the period waiting for the order to advance was one of inertia driven by fear. 'I knew that I would never get moving,' he says. 'I was terrified. Then a voice came along the line, "Fix bayonets, fix bayonets." Click,

click, click, click . . . the most wonderful sound. And suddenly all the fear left and I felt so strong and almost intoxicated.'[72]

The two battalions advanced in parallel along the coastal strip towards German troops concealed in villages forward of the airfield. Moving with the New Zealanders at infantry pace were three English light tanks. The Maoris passed through groves and clusters of cottages, joined from time to time by shadowy figures: armed Cretans. They encountered scattered Germans firing from windows and from behind stone walls. The tanks shot at the flashes from houses and the Maoris followed up with grenade and bayonet.

Moving forward, the other, smaller New Zealand formation was delayed by groups barricaded in farmhouses or dug in among bamboo stands and olive groves. Charlie Upham's diary notes, 'Went on meeting resistance in depth—in ditches, behind hedges, in the top and bottom stories of village buildings, fields and gardens. We had heavy casualties but the Germans had heavier. They were unprepared. Some were without trousers, some had no boots on.'[73]

Under heavy fire from two machine guns firing out of a farm- house window and a shed, Upham dashed to the side of the shed under covering fire and edged along the wall to the shed's open door where a dead German lay with arm outstretched. He pulled the pin, put a grenade in the dead man's palm and jumped back, screaming as it exploded, 'Come forward, come on.' Six Germans came out of the house with hands in the air; eight were dead in the shed.[74]

Where a stream of tracer crossed their path, Upham told his platoon, 'It's chest high. That won't hurt anyone. Crawl underneath it.' They did. And when he saw a large enemy soldier grappling with his batman, Upham hit the German repeatedly and savagely with his pistol butt, like a man possessed. The lieutenant went on to clear a captured Bofors gun near the airfield. While his men's covering fire kept the gunner's head down, he crawled on his stomach near enough to lob a grenade, killing the gunner and putting the gun out of commission.[75] The outcome in due course was a Victoria Cross.

A 32-year-old land valuer from Canterbury, Charlie Upham was obstinate and argumentative with a level gaze. He regarded Germans as arrogant and robotic. 'The Huns wouldn't fight at night because their officers couldn't direct operations and the German soldier was unused to doing much on his own,' he claims. 'With another hour of darkness, we could have reached the far side of the 'drome.'[76]

Not all had Upham's steely resolve, but some surprised themselves. Fred Carr's diary notes, 'Jerry would file out of houses with his hands in the air, but we'd just mow him down. Strangely enough though, I, who wouldn't hurt a fly, was just as bloodthirsty as the others. I seemed to be in a trance for I remember that blood and guts didn't worry me in the least. We had received orders to take no prisoners—not that we wanted to—and we left no wounded. We bayoneted those still living; it was a safety measure anyway.'[77] Carr was a commercial artist back home.

The counter-attack forces were held up getting around scattered groups of defenders and daylight was soon upon them. Shouting could be heard from Maoris inland, and shouts and shooting from the beach where there was less opposition. After a few skirmishes, the shoreline unit reached the edge of the airfield, but under heavy mortar and machine-gun fire with increasing casualties. As the rest of the advance was still two kilometres back, the platoon pulled back to bamboo cover.

Coming into a village, the lead English tank was hit by a Bofors, killing its commander and gunner, wounding the driver and setting the tank on fire. Its driver managed to back out of Bofors range and put out the fire. The second tank turned to avoid a Messerschmitt 109's strafing run by backing into a bamboo clump and broke a bogey wheel. The tank leader, Roy Farran, signalled the third tank not to go on alone, and tank support for the mission ended.[78]

Jimmy Hargest watched the airfield through binoculars from his headquarters, seven kilometres away, and concluded that the transports landing and figures dashing under Australian artillery fire were a German evacuation. They were actually unloading. He messaged Puttick at Division HQ, 'Steady flow of enemy planes landing and taking off. May be trying to take troops off. Investigating.' A dubious headquarters responded, 'No other indication as you suggest, but it is possible.'[79]

Hargest persisted in his fantasy until early afternoon, despite reports contradicting it, eventually advising, 'Officers on ground believe enemy preparing for attack and take serious view. I disagree but of course they have a closer view.' With no contact with his battalions, he relied on garbled reports by stragglers and what he thought he'd seen with his field glasses. Later in the afternoon, Hargest was conceding the counter-attack had failed.[80]

In daylight, and with no tank support, the Maoris had made slow progress despite repeated bayonet charges. George Dittmer was always at the head of the pack, urging them on, at one point yelling at men forced to ground by enemy fire, 'Call yourself bloody soldiers!' and going forward. They got to their feet and the attack went on.[81]

Realising crossing the airfield in broad daylight was suicidal under fire from the hill and the air, Burrows ordered his battalion to divert and support the Maori assault on Hill 107. However, his men were scattered and not all got the message, relayed by runners and Bren carriers. Some misunderstood it and withdrew to the start line, some to higher ground.

After conferring with Burrows, Dittmer went back to the battalions in reserve to ask Leckie and Andrew for support in an afternoon attack. Brigadier Hargest wasn't brought into the discussion. The two colonels thought the manoeuvre unlikely to succeed without more artillery and air support, preferring to hold the ground they had.[82] For the third time, the initiative was not taken to seize the ascendancy at Maleme.

As dusk approached, with the Maori battalion near the foot of Hill 107, the Germans counter-attacked carrying a red swastika flag on poles. A group of Maoris rushed forward from under trees with deep throaty shouts of 'Ah! Ah! Ah!', bayonets drawn and firing from the hip. It was too much for the Germans who turned, abandoned their flag and headed back across a gully. Soon, machine guns and mortars opened up on the Maoris and they moved back quickly.[83]

In the late afternoon, Freyberg had given orders to Puttick for a new attempt to regain the airfield. It would be carried out by three fresh New Zealand battalions and an Australian one. Lindsay Inglis would take command of the operation; Hargest and his units would pull back, reorganise and form a reserve force for Inglis's attack.

On returning from Creforce, Edward Puttick met with Inglis and was told that the Germans in Prison Valley had been advancing towards Galatas and the coast road was blocked by a detachment of mortars and machine guns. Hargest had earlier said his men had been 'severely attacked' and were 'considerably exhausted and certainly not fit to make a further attack', although he'd not gone forward at any stage to see for himself.[84]

Puttick decided the action was too risky without bothering to discuss it further with Hargest. He didn't consider that the paratroops might be equally exhausted or note that one counter-attacking group had made it through to the Tavronitis River. Instead, he phoned Freyberg to recommend withdrawing Hargest's force across the Platanias River, halfway between Maleme and Galatas. Freyberg apparently didn't argue, although he must have been aware of the implications of this move, perhaps concerned at the possibility of four battalions cut off at Maleme and taken prisoner. Perhaps, as with other senior officers, weariness had set in. He knew the Germans had the capacity to bring in fresh troops now that they had control of an airfield, a luxury not available to the island's defenders.

Darkness came, the infiltrating enemy fell back to a line indicated by signal lights and the New Zealanders settled where they were—in a creek bed, an olive grove, wherever—to wait for daylight and the resumption of battle. There had been no thought of a night counter-attack, when the Germans had a dislike of fighting and would have no aircraft support. At 10 pm, the decision was circulated to withdraw all Allied forces east to Platanias.

The enemy was left to use Maleme airfield unhindered, to continue landing reinforcements and supplies. And the loss of Crete to the Germans had become inevitable.

9

FIGHTING WITHDRAWAL

'We withdrew under orders soon after midnight, carrying our wounded on improvised stretchers, down a steep cliff face and then along a difficult clay creek bed to the road,' New Zealander Sandy Thomas recalls. 'Then we marched until nearly dawn. Everyone was tired. All were vaguely resentful, although none of us could put a finger on the reason.'[1]

News that the New Zealanders were withdrawing had spread slowly and was greeted with incredulity in the field. Expecting to take part in another night attack, they had seen so many of the enemy die their confidence was holding. Instead, they were moving back . . . past dead parachutists still swinging gently in their harnesses, past parachute silk and cord tangled on branches of olive trees, past bodies in the grass and along the road. They had turned black in the heat. Cottages were shattered and dead donkeys were covered in debris. Equipment was strewn everywhere as if a party had got out of hand. Blowflies buzzed about and a rancid stench seeped into every nook and cranny. One soldier's diary notes, 'Crossing stream . . . found several Jerries in water, smelt awful, had drink anyway.'[2]

The growl of Junkers 52s bringing in fresh reinforcements grew more distant behind them as they trundled back to new positions.

Roy Farran, the English tank commander, watched the Maoris coming back. 'As they passed, they winked and put up their thumbs,' he remembers. 'Some fifty yards behind the rest came two Maoris carrying a pot of stew across a rifle.' The outcome could have been different if Creforce had been properly equipped and different options taken, the same story as the Greek campaign. 'They had not been beaten and they knew it,' Farran comments, 'but here they were, going back again—back, always back. They had fought like tigers. The Maoris had executed one bayonet charge after another and they all knew they were more than a match for the Germans. The surprise and the shame of the retreat was written on all their faces.'[3]

The reported advances towards Galatas that had determined Edward Puttick's proposal to withdraw had only been patrols, dispersed by evening. The force that had 'blocked the road' was still a couple of kilometres from it by the next morning.

———

There were arrivals and departures. General Ringel, now field commander of the German Crete operation, arrived at Maleme on its third evening with a heavy fighter escort and had to land on the beach as the airfield was still under artillery fire. General Student, out of favour, was refused permission to go to Crete by General Löhr and had to cool his heels in Athens.[4]

The second convoy for Germany's planned amphibious reinforcement didn't get to arrive, however. Delayed by the late arrival of its Italian escort, the flotilla didn't leave Milos until the morning after the first convoy had been scattered by the British. Heading for Heraklion with 4000 mountain troops in its thirty-eight caïques, it was met by a British naval force soon after leaving the port. The British came under intense air attack while the convoy and its escort slipped away under a smokescreen, returning to Milos.[5]

Admiral King elected not to pursue the caïques. The severity of the bomber attacks persuaded him it was a doomed venture with his ships low on anti-aircraft ammunition. Calling for support from another fleet in the area, both fleets soon suffered serious damage. Some ships were sunk before they could get away. The remnants of the naval force limped back to Alexandria. The sea landing of enemy troops had been prevented, but the mountain troops brought back to Milos were simply added to those being brought by air to Maleme.

A third planned convoy, to land tanks and other heavy equipment west of Maleme, was postponed. The paratroops dropped at Kastelli on the first night to protect it had either been captured or killed. A sea landing there was no longer feasible for the time being.

The defenders were only able to bring in what reinforcements could be carried on the smaller warships, fast enough to get in and out before daylight, but General Freyberg had managed to offload one liability. Before the invasion the royal party had moved into the house near Galatas of new prime minister Tsouderos, a Cretan. On the morning the paratroops were dropping, Jasper Blunt of the British Military Mission instructed the New Zealand platoon, guarding the royal party and the government in semi-exile, to escort their charges up to the mountains, out of harm's way. It was a steep climb in the blazing sun with the king wearing the gold braid and ribbons of a Greek general. The platoon commander, Winton Ryan, eventually plucked up the courage to ask him to take his coat off before it attracted attention from the air.

In the rush to leave, King George had left private papers behind that would alert the Germans to his presence in Crete. Blunt and a Kiwi sergeant went back and, finding the house now occupied by paratroops, thought better of trying to get in. Blunt managed to find a working telephone and was told by the navy at Suda that a ship would pick up the party at Ay Roumeli on the south coast in two nights' time.

After five hours trekking, mules were found for the fifty-year-old king and 58-year-old prime minister. The royal party spent the night in a mountain village with a humble meal of cheese, bread and red wine, sleeping on a bare floor. The journey continued with unaccustomed hardship for royals and government officials, sleeping in the clothes they wore in the bitter mountain cold and eating a spit-roasted mountain sheep. The New Zealanders lugged machine guns and ammunition over the towering mountain range. From their high position, the party saw the flares and tracer of the naval battle off Canea.

Getting down to the coast on the third day, boots and feet suffering, they met up with a British legation party that had made the journey separately. They dined that night on tinned food while a signal light was used to try to contact the promised British warship. After an anxious wait, an answering flash eventually came at 2 am. Royal, government and legation parties, along with the New Zealanders, were taken on board two destroyers making their way back to Alexandria after encounters with the Luftwaffe.[6]

Michael Forrester had continued to work with the Greek regiment after the rush of blood on Pink Hill on the first afternoon of the invasion. With an English-speaking officer from the Greek army, he put them through basic infantry training. Cretan villagers listened in, both men and women. The soldiers were given commands with blasts on the Englishman's whistle and he suggested yelling '*Aiera!*' like the Evzones—the Hellenic royal guard—when charging the enemy.

Meanwhile, running short of supplies in Prison Valley, Colonel Heidrich ordered the recovery of Pink Hill so he could launch an attack on Galatas. Kiwi defenders were blasted off the hilltop by mortar and Messerschmitt, allowing the enemy to set up two machine-gun posts facing the town's walls. Word that the counter-attack at Maleme had stalled, along with their own heavy losses, chewed at the men pushed off the hill, specialists armed as infantry. Howard Kippenberger noticed 'an increasing number of cases of slightly wounded men being brought in by three or four friends in no hurry to get back'. To retrieve the initiative, he ordered the storming of two sides of Pink Hill in the late afternoon.

Waiting for the order to charge, Arthur Pope, a driver armed as infantry, watched in amazement as Forrester came out from the trees in shorts and a long yellow army jersey, followed by a mob of Greek soldiers and villagers, including women. Tall, thin-faced and fair-haired, with no tin hat, web belt in place and brass polished and gleaming, the Englishman was 'the very opposite of a soldier hero; as if he had just stepped onto the parade ground. He looked like a Wodehouse character.'[7]

Waving his revolver and blowing on his whistle, Forrester led his horde up the hillside, yelling like Evzones. One villager had a shotgun with a serrated breadknife tied on like a bayonet, but the soldiers were now armed with Tommy guns and rifles. Peter Winter, another reassigned driver, was there. 'They went on regardless of a hail of machine-gun and small arms fire and a shower of mortar bombs,' he says. 'They seemed to go unscathed. A German machine gunner arose from his hiding place firing from the hip. A Greek walked up, bayoneted him and the machine gun seemed to continue firing as it fell to the ground. I could not believe the Greek soldier wasn't hit but he continued on his way.'[8] The composite unit joined with Forrester's Greeks and drove the enemy off Pink Hill. For the second time the pendulum had swung back to where it started.

Replenished with air-freighted troops, the main German force on the coast was moving hard on the heels of the New Zealanders retreating from Maleme. The new line at Platanias was peppered with machine-gun fire and mortar before the defenders had time to settle into position. Continuing to worry about the Germans outflanking to the south and cutting off Hargest's battered and weary battalions, Puttick met with Freyberg and got agreement to bring the men back as a reserve force behind a defensive line pulled back nearly to Galatas. The possibility of being isolated had been eliminated by conceding the ground where they might have been isolated.

After the optimism of the nullified seaborne attack, Freyberg now introduced a pessimistic note into his report to Wavell, 'I have heard from Puttick that the line has gone and we are trying to stabilise. I don't know if they will be able to. I am apprehensive.'[9]

That same day, Freyberg got a message of encouragement from an old friend. 'The whole world watches your splendid battle on which great things turn,' wrote Winston Churchill. Freyberg would later comment tartly, 'However splendid the battle might appear in the eyes of the world, I knew the situation was deteriorating fast in the Maleme sector.'[10]

———

Initially, Freyberg had felt that Kastelli Kissamou, the small port west of Maleme, needed nominal defence. A thousand local men were given rudimentary training by a group of New Zealand officers and NCOs. With fewer rifles than men, the new regiment supplemented its armoury with axes, curved Syrian knives, old shotguns and home-made grenades, but these raw soldiers were also armed with the spirit of defending their own soil and a tradition of mountain toughness. They were the regiment whose move to the Tavronitis bank Freyberg had cancelled.

On the morning of the German invasion, seventy-four paratroops had dropped east of the town and were set upon by the newly recruited soldiers, the local gendarmes and villagers, who shot them in the air, knifed or clubbed them in olive groves, and stalked those who landed by crawling along drains on their stomachs. The New Zealanders attached to the local force had Bren guns for covering fire but soon the Cretans had weapons taken from dead paratroops.

Within an hour, surviving Germans were holed up in a farmhouse, firing through the windows. Geoff Bedding, the senior New

Zealander, advised laying siege and letting hunger force them out, but the Cretans' blood was up. They rushed the building overwhelming its occupants by weight of numbers but with considerable casualties on both sides. The seventeen unwounded survivors of the paratroop force were captured and, for their own protection, taken by Bedding into custody in the town jail.[11]

On 23 May, the fourth day of the invasion, freshly landed German mountain troops began a push towards Kastelli. The following morning, Stukas circled the town, machine-gunning the streets and dive-bombing buildings. One bomb struck the jail, allowing the German prisoners to escape, find weapons and capture Major Bedding and a lieutenant leaving their headquarters to rally the Cretans. Short of ammunition, the garrison and armed villagers launched bayonet charges against mountain troops advancing through rubble-strewn streets, but the locals were mown down by machine-gun fire. Sporadic fighting continued on the outskirts of the town for a couple of days, denying the use of Kastelli's jetty for the postponed landing of German tanks. It wasn't until 27 May that it became possible but, by then, their need for tanks was greatly diminished.[12]

For a few days, occupation of the hills around Galatas swung back and forth between two battling armies without the German invaders gaining a strong enough footing to take the town. By 24 May, the fifth day of the invasion, the air attacks there eased and warplanes turned their attention to nearby Canea. Over more than four hours, waves of ruthless bombing left the town under a cloud of smoke and dust, with flames reaching through. Fighter planes swept up the roads out of Canea, machine-gunning townspeople fleeing into the hills and raking adjacent woods. There were no British or Greek troops in the town, so no military purpose to the attack.

Geoffrey Cox went down to the burning town to see if his *Crete News* printers were safe. An Auckland journalist before the war, he had been asked by Freyberg before the paratroop attack to put out a news-sheet as a morale booster for the troops offloaded at Crete. Working cautiously now along the water's edge, and sheltered by an old Venetian wall, Cox came across a man, naked and dripping wet, arguing with three women. Diving back into the water, the man tossed out fish killed by the bomb blasts.[13]

Cox found the cellar where the printing presses operated, now packed with women and children. His printers were safe among them. A drunken Australian private, probably a deserter, wandered in and out 'with the cheerfulness of the brave as well as the drunk'. He'd go out after each air attack to see what he could find, coming back with bread, wine and tins of army rations which he shared with the sheltering refugees. 'All this the people needed,' Cox comments, 'but even more they needed the cheerful indifference to danger which he spread around.'[14]

After the distraction of the heavy air attack on Canea, the arm-wrestle got back to business in the morning. New Zealanders on the north side of Galatas were bombed and strafed from the air, with mortar bombardment backing it up. Counter-attacks failed to recover ground and the defenders began dropping back. 'By this time, the troops were tired beyond feeling anything,' says Jim Carstairs, 'and nerves were so taut they were at breaking point. I was frightened to get into a slit trench lest I could not bring myself to get out again, so I moved all the time from tree to tree.'[15]

Kippenberger brought reserve units in from the other side of the town and temporarily restored the line, but the barrage continued. Runners came twice from Wheat Hill for permission to withdraw and were refused. The Kiwi commander went forward to observe the struggle and was long haunted by what he saw instead: 'In a hollow, nearly covered by undergrowth, I came upon a party of women and children huddled together like little birds. They looked at me silently, with black terrified eyes.'[16]

Facing Galatas like Pink Hill, Wheat Hill was overrun during the afternoon and groups of defenders fell back, 'filthy with dirt, sweat and blood, shaken nearly out of their senses by continual bombardment'.[17] A trickle of stragglers began and the RAP (Regimental Aid Post) filled with wounded men, trucks taking them down to the Advanced Dressing Station 'like loads of butchers' meat'.[18]

Asked to send more reserves to the defence of Galatas, Lindsay Inglis was able to offer only small scratch formations from the composite units: labourers, signalmen and a brass band armed as infantry. When two platoons arrived, a captain in one asked a lieutenant with the other to position the troops as he was only a signals officer. 'What the hell do you think I am?' was the reply. 'I'm only a bloody bandmaster.'[19]

Germans moved around the edges putting Galatas under siege. With the line wavering, John Gray, commanding New Zealanders in the thick of the onslaught, went forward shouting, 'No surrender, no surrender!' The men rallied for a short time before the trickle of stragglers turned into a stream. 'Hundreds of New Zealanders were running hell for leather through the grapevines,' a driver in the composite infantry wrote home, 'so I took off too and never ran so hard in my life before.' Soon he ran out of wind, bullets flying overhead and muttering to himself, 'To hell with them.'[20]

Kippenberger moved among the panicked mob, shouting 'Stand for New Zealand!' and 'Stand every man who is a soldier!' with such calm resolve that it stopped the defence disintegrating altogether. With two sergeants, he rallied the men back across the next valley to form a new line along the ridge.[21] When that was achieved, one of the sergeants, George Andrews, came up to 'Kip' and said quietly, 'I can't do any more, sir.' Asked why, he pulled up his shirt to reveal a neat bullet hole in his abdomen.[22] Twice wounded, the Waikato farmer survived the war and lived to the ripe old age of ninety-one.

On the south side of Galatas, the tug-of-war over Pink Hill had continued all day but, as twilight slid in, the fighting drivers were finally overrun. At the same time, the enemy was climbing the slopes and pouring into the town. It had taken six days, but Heidrich had finally reached a position where he could launch an attack on the smouldering ruin of Canea. Suda Bay waited beyond it.

Howard Kippenberger knew he had to reclaim Galatas or the road to Canea would be wide open. In the early evening, he assembled a force along a stone wall facing up towards the town. Inglis had sent him two more companies and two light tanks. While Kippenberger organised his soldiers, the English tanks drove into Galatas on an armed recce of the town.

As the men gathered for the attack, Sandy Thomas thought his platoon seemed to have grown. Peering into the gloom he made out several unfamiliar faces. His sergeant said to him, 'We've got some reinforcements, sir. These chaps are from the Eighteenth and Twentieth and want a crack at the Hun.' A lance-corporal chipped in, 'Is it okay, sir? They got my brother today.'[23] It was okay. Trained infantrymen weren't going to be turned back.

Firing on both sides, the tanks reached the other end of the village, turned round and came back still firing. An anti-tank rifle pierced the second tank's turret, wounding its commander and gunner, but both tanks made it back. 'The place is stiff with Jerries,' reported Roy Farran, their leader.[24] He agreed to spearhead the infantry attack but needed a replacement crew for the second tank. Kip called for volunteers familiar with Vickers guns and selected Charlie Lewis, a machine gunner, and Ernie Ferry, a driver. The two volunteers were taken down the road for a quickfire course of instruction by Farran, finishing with, 'Of course, you know you seldom come out of one of these things alive.'

'Well, that suited me all right,' Ferry writes. 'It seemed a pretty hopeless fight with all these planes knocking about and a couple of my bosom friends had been knocked.'[25]

Gathering in the dark behind the two tanks, everyone looked tense and grim. 'I wondered if they were feeling as afraid as I was,' says Thomas, 'whether their throats were as dry, their stomachs feeling now frozen, now fluid. I hoped I appeared as cool as they did.'[26]

Kippenberger gave the signal to fix bayonets and shouted at Farran to 'get cracking'. The infantry followed. For once it would be men against men on the ground, with no dive-bombers to contend with. First they walked, then they broke into a run up the hill towards Galatas. The Maoris did a haka as the tanks disappeared into the village in a cloud of dust and the running force took it up, blood-curdling yelling and battle-cries swelling to a crescendo ringing across the olive groves. 'Heaven knows how many colleges and schools were represented by their hakas but the effect was terrific,' says Thomas. 'One felt one's blood rising swiftly above fear and uncertainty until only inexplicable exhilaration remained.'[27]

Farran's tank, first to the town square, was hit in the turret, wounding him. Another shot broke his tank's track, immobilising it, and wounded the driver. Farran dragged himself to the shelter of a stone wall while the crew crawled out of the driver's hatch. New Zealanders came up the main street in a yelling rush, charging at Germans with bayonets and grenades. Slumped by the wall, Farran shouted, 'Come on, New Zealand! Clean 'em out, New Zealand!'[28] Attackers lunged into darkened streets and alleys as stretcher-bearers put Farran on a door and took him back to safety.

The Germans had thought their capture of the town was so emphatic that the night's fighting was over. Unprepared for a counter-attack, they were still forming up when the New Zealanders swarmed into the square, the ferocity of the attack at bayonet point catching the Germans off balance. Many in houses opposite the square fled, one staying to throw grenades from a rooftop. The second tank, with its volunteer crew, stalled in a gutter, retreated then turned back into the village as the infantrymen surged forward.

Dave Seaton, a 33-year-old tractor driver from Oamaru, strode forward, firing his Bren gun from the hip in steady bursts, while others moved around the side of the square knocking out machine-gun nests with grenades.[29] Seaton was eventually brought down,

FIGHTING WITHDRAWAL   245

but the attack surged on with bayonets, rifle butts and bare hands
in frenzied hand-to-hand fighting around darkened houses. Some
soldiers jumped stone walls and ran through back yards to get at
gun nests. Some of the enemy, shooting from rooftops, were picked
off and tumbled down to the cobblestones below. Men stepped over
groaning forms. If one of the forms rose, it was knocked back down
with a bayonet thrust.

'It was pretty intense,' says Ted Martin-Smith. 'I'm sure that a
lot of our fellas were killed by their own side. It was so mixed up.
Anybody in front of you, you knocked down. It's not as if you had a
target—you were just going through the whole place and anybody
in front of you was regarded as the enemy.'[30]

Cretan women ducked between exploding shells to bring
water to the wounded. Girls brought casualties indoors, dressing
them with torn sheets from their dowries. Asked later why they'd
destroyed these important belongings, one replied, 'What's the
point in having a dowry if we become slaves?'[31]

Gunfire was coming from all directions, frenzied and inaccurate. The Kiwis' yelling, incomprehensible to many of the Germans,
added to the confusion and many of the enemy started to run. They
climbed out of windows and through doors, falling over each other
to escape the charging melee.

Galatas was regained by midnight, silent apart from the
muffled sounds of the wounded. Stunned by their success, the New
Zealanders were unsure what to do next. A Cretan girl, about twelve
years old, crept out from broken masonry and covered the bodies
in gutters with rugs. Whenever she heard a human response, she
returned with sweet goats' milk.[32]

Kippenberger put Major Thomason in charge and walked down
the road to report to Inglis, 'Exposed to attack from both sides and
with no fresh troops, Galatas can't be held.'[33] Thomason deployed
troops around the outskirts of the town but no fresh attack came.
Orders arrived to evacuate Galatas and move back as Puttick had

ordered another general retreat. The new line would link with the Australian positions at the entrance of Prison Valley.

The wounded were carried out on doors, on stretchers made of battle jackets slung on two rifles and on the backs of comrades. A high price in casualties had been paid to retake a town they couldn't hold, but the New Zealanders had stabilised themselves and Kippenberger's resolve had brought fresh courage to men at breaking point.

Martin-Smith and a mate had been sent out of town by Thomason to watch for the enemy coming back from that direction. After several hours, they returned to find the Germans had moved into the vacated town from another direction. 'We walked through the buggers,' says Martin-Smith, a stock agent from the Bay of Plenty. 'How, I don't know, but my back felt very wide. We still had our rifles, slung on our shoulders. It was dark, of course, and we were coming from where they knew their own people were. You could get away with anything if you looked like you should have been there. Nobody challenged you. We walked right through them.'[34]

In the other two theatres, Retimo and Heraklion, the invasion had receded to a stalemate of sorts, but it was a stalemate in which the Germans had suffered high casualties and gained nothing. They were doing no more than hanging on to a precarious position.

In Retimo, Colonel Campbell ordered an attack with two Bren carriers and artillery support on the thick-walled olive oil factory sheltering about 150 Germans. The carriers were destroyed by anti-tank guns and shellfire had little impact on the building's walls. In an infantry charge, Greek casualties lost them momentum. Red and white flares were fired from within the factory when six Junkers appeared but the canisters of supplies were dropped in no-man's land outside the factory.

Campbell ordered another attack in the late afternoon, two hundred Greeks from the east side of the factory, forty Australians from the west, with artillery and mortar support. The Australians rushed forward with losses to within 40 metres of the factory wall and waited for the Greeks. There was much shouting and after thirty minutes it was clear they weren't going to attack. Ian Campbell called out to his men to withdraw after dark and decided to starve the enemy out rather than try to take the factory. Ordered to make sure no one left the factory, the Greeks crept forward in the dark and brought back the parachuted supplies.[35]

On the other side of the airfield, Greek police cadets had isolated the enemy in St George's Church near Perivolia. Guns on Hill B knocked out the church's windows, one by one, then brought the steeple crashing down in a cloud of dust.[36] The next day, further Australian shelling forced the Germans to abandon the church and set up in the village.

Vacated areas were littered with the debris of battle, the stench overpowering. Calamity and suffering prevailed. Returning to his unit at night, Australian bombardier Lew Lind stumbled on a heap of Germans, their bodies swollen and bursting from their uniforms after a few days in the sun. Already finding it difficult to avoid stepping on spongy flesh, the stench made Lind vomit.[37] Elsewhere, a group of Australians clearing vacated ground came across a dingy house where a blind lady sat whimpering, too old and helpless to move when her neighbours fled. A goat nearby needed milking. The soldiers put food and water beside the lady, milked the goat and tethered it within her reach.[38]

After the Australians overran an enemy dressing station near the olive oil factory, the medico Alan Carter arranged a three-hour truce for both sides to collect their wounded. The German RAP was moved into the Australian station in a two-room shack and the wounded from both sides were taken there in trucks draped with the Red Cross. One truck was attacked by a German bomber, killing wounded men and a German doctor.

The arrangement remained in place nonetheless, with those able to be moved taken, along with German orderlies, to an Australian field hospital in a village further inland. Staff shared rations and German-supplied drugs and equipment. Carter remained at the dressing station with two German doctors until the end of the battle.[39]

By 26 May, Campbell's two immobilised Matilda tanks had been recovered and hastily patched up to be sent with volunteer crews as support for a dawn infantry attack on Perivolia. They fared no better this time—one tank hit and set on fire, the other disabled by a mortar. Commanding the attack, Major Ralph Honner decided to pull back but was then told a platoon had broken through the German line. Honner felt obliged to support the platoon's success or extricate its survivors, despite the inevitable casualties.

A unit was ordered forward to set up a Bren gun on a stone well close to the German line. The section leader and then the Bren gunner fell. The gun was picked up by a soldier who was shot and the next man picked it up. This pattern continued until the last man of the nine-man crew got to the well with the gun and was killed.

The missing platoon hadn't, in fact, entered Perivolia but was found further down the line, lying 'doggo' under German fire.[40] While Ralph Honner barely contained his rage, the regimental medico, Jim Ryan, went forward with a Red Cross flag and stretcher-bearers to collect the wounded, unsure if the enemy would allow them that close to its line. They found only one man still alive. While collecting him, Ryan looked into the German line 'bristling with machine guns' and was waved away.[41]

In Heraklion, the invaders were in a more desperate position but little advantage was being taken of it. By the third day, less than six hundred of the 3000 paratroops who had been dropped were still capable of fighting. Brian Chappel was content to deny the enemy the airfield and the port, with no serious attempt to chase the Germans out of the town until ordered by Freyberg to do so. 'We were wondering why we didn't attack the remaining Huns and wipe them out,' Norm Johnstone wrote home.[42]

An Australian unit at Heraklion found a codebook for ground-to-air signals in an air-dropped canister, along with a Very pistol, cartridges and signal strips. To see if they could induce the enemy to drop supplies, Ivan Dougherty told one of his officers to fire the pistol when the next formation of planes approached. Brian Rolfe did as ordered and the planes turned in their direction. He fired the pistol again and canisters rained down on the signal strips they had laid out. Inside were ammunition, medical supplies, a wireless and a set of chairs and tables. A motorcycle and sidecar also floated down.[43]

It was a one-off. The Germans on the ground must have spotted the ruse and advised their base by radio. The next day Rolfe fired the signal gun again and they were machine-gunned for their trouble.[44]

Crete's south coast offered the only relief from the predatory Luftwaffe to allow the Allies some chance of landing supplies and reinforcements safely. The rugged rocky mountain spine fell steeply down to the Mediterranean on that side, but it opened around Timbaki, across from Heraklion. Without bothering to tell General Freyberg, Middle East Command had sent a Scottish battalion and three new Matilda tanks to Timbaki, landing the night before the paratroop invasion.

The remnants of the German force around Heraklion had grouped around the road from Timbaki, so tanks and troops had to push their way through them. One of the tanks broke down and never left Timbaki, but the other two arrived at Heraklion on the fourth day of the invasion, the Argyll and Sutherland Highlanders following in batches a couple of days later. The tanks were taken down the coast by lighter to Suda Bay, too late to affect the outcome of the battle there.

The Highlanders were positioned alongside Australians holding the enemy away from Heraklion airfield. In their first action, against three hundred paratroops east of the town, the newcomers fared badly, mistaking Australians alongside them for Germans and directing friendly fire at them. An Australian sergeant had to creep forward under fire and explain to the Scotsmen 'who was who', while an English unit counter-attacked and restored the position.[45]

The RAF reappeared for the first time for a few days with much the same effectiveness as the tanks. A small formation of Blenheims and Marylands bombed and strafed Maleme airfield, but that had little impact on enemy operations there, no more than nuisance value. Then two flights of six Hurricanes arrived, so unexpected by the Heraklion defenders that anti-aircraft gunners shot two of their compatriots down. Three landed at Heraklion but, with insufficient fuel and ammunition there, returned to Egypt the next day.[46]

The stalemate continued at Retimo and Heraklion, with tanks constantly breaking down and occasional ineffective sorties by RAF planes. The remnants of the German invasion force were able to do little more than stay in the fight, but there were ominous signs of a shift in this balance at this eastern end of the battle zone. The Germans were air-dropping reinforcements to the west of Heraklion and preparing for a major attack on the isolated garrison. However, it was in the flow-on from Maleme that the battle for Crete would be finally and irrevocably determined.

————

As near to exhaustion as anyone else in Crete, Bernard Freyberg had already advised Wavell that the Galatas line had gone, Puttick was falling back to a new line outside Cánea and General Skoulas, the Greek commander, had warned that his units were disintegrating. On 26 May, the seventh day of the battle for Crete, he signalled Wavell, 'I regret to have to inform you that in my opinion the limit of endurance has been reached by troops under my command here at Suda Bay. No matter what decision is taken by the Commanders-in-Chief, from a military point of view the position is hopeless.'[47] He wanted an orderly naval evacuation after holding Suda port for another twenty-four hours to land supplies and a small commando force.

Wavell, under considerable strain trying to hold Tobruk against Rommel, suppress a revolt in Iraq and deal with the Vichy French in Syria, was now trapped between Churchill's insistence on holding Crete and Freyberg's desire to abandon it. Churchill had sent a message to hurl reinforcements at Crete regardless of cost . . . but there was little to hurl and little would escape the claws of the Luftwaffe.

Wavell and Air-Marshal Tedder, who had replaced Longmore, met with Cunningham at Alexandria and advocated instructing Freyberg to surrender. A sea evacuation could well finish off the Mediterranean Fleet. General Blamey and New Zealand prime minister Fraser were there, but felt unable to disagree. The admiral wasn't so constrained. 'It's the duty of the Navy to take the Army overseas to battle,' Andrew Cunningham said, 'and its duty to bring them back.'[48]

The battle had advanced to the vicinity of Canea and Suda, with Hargest's weary brigade in need of relief. Freyberg put the Royal Marines general, Eric Weston, in command of the battle front line now that it had moved into his area of responsibility, but it proved unproductive. Unnerved by the constant aerial bombardment, Weston was argumentative when he could be found, although much of the time he couldn't. He'd had limited involvement with the ground battle to that point, and perhaps continued to resent not being given command of Creforce.

Freyberg put Lindsay Inglis in charge of Force Reserve, made up of the relatively fresh British units around Canea: the Welsh, the Rangers and the Northumberland Hussars. Inglis met with Weston, his new field commander, to be briefed. 'He was hurried and worried and very short with me, but I gathered that he intended to use these troops himself and not through me,' he says. 'In any event neither then, nor at any other time, did he give them any orders through me.'[49]

Men from Suda Bay base units were being told by their officers to make their way over the mountains to the fishing village of

Sphakia, adding to the general confusion. Some of the stragglers from combat units moved along the road with them. There had been no announcement that Creforce would be evacuated through Sphakia, or even a decision to do so, but word had drifted about that this would happen. Non-combatants knew they wouldn't be put at the front of the queue for embarkation. They would have to put themselves there.

Concerned the enemy was moving around their flanks and that their respective units couldn't remain cohesive for long, Vasey and Hargest proposed to Puttick that they withdraw to a more secure line that night, rather than risk having to do it in daylight the next day. Puttick put that plan to Weston, with Inglis's Force Reserve to cover the withdrawal, and the general said he would discuss it with Freyberg.

Eric Weston had a problem. That morning, he'd ordered Force Reserve forward to relieve Hargest's New Zealanders, using Vasey's Australians as protection for their flank. If Vasey's men pulled back, Force Reserve would be vulnerable from its side. Weston was unable to find his commander, who had gone down to the quay at Suda to make sure two warships made it from Alexandria. By this time, ships had to be fast enough to get into Suda Bay and away before daylight brought back the marauding German planes. A minelayer and a destroyer arrived that night with a cargo of ammunition and 750 men of an English commando unit under Colonel Robert Laycock. A 200-strong advance party of the commandos, led by Felix Colvin, had disembarked two days earlier.

After a wait of forty-five minutes, anchored out from the quay, a lighter came out loaded with walking wounded. Laycock and his intelligence officer, Evelyn Waugh, already well regarded as a novelist, were with their ship's captain when a dishevelled naval officer burst into the room in shorts and greatcoat. 'I've got my orders to pull out,' he spluttered, 'and by God I'm pulling out. I've only got what I stand up in. The whole place is a shambles.'[50] Bob Laycock had been told by Winston Churchill's son, Randolph, that everything in Crete was under control and the battle was as good as won. He couldn't reconcile that rosy report with what he was seeing.[51]

On the deck, hobbling men from the lighter pushed their agitated way through the waiting commandos. There were angry shouts to move gear off the deck. The lighter's skipper called out to 'look slippy', he was casting off in fifteen minutes as he had another load of wounded men and a Greek general to bring out. Laycock's commandos, known as Layforce, were told to ditch their wireless sets and heavy equipment, and take with them only weapons, ammunition and food. This pandemonium was not what they had been led to expect.[52]

The quay, where they met Colvin, was cratered and littered with loose stones. Freyberg tracked down Laycock and told him there was no hope of holding Crete. The commandos were to be part of a rearguard and take up their positions in the morning covering a withdrawal to Sphakia. A disorientated Layforce marched along the coast with what they had salvaged to join Colonel Colvin's advance party.

Having heard nothing from Weston, Puttick signalled Creforce HQ to be told General Freyberg hadn't returned and that General Weston would issue orders. By then, it was well into the night and time was getting critical. An exasperated Puttick proposed, with Vasey's agreement, to order an Anzac withdrawal on his own authority, starting at 11.30 pm. They would move back to a long sunken track running through thick olive groves. Called 42nd Street by the British after the 42nd Field Regiment of the Royal Engineers who had been stationed there the previous year, it was the Tsikilaria road to Cretans.

Edward Puttick sent his intelligence officer to Weston's HQ, wherever it had moved, to advise the steps he was taking. After some searching, the new headquarters was located in a peasant cottage near 42nd Street. Weston had returned after a chance meeting with

Freyberg, who was adamant troops were to hold their line until the following evening. He wanted supplies and commandos landed at Suda quay without interference and the wounded evacuated. Almost incoherent with fatigue, Weston had fallen asleep on the cottage's earthen floor before he issued any further orders. Soon after that, Puttick's messenger arrived, his message handed to a staff officer who said the general was not available.

Weston slept on while Force Reserve moved forward and, unknown to them, their Australian cover on their flank moved out. At about one in the morning, Weston was woken by the arrival of Laycock and Waugh. He was told then by his staff officer that the Australians were moving back as well as the New Zealanders and, realising that Force Reserve would be unprotected, Weston sent an order to the force's senior commander, Colonel Duncan of the Welsh regiment, to withdraw immediately. Laycock apparently didn't get much out of the meeting with Weston, who Waugh's batman describes as 'flapping about on his own'.[53]

Puttick arrived an hour later. Asked why an order had not been given earlier, Weston petulantly responded, 'There's no point sending orders when the division commander has made it very clear that the New Zealand Division is retiring whatever happens.'[54] The division commander in this instance was General Puttick. He replied that orders were necessary to know where to retire to and how to coordinate with other units.

Force Reserve had meanwhile moved forward under cover of darkness. Its troops were in position by midnight, believing Australians covered their left flank, but just before dawn a patrol found the Australians gone. Before they could digest this unexpected turn of events, a fierce ground attack was launched by the enemy from where the cover had been thought to be. Two runners had been sent through Canea by Weston with an order recalling the British force but neither got through. Unable to make radio contact with Weston, Duncan sent runners, but they couldn't find a way past the Germans. The enemy had moved through the undefended flank and behind the advancing units of Force Reserve, by then threatening to cut them off completely.

By midday, with no word from his commander, Colonel Duncan decided they had to withdraw, with or without orders. Nearly surrounded and fighting grimly, it was too late for some of the British force. The men fell back, many cut to ribbons under fire from mortars and captured Bren carriers; others were taken prisoner, but some four hundred of the force of 1500 managed to work their way through the bursts of machine gun. Reaching a clearing among thickets of olive trees, they became aware of a line of riflemen waiting silently ahead of them. They moved forward cautiously, thinking their determined lunge for safety had come to nothing, until they were close enough to see these men had flat helmets. It was the Anzac defence line at 42nd Street.

Soon after his troops began withdrawing, a runner had come to George Vasey with a belated order from General Freyberg to hold their previous line 'at all costs'. The Australian decided that was no longer feasible. 'The Greeks dispersed on my left flank and the New Zealanders withdrawn on my right,' he explains, 'would only result in Seventh and Eighth Battalions being captured.'[55] He and Jimmy Hargest worked together organising the withdrawal in the leadership vacuum.

Hargest was a man reborn, relishing working with the confident and decisive Vasey. Freyberg's chief of staff, Keith Stewart, noted the changed demeanour. 'At Maleme, Hargest had seemed jaded beyond all recovery, his lack of grip or urgency on the first and second days had pointed the way to disaster,' he writes. 'Now he imposed his authority on the rearguard.'[56]

The Aussies and Kiwis were at less than half their normal strength, the men exhausted, hungry and dehydrated. They fell back to 42nd Street through an area 'filled with the stench of thousands of dead paratroops, burnt out gliders everywhere'.[57] Arriving at the sunken road, they put down their gear, ate what hard rations they could find and lay down. Units had become mixed during the night march but managed to get themselves into platoon areas.

There was water nearby, suitable for drinking and a morning wash of both body and clothes. For many, it was their first wash for seven or eight days. Ammunition was distributed and men swapped experiences for the first time since the battle began, comfortable in the belief they weren't the front line. They thought they had the British troops of Force Reserve as their rearguard but those men had been sent further forward and were fighting for survival elsewhere. Forty-second Street was now the front line.

The morning 'hate' was relatively light. Greeks holding the village of Alikianou at the end of Prison Valley had finally been driven out by German mountain troops who were then attacked by mistake by their own bombers.[58] About the same time, dive-bombers blew up an ammunition dump unaware the area was occupied by Germans, reportedly killing at least seventy.[59] The pilots had temporarily lost their swagger.

Two of the New Zealand battalion commanders, George Dittmer and John Allen, placed men along the bank on the far side of the road. Both sides were thick with olive trees, so that the road was the best opportunity to get a clear view of troops approaching. Those resting on the near side were pulled across behind this line. If the enemy approached, the line would fire across the open space, then charge with bayonets, a bold plan when morale was fading with the constant retreat . . . but Dittmer and Allen knew their men.

While the Kiwis were being moved into position, a runner came from Australian battalion commander Theo Walker asking the New Zealand intention if the enemy broke through. Told of the decision to counter-attack, the runner soon returned with the message, 'Wait a little and the Australians will be pleased to join you.'[60]

While the British units were trying to extricate themselves around Canea, some four hundred German troops moved around them towards 42nd Street, unaware of the defensive line forming along it. An Australian patrol from the line, led by Sergeant 'Blue' Reiter, probed the olive grove. Reiter headed towards an abandoned British supply dump. 'After being bombed all round Greece, we were really browned off with the Germans,' says Reiter, 'and wanted to close in on them. Well, we got to this food dump and one of the boys spotted Germans at the other end doing the same thing.'[61]

The Australians opened fire and the handful of Germans went to ground, fired back and pulled out quickly. A second patrol, also from Walker's battalion, heard the brief exchange of gunfire somewhere in the vicinity and urgent German voices nearby. Mountain troops were spotted through the trees, bustling over a rise 50 metres away. The Aussies opened fire and soon, in the rattle of small arms, leaves were being shot off olive trees in front of them.

Reg Saunders was in this patrol. His battalion had seen limited action apart from replacing New Zealanders who took part in the failed counter-attack at Maleme. When a German soldier stood up a short distance in front of him, it became a defining moment for the young man from rural Victoria. 'He was my first sure kill,' Saunders recalls. 'I can remember feeling for a moment that it was just like shooting a kangaroo. Just as remote.'[62]

For those back on 42nd Street, it was the first indication there was no rearguard. 'Yarns were being swapped,' says Keith Cockerill, a Kiwi lieutenant, 'washing was being done and bodies were being washed when, without any warning whatsoever, the enemy opened up with Spandau fire from about three hundred yards.'[63]

When the first German soldiers appeared at the edge of the olive grove and saw a large contingent waiting, they stopped abruptly and hastily dropped back. It set off Hemara Aupouri, a 36-year-old from Rotorua in the Maori battalion. Clutching a Bren gun magazine like a greenstone *patu* (club), he began a haka, shouting a challenge in Maori, stamping and gesticulating, poking out his tongue and rolling his eyes. Soon seventy kinsmen were yelling, '*Ka mate! Ka mate! Ka ora! Ka ora!*' ('I may die! I may live!').[64]

A call to fix bayonets went out along the line. Among the Australians was Harold Passey, Colonel Walker's batman. 'When this order went out,' he recalls, 'it seemed to lift the tension that had been hanging over us for the past few days. The time had come when we were going to show Jerry a few tricks.'[65] The line resounded with the click, click, click of bayonets fixing on rifles.

Seventeen-year-old Rangitepuru Waretini, known as Sonny Sewell, was standing by as Rangi Royal signalled the Maori charge. 'He blew his whistle and no bugger moved,' the runner says. 'It wasn't until he blew it again and he jumped up himself and Sam O'Brien from Te Puke got up with him and started to *mea* (gesture) with his rifle. You wouldn't think he was a soldier at all. He had two left feet, but something must have stirred inside him.'[66]

Waving a bamboo pole like a *taiaha* (staff) in one hand and a revolver in the other, Captain Royal led his company into the fray, yelling, 'If anyone falls, leave him. There's people behind to pick him up.'[67] Two more Maori companies merged with Royal's men, fanning out to confront the Germans. Further along the line, Australians joined in, advancing with bayonets drawn to link with their two patrols. Other New Zealand units and some stray Greeks were spurred into swelling the moving line.

The haka had set the tone. 'When Jerry saw us coming and someone gave himself a yell to give himself more courage, everyone took it up. Before you could say it, we were bolting along screeching at the top of our voices,' says Reg Saunders. 'It was crazy, crazy, the most thrilling few moments of my life. It wasn't like killing kangaroos any more.'[68]

The front of the enemy force was closing in on the sunken road in scattered groups, unsure what they were dealing with or how to deal with it. Machine-gun fire opened up on the yelling, surging mob, but it kept streaming like a dam had burst, spilling across the sunken road. There was no hesitation and no supporting fire except Bren and Thompson guns firing from the hip.

'We walked all the way,' says Fred Baker, 'jumped into his first position and bayonetted or Tommy-gunned them, then walked on to his next line.'[69] Germans fell back in disorder. Some stood their ground as they were overrun by the horde sweeping around them, a screeching mob in a crazed charge with bayonets, firing as they ran.

'We used our knees and our rifle butts and our blades,' says Saunders. 'For a while we stopped being ordinary blokes and became blood-lusted creatures. We had never been at close grips with the enemy before.'[70] It was the first time many of these men, always under air and land bombardment, had been in hand-to-hand combat. They were unbeaten men in a beaten army.

Johnny Peck, a nineteen-year-old Australian, recounts, 'They didn't just turn and run, they fought back. I got a bayonet through the arm. Hand-to-hand combat was very frightening. You knew without a shadow of doubt that if you made a fraction of a mistake, then you're dead. The German knew it and I knew it.' Peck felt no pain in the heat of battle, adrenaline masking the loss of blood.

As the shouting lines advanced, forward enemy troops were unnerved but had little time to flee. Some chose to keep firing and face the onslaught with shorter bayonets, some turned and risked being shot in the back. Where Germans dropped their automatic weapons and ran, the weapons were seized and turned on the fleeing enemy.

'They ran and we kept running after them,' continues Peck. 'We were absolutely exhausted; we'd gone from a gallop right down to a crawl. If we'd suddenly struck a fresh batch of troops, we would have been dead.'[71]

By then, the Germans had been driven back more than a kilometre, but the olive grove was thinner there, exposing the advancing troops to air attack. The further they advanced the less cover they would have and they'd be at greater risk of being cut off. Dittmer knew that military action couldn't be sustained by uncontrolled aggression alone and sent his second-in-command, George Bertrand, out to recall the Maori battalion. Bertrand got to the forward men and told them, 'The old man is going fair dinkum crook. Come back now.'[72]

Other unit commanders drew the same conclusion as Dittmer and called their men back as well. The attackers walked back, exhilarated and grumbling, collecting food, cigarettes and equipment left by the enemy.

In the afternoon, the Germans fired mortar and machine guns in the direction of the defensive positions but made no attempt to regain the ground they had been driven back from. They set up a roadblock east of Canea but only a remnant of Force Reserve was trapped behind it by then. Men and mules were seen crossing ridges to the south, too distant to tell if they were Germans setting out to cut off the road south or refugees.

After the 42nd Street action, Doug Chitty, a sapper who worked with an Auckland engineering company before the war, came to a clearing where a German medico was attending to two or three wounded men. 'He greeted me in a quite friendly fashion,' says Chitty, 'and offered me a glass of wine, which I readily accepted. One of the Germans had been bayonetted in the thigh and his leg had swollen to elephant size. They didn't seem to worry about me, even though I had a rifle. I tried to make conversation with the medic fellow, then he gave me some ointment to put on some open wounds I had on my legs and with that I continued back to 42nd Street.'[73]

War is brutalising . . . and yet . . .

Word was spreading that the entire British force would be moved to the south coast and—hopefully—evacuated by the Royal Navy. A disorganised, panicked rabble was already heading that way; although the withdrawal hadn't yet been formally authorised.

10

DESPERATION

Late on 26 May, the night before the bayonet charge on 42nd Street, Cairo suggested the 20,000-strong Suda–Maleme defence should retire to Retimo and hold eastern Crete as an alternative to General Freyberg's proposed evacuation. It showed how little Middle East Command understood the reality in Crete. A frustrated Freyberg signalled Wavell that Retimo was without food and nearly out of ammunition. The enemy had set up roadblocks between Suda and Retimo and, without gun tractors, artillery had been left behind in the retreat from Maleme.[1]

The next morning, Wavell advised Winston Churchill that withdrawal south was the only chance of survival for the men around Suda, then waited all day for authorisation from London to evacuate forces from Crete. By the late afternoon, his patience ran out. On his own initiative, General Wavell authorised a withdrawal to the south coast and informed London. Churchill's assurance to the two dominion governments at the outset, that all their fit troops would be evacuated if that became necessary, was no longer discussed. Already, thousands had been left behind on the Greek mainland.

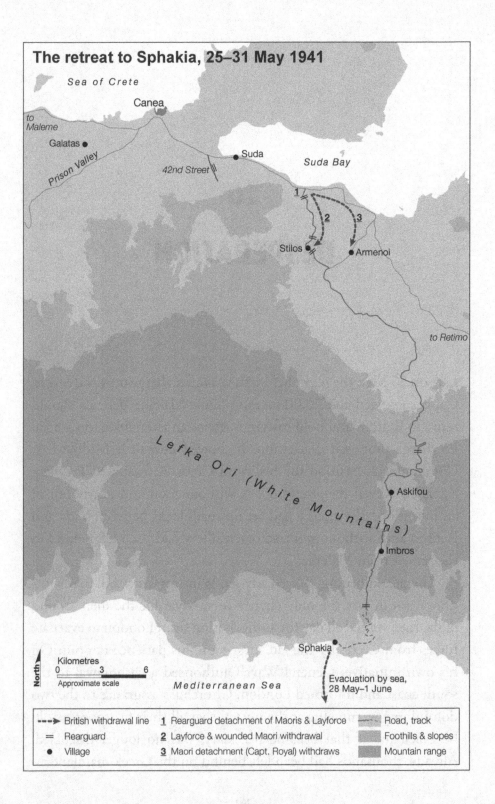

The retreat to Sphakia, 25–31 May 1941

Sea of Crete

Canea

to Maleme

Galatas ●

Prison Valley

42nd Street

Suda

Suda Bay

1

2

3

Stilos ●

● Armenoi

to Retimo

Lefka Ori (White Mountains)

● Askifou

● Imbros

Sphakia ●

Evacuation by sea,
28 May–1 June

Kilometres

0   3   6

Approximate scale

North

Mediterranean Sea

--▶ British withdrawal line	**1** Rearguard detachment of Maoris & Layforce	Road, track
= Rearguard	**2** Layforce & wounded Maori withdrawal	Foothills & slopes
● Village	**3** Maori detachment (Capt. Royal) withdraws	Mountain range

Even before the decision was made to evacuate, Jack Ryan brought orders back to his radio intercept team to destroy all equipment and burn all sensitive documents, urinating on the ashes and turning them over.[2] The Australian unit set out over Lefka Ori, the White Mountains, dealing with circumstances as they arose. Water was drawn from wells with a tin hat on a bootlace rope. A junior soldier swapped boots when Ryan's shoes began to disintegrate. The paws of the fox terrier, Micky, rubbed raw on the rocks and he had to be carried, tucked inside tunics.[3]

First to head south when talk of evacuation gathered momentum were base personnel without leaders or arms, and members of the composite units that had mostly disintegrated after the taking and abandoning of Galatas. Starting out with jokes, laughter and bursts of singing, the heat soon drained their strength and they spent increasing time hanging around wells. These men, including stragglers, deserters and others detached from their units, knew they would be a low priority for evacuation. The quartermaster of one Australian battalion had disappeared some time before. He reappeared and asked the battalion's second-in-command if they could take him with them. 'No way,' was the reply. 'You deserted us. Now you can find your own way.'[4]

When the withdrawal was officially authorised, infantry and gunnery units were allocated roles in a series of rearguards to slow the enemy's pursuit of a retreating force already evolving into two distinct classes: the organised and the disorganised.

Howard Kippenberger returned to his own battalion after the disintegration of his brigade of composite units. Assembling his troops, he told them they would be heading south in rigid march discipline, Kippenberger leading. They would halt every hour for ten minutes.[5] 'There were units sticking together and marching with their weapons,' Freyberg would later report, 'but in the main it was a disorganised rabble making its way doggedly and painfully to the south. There were thousands of unarmed troops including

Cypriots and Palestinians. Without leadership, without any sort of discipline, it is impossible to expect anything else of troops who have never been trained as fighting soldiers. Somehow or other the word Sphakia got out and many of these people had taken a flying start in any available transport they could steal.'[6]

Some curious 'ring-ins' were among the growing mob heading south. Two Greek nurses in borrowed battledress and helmets were with a group of New Zealand soldiers, laughing and joking in broken English, and a blonde woman, Niki Dermetzi, from the Argentina nightclub in Athens was spotted in a khaki uniform.[7]

Many of Kippenberger's men were physically exhausted from fighting at Maleme and Galatas, deprived of sleep by the daily air raids and the consequent need to move at night. At one point, they were overtaken by three Australians singing, 'When there isn't a girl about, you do feel lonely'[8] and their spirits rose. The New Zealanders began singing, joining Australians with 'Waltzing Matilda'.[9]

As the road climbed the mountain spine, winding and steep with hairpin bends, the jollity seeped away. The unattached walked alone or formed small groups, many just in twos and threes, short of water, food and tobacco. The heat was suffocating under the cloudless sky. Only a few kept climbing during the day despite observer planes sniffing around. The rest hid under trees or behind rocks, nibbling anything they could find—broken biscuits from trucks that had been hit or vegetables from gardens that hadn't already been raided. Stirring from their shelters at dusk, they swarmed onto the mountain road like a football crowd after a game.

The ascent was too gruelling for some of the wounded. They dropped out, hoping for transport. After each rest stop, some men couldn't get to their feet again and had to be left. The march became a dogged fight against the desire to sleep, always expecting the next summit to be the top of the mountain range and instead seeing a winding road rising ahead. 'At times I didn't care if I went on or not,' says Allan Christoffersen, a driver from Hawkes Bay.[10] One young

Kiwi soldier thought he was going to crack. Colonel Andrew sat with him and, learning they'd gone to the same school, yarned about Wanganui College. 'I was okay after that,' the soldier says.[11]

Jimmy Hargest wrote home, 'We loaded our wounded and sick on to lorries and took them as far as we could. Poor chaps, little could be done for them but move them—the seriously wounded we had to leave.'[12]

Wounded soldiers in filthy, bloodstained bandages walked past bodies in ditches and among olive trees, the sickening smell of death mixed with the sweet smell of thyme. Little was said. Charlie Jager, a gunner from Melbourne, noted, 'Only a curse, or the clash of equipment, breaks the sound of boots trudging in the dust.'[13] Resting by farmhouses and wells, there was little talk. The red glow of cigarette ends in the dark darted about like insects. Herbert Longbottom and his mate Tom Hutchesson found a bottle of gin in an abandoned jeep and bathed their sore feet in it. It helped harden the skin.[14]

A line of vehicles slowly passed the marching column, some cars and ambulances, a number of trucks and lorries. A truck filled with base troops honked and pushed those on foot off the road, choking them with swirling dust, walking wounded included. The roadside was strewn with discarded equipment, packs and steel helmets cast aside, empty water bottles, officers' valises and burst-open suitcases, all half-buried in dust. Lorries and cars had been abandoned along the way, some hit by aircraft fire and burnt out, others out of petrol or broken down. Some had been pushed off the road into jagged ravines, gear spilling out on the rocks.

It was disorganised and desperate, and it was all headed towards a small fishing village.

———

General Weston, commanding the rearguard, drove south to recce the road winding up the mountains and didn't reappear until late afternoon, his return blocked by the tide of vehicles and troops streaming along the road. In Weston's absence, brigadiers Vasey and Hargest stayed together, coordinating the withdrawal and its rearguard. Two Maori companies and a commando detachment were positioned around a key bridge at the junction where the road forked south to the coast. Australian and New Zealand troops were placed around Stilos, further up the road before it started climbing.

Told to disable his field gun and withdraw, Jack Gordon removed the firing pin and hid it in a tree. He moved on in the dark to be told a truck had towed his gun out. Its firing pin's hiding place was by then in enemy hands, but the New Zealander slipped back to the tree, tiptoeing through snoring Germans. He reached cautiously in the dark between the tree and a sleeping body, found the pin and put it in his pocket, gingerly picking a path out through the sleeping enemy. The field gun was firing again the next day.[15]

Medical stations had been set up along the route and trucks, marked with crude white crosses stretched across grey blankets, were used as ambulances. At Stilos, a barn served as a dressing station, packed with men lying on stretchers, blankets and sacks.

Four men fell asleep beside the road, having fought at Maleme for several days without rest. A passing truck carrying retreating soldiers ran over their legs, causing broken thighs, ankles and, in one case, probably a broken pelvis. There were only morphine tablets and field dressing to treat them. It was risky moving the two thigh cases, so they were edged gently to one side to await treatment by the better-equipped Germans when they came through.[16]

The Layforce detachment at the road junction included sixty Spaniards, veterans of the Spanish Civil War. At sunrise it was found the Spanish volunteers had moved off, probably on the tail of relocating Anzacs.[17] Within a short time, the rest of the commando detachment had gone. The Maoris, under Captain Royal, held off the enemy unassisted until German mountain troops found a way around them, capturing some of the retreating commandos as they did so. Cut off from the main body of the retreat, Royal looked at how to extricate his men. He gave the wounded a chance by sending them on. A few walking wounded and two stretcher cases, having discarded their rifles and trusting to luck, marched straight up the road and were left alone by the Germans.[18]

By the middle of the day, the firing on the Maori defenders had died down, the enemy being in no hurry when there appeared to be no escape route. Royal saw a lizard he took to be a tuatara, a reptile found only in New Zealand, which he might or might not have known. The tuatara's head pointed directly over a cliff at the rear of the plateau on which they were set up. To 43-year-old Rangi Royal this was a sign from the old-time Maori god of war, Tumatauenga. He led his men down a cliff that wasn't as sheer as it first appeared, over a river at the bottom and eventually took a wide berth to arrive at an occupied village near the Sphakia road. They marched through the village with bayonets drawn, the only reaction a brief exchange of fire as they left. Eventually they caught up with the tail of their battalion further along the road.[19]

The main body of the rearguard, having marched through the night, was settling into positions around Stilos when Kiwis spotted the enemy coming up from a creek bed. Men rushed to a stone wall across the top of the hill. One of the first there was Sergeant Clive Hulme, opening fire at the Germans as they neared the ridge and rolling grenades hurriedly primed by his men. As the enemy turned back, Hulme, a thirty-year-old farm labourer from Nelson with a reputation already for picking off snipers, sat astride the wall like a cowboy on horseback, shooting at the Germans scuttling down the slope.[20]

Shortly after, Hulme volunteered to deal with five mountain troops firing in the vicinity of battalion commanders coordinating the day's march south. Wearing a camouflage suit he'd taken days before from a dead paratroop, he climbed a hill above the group and shot its leader. When the Germans looked to see where the shot had come from, he looked around too, creating the impression in his paratrooper clothing he was one of them. When they looked down again, he shot two more, then a fourth coming up the hill to investigate and the fifth as he tried to come around the hill.

After that, Hulme went forward, shooting a mortar crew and disabling the mortar. Working back on the German side of the hill, he took out three snipers, but was seriously wounded in the shoulder and eventually evacuated. He was awarded a Victoria Cross.[21]

Julius Ringel's plan was for his German troops to encircle Canea and drive on towards Retimo. He was convinced the British aim was to prolong the battle by falling back to Heraklion. He assumed enemy troops going south were a flanking movement towards Retimo. The general had planned for that flank to be covered by troops coming round from Prison Valley, but repeated attempts to dislodge the Greeks from Alikianou took eight days to achieve. A quick success there would have allowed Germans to move across to the Sphakia road and block the retreating troops. Instead, by the time their forward detachment got to Stilos, they had a rearguard to deal with and were driven back.

The stand at Stilos had become tenuous and was no longer needed once the bulk of the withdrawal had passed through. Vasey and Hargest conferred in the evening with their battalion commanders, debating whether to stand and fight at Stilos or risk marching on the road by day. The commanders had no confidence that at this stage of the gruelling campaign their men could fight all day and then march all night. 'Well, we'll march at ten,' said Hargest.[22]

Australian, New Zealand and commando rearguard units started withdrawing that morning, leapfrogging through each other on a tortuous zigzag climb. At the same time, 3000 Italian PoWs marched down through the retreating horde, frantically waving improvised white flags. Captured months before in Albania by the Greeks, they had been released and demanded passage when they got to the withdrawing rearguard. Hargest allowed them through, hoping it would interfere with the German advance, which it did.

When the Italians got to Stilos, they came under German mortar fire and scattered.[23]

The Royal Engineers had been ordered to remove a rocky obstruction further along the road, but in doing so they cratered part of the road before the rearguard pulled back. The sappers said they'd been ordered to detonate by an officer claiming to be in charge of the rearguard. That could have been General Weston but, even so, his instruction would have been to make the road easier for trucks carrying the wounded, not to make it impossible. Communication was getting ragged.

It took the infantry two hours to scramble around the rockfall and vehicles couldn't get past at all. The road was eventually repaired sufficiently to get the wounded across and into ramshackle lorries waiting on the other side. Jimmy Hargest, meanwhile, rode on a Bren carrier, looking out for enemy planes, but there were remarkably few that day. There were reasons for that, the good news being that Hitler had sent much of his Stuka force from the Mediterranean to Poland for the coming secret operation against Russia. They would not be coming back. The bad news was that most of the warplanes that remained were heading for Heraklion.

Admiral Cunningham's staff decided the entire garrison of about 4000 in Heraklion could be evacuated from its quay in a single night, instead of marching down to the south coast. The garrison force was made up of the original garrison of English and Scottish units, Dougherty's Australians and the late-arriving Highlanders. The Germans had been driven out of the port town, but were building strength around it with air-dropped reinforcements. Brigadier Chappel at Heraklion was told by Cairo on 27 May that Crete was to be abandoned. Nine fast warships would arrive the next night to evacuate all his men. Chappel didn't bother to pass this on to his officers until dawn the next day, Colonel Dougherty and his adjutant among the officers told.[24]

Before leaving, the Australian battalion put its vehicles out of commission, destroyed its stores and set charges on petrol and ordnance dumps, timed to explode the following morning. Trip wires and mines were laid to delay enemy patrols. Rifles were rigged with water dripping into cans tied to triggers, so they would fire at intervals to give the impression the defences were still manned, a ruse that had been used at Gallipoli.[25]

Messages were sent by runner to the dressing station at Knossos, out of town, and to an Australian officer working with the Greek force. The Greek commander, however, was not notified that the British were evacuating that night. Chappel's explanation for this was that the ships didn't have room for more troops and the message couldn't be safely sent.[26]

The naval flotilla arrived from Alexandria at 11.30 pm and its six destroyers went into the quay, four at a time, to ferry the English, Scottish and Australian soldiers out to the two remaining cruisers. An air attack on the way had put the third cruiser, *Ajax*, out of commission and it had returned to Alexandria.

Troops were to file out quietly in the darkness, unit by unit until the last defensive post was abandoned, water-triggered rifle fire disguising the departure. The embarkation went smoothly alongside a town in ruins. 'Heraklion was one large stench of decomposing dead,' recalls Paul Tomlinson, a medico who had come in from Knossos. 'Roads were wet and running from burst water pipes, hungry dogs were scavenging among the dead. There was a stench of sulphur, smouldering fires and pollution of broken sewers.'[27]

Ivan Dougherty received word just after midnight that the navy wanted to leave at 3 am, half an hour earlier than originally planned. Doubting that men from the forward positions could get there by that time, he stood in plain sight on the quay to delay the ships' departure.[28] Max Rungie, an officer in the last company to leave, remembers 'the three-odd miles to the wharf were done at a jog trot all the way and we made the destroyer just as they cast off the first hawser'.[29] It was 3.20 am. In a smoothly run operation, the whole garrison had boarded, apart from a detachment guarding a roadblock, and the wounded still in the dressing station at Knossos.

The good fortune couldn't last. The destroyer *Imperial* was the first to go, its steering gear, damaged by the air strike on the way to Crete, jamming on leaving. It nearly collided with two other ships, then lost power. The captain of *Hotspur* was ordered by the squadron's commander, Admiral Bernard Rawlings: 'Take off crew and sink *Imperial*.' *Hotspur* drew alongside. Three hundred troops, mostly Australian and Black Watch, were transferred in the pre-dawn gloom before *Hotspur* moved away and fired two torpedoes at the stricken vessel.[30]

A 33-year-old Sydneysider, Percy Webb, had been sleeping soundly in the bowels of *Imperial* after an evening's solid drinking and hadn't been noticed in the clamour to get off the ship. He awoke to an eerie quietness after the first torpedo slammed into the vessel. Clambering onto the deck, Webb found the ship was listing. When *Hotspur*'s second torpedo struck, he jumped clear of the sinking *Imperial* and found a raft floating in the wreckage. He drifted all day. Washed ashore the following morning, he was handed over to the Germans by Cretan police.[31]

With the dawn came the remaining Stukas. Starting about six, they soon hit the funnel of the destroyer *Hereward*. Malcolm Webster, who'd had his twenty-first birthday four days earlier, had been lying on the deck with other evacuees when the order came to abandon ship. He folded his clothes neatly, put his tin hat on top in good military fashion, and climbed down a rope into the sea. 'I looked up, there was a gun crew lolling about, all dead,' he says. 'The Germans were flying around strafing the ship.'[32]

There were no life jackets; the crew were throwing everything wooden overboard. Webster joined two sailors holding onto a wooden plank, but cramps set in and the sea got rougher. A Stuka was strafing survivors in the water until an Italian Red Cross plane circled around and kept it away. One of the sailors lost his grip on the plank and drifted away. After some six hours in the water, Webster was near the end of his tether when an Italian torpedo boat appeared, its crew pulling bodies out of the water. If they were dead, they were thrown back like undersized fish; if not, like Webster they were taken into captivity on Scarpanto, an Italian island east of Crete.[33]

While Malcolm Webster floated into captivity, the Germans continued their attack on the larger cruisers. A bomb hit a gun turret on *Dido* and exploded in the crowded 'tween decks. Bill Williams was there. 'The PA system was belting out a popular tune, "It's a Hap-hap-happy Day",' he remembers, 'when a tremendous explosion took place, everything turned red and black, I couldn't breathe and I remember little or nothing else until Reg Angel, who came down immediately the bomb exploded, grabbed me and carted me on deck.'[34]

Ken Moses was also down there. 'The lights went out, water pipes burst and the confined space was filled with cordite fumes and the sweeter smell of burning flesh,' is his memory. 'There was no panic. Those that were left filled the empty five point two shells with water from the broken pipes and began putting out the fire that started to lick the walls of the magazines.'[35]

A warplane raked the bridge of the cruiser *Orion*, killing its captain and wounding Admiral Rawlings. Later bombs destroyed the forward gun turrets and exploded in the stokers' mess-deck crowded with soldiers. Black choking smoke billowed across the decks as *Orion* limped on with a list. The convoy slowed to stay with the cruiser and the badly damaged *Dido*, reaching Alexandria by evening.

Eight hundred of the troops from Heraklion had been lost— killed, wounded or captured. As the battered convoy neared Alexandria, a mass burial at sea was carried out in a deep and moving ceremony,[36] underscoring how the odds are stacked against any fleet without aircraft protection. As if to rub salt in their wounds, an

RAF plane later flew up to the convoy and the ships' guns—or the soldiers on board—opened fire on it. The pilot sent out an identification flare and flew off.[37]

_____

While the evacuees from Heraklion made their ill-fated way to Egypt, those from Suda were streaming across Askifou Plain, high on the White Mountains. This long ribbon of retreating men spread all the way to the coast. After the wearying climb for already exhausted, hungry men, the road to Sphakia ran through a narrow gorge to Askifou's mountaintop plateau, a patchwork of fields dotted with farms, scattered wells and little villages. The sounds of birds and tumbling streams and the heady aroma of Cretan herbs and shrubs provided a respite in which the men could hope for an end to their agony of endurance.

There were acute shortages of food and water. When the men did get a food issue, it was typically a tin of bully beef between six men and two biscuits each. Bully beef was compact and lasted a whole day; tinned pineapple was bulky and had to be eaten once it was opened. Several men suffered diarrhoea from the juice of tinned beetroot. 'Food dumps were supposed to be along the road, but I never found them,' says Melbournian Arthur Wallace, 'neither did other men I asked.'[38]

A group of Kiwis had no means of filling their water bottles at a village well. They improvised a rope by tying their bootlaces together then adding their braces, but they still couldn't reach the water. They needed the sergeant to take off his trousers, tie one leg on and hold the other.[39] Another group was equally inventive, tying together pull-throughs, used to clean gun barrels, and lowering a tin helmet. 'I can still remember the taste of perspiration as I drank that water,' says one.[40]

The leaderless and unattached drifted about, some in despair, some teetering on the edge of anarchy. Those in formed units set up camp, having marched all day with officers and NCOs. Howard Kippenberger halted his men and took out a torch to consult his map. There were threats and curses from the surrounding darkness. A man leapt at him and kicked the torch from his hand. Kippenberger grabbed him by the throat, nearly throttling him. Addressing the sullen shadowy forms, he said, 'I'm going to use that torch again. If anyone objects, I'm prepared to shoot.'[41]

For the unattached, it was a story of survival. Charlie Jager and Ben Travers, two gunners from the Melbourne suburbs, scavenged in a deserted village, found a barrel of wine, caught and plucked a cockerel and smashed a chair for firewood to cook it. A Maori poked his head in the kitchen door and sniffed, calling out, 'Hey, Tama, it's a hangi.'

Kiwis crowded into the kitchen, around the pot hanging over the fire. Along with their own weapons, they had souvenired a Schmeisser machine gun and Zeiss cameras and binoculars. Tama, short and stocky, had a tattooed face and a cord hanging from his belt, threaded with German ears. The room filled with laughter and animated conversation over a shared chicken stew, the New Zealanders bemoaning the failure to push the Germans off Hill 107 at Maleme. 'We started off too late and there weren't enough of us,' said a corporal they called Hone. 'Your Seventh [AIF 7th Battalion] were kept in reserve but, if they'd been with us, they'd've made the difference.' After dinner, the Maoris sang and did a spirited haka. 'Thank God they're on our side,' thought Jager. Travers did a Charlie Chaplin impersonation which the Kiwis thought hilarious. They all went to sleep out in the open, Jager using his boots as a pillow.

In the morning, Jager woke to the thud of enemy mortars and found the Maoris and his boots were gone. 'Charlie, didn't you see their boots?' said Travers. 'Those blokes were on their uppers. I slept with mine on. And with the laces done up.'[42]

A church in Imbros, a village on the far side of Askifou Plain, was set up as a dressing station with thirty seriously wounded inside and a further twenty outside under a tree. Officers were kept busy ordering retreating troops away to avoid drawing enemy fire on the church. As it would be impossible to evacuate these wounded, a party of orderlies and stretcher-bearers volunteered to stay with the medico, Kiernan 'Skipper' Dorney, to be picked up by the advancing Germans.[43]

Freyberg had kept command of the embarkation phase, while assigning command of the rearguard to Weston, and set up headquarters in Imbros before the ships arrived. From there, staff officers coordinated the naval rescue with Fleet HQ in Alexandria. Portable wireless sets and naval ciphers had been sent to Sphakia by a motor launch that was sunk before getting there. Freyberg had to get by with intermittent contact with Wavell on a single RAF wireless with a fading battery. Cairo sent some supplies with the evacuation ships but that never included an extra wireless or batteries.

The road to Sphakia ended with a series of acute hairpin bends, stopping abruptly on top of a cliff two kilometres from the beach. A goat track ran down to the village, which was on a flat area of rough coastal scrub crossed by ill-defined tracks continuing down to a small shingle beach. There was no jetty. Fishermen dragged their boats up onto the pebbles.

By the time sufficient troops had gathered at the end of the road to start evacuating, Freyberg had moved his headquarters to three small caves overlooking the village. Captain John Morse, the naval liaison officer in Crete, signalled Admiral Cunningham from there, advising, 'Up to 1000 troops ready to embark'. Four destroyers were despatched from Alexandria. It was the same night a larger flotilla was sent to pick up the entire garrison at Heraklion.

Wounded men, having trudged all the way from Maleme–Suda, were assisted with extreme difficulty down the track to the beach, a chubby Padre Youll from Taree cheerily encouraging them not to give up. Some of the unattached had wrapped field dressings around uninjured heads and tried to join them.[44] Formed units also made their way down in the dark, told to keep a hand on the shoulder in front of them so outsiders couldn't break into the line.

The four warships anchored out from the beach shortly before midnight, sending in whalers and a landing barge. Embarkation staff on both sides of the tracks waved the men in. Ahead, English accents called out, 'Come on, there's room for more that side. Step on it! Move along!' The pace quickened at the sight of the dark form of a vessel to ferry them off Crete. Jogging troops jumped aboard in utter relief.

The call went out, 'There, that's our tally,' and it was all over, the unlucky next man cut off by a sailor's outstretched arm. The ramp creaked up and they were soon sliding across water. Pulling along-side a ship, they clambered up scrambling nets, some so exhausted they struggled over the last few metres to the top. Sailors leant over, grabbed their shirts and pulled them up and over, like they were loading sacks of grain. On board cocoa and tea were offered while a wonderful reality sank in. They were leaving Crete.

There were over 20,000 men from Maleme–Suda to be evacuated. On that first night, only 724 troops, many of them walking wounded, and twenty Greek civilians were embarked from Sphakia's pebbly shore. Among the evacuees was Jack Ryan's Australian radio intercept team with, tucked away in the tunic of one of them, a fox terrier called Micky.

By this time, the rearguard had pulled back to Askifou Plain where the Australians were given their first rations for two days, bully beef and biscuits. Gunners found an abandoned truck with tinned bully beef and vegetables. 'We humped a good quantity back to the guns,' says Michael Clarke, 'opened the beetroot and potatoes and drank the juice. It tasted lousy but by God it was thirst-quenching.'[45] Supplies left by the evacuation ships were found to have little of the food concentrates desperately needed. Cairo quartermasters had hurriedly packed bags of flour and cases of matches.[46]

A commando, Arthur Swinburne, recalls twenty-seven men sharing a tin of sausages, half a sausage each, and nine sharing a tin of potatoes.[47] 'The commandos fared better for they had been taught to live off the country and do without rations and I never saw any of them faint from hunger,' says Colonel Laycock, adding, 'My servant gave me two roast fowls for dinner, with rice,'[48] the alumnus of Eton and Sandhurst apparently oblivious to any irony there. Later, the Spanish commandos, having deserted their post and headed well down the road to Sphakia, would find a pig and invite Bob Laycock and Evelyn Waugh to dine on roast suckling pig and rice.[49]

The Layforce commandos were fish out of water, dilettante soldiers where gritty determination was needed. Alan Lomas, a New Zealand medico, relates, 'While I was sheltering from an air attack, I chatted to an indignant Commando other rank [non-officer]. "We have not been trained for this type of war," he expostulated. "We are Commandos, Churchill's own, we fight at close range in the dark, with the dagger or the pistol. This is not the place for us." I didn't bother to argue.'[50] Laycock had made a similar complaint to Weston and Freyberg.

Ian Stewart, a medico with the Welsh regiment, says scathingly that infantrymen had little faith in men 'in baggy shorts and bandeaus, their belts hung about with dirks and daggers and throttling ropes, and their training, so it appeared, more appropriate to the silent assassination of a drowsy nightwatchman on some deserted dockside than to the serious business of holding the Germans in the open'.[51]

In the reality of this encounter, where you didn't get an agreement with the enemy on the type of battle to be fought, the rearguard was occupied dealing with German infantry and motorcycle troops probing its defence. One of the Matilda tanks brought across from Heraklion had broken down within 15 kilometres of Suda, but the other had been brought back along the Sphakia road and its guns, along with the Anzac artillery, forced the enemy patrols back. Three of the English light tanks had also come back to strengthen the rearguard.

Meanwhile, preparations for the second night of evacuation were proceeding. To cope with the expected numbers, a troopship was sent with seven warships, four of them the larger cruisers. Captain Morse had signalled Cairo that up to 10,000 troops were ready to leave that night, although only about 2000 of them were organised units of combat troops. They were waiting on the clifftop until called down, but thousands were milling around the village below and the surrounding slopes.

Discipline had collapsed and panic had taken over the mob. Hargest posted a cordon of troops with fixed bayonets around the beach to keep lanes open and to control the unattached pushing forward in a desperate attempt to get away. The combat units and the wounded assembled at the top of a gorge to make their way down goat tracks to the beach when darkness approached.

The English medico, Theo Stephanides, had been trucked to the end of the road with the walking ('just, in some cases') wounded in his charge. They were ordered to stay bunched together, not take cover or drop to the ground if planes approached, while a corporal waved a Red Cross flag from side to side to keep it open. An enemy formation did approach, machine-gunning randomly, and the men held their nerve with the corporal waving his flag. The planes stopped firing, circled low a couple of times and flew off, several dipping their wings in acknowledgement.[52]

Jack Buxton, a gunner from South Australia, was among the troops embarking that night. His diary describes going down in the twilight: men 'stumble over the rocks, but are too tired to even curse. We walk automatically, we don't know where we are going, we just follow the men in the front and hope for the best.'[53] The line would occasionally break when the front moved too fast for some of the wounded, then with whistling and shouting in the dark, it would reassemble, reach the edge of the fishing village and wait in an olive grove.

The convoy arrived at 11.30 pm with the troopship, *Glengyle*, and two of the cruisers anchoring off Sphakia. The other warships patrolled, the commanders aware of the previous night's disastrous evacuation from Heraklion. Landing barges came in to the shore and their ramps dropped down. Naval officers came up, quiet and businesslike, to the waiting groups and waved them down a slope and through a narrow, deserted street full of rubble and smashed brickwork, then hurried them through the cordon of guards.

'After many delays, we neared the beach and I could make out the shadowy outlines of several ships looming faintly through the night some distance from the land,' recalls Stephanides. Small craft were moving around in the darkness and soldiers and sailors pushed and shoved each other on the shore. Pale lights flashed out at sea, answered from the water's edge. Once on the beach and herded by sailors, the troops filed aboard a waiting barge. 'What struck me most when we set foot on the barge was the efficiency of every-thing,' comments the Englishman.[54] The barge filled, there were curt orders, a bell clanged and they slowly left shore.

The last stage of the escape from Crete was to clamber up netting hung on the side of *Glengyle* and the cruisers. Arthur Midwood, a Maori soldier from Rotorua who had been shot in the chest, had walked over the mountains to Sphakia and been ferried to *Glengyle*. 'I had to climb up this rope netting on the side of the boat,' he recalls. 'I had difficulty getting to the top because my arm was in a sling and I could only use one arm. I held on by the back of my head while I grabbed another rope. I got on board and crawled two metres across the deck and stayed there.'[55]

With the New Zealand Division HQ absorbed into Creforce HQ, General Puttick, his adjutant Colonel Gentry and most of their staff embarked that night. The convoy sailed at 3.20 am with over 6000 departing, including 550 wounded. On board, the evacuees were offered the traditional mugs of hot cocoa and tea. The cruiser *Perth* went one better, giving the men 'hot soup, bread and bully beef on a clean white china plate with mustard and pickles'.[56] Also on board *Perth*, some New Zealand officers noted, were several commandos who were supposed to be part of the rearguard.[57]

While 30 May dawned on the remnant of the Maleme–Suda force, preparing across the mountains at Sphakia for its third night of naval evacuation, the Australian force at Retimo was still in place, unaware of what was happening elsewhere on the island. Their predicament would soon become clear.

General Freyberg had endeavoured to instruct Colonel Campbell to retire his force to the south coast, but the message couldn't be sent by wireless. With Campbell having no ciphers for a coded message, there was a risk of the evacuation plans being picked up by Germans. As a runner would have taken three days to get to Retimo, if he survived, Freyberg had proposed to send the order with Lieutenant Haig, who was waiting at Suda until nightfall to take provisions to Retimo by landing craft. When it was found Haig had already gone, Freyberg arranged with Cairo to drop a message to Campbell by plane but the aircraft was shot down on the way. Further planes had been sent but there was no way of knowing if the message had been received.[58]

It hadn't. Not knowing of movements elsewhere, Ian Campbell had decided to make no further attempt to take Perivolia. Food and ammunition were low, as were the enemy's, and both forces were seriously reduced in numbers. The remnants of the German force were several kilometres on either side of the airstrip and, Campbell thought, not threatening it. Bob Haig's landing craft had delivered two days' rations overnight but the Retimo force was now having to feed its 450 German prisoners as well as nearly a thousand of its own men.

Major George Hooper was liaising with the Greek units. Late on 29 May, he passed on to Campbell that a large force of German mountain troops and tanks had been seen approaching from Heraklion.

As reports by the Greeks tended to be exaggerated, Campbell took no action. During the night, one of the Greek regiments dispersed into the mountains and the other warned that about a thousand German troops had arrived in the afternoon at Retimo from the other direction.[59] With a reinforced enemy approaching from both sides, the colonel realised his position was deteriorating rapidly.

After sunrise, motor engines were heard approaching from Retimo township to the west. Infantry were reported moving along the shoreline from Perivolia, then two tanks with their sinister black cross insignias appeared on the coastal road. Motorcycles followed, pulling light field guns. Covering the road from Perivolia, a company under Major Honner waited for the tanks to pass and then fired at the motorcycles and infantry coming behind. Further on, enemy troops sheltering behind the tanks' turrets came under Bren and small arms fire and leapt into ditches and bamboo thickets. Having exhausted the benefit of surprise, the Australians were soon under heavy mortar and artillery attack. The tanks moved up to the airfield runway.[60]

Ian Campbell calculated the airfield could be held against German armour for no more than an hour and then at high cost in lives. He conferred by phone with Ray Sandover, commanding the other battalion in the Retimo sector. Sandover agreed with Campbell's assessment but the two had differing views about what to do next. To Campbell, a regular soldier, it was unreasonable to expect Cretan villagers to risk their lives feeding soldiers on the run. He proposed, as Retimo's senior commander, to surrender. Sandover, a Perth businessman, believed the men should be allowed a choice of surrendering or getting away.[61] The two officers agreed to differ and wished each other luck.

Dug in overlooking the airfield, defenders saw Colonel Campbell walk across the runway, followed by his adjutant waving a dirty white towel. At the same time, a breathless runner arrived at the trenches, calling out, 'Stop shooting! We've just surrendered.' The Bren gunner and riflemen removed bolts and breech blocks from their weapons and threw them away. Unsure what to do next, they remained where they were until their platoon leader arrived. 'I suppose we'd better go down and get it over with,' he said.[62]

The sound of fighting ceased. Only the drone of planes in the middle distance continued. Various groups converged on the airstrip, Germans having replaced their steel helmets with peaked caps. Campbell was in a long conversation with a young German officer. Michael Kennedy noticed on arriving at the runway that 'three dead Germans lay where they fell. Their blood-sodden faces were already covered with so many flies that they looked as if they had been smeared with blackberry jam. This didn't seem to distress their comrades. It was like the end of a hard-fought football match with the Germans laughing and joking and taking souvenirs.'[63]

The German commander told Campbell to assemble his troops. A whistle was blown and the command shouted, 'Battalion! Fall in!' There was an awkward pause as men groped automatically for rifles they'd tossed aside.

The prisoners were herded down the road to the township, past fields with scattered dead. German bodies had been cleared from the roads and heaped three or four deep on the roadside. A paratroop still attached to his parachute hung from phone wires, half his head blown off. The silence was broken by the tramp of boots. In the town, Cretans searched fire-blackened ruins for missing family. The prisoners were halted in front of a Retimo schoolhouse where they were to be temporarily held. There they were given a ration of uncooked rice and raisins. There was nothing to do and nothing to talk about.

Four destroyers left Alexandria on 30 May for the third evacuation from Sphakia. One broke down with mechanical defects and another was damaged in an attack by three Junkers bombers. Those two turned back, leaving an evacuation fleet of two. As a result, some of the New Zealand battalions were told they wouldn't be leaving that night but would join the rearguard. There was no certainty of further evacuations.

When his men were told, Major Jim Leggat says, 'No one spoke for a while and then we just rolled our pipe tobacco in our newspaper cigarette-paper.'[64] There were unexpressed reactions though. Stan Johnson had led one of the two companies still fighting when Les Andrew had withdrawn his defences around Maleme airfield on the first day of battle. 'After the exhaustion of the fighting of the preceding ten days,' Johnson says, 'and with that hollow feeling in one's stomach resulting not only from the knowledge of failure, but also of the feeling of having been let down some ten days earlier when the counter-attack at Maleme did not eventuate as promised, this was almost a knockout blow.'[65]

The Maori battalion was told that little more than half of them would be embarking that night. Their commander, George Dittmer, argued that all should go or all, including himself, should stay, but he was overruled by his superiors. With each company commander to nominate who stayed behind, volunteers exceeded the number needed and some had to be ordered to embark.[66]

The rearguard, reorganised with troops that weren't being evacuated that night, had pulled back to cover approaches to Sphakia. Lindsay Inglis, a former machine gunner, joined the rearguard gunners, with two fellow officers as observers.[67] 'Bloody George' Vasey was up the road beyond Imbros positioning English cruiser tanks, Australian Bren carriers and Australian artillery. Cheerful and unhurried, he was watching the German advance through binoculars when written orders were brought from Freyberg. He said, 'Tell your general we can hold the bastards for at least twenty-four hours,' and signed for receipt of the orders.[68] By afternoon, Inglis was back with Kippenberger setting the rearguard in the hills covering Sphakia.

In charge of the German detachment moving down the road to Sphakia while General Ringel took the main invasion force towards

Heraklion, Colonel Utz found himself up against infantry supported by tanks and artillery. He called for dive-bomber and artillery back-up, but the Stukas had gone to Poland and never came. While he waited another day for the artillery to arrive, he sent out patrols.

One patrol was seen making its way down a ravine thick with rhododendron bushes. It was heading towards Creforce's temporary HQ in the caves. Men were rushed to the ravine's near side and Kiwi company commander Den Fountaine was ordered to get some of his men up on its far side, above the enemy. Charlie Upham led a dog-tired group up a cliffside climb to a point where they could see the patrol moving from cover to cover below. Gunner Brown was held by his legs so he could lean over the cliff edge enough to direct his Bren fire at the enemy. The Germans moved into the open to shoot back and found themselves shelled from two directions. Running desperately for cover, they were picked off one by one.[69]

Three Bren carriers joined the three light tanks as a front line covering a bend in the road forward of the rearguard. Trucks with enemy troops came round the bend, followed by walking troops. They were fired on by the front line and by three Australians and a New Zealander who'd moved even further forward. Unable to locate the sources of fire, the Germans tried to move around them, but their cover was thin and they were picked off. While the enemy explored wider flanking in the late afternoon, Vasey ordered the defenders to ditch their carriers and retire to the clifftop overlooking the beach.

At the top of the slope behind the fishing village, Maoris passed arms and tins of foraged golden syrup and jam to their comrades who were staying. Rangi Royal was presented with a rabbit caught that day. In the late afternoon, troops who were leaving were ordered down the narrow, rocky track. At the bottom they were divided into groups of fifty and told to wait until dark.[70]

The two destroyers arrived about midnight. Lights flashed across the water and engines could be heard, then a landing craft slid onto the shingle beach. Given the order to go forward, the men were counted in by their unit commanders and walked between lines of Maoris as an inner cordon standing shoulder to shoulder, facing outwards with bayonets fixed. Small groups of the unattached had come down to the cordon. Some begged to be taken into the departing column, most simply stared stonily at those leaving. A group, lawless and fear-stricken, rushed the cordon line at one time. 'Back! Back!' shouted 'Guv' Matthews as he and Jack Tainui fired bursts of Tommy gun in the air and bayonets were pointed towards the agitated swarm. 'There was a shot, a yelp and the mob went back the way they came,' says one departing Kiwi.[71] The destroyers left about 3 am with 1500 troops embarked.

Having handed command over to General Weston, Freyberg, Morse and the Creforce staff officers were ferried out to two Sunderlands before midnight and flown to Alexandria.[72] On arrival, Freyberg sent an urgent signal to Wavell in Cairo, pleading for another lift the next night with up to 7000 still to be evacuated.

Peter Fraser was in Egypt, on that day visiting the wounded in Alexandria. The New Zealand prime minister returned to Cairo, exclaiming that 'it would be a crushing disaster for our country and its war effort if such a large number of our men fell into the enemy's hands'.[73] That set a cat among the pigeons in Middle East Command and in the Admiralty in London, where antennas were detecting a political storm in the making.

Concerned about the strain on men and ships from being at sea for extended periods, Cunningham had advised Admiralty that the evacuation that had just taken place would be the last. During the day, the First Sea Lord, Admiral Pound, cabled that the British government wanted a further evacuation if it was likely a reasonable number could be embarked. About the same time, Weston messaged that 9000 troops remained. If there was to be no further evacuation, the exhausted men would have no option but capitulation and capture. Concerned by the small number of Australians who had embarked, Blamey was pressing Cunningham to send a ship to the south coast where the Retimo garrison should be waiting if it had got Freyberg's air-dropped message. Churchill had bought into the argument, perhaps recalling his undertaking to the dominions. He told the navy's deputy chief that 5000 men could not be left behind without an attempt to save them. Still hesitant, Cunningham was cornered.[74]

The rearguard at Sphakia was ordered to hold the hillside at least until dark. The Germans resumed mortar and machine-gun fire, but they too were worn out and didn't advance on the rearguard positions, preferring to explore encirclement of Sphakia. It turned out to be a quiet day with only sporadic shelling and few aircraft.

It wasn't until late in the afternoon that Eric Weston was advised by Cairo of a convoy arriving that night for a final evacuation. Leaving written orders to capitulate, he was to fly out in a Sunderland already on its way. Colonel Laycock, as senior officer remaining, was to surrender the next morning.[75] Told the ships had been authorised to take 3500, Weston advised Cairo 5400 troops would have to be left behind without rations. His wireless batteries died soon after, with order and discipline on the beach crumbling.

Bob Laycock had met Freyberg in front of the caves the night the general left. Enquiring about evacuation priority, he was told combat troops were to leave before stragglers, but 'you were the last to come so you will be the last fighting unit to go'.[76] Layforce was relieved on that final afternoon by the Maori battalion and told to cover the gorge coming down to Sphakia. The Maoris were to cover the night embarkation and then be taken off themselves.

Layforce's brigade major, Freddie Graham, arrived at force headquarters after dusk for instructions, not having seen Laycock all day. A voice called out from inside the cave, 'Please come in and bring a notebook.' With paper, pencil and carbon paper in his haversack,

Graham went in and found Weston there with Felix Colvin. Colonel Colvin had suffered shell shock in Layforce's early action and been relieved of his command.

Weston said, 'Sit down on that suitcase. Take this letter I'll dictate and make three copies.' He dictated an order, addressed to Colvin, for the capitulation of British forces in Crete. Weston took the two carbon copies, handed one to Colvin and kept the other, saying, 'Well, gentlemen, there are one million drachmae in that suitcase. There's a bottle of gin in the corner. Good bye and good luck.' He walked out of the cave and down the hill to the waiting flying-boat.[77]

Soon after, Laycock 'came panting up the hill'. He cut Graham off trying to bring him up to date. 'I have counter-orders this evening. That's why I'm so late back,' he puffed. 'As we have two battalions in Egypt [the balance of Laycock's commando force], we are to be evacuated tonight, taking as many troops with us as we can.' He had met with Weston earlier that evening and been told Weston intended to surrender in the morning.[78]

Laycock took Graham's copy of Weston's surrender order, crossed out Colvin's name and inserted 'Senior officer left on the island'. He had it sent to Colonel George Young, Colvin's replacement in the field, still out with the rearguard.[79] Laycock, Graham and Waugh, 'with servants', went down to the beach, pushing their way 'through the crowds who were too spiritless even to resist what they took to be an unauthorised intrusion'.[80] Colvin left too, although there is no mention of that in the unit diary or Waugh's.[81] He had become a non-person as well as a political liability.

Different versions have been put forward over the years of who proposed Laycock should suddenly have evacuation priority—that it was Weston, one of his staff or Laycock on his own initiative. Whichever it was, the outcome was that Felix Colvin briefly became the senior officer to surrender to the Germans. Laycock at least seems to have recognised that appointing an officer relieved of command

and suffering shell shock to handle the surrender negotiation might not play out well in reports of the Crete campaign.

————

When night came, Australians on the hill had dumped anything that would rattle or clink and waited silently for the order to withdraw. German voices floated up from the darkened gully below. Vasey and his headquarters staff started moving down the narrow track but it was blocked by thousands of waiting men and a self-appointed movement control officer brandishing a pistol. Vasey went forward with two other officers to investigate.

Meanwhile the convoy of five warships arrived about 11.30 pm, with whalers and three landing barges to ferry embarking troops to them. The beach had to be cleared of the surging mob, but liaison between embarkation staff and the navy was disintegrating. Vasey found embarkation proceeding haphazardly with delays in getting the boats filled from the crowded beach.

A whispered order finally came to the Australians on top of the hill. The last of the rearguard crept over the ridge and groped their way down the track in the dark. There was no sign of the promised guides. The path was choked with men trying to get down to the beach, unarmed and desperate to get away. The column on the track moved forward a few paces and stopped. It moved again, then an order to halt was given from somewhere. The Australians were confronted by a British officer threatening to shoot. Theo Walker, the battalion's commander, tore strips off him; he should have been keeping the path clear for the rearguard to come through.[82] Walker went forward to find out what had happened to the promised clear path.

Getting no useful answers, Walker returned to his men, told them to stick together as an armed column and led the men down, pushing their way to the beach. Stragglers trying to infiltrate the unit were forced out, but that broke the unit into smaller groups.

Johnny Peck was a private in Walker's battalion. 'We were hopelessly entangled in a mass of milling panic-stricken men,' he says.
'Hundreds of stragglers were determined to get away at any price
and bugger the arrangements and controls for an ordered embarkation. Now it was every man for himself and now there was chaos.'[83]

Many of the stragglers were turned back at the barges, but many
managed to get on board in the confusion. There were few officers
and little effective control. The remaining New Zealand infantry
battalions had boarded and one of the two Australian battalions.
Told that Theo Walker had arrived at the beach, Vasey and his staff
boarded a naval launch, believing the remaining Australian battalion was on a barge.[84]

Walker had arrived at the beach at the front of his battalion
with separated groups still pushing their way through the swirling
mass. Sixteen of his men were already there and boarded the waiting
barge. Walker was told the barge could take no more but would fit
him on. The colonel refused the offer. 'I'm not going without my
men,' he said.[85]

The Maoris held over from the previous night's evacuation were
among the last to leave, with Royal Marines covering this late stage
of embarkation. The last barge, that Theo Walker had declined to
board, was too weighed down to get off the shore at first. Some of
the Maoris got off so it could move, then leapt back on again.

More Australians arrived as the packed barge was leaving.
Warship anchor chains rattled through hawsers out in the darkness.
'I was supposed to have been on the next bargeload off,' says Reg
Saunders, 'but there wasn't any. The last boat left not twenty yards
from me. I was too fatigued to worry about it, even as we stood and
watched the barge go with some of our mates on board.'[86]

Time was running out and naval officers, with the evacuation from Heraklion in mind, wanted to be well clear by sunrise.
Although nearly 4000 men were lifted on that last night, some
units were in notably small numbers. As well as the sixteen men

from Walker's battalion, there were only a hundred Marines and twenty-seven from Layforce,[87] but Bob Laycock, Freddie Graham and Evelyn Waugh were safely on board. The naval operation over four nights had evacuated 12,000 troops. Half as many were still on the shore.

Part IV

AFTERMATH

11

LEFT BEHIND

'Shocked, shamed and humiliated to a state of abject misery, we milled about the tiny village of Sphakia,' remembers Kiwi driver, Peter Winter. 'Our brains could not cope with the truth. We snarled at each other and hated each other. A fury, like sickness, dulled the senses. My hatred was greater than my hunger.'[1]

Jack Ulrick from rural New South Wales was just as angry. 'We thought, "Well, that's bloody lovely. Here's the mob, they've cleared out, they've left us here",' he says, 'and I think if the Jerries had asked us then, we would have joined their flamin' army.'[2]

Australian gunners, Michael Clarke and Roy Macartney, simply lay down on the ground, the latter debilitated from drinking tinned beetroot juice. 'We were almost at the end of our endurance,' says Clarke. 'He went straight to sleep. I listened to the arguments going on in the darkness, recognising the voices.'[3]

Over 6000 men were left waiting on the shingle beach, in the village and on the slopes overlooking Sphakia. The area was covered with debris left by the departed troops, empty tins, discarded boots, helmets and tattered clothes. Abandonment numbed the fears of some. They considered options. Most wandered aimlessly . . . or did nothing in a state of suspended animation. 'We abused our leaders and bemoaned our bad luck,' continues Winter, 'but like sheep we waited patiently for the enemy to arrive and take formal possession. Why I didn't walk off with my rifle and forty precious rounds, I don't know. The thought didn't occur to me.'[4]

In discussion with George Young, the commando officer who had inherited Weston's capitulation order, Theo Walker found he was actually the senior of the two colonels. Taking Young's order, he made his way up the cliff at sunrise with the German-speaking Layforce medical officer, Captain Cochrane. Walker's appearance with a white flag at Colonel Utz's command centre came as a surprise to the German. He had expected it would still take a day or two to overcome the rearguard resistance. In the discussion that followed, Utz asked, 'What are you doing here, Australia?'

Walker replied, 'One might ask what are you doing here, Austria?'[5]

'We are all Germans,' said Willi Utz.[6]

On the beach, men were being told by junior officers left behind that they had capitulated. The men were instructed to put arms and helmets in a pile, then wait to be collected. Improvised white flags started flying at dawn to discourage strafing. An angry murmur trailed around the crowd.

Soon, German soldiers came down the slope and walked among the defeated army, Schmeissers on their shoulders and bellowing orders, '*Raus! Raus! Mach schnell!* [Out! Out! Hurry up!]' A thin line formed and moved slowly up the slope to an assembly area with guards by a pile of surrendered weapons. Once the mob started moving, the Germans allowed it to move at its own pace. Still without boots, Charlie Jager was part of the crowd, 'mortified by the contrast between our bedraggled selves and the superbly equipped and seasoned eighteen-year-olds [Jager was twenty-one] who've taken us'.[7]

Two Stukas arrived after the mustering of prisoners had begun and bombarded the assembly area, causing severe casualties including a German officer trying to unfurl a Nazi flag. The Germans on the ground were apparently caught by surprise as much as their captives and apologised for the attack.[8] Nobody had thought to tell the Luftwaffe of the surrender.

After a rudimentary search for arms, the prisoners were marched along the road back to Canea. When they got to Imbros, they milled around the nearly empty well, its windlass chain broken and its bucket at the bottom. An Australian jiggled his water bottle on a length of twine he still carried until the bottle was filled. After that, he had to deal with the clamour for his string.[9] Others drained the radiators of smashed trucks for drinking water. The main body of prisoners got to the top of the pass by nightfall and slept by the roadside.

It took three days to get to Canea, stopping from time to time to let stragglers catch up. The victorious soldiers were in no hurry. Peter Winter's lasting memory of the journey is of 'the bodies of hundreds of our compatriots lying unburied in the olive groves and at the roadside, bloated, flyblown and obscene in the heat of day'.[10] By contrast, the two Greek nurses were coming back in British shorts and shirts, still smiling with adventure and unfazed after being stopped by an embarkation officer from boarding a barge.[11]

It wasn't until the third day that the prisoners got their first issue of rations, a packet of biscuits for each man. Barely enough to live on, but their own army hadn't fed them much better on the journey there. Sam Payne, a driver from Wellington, hadn't eaten for seven days. He found an egg and a tin of bully beef run over by trucks. 'It was as flat as a pancake and the meat was a brilliant yellow,' he says, 'but I ate it.'[12]

In Canea, bully beef was added to the rations before the Anzacs and Marines were marched 18 kilometres to Skines at the end of Prison Valley, to a small compound built by the Greeks to house

Italian PoWs from Albania. Here the reality of being a PoW sunk in quickly. Living conditions were filthy, especially the latrines, and rations—rice, beans and lentils—were reasonable for a few days before falling off dramatically, perhaps easing the latrines. Discussions about escape started.

————————

About 6500 troops were captured by the Germans at Sphakia and Retimo, but that left over one thousand on the loose in Crete, some six hundred Australians and four hundred New Zealanders who had decided against surrendering and were looking for a way off the island. A group from Theo Walker's battalion had moved into the hills to one side. From there they could see German soldiers rounding up those still on the beach.

Reg Saunders, the Aboriginal sergeant, was in a group of fifteen who filled water bottles and hiked three kilometres to an olive grove where they hid for the day. That night they made their way to a beach east of Sphakia, hoping to be seen by a passing British ship. They flashed their only torch continuously until its battery ran out. Still trying to assemble a survival plan, they came across goats grazing near a remote village. 'Bluey' Reiter, a rural labourer from Gippsland, cut the throat of one with a bayonet. While he was skinning it, someone called out, 'Here comes a couple of Greeks.'

They sat on a bag draped over the carcass but the Cretans weren't fooled and menaced the Australians with their rifles. The matter was resolved by paying the goat's owners all the drachmas they had between them. They lit a fire and enjoyed an unaccustomed meal of roasted goat, but after that they had no money, nothing beyond the filthy clothes they were standing in. The decision was made to double back to Suda Bay where Saunders had buried tins of food before leaving for the south coast.[13]

While the infantrymen went one way, a group of Australian gunners set out west before dawn, stumbling in the dark along a goat track. The lieutenant, Michael Clarke, was with them. As the sun rose, they came to an open space on a clifftop, with a stone bench overlooking the Mediterranean. German planes were starting to snoop around, so they hid in the scrub, ate some of their meagre rations and slept until afternoon.

At dusk, a man came along with a large black dog and sat on the bench, gazing out to sea, oblivious of the men hiding nearby. The dog sensed the fugitives, however, and barked, prompting the man to investigate and find the Australians. Clarke knew no Greek and tried other languages without success. '*Afstralós?* [Australian?]' the man asked and gestured drinking and eating. The fugitives nodded and he indicated for them to lie back down, then wandered off. He returned after dark with a big water flask and a wooden platter of cheese.

The Australians spent the night signalling out to sea—futilely— and in the morning returned to the undergrowth cover and slept while aircraft patrolled overhead. The Cretan came back at dusk with bread and more cheese, accompanied by a young man who spoke broken English. They indicated the fugitives should come to their village but the gunners shook their heads. They wanted to resume signalling and did so until a flat battery put an end to it.

Before dawn, the two Cretans returned to warn that a German patrol was moving along the cliffs looking for evaders. They'd halted for the night a few kilometres away. This time the Australians followed the Cretans to a bustling village where they washed, break-fasted and had Clarke's offer of payment waved away. They were shown into a small room at the back of a tavern and slept until they were woken in the afternoon.

The visitors were ushered into the tavern, which was filled with chattering villagers eating lunch. Some called out greetings to the Australians who nodded, then sat at the back where they were served onion soup, veal and potatoes and carafes of retsina. The youth came over and said they would move out at dusk. As the villagers were beginning to depart, there were sudden gasps of dismay.

A truck had driven up to the front door and six German soldiers walked in, laughing and joking. They sat down, taking no notice of the group at the back, and busied themselves trying to order their meal.

A fair-haired *oberleutnant* stood up and looked around, spotting the group at the back. He walked over and said '*Gruss Gott* [Good day]' to Clarke, who replied in fluent German, then was asked if he was enjoying Crete and if he had visited Austria, the German soldier's homeland. Clarke replied that he had and they exchanged pleasantries about skiing.

'May I ask you, sir, which unit you are with?' the German asked.

'The artillery,' Clarke replied.

He peered at the Australian's shoulder insignia, then straightened. '*Mein Gott*. Can it be that you are Australian soldiers?'

'Yes, Herr Oberleutnant.'

Momentarily speechless with mouth open, he gathered his wits, saluted and said, 'I have to inform you, Herr Oberleutnant, that you and your men are prisoners of the German army.'

Michael Clarke nodded and stood up. He was waved back to his chair. 'Finish your meal, sir. It may be your last good one for some time.'

'Thank you for your courtesy, Herr Oberleutnant.'

'We shall eat our dinner but I regret I must send my *feldwebel* [sergeant] to guard you,' he concluded, adding, 'please tell your men that the Australian soldiers fought very bravely and allow me to congratulate you on your German speech, sir.'[14]

———

Three barges used for evacuation had been left near Sphakia by the navy. Looking for his brother Keith, Ian Walker found him with a group planning to try to get away from Crete. They headed for a barge Ian had spotted earlier and found it off the beach and now packed with fugitive soldiers. An English voice called out, asking if anyone could repair engines. Keith, a Mildura car salesman, volunteered and boarded the drifting barge. He got an engine going by unfouling its propellor. The Australians climbed onto the already packed vessel.

A Royal Marines major, Ralph Garrett, had taken charge and the landing craft set off with 137 on board, mostly Marines and including Roy Macartney, recovered from his beetroot juice poisoning. Using a navy chart left with the barge, they headed south towards Gavdos, an island 48 kilometres away. A short distance out, they picked up a naked New Zealander, Wilfred Hancox from the Medical Corps, paddling on a large plank. He had stripped and swum towards an empty rowboat he saw offshore but it was taken before he could get to it.

After three hours of slow motoring, they got to Gavdos where they stocked up with food and water, fixed the second engine and set off into the night. By morning, fuel was getting low. Mixing with paraffin extended its range but it eventually ran out and the vessel drifted for several windless days. Men plunged into the sea to escape the heat and a Palestinian shot himself after ignoring advice to not drink sea water. When a plane passed nearby, cordite flares were burned to no avail. The next day, a bowl of cordite was accidentally ignited with four men severely burnt. A rough sail was rigged with blankets, but steering was difficult. When wind gusts blew the barge off course or the wind died, the stronger men jumped into the sea and turned the vessel back on course.

By the eighth day, all men on board were very weak, their daily rations down to half a biscuit with a sliver of bully beef, and half a cup of water. Most were in a bad state. Ralph Garrett held a church service. 'It was really marvellous,' Keith Walker wrote later, 'all knelt and prayed together—all creeds, denominations, Jews, Greeks and all together. It was great, it seemed to raise the spirits of the lads one hundred per cent.'

The wind came up in the afternoon and a more robust sail was rigged up with bootlaces and blankets by two Australians, enabling the vessel to run with the wind. Before the sun went down, land was in sight. The barge beached in the morning. Macartney took a group along the shore and found a British armoured column. They were west of Sidi Barrani, ashore in Egypt after nine days at sea.[15]

The other two landing barges beached near Sidi Barrani, one half an hour after Garrett's vessel and the last the day after, both with similar stories of running out of petrol and food, severe water rationing and sails improvised from blankets. Those on all three barges had experienced outbursts of irrational temper with nerves on edge as hopes dimmed and hunger took hold, but all on board survived to reach the north African coast, apart from the suicide and a Briton who died of exposure.

Even more remarkable is the voyage of two Australians and two New Zealanders who left Crete's south-west coast in a small open boat. As the British force withdrew to Sphakia, a New Zealand machine-gun detachment had been picked up by landing craft from an island at the entrance to Suda Bay and taken around the coast towards Sphakia. The vessel was sunk by a Stuka while stopping on the west coast. Brendan Carter was among the men captured and taken to Kastelli. He was moved to Canea to work in a kitchen, then transferred to the PoW camp at Skines.

Slipping out of the camp in the dust of passing trucks, Carter made his way to the south coast. On his way, he ran into another New Zealander who had been wounded and captured in the main hospital near Canea, then escaped three weeks later.

On the coast the two Kiwis linked up with two Australians and found a derelict 18-foot (5.5-metre) dinghy. The four escapees knew nothing about boats, but they patched this one up, blocking holes with socks. It was mid-July when, with little food, they started to row across the Mediterranean, bailing as they went. When wind came up, they lashed the oars as a mast and rigged a blanket as a sail. The wind built up to a gale and blew them south, dying off as they came within sight of the coast near Sidi Barrani. At the end of the four-day voyage, soldiers waded out to help pull in the boat. As they did, the gunwale broke off. The next day, the soldiers tried to use the dinghy out of interest. It fell apart and sank.[16]

The men in Ray Sandover's battalion at Retimo who chose not to surrender—which was most of them—headed south through a mountain valley in two groups, one led by Sandover, the other by Ralph Honner, his second-in-command. The Western Australians kept much of their battalion structure and headed to Ay Galini, a fishing village near Timbaki where reinforcements and tanks had been landed for Heraklion just before the battle. Honner's party got there on 31 May; Sandover arrived that evening, the night of the final evacuation from Sphakia. About 300 British troops were already there, most of them Highlanders. For the first time, the Retimo contingent heard of the evacuations from Heraklion and Sphakia.

Ay Galini had two abandoned landing barges and not much food, most of the villagers having gone. Those remaining sold what little they had. The Retimo groups decided to move away from the large and growing crowd already there. It was unlikely to escape detection for long.

John Fitzhardinge, an artillery officer, planned an escape on one of the barges if it could be made seaworthy. The former Perth architect oversaw the repair work. One barge, beyond repair, was stripped for parts while a team of mechanically minded troops worked on the other. Told by Highlanders there were abandoned trucks with batteries at Timbaki, two Australians walked barefoot up the coast for three kilometres to retrieve them. They found the trucks, as well as cases of rations in an olive oil factory, and struggled back with two batteries, returning to find the engine repaired and powered by fuel drained from a crashed Glenn Martin patrol plane.

While the hull was being patched, one of them, Bill Mortimer, returned to get the provisions with Fitzhardinge and Tom Bedells.

Sailing to Timbaki in a small boat they'd found, they filled tins with water and loaded rations from the factory. As Fitzhardinge and Mortimer were pushing the boat out, a German motorcyclist arrived and began shooting at them. His fire from a distance was largely inaccurate but he managed to wound Bedells twice before they got out of firing range.

With the barge now seaworthy, Colonel Sandover had the task of selecting seventy-seven men for the voyage to North Africa. After excluding himself, the packed barge left Ay Galini at dusk on 2 June.

Shortly after midnight, an Italian submarine surfaced, slid past and turned around, directing machine-gun fire across the barge's bows. The escape, so near to success, seemed headed for heartbreaking failure with Italian submariners boarding the craft. As there were too many fugitives to fit in the submarine, the Italians just took off nine of the officers, leaving on board the wounded Bedells, an English officer who couldn't swim and the sixty-six lower ranks. Ordered to follow their captors back to Crete, the barge's course was re-set for the Egyptian coast when the submarine dived.

On 5 June, land was seen in the distance and, as they got closer, unfamiliar vehicles moving about. One of the Western Australians swam to shore to investigate and, shortly after, beckoned the vessel in. They were South African troops, 15 kilometres from the voyage's planned landing point.[17] Along with the three barges from Sphakia, a total of 300 soldiers had made it to the North African coast.

———

By the time the Germans were victorious, anger had built within their ranks at the resistance of armed Cretan civilians during the invasion, fuelled further by stories of mutilation of German soldiers by Cretans and even by British soldiers. The stories originated with the young mountain troops who had been confronted on arrival with the bodies of soldiers in fields and groves where they'd been lying in the heat for a few days, black, bloated and pecked at by ravens. Many of the new arrivals had never seen a dead body before. Some senior German officers encouraged the spread of these misconceptions.[18]

After surrender, General Student ordered reprisals against villages where civilians had participated in the battle and as a response to the 'mutilations' of German soldiers. During the battle, a motorcycle detachment trying to get through to the coast had been held back by villagers at Kandanos for three days. Later, on 3 June, 180 men, women and children were massacred at Kandanos and the ancient village burnt to the ground.[19] It was the day after seventy-nine men were shot in front of relatives in a churchyard at Alikianou, where the German flanking movement through Prison Valley had been thwarted for several days. Two months later, a further 118 civilians from the far end of the valley were shot. Males were made to dig a mass grave before their execution.[20] At Galatas, Germans ripped dresses from the shoulders of women suspected of fighting against them. If they had a bruise from rifle recoil, they were executed with the men.[21]

Cretan townspeople and shepherds sheltered the Australian and New Zealand soldiers evading the occupation force, assisting them at great personal risk. At first, troops left behind lived with villagers, sharing their scanty food and clothing. The numbers on the run increased as PoWs escaped from the poorly guarded camps. When the occupation force circulated posters proclaiming harbouring fugitives as a capital offence and advising that civilians caught would be shot, many villagers along the main routes became too fearful for evaders to stay with them, but they would still give food and medical assistance to the men as they passed through.

The Germans knew there were soldiers hiding in the hills and mountains but it was difficult terrain to patrol. They were slow to occupy the mountainous south of the island and for several months their patrols rarely went there. People in the more remote villages and shepherds in mountain huts continued to provide shelter, if not in houses, then in nearby caves, taking food to those evading the Germans. Many villagers had sons who had been fighting the Italians in Albania and had not returned. Passing locals would warn fugitives if Germans were in the village they were approaching. One villager, Adonis Paterakis, hung a rug over a wall on the outskirts of his village when Germans were about.

'As long as the Cretans had anything they would give it to us. When we went hungry we knew they were going hungry too,' says Johnny Peck. 'They would share their last piece of bread with us and we would all sit around the table dipping the hard crust into a cup of olive oil and vinegar.'[22]

––––––––

Most of the Allied soldiers had been aware they might be wounded or even killed in Greece, perhaps heroically, but many hadn't contemplated they might be taken prisoner. They dealt with the twin feelings of shame and helplessness in the first instance. Once that was overcome, they could settle into camp life with its discomforts but also its continuing camaraderie. The guards at the camps in the early days were sometimes surprisingly lax, probably because they were combat soldiers, paratroops and mountain troops, not garrison soldiers. It was almost as if they were happy to be rid of some of their charges when they escaped.

After a few days, the camp commander at Skines, a lieutenant, went to Athens, leaving his second-in-command, a sergeant, in charge. The prisoners were allowed to go into the village where they mingled with residents. The whistle went to return to camp, but some prisoners were still drifting back when the commandant returned. The sergeant wasn't seen again.[23]

Paratroops and mountain troops, soldiers rather than Nazis, moved on to the Russian front in due course and were replaced by the eager young ideologues of Hitler Youth. Prison escapes had initially occurred because they were easy. Soon it was to get away from the wave of indiscriminate brutality. The prisoners were gradually being shipped to the crowded and unhygienic camps at Corinth and Salonika, then on to the big stalags in central Europe. That became another reason to get away.

Lew Lind had been put on a PoW work party, clearing Maleme airfield. After a month there, he was in a group of four who cut through barbed wire while guards were patrolling in the opposite direction.[24] Charlie Jager and Ben Travers, the gunners from Melbourne, had it even easier. They just slid under the barbed wire at the Skines camp. Woken by children in a garden the next morning, they were taken to a farm where three other Australians were hiding, dressed as farm workers.[25] Warned of reprisals brewing in Skines, the five fugitives moved on and heard the next day that Germans had massacred old men and boys in Skines and put the women who had sheltered them in prison. 'A strange horrible feeling persisted in my guts,' Jager says. 'I was alive, but better men than me, perhaps, had died. I felt the guilt of a deserter or malingerer.'[26]

Western Australians Geoff Edwards and Bill McCarrey found a dry creek bed running under the barbed wire at Skines and watched the pattern of the sentries to work out when to slip through.[27] At the Galatas camp, two Christchurch drivers, Tom Cumming and Jim Toon, waited at night in the latrine pit for the guards to pass, then clambered through barbed wire and a culvert under the road and into a vineyard, hiding in a farm building.[28]

From time to time, fugitives would cross paths with the German military on the lookout for them, with an outcome that was largely a matter of luck . . . or of luck running out. Pat Minogue, a Christchurch baker in another life, was working in the stables at the Salonika camp on the mainland. One day, when no guards were about, he simply dropped his broom and walked slowly down the road to the first corner, then ran until he was out of breath. A woman beckoned him from a house and took him to Madame Lappa who coordinated the movement of fugitives through a network of Greek homes. While he waited with other fugitives in a dockside warehouse to board a submarine, two armed Gestapo arrived at the door and shouted, 'Hunds oop!' Minogue was taken in a locked cattle truck to Germany, finally escaping through Prague. Madame Lappa was sent to a concentration camp.[29]

Jim Carstairs was in a group of four Australians left on the beach at Sphakia. They had moved into the hills and drifted around mountain villages and shepherds' huts for five months. By then looking like a shepherd himself, he was in the mountains above Heraklion when he took a New Zealander with malaria down to a nearby town for treatment.

While waiting in the town, he saw a uniformed man too late to slip away unnoticed. The man said '*Kalinychta* [Good night],' and Carstairs replied, 'Good night to you,' in good Greek.

The man peered at him. 'You're an Australian,' he said.

'No, no. I'm a poor shepherd from the hills. I'm only a poor man, sir.'

The man laughed. 'You'd fool a German but I'm a Greek police officer working for the Germans. My job is to catch you escaped PoWs.' As it turned out, he loathed the Germans and used the job as a cover while he helped escapees hide.[30]

Reg Saunders, from the same battalion as Carstairs, had been on the run for a similar time, sometimes alone, sometimes in small groups. He was holed up in an olive mill in the mountains south of Retimo, half a kilometre from a village, with two Australian prison camp escapees, 'Dodger' Vincent and George Burgess, along with a New Zealander, Arthur Lambert. They could look down from their loft and see German soldiers lounging around in the village. A villager, Vaselichi Zagarchis, brought them food, often a delicious soft white cheese riddled with maggots, and kids sometimes brought eggs and cigarettes at night. Vaselichi came one night and found Lambert shivering with yellow jaundice. The men could understand Greek by then and she said he should sleep in her one-room house in the village. Saunders and Burgess helped her get the sick man to her house that night.

The Australians were having a meal in a neighbour's house when a man burst in, warning that the Germans were conducting a house-to-house search of the village. The two fugitives decided that if they ran it might put a halt to the search so Lambert wouldn't be found. There was nothing to be gained by staying where they were anyway. Heads down, they dashed into the dark in different directions for cover outside the village, with hasty gunfire hot on their heels. Burgess jumped down a bank, twisted his ankle and was caught. Saunders got away and the action achieved its aim. The search was stopped to pursue the runaways and wasn't resumed. Lambert went undiscovered.

Next morning, Burgess and two Greek partisans were marched from the house used by the German commander. Village women screeched and spat at the armed escort as it tied the two Greeks to kitchen chairs in the village square. Seven German soldiers lined up and shot the sitting pair, but Burgess wasn't shot. He was kept in a compound for a week, well treated and given rations until he escaped and got back to the olive mill's loft. The three moved on.[31]

The Antipodeans were admired by the Cretans for coming so far to help defend Greece and for their bravado, their audacity in dealing with the Germans. Hiding out for a while in Canea, for example, Charlie Jager went into a barber shop for a shave. A German soldier was in the chair with two more standing by. Jager sat away from them and waited. The barber looked up and was astonished to see the Australian, then got back briskly to the job in hand. After the German paid and the three of them departed, Jager was shaved hurriedly with no payment asked.[32]

In another incident, Murray McLagan, a Kiwi gunner on the run, tells of two Australians drinking in a tavern when a tipsy German walked in and asked if he could join the 'Greeks'. The party got merrier and the Aussies got bolder, singing 'Roll Out the Barrel', 'Tipperary' and other soldiers' songs. The German had a great night, commenting that Greek songs were similar to German and English ones.[33]

In the dead of night on 26 July, the British submarine *Thrasher* rose from the black water out from Preveli beach on Crete's south coast. A light on the hillside flashed 'SOS' repeatedly. Two passengers were landed on the tiny, secluded beach by folboat, a folding military kayak. One was Royal Navy reservist, Francis Pool, the other his Greek guide. They made their way up a gully to the nearby Holy Monastery of Preveli.

Pool was from the Special Operations Executive (SOE), a clandestine organisation set up by Churchill in mid-1940 to conduct espionage and sabotage in Axis-occupied Europe and to encourage local resistance. The landing barges that had beached in Egypt loaded with troops left behind at Sphakia and Retimo had brought reports of hundreds of British and dominion troops on the run in Crete. It was not something the British could ignore. Their presence put Cretans in peril and raised questions, already being asked, about Britain's capacity to help its allies if it abandoned its own soldiers.

Pool had been sent to arrange the naval rescue of these evaders and escapees. He was taken to meet the abbot at Preveli, Father Agathangelos Lagouvardos, a giant of a man who was just concluding mass. Wary of German spies, the white-bearded abbot was initially cautious of the visitor who looked more Mediterranean than English and spoke fluent Greek with a Cretan dialect. Before the war, 'Skipper' Pool had for many years managed a flying-boat station for Imperial Airways on Crete's north coast. After establishing his bona fides, the Englishman told the abbot that the submarine would return the following night to take as many troops as could be brought to the beach.[34]

Francis Pool was the first English operative to cross to Crete, nearly two months after the surrender. An extensive network had built up within the Cretan population, guiding fugitive soldiers to anticipated evacuation points. These groups would have had to communicate with Cairo, either by radio or through undercover operatives in mainland Greece, for Pool to know to land at Preveli.

The waiting men had been guided to the area through Crete's bush telegraph. Alan Hackshaw, a Perth truck driver, was one of the signallers at Preveli beach. He'd been told by a Cretan that British ships were sailing off the coast each night, contactable by signal lamp, then was told a submarine had seen the signal and he should get to the monastery.[35]

Geoff Edwards and Bill McCarrey, having escaped from Skines, had been told by a local to head towards Preveli as other Australians were gathered around there. As they approached, they were intercepted by an agitated Cretan who said Germans were around the monastery. He took them to a hideout already holding a group from Retimo. Village men acted as guides and the women brought food. Schoolboys were used as runners.

While they were waiting, Edwards and McCarrey began to worry there were too many fugitives about and security was getting slack. They decided to move down the coast, but were persuaded to wait three more days. On the second of those days, Pool arrived and the following night the two joined the seventy-odd men assembled on the beach.[36]

A 21-year-old Australian warrant officer, Bill Ryan, had led a group away from Sphakia beach after the initial surrender, taking some of the revolvers from the pile of surrendered arms. They'd headed into the mountains, eventually banding with a party of Retimo fugitives. After six weeks on the move, Ryan was brought a note from an Australian officer, 'Be at the beach [Preveli] at ten o'clock, there's a good chance of getting off.' Having heard repeatedly from locals about a boat that went underwater, the group was at last setting out for one. They walked in single file, Cretans at front and back with small boys as scouts either side.

Arriving at a deserted beach, other evaders soon joined them— some had been hiding in villages, others constantly on the run. Given a number for each man, they were lined up in groups of ten. While they chattered softly in nervous excitement, worrying about how many men the sub could hold, the Cretans produced eggs, cold meat and bread for a last supper. Suddenly and silently, a black shape emerged on the sea's surface about 200 metres out. A folboat brought in a line from the submarine and would ferry non-swimmers out. The rest were to swim out, using the line as a guide.[37]

Geoff Edwards, a Kalgoorlie truck driver, was not a strong swimmer and had an anxious moment on the way out. 'I pulled myself along the rope to the sub,' he remembers. 'Halfway out there, the soldier in front of me panicked, as he couldn't swim a stroke, and he started splashing around and shouting out. A sailor quickly quietened him with a terrific punch to the jaw and then guided him along.'[38]

Along with the others, Ryan took off his clothes and gave them to a Cretan boy, clothing by then being in short supply on the island. The Armidale shop assistant's last action in the Greece campaign was to swim out to his rescuers. On 1 August, seventy-eight rescued men, mostly Australians and Britons, disembarked at Alexandria.

———

Francis Pool remained in Crete to arrange further evacuations and contact resistance groups through Father Lagouvardos and a local resistance leader. While he did that, further bands of fugitives were finding their way to Preveli.

Tom Cumming and Jim Toon had been told in a village about a British officer who was getting evaders off Crete in a submarine. A Cretan guided them by night along steep tracks winding through thick scrub to his village where he was the local blacksmith. Taking them to a hideout outside the village, he didn't return. The pair risked going into the village where they found their guide, dead drunk.

Pushing on without him, they found new contacts who got them to a cave already occupied by eight fugitives. They could look down from there on Germans swimming and at the monastery, across in the distance, looking like a group of toy houses. Monks came down to attend to livestock and vineyards.[39]

After the Fitzhardinge barge had left Ay Galini for Egypt, Ray Sandover, Ralph Honner and the Retimo fugitives still in Crete were befriended by an English-speaking Cretan, Costas Folakis, and taken to a cave where Folakis brought food regularly. In late July, a villager gave Sandover a cryptic message on torn-off paper. 'To the English Major,' it said, 'Do you remember the young lady who swam naked to the Elaphonesos Islands? The man who entertained you then is waiting to greet you now. Follow this guide, he can be trusted.'

Sandover, schooled in Germany, was suspicious that the '7' in the date was crossed through, European-style. He had no memory of a young naked swimmer but doubted a German would write such nonsense. He decided to take a chance and, travelling by donkey, met Pool in a small hut out from Retimo. It turned out the message had been addressed to John Pendlebury, the archaeologist appointed to create a Cretan regiment before the German invasion. Unknown to the SOE man, Pendlebury was already dead, killed by the Germans. Pool had somehow got in his mind that Sandover must be him. Told that Australian soldiers from Retimo were hiding within two days of Preveli, Pool instructed the party to report to Brother Dionysius at the monastery on 18 August. A submarine would be there the next night.[40]

The small group with Cumming and Toon moved silently along the road to Preveli that night, merging with another group coming down from a village with a crowd of Cretans following. A searchlight on a nearby headland swept the bay a few times, then lost interest. By the time the Retimo group got to the small pocket of sand, about 120 fugitives were crowded on it. As the senior officer there, Sandover divided the mob into three parties which drew lots for boarding priority. The abbot came down on a mule and blessed the evacuees. Told they would be swimming out to the submarine when it came, the men stripped off, their clothes whisked away by the Cretans, then found themselves waiting naked in a cold wind.[41]

Half an hour later, there was a swishing sound and a conning tower appeared against the dark sea. Sandover waded out to meet a naval officer in a folboat, while a sailor jumped out with a rope around his waist and secured it to a rock. The officer asked, 'How many?' then added, 'Keep them quiet or we'll go away.' He said he could take 120, 'but no Greeks'.[42]

Two wounded men were put in the folboat and ferried out to the submarine *Torbay*. The rest had to follow the rope out, a man sent from the beach every twenty seconds. Non-swimmers were given lifebelts and had to pull themselves out on the rope, with a swimmer behind for encouragement and to assist if needed. Lew Lind was one of the evacuees but he couldn't find the rope. He'd swum most of the way when he heard thrashing in the water to one side. A Greek was gripping the rope, but he was stopped from boarding and was eventually dragged ashore half-drowned. One of the Australians who had been a lifesaver at home brought him round before heading into the water.

Lind got to the black shape heaving in the swell, but the sloping deck was slippery with grease. After trying to get a footing at several points without success, he yelled out. Immediately a rope slapped the water beside him and he was pulled up. At the conning tower, two sailors took name, rank and serial number. The inside of the submarine was full of naked men in the dull light, hazy with cigarette smoke. Time ran out on that first night before all on the beach had embarked and *Torbay* submerged for the day, returning the next night to complete embarkation. Some 130 fugitive troops were squeezed on board, along with Francis Pool.[43] In the morning, monks took flocks of sheep and goats down to the shore. Any visible footprints disappeared under their tracks.

After a week in dim, sepulchral light, the evacuees arrived at Alexandria. 'When the hatch was opened to admit the blinding sunlight,' remembers Lind, 'it was as though we had been given a glimpse of paradise.'[44]

_____

An informer told the Germans of the submarine rescues soon after *Torbay* had gone. A few days later, they came to the monastery to arrest the abbot, but he'd been made aware of the German plans and got away in time, allowing the monks to claim he was pro-British but they weren't. The monks were interrogated nonetheless and some arrested, to be released later. The monastery buildings and much of their contents were vandalised, furniture and vestments destroyed. Goods and livestock were taken away.[45]

With the Germans setting up a post near Preveli, new landing sites had to be reconnoitred and, when the Royal Navy cut back on use of its submarines, new rescue vessels found. Late in the year, the SOE started landing operatives, including Francis Pool, to continue supporting local resistance and extricating fugitives at large on Crete. Two boats were found, the motor lifeboat *Escampador* and a 60-tonne fishing boat *Hedgehog*, to look for new landing sites and to pick up Allied soldiers. One trip by *Hedgehog* in November 1941 picked up ninety soldiers and Father Lagouvardos, the abbot of Preveli, and took them to Egypt.

Reg Saunders, the Aboriginal sergeant, was on the run in Crete for eleven months, living mostly in caves. At one time, he and his two companions were approached in an olive grove by a fair-haired 'Greek' who wanted to contact Cretan resistance. They told him he would have to wait for a Greek soldier to confirm he was Greek. The man disappeared that night and the Australians left in the morning. Saunders was later told a German patrol searched the area soon after and, later, the man was killed by Greek resistance. His body was dumped outside a German army post.[46]

In May 1942, a year after the German invasion of Crete, a message came to Saunders from a shepherd who'd previously given him food and information. The Australian was told to contact a man in the next village. He did so and was told to return at dusk 'for a meeting'. Coming back with Burgess and Vincent, the trio were taken with fifteen other fugitives to a beach where more escapees were being organised into three batches by agents with clipped British accents and dressed in scruffy peasant clothes. They were told to strip off on the beach so that lice weren't taken on board.

They sat around in naked groups until *Hedgehog* arrived at dawn. Cretans waded out and unloaded supplies for the resistance units in the hills, then the evacuees climbed on board. Saunders, Burgess and Vincent were given their first change of clothes in a year. At last, they could drink, laugh and talk loudly in English. Drunk on overproof rum, Saunders and Burgess got into an argument with fisticuffs but little damage.

They arrived with hangovers in Egypt where Reg Saunders heard for the first time that they were at war with Japan.[47] The world was forever changing, the war was rolling on.

12

THE WAR ROLLS ON

No story of human activity and affairs comes to a standstill. Parts come to a conclusion; other parts move on into new stories. The battles for Greece and Crete may have ended with the surrenders at Retimo and Sphakia but for the participants, those who survived the battles, there were new ventures to play a part in.

After the evacuation from Crete, the Australian force continued rebuilding in Palestine. Two of its battalions took part in the Allied invasion of Syria and Lebanon, at that time controlled by the Vichy French. German planes had been allowed use of Syrian airfields to attack the British in Iraq. Still unaware Hitler was planning an invasion of Russia, the British feared that these airfields would be used to attack Egypt with its canal that brought the Empire's spoils to Britain.

When the Vichy French capitulated in July 1941, the Australians provided a garrison for Syria until the simultaneous Japanese invasion of Malaya and raid on Pearl Harbor. In January 1942 the decision was made to withdraw the force back to Australia to meet the new threat. By then, the Menzies government had been tipped out of power, in part for allowing Australia to be drawn into the disastrous Greek campaign.

John Curtin, the new prime minister, was not in awe of Britain, nor of Churchill who regarded dominion armies as being at his disposal. When, without consultation, the British leader diverted returning Australian troops to Burma to curry favour with America, Curtin stuck to his guns and Churchill had to back down. On their government's insistence, Australian troops were brought back to defend their homeland against the threat of Japanese invasion.

The two Anzac armies didn't fight together again in the war. The New Zealanders remained as part of the British Eighth Army and fought in North Africa, where they were left unsupported by British armoured units at El Alamein. General Montgomery ordered a subsequent assault by British infantry and armour under New Zealand HQ's tactical planning and Rommel was forced to withdraw. By November 1942 the Axis was in full retreat in North Africa.

In late 1943, 6000 battle-weary New Zealand soldiers were brought home on leave. In agreeing to a British request to join the Anglo-American push through Italy, the government was pressured to release the returned men and send men who'd not yet served, the RSA—the Royal New Zealand Returned and Services' Association, the equivalent of Australia's RSL—leading protests to 'get at the shirkers'. Only 1100 returned to the fray, the new arrivals fresh but untested in battle.

The Maori battalion spearheaded a pivotal assault on Cassino, a brutal and costly battle at a German strongpoint on the path to Rome. In house-to-house fighting after the intense bombardment of the town, the Kiwis continued to reconnect to their warrior heritage and kept their distinctive sense of humour. On one occasion they found themselves on the ground floor of a ruined building, exchanging gunfire with Germans holding the floor above. The battle suddenly went quiet and, in the silence, a German voice called out in a stage whisper, 'Heinrich? Heinrich?'

There was no response. The voice called again and, in the silence that followed, a Maori voice shouted from the floor below, 'Heinrich! Answer him, you bastard!'[1]

When General Student reported to his Führer that Crete had been conquered, Hitler replied, 'Yes, but at what cost?' The price had been nearly 6000 casualties from a force of 22,000, greater than that paid by the ragged force defending it. Concluding from the experience that airborne invasion wasn't viable, Hitler refused to consider it as an option again, rejecting a proposal for a similar attack on Cyprus, thinly held by a small brigade. In truth, the invasion of Crete was not hamstrung by the shortcomings of paratroop operation, but by the failings of German intelligence.

After the war, Kurt Student was tried for the treatment of PoWs and reprisal killings of civilians by his men in Crete. He was found guilty of the charges relating to PoWs, but acquitted of crimes against civilians after Lindsay Inglis gave surprising testimony in his favour. Sentenced to five years imprisonment, Student was given an early discharge for medical reasons in 1948 and lived another thirty years.

The offensive against Crete had been largely a cover for the preparation of the upcoming attack on the Soviet Union and to protect that operation's perimeter. Operation Barbarossa was launched on 22 June 1941 with the bombing of cities in Soviet-occupied Poland and Crete became a backwater in Germany's planning. Paratroops were used in Russia as ground troops only.

Greece was divided by the victors into three occupation zones. The most strategically important regions, including Athens, Salonika and most of Crete, were administered by the Germans. Other regions were given to Germany's junior partners in that campaign, Italy and Bulgaria. Within three weeks, large quantities of food and materials were being transported north by the conquering army, either looted or bought with worthless paper marks, issued locally.

Greek factories closed for lack of raw materials. Distribution of produce was disrupted by German and Italian roadblocks and seizure of crops, so farmers didn't take their produce to market, leaving towns without food. Prices rose and hoarding became widespread[2]. Nearly 50,000 civilians died from starvation in Athens–Piraeus alone in the first year of occupation, increasing in the years following. Thousands more died from reprisals by Nazis and their Greek collaborators.

With the defeated Greek government in exile in Egypt, a puppet government was set up by the Germans with General Tsolakoglou its prime minister. Whatever benefit the Greek people might have gained from his ending of the German onslaught was forgotten in his servicing of its occupation. Arrested and tried for war crimes in 1945, Tsolakoglou's death sentence was commuted to life imprisonment. Three years later, he died of leukaemia.

At the same time, the Greek resistance was formed, launching guerrilla attacks against the occupying powers, fighting collaborationist groups and setting up espionage networks. By late 1943, the resistance groups were starting to fight among themselves, so that by the time of liberation of mainland Greece in October 1944, the Greek civil war had already begun.

––––––

Immediately after the defeat in Crete, the English and Australian press began to look critically at the Greek expedition. At issue was the preparation for the campaign and its viability. Of particular concern was the RAF's role. 'The conclusion cannot be avoided that there was an under-estimation on the British side of the power of the enemy to strike at Crete by air,' editorialised *The Sydney Morning Herald*, 'and a failure during the last six months to equip the island aerodromes with adequate anti-aircraft defences.'[3]

In Britain, *The Times* posed a rhetorical question: 'Success or failure in the defence of Crete depended to a very large extent upon constant air support. That is the point where criticism deserves an answer, and the one essential question is whether—and if so from what moment—it was known that the defence would have to be conducted without that support?'[4] The answer is, of course, that it was known from the outset.

The New Zealand press was more circumspect. With any moral obligation already honoured in defending Greece's mainland, Wellington's *Evening Post* saw the decision to fight on in Crete as a purely military judgement. Germany's overwhelming air superiority and the Crete garrison's weak defence made it a poor decision, ensuring 'hand-to-hand fighting against a constantly reinforced enemy'.[5]

The only positive the press could find in the immediate aftermath was that the two weeks of fighting on Crete had delayed Germany's plans to capture the Suez Canal and Iraq's oilfields. Within a few months, that glimmer faded. Hitler's invasion of the Soviet Union made clear there was no intention to press on to the south. That objective would be left to Rommel, then making significant progress in North Africa.

There wasn't much left to justify the expedition. The *Lend-Lease Act*, the core reason for embarking on the operation, had been passed in both US Houses of Congress by 11 March, four weeks before the German invasion of Greece. The Balkan front had been only a fleeting possibility, Turkey never indicating any serious interest and Yugoslavia's position constantly shifting. Britain simply didn't have the resources it promised in order to stop the German advance it had frog-marched the Greeks in to resisting. Middle East Command was already tied up on several fronts in its over-extended area of responsibility, its bare RAF support spread thinly with mostly obsolete aircraft.

The defence of the Greek mainland had been a series of withdrawals by an army still trundling into position when the

invasion began. Beginning on the first day of engagement with
the German army, the retreat continued until the entire British
force had been evacuated from the Greek mainland or abandoned.
Withdrawals had mostly started before the previous one was
completed, the speedy retreat difficult to explain in the changing
situation to field commanders and then to the men. The decision
to resist the inevitable invasion of Crete was even more indefen-
sible, with an inadequately equipped force in a patched-together
command structure. Troops were exhausted, demoralised and
embittered, the Luftwaffe air supremacy bound to continue.

'We lacked much vital equipment necessary to support the
army; for example, only one tank brigade could be spared for this
hair-brained adventure,' writes Australian artillery commander, Bill
Cremor. 'But worst of all, we buoyed up the heroic Greek people
with illusory hopes and advertised to Turkey our inability to give
adequate help to our friends.'[6]

The British military conducted several inquiries into its Greek
'adventure' until, carefully managed, it got an outcome it could live
with. Colonel Freddie de Guingand, a Middle East Command staff
officer, headed a committee to assess lessons to be learnt. The prin-
cipal finding was the lack of preparation in Crete by the British
garrison force in the six months prior to the island's invasion. The
report was sent to London and buried.[7]

A Court of Inquiry reported in early July. Chaired at Churchill's
insistence by Brigadier Guy Salisbury-Jones, a former chief of the
British Military Mission in Athens, it was highly critical of GHQ
and the RAF in the Middle East, particularly the failure to consider
future requirements for the defence of Crete. General Wavell, by then
relieved of his Middle East command and appointed commander-
in-chief in India, didn't read the inquiry's report until he was on the
plane to Delhi. He was furious, demanding its withdrawal.

Given the antagonism that had existed between Middle East
Command and the Athens mission, Salisbury-Jones wasn't a very

astute choice to chair the inquiry. GHQ, under its new commander-in-chief, General Claude Auchinleck, demanded the War Office disregard the report. Although the facts weren't questioned, superior officers had been criticised by their juniors and there had been an unwitting breach of Ultra security.[8] The report was suppressed and a second Court of Inquiry was held in secret under Brigadier George Erskine, an infantry commander in North Africa. It removed twenty-nine paragraphs from the earlier report, those parts compromising Ultra and those critical of Middle East staff.[9]

In the search for scapegoats that followed, the New Zealanders were the obvious target with their flawed defence of Crete, although they were working with the hand dealt them by random troop and equipment arrivals, an unfettered Luftwaffe and Britain's complacent defence preparations. No doubt aware of the political danger, some senior New Zealand officers moved quickly to protect their reputation.

On his return by flying-boat from Crete, Jimmy Hargest went straight to Cairo. 'Dirty and unshaven with only the clothes I possessed not having been removed for twelve days, I pushed my way to the Embassy and told General Wavell and Admiral Cunningham the truth of many things without once knuckling down,' recalls Hargest, the genial politician. 'Peter Fraser stood by me God bless him and instead of being ashamed of my appearance was loyally proud.' He met Fraser again the next day and complained about Freyberg's retreat in Greece and leadership in Crete, his deployment at Maleme and the ineffective counter-attack there.[10] Hargest had a politician's gall.

Asked by Wavell to send a senior officer to London to lecture on containing German airborne troops, General Freyberg chose Lindsay Inglis. At a 13 June meeting with Churchill, Inglis was critical of Middle East GHQ's lack of preparation and strategic thinking. It has been inferred that Inglis was also critical of Freyberg from remarks by Churchill the next day but, while Inglis was highly

opinionated, his performance wasn't under scrutiny and some of
the opinions Churchill expressed are unlikely to have originated
with Inglis. It's possible Inglis criticised Freyberg to Churchill, but
there's no direct evidence for it. It's just as plausible that Churchill's
comments were his own.

Freyberg took responsibility for the failure to hold Crete
against the Germans, reluctant to pass the blame on to his subor-
dinates. His prime minister, Peter Fraser, considered replacing him
as New Zealand commander-in-chief, but strong endorsements
from Wavell and Auchinleck dissuaded him. Nonetheless, post-war
writers looking for a scapegoat for the defeat, preferably one who
is not English, tend to single out Freyberg. Antony Beevor, perhaps
the best known, is preoccupied with what he sees as Freyberg's
unwarranted fixation on a possible seaborne invasion to the neglect
of measures against the airborne attack. Yet the seaborne invasion
was constantly appearing in Ultra reports in conjunction with the
airborne invasion and with near equal strength. A seaborne landing
was in fact attempted, to deliver the element Freyberg most feared:
German tanks.

It's been said of Freyberg that 'few commanders in history had
enjoyed such precise intelligence on their opponents' intentions,
timing and objectives'.[11] This is tendentious nonsense. Ultra was then
in its infancy, its reports an undifferentiated mix of limited decrypts
and speculation by intelligence officers with no military background.
The information Freyberg was getting was piecemeal and incom-
plete, sometimes inaccurate, often merely confirming what had been
inferred without Ultra six months earlier. At this time, of the three
German military services only the air force's Enigma had been pene-
trated. Later in 1941, with the other two service codes broken and
the processing of this intelligence refined, Ultra started becoming a
formidable weapon, but its time hadn't come by May 1941.

Howard Kippenberger, who emerged from the war with an
enhanced reputation, has been scathing about some of his fellow

officers, noting 'Hargest's flabbiness and lack of grip dreadfully evident. Puttick not much better. Inglis all talk . . . and nothing done.[12]

'The failure in each case seems to me to have been that they answered all questions pessimistically,' a bitterly disappointed Kippenberger comments, 'that they saw all dangers real, imagined or possible, that none made any effort to dictate or control events, that they were utterly without any offensive spirit, and that invariably in each case, they adopted the course that made victory impossible and defeat inevitable. Not the minor mistakes all commanders make, but fundamental mistakes.'[13]

In particular, Kippenberger has in mind the abandoning by Les Andrew of Hill 107 at Maleme and Jimmy Hargest's tardiness in assembling a counter-offensive to recover it. However, the German invasion would probably have succeeded even without those blunders in defence. Unless General Löhr chose to cut his losses in the first couple of days and abandon the attack—and that would have been out of character—then it would have eventually succeeded with the defenders unable to be reinforced and their supplies exhausted. The Royal Navy couldn't afford the losses it would sustain in resupply or preventing a seaborne attack by day. With the Maleme airfield captured, the Germans didn't need to renew the seaborne attack because they could land reinforcements by air.

The men defending Crete were little more than weary refugees improvising defence at short notice . . . and that included General Freyberg. It's quite astonishing that, despite that, they came as close as they did to repelling an invasion that had the initiative and superiority in the air, that was fresh to the task and not traumatised by constant bombardment from the air.

———

The soldiers who fought in this twin campaign largely escaped the recriminations that dogged it through and beyond the war. They were heroes who had fought valiantly against impossible odds under arguably questionable leadership, although whose questionable leadership would often depend on the comment's source. It's not an unreasonable assessment of the men, a mixed bag of volunteers from all walks of Australian and New Zealand life.

An observation by a German officer on the footsloggers of the two dominion armies is interesting. 'Australian soldiers always grin when they are attacking,' Colonel Erhard Löhter told Berlin Radio. 'On some occasions our boys thought the Australians would not take a bayonet charge seriously because they smiled so broadly. We don't know whether the Australians think fighting is funny, but we are not deceived any more by these obliging grimaces. New Zealanders are as wild as if all of them are Maoris. They don't smile but shout their heads off. They are quicker than Australians and not so congenial when captured. New Zealanders are tough and our boys don't try to be polite with them.'[14]

When you grow up in what feels like the far end of the world, you develop a curiosity to see what is elsewhere on the planet, a characteristic of young Australians and New Zealanders that persists to this day. Robert 'Bon' Gillies enlisted in 1939 as a sixteen-year-old labourer from Rotorua. Like Vic Hillas, the butcher's apprentice from rural Victoria, it had nothing to do with God, King and Country. 'I think we all went for the adventure,' Gillies says. 'We hadn't even been out of town, most of us. We didn't go to fight a war; we went to have a look around and ended up in a war.'[15]

Unworldly young men went to a war and came back with a range of deep emotions imprinted in them by the experience. One aspect was the adversity shared with Greeks and Cretans, their enduring gratitude and the sacrifices they were prepared to make to defend their homes and people. Those soldiers who survived the war brought it home with them, sometimes keeping the experience bottled up inside them, unable to share it with or explain it to those nearest and dearest to them. The camaraderie and horror of war moulded them for the remainder of their lives, for better or worse, but it was more easily shared with those who had also been through and understood it.

'It was something you would never want to go through again,' says Keith Newth, a signaller in the war, previously a Nelson bus driver, 'but I wouldn't have liked to have missed it either. It was a wonderful experience to realise what a ghastly thing war was and how it made men act as heroes and some as animals.'[16]

ACKNOWLEDGEMENTS

This is the sixth book I have written with the support and guidance of Richard Walsh and Rebecca Kaiser. Bec retired from Allen & Unwin part-way through the project and Tom Bailey-Smith has taken it through to completion. I value the insights, advice and encouragement of all three.

My interest is less in the structures, equipment and strategies of military history and more in the personal experiences of battle, how people deal with that and the relationships they form with each other and with the surrounding populace. Anecdotes are the heart of these social histories, although judgement is needed to sift out authentic reflections from exaggerations, mythology and self-promotion.

Very few of the participants in this story are still alive. The contacts I did make were through Nick Andriotakis of the Greek Australian Alliance. Nick is a man of daunting energy but his assistance and enthusiasm were invaluable to me. Through him I contacted Eleni Blouchou and her family (Vassiliki, Katerina and Stelios) in Ambelakia, Costas Mamalakis in Crete and the Spyrakis (John, Kathy and Nick) and Minas (Fiona, Theodora and Helen) families in Sydney. Nick also put me in touch with Les Cook through Rania Kalimeris.

As most of this story has drawn from existing records in a variety of obscure and not-so-obscure sources—diaries, memoirs, unit histories, oral histories—a number of people have pointed me in useful directions in the hunt for anecdotal material. I thank Geoff Barnes, Paddy Conroy, Denis Lenihan, Maggie Paxton-Love, Kel and Phil Bourke, Roger Selby, Wes Olson, Christine Melville, Brian Nicholls, Ruth Hall, Michael Osterberg, Lou Kissajukian, Wendy Charell and Kiriaki Orfanos for passing assistance in locating some of these sources.

I'm also grateful to Jennie Norberry, Kellidie Saunders and their colleagues at the Australian War Memorial Research Centre and to Paul Irving at the Ursula Davidson Library (RUSI, NSW) in Sydney. Annie Howard assisted me with some of the archive research.

The other side of the equation is the writing of the story and its packaging as a book. Jan Stretton, Sue Murray and Tony Biddle went through early drafts of the manuscript as proxies for you, the reader, suggesting changes that will make it more understandable and more readable. That process has been continued by the copy editor, Deonie Fiford, in her work on the delivered manuscript, improving its narrative flow and highlighting where the story has punch. These word police make the book more pleasurable to read than the version I wrote. I'm grateful to them for that. Why would I not be? For their role in the physical production of the book, my thanks to Luke Causby for the cover, to Kim Wright for the maps and to Midland Typesetters for typesetting and the production of the photo section. All these components add to the reader's enjoyment of the book.

Finally, I'd like to thank all the individuals who have left their recollections for me to scoop up into this human story. No matter how undesirable it might be, war can be a crucible of character . . . one way or the other.

NOTES

PRELIMINARIES
1 Adam-Smith, *Australian Prisoners of War* (2014), pp 140–1

CHAPTER 1   Boys far from home
1 Holt, *From Ingleburn to Aitape* (1981), p 16
2 Uren, *Kiwi Saga* (1944), p 35
3 Uren, *A Thousand Men at War* (1959), p 26
4 Robinson, *Journey to Captivity* (1991), p 17
5 McLean & McGibbon, *The Penguin Book of New Zealanders at War* (2009), p 252
6 Johnston, *Anzacs in the Middle East* (2013), p 42
7 Robson, 'The Australian Soldier: Formation of a Stereotype' in *Australia: Two Centuries of War and Peace*, eds McKernan & Browne (1988), p 313; McLean & McGibbon (2009), p 253
8 Johnston (2013), pp 37–8; King, 'Half a World Away' (2019), p 77
9 Charlton, *The Thirty-Niners* (1981), pp 91–2
10 King, 'Certainly getting about the world' (2020), p 120
11 Uren (1944), pp 293–4
12 Puttick, *25 Battalion* (1960), p 34; Semmler, *The War Diaries of Kenneth Slessor* (1985), p 207
13 King (2020), p 122
14 Dawson, *18 Battalion and Armoured Regiment* (1961), p 71; Pringle & Glue, *20 Battalion and Armoured Regiment* (1957), p 22
15 Holt (1981), p 27
16 Thompson, *Anzac Fury* (2010), p 50
17 Howie-Willis, 'The Australian Army's Two "Traditional" Diseases' (2019); Charlton (1981), p 89
18 Bellair, *Amateur Soldier* (1984), p 49
19 *Ibid*, p 47
20 *Sydney Morning Herald*, 'War and lust in the dust – a digger's story makes the stage', 14 April 2003

330

NOTES

21 Charlton (1981), p 59
22 Horner, *General Vasey's War* (1992), p 54
23 AWM52 18/2/19
24 Wahlert, *The Other Enemy?* (1999), p 92
25 Clift, *The Saga of a Sig* (1972), p 27; Bowden, *Larrikins in Khaki* (2019), p 66
26 King (2020), p 125
27 Ewer, *Forgotten Anzacs* (2016), p 104
28 Barrett, *We Were There* (1987), p 334; Wahlert (1999), p 90
29 King, (2020), p 125
30 Gordon, *The Embarrassing Australian* (1962), p 54
31 Charlton (1981), p 87
32 Wahlert (1999), p 89
33 Clifton, *The Happy Hunted* (1952), pp 61–2; Beevor, *Crete* (1991), p 32
34 Dawson (1961), p 71
35 Cody, *21 Battalion* (1953), p 34
36 Bellair (1984), p 48
37 Ewer (2016), p 103
38 Baker, *Paul Cullen* (2005), p 62
39 Wick, *Purple Over Green* (1977), pp 89–90; AWM52 8/3/2
40 Unit History Editorial C'tee, *White Over Green* (1963), p 104; Bishop, *The Thunder of the Guns* (1998), p 177; Bentley, *The Second Eighth* (1984), p 48
41 Bowden (2019), p 93; Ryan, *POWs Fraternal* (1990), p 151
42 Sinclair, *19 Battalion and Armoured Regiment* (1954), pp 57–9
43 Green, *The Name's Still Charlie* (2010), p 88; Marshall, *Nulli Secundus Log* (1946) pp 32–3; Wick (1977), p 90
44 Simpson, *Operation Mercury* (1981), p 85
45 Johnson, *The History of the 2/11th (City of Perth) Australian Infantry Battalion 1939–1945* (2000), p 86
46 *Australians at War* Film Archive, 'Frank Roy'
47 Johnson (2000), p 87; Olson, *Battalion into Battle* (2011), pp 106–7; Le Souef, *To War Without a Gun* (1980), p 89; AWM52 8/3/7
48 Gullett, *Not as a Duty Only* (1976), pp 40–2
49 Bracegirdle, 'A Visit to Piraeus, Greece 1941' (1990)
50 MacDonald, *The Lost Battle* (1993), pp 106–7; Vial, *The War I Went To* (1995), p 123; AWM54 534/2/32
51 Johnson (2000), p 88
52 Johnston, *Anzacs in the Middle East* (2013), p 75
53 Cody, *28 (Maori) Battalion* (1956), p 43; Wikipedia, 'The Woodpecker Song'
54 Stuart & Arnold, *Letters Home 1939–1945* (1987), p 128
55 Barter, *Far Above Battle* (1994), p 82
56 Marshall (1946), p 41
57 Stuart & Arnold (1987), p 128
58 Henderson, *RMT* (1954), p 47; Norton, *26 Battalion* (1952), p 20
59 Clift, *War Dance* (1980), p 117
60 Marshall (1946), p 34
61 NLA MS8436 Series 1, file 34
62 Hill, *Diggers and Greeks* (2010), p 129
63 Simpson (1981), p 93

64 Barter (1994), p 83
65 Clift (1972), p 54
66 Dawson (1961), pp 76–7
67 Holt (1981), p 90
68 Cody (1956), p 44
69 Holt (1981), p 91
70 *Australians at War* Film Archive, 'Bill Robertson'
71 Ballard, *On Ultra Active Service* (1991), pp 42–3; Collie, *Code Breakers* (2017), pp 51–2
72 Pringle & Glue (1957), pp 46–8

CHAPTER 2   Machinations

1 Thompson, *Anzac Fury* (2010), p 51
2 Playfair, *History of the Second World War* (1954), p 207
3 Kershaw, *Fateful Choices* (2007), p 164; 'Athenian', *The Greek Miracle* (1942), pp 31–3; Reid, *Last on the List* (1974), pp 100–1
4 Playfair (1954), p 223
5 *Ibid*, p 257
6 Clark, *The Fall of Crete* (1962), p 11
7 Kershaw (2007), p 172
8 Kiriakopoulos, *The Nazi Occupation of Greece, 1941–1945* (1995), p 13
9 Playfair (1954), p 226; 'Athenian' (1942), pp 39, 46–7; Simpson, *Operation Mercury* (1981), p 32
10 MacDonald, *The Lost Battle* (1993), p 52; Beevor, *Crete* (1991), pp 6–7; 'Athenian' (1942), p 12
11 Playfair (1954), pp 233–4; Hunt, *A Don at War* (1966), pp 25–6
12 Simpson (1981), pp 51–2
13 Playfair (1954), p 255
14 *Ibid*, pp 259–60; Lewin, *The Chief* (1980), p 59; Thompson (2010), p 64
15 Thompson (2010), p 67
16 Playfair (1954), pp 265–71
17 Thompson (2010), pp 72–5; Murray & Millett, *A War to be Won* (2000), p 99; Playfair (1954), p 271
18 Playfair (1954), pp 277–87
19 *Ibid*, p 289
20 MacDonald (1993), p 89
21 Connell, *Wavell* (1964), p 22
22 Lewin (1980), p 57
23 Rowell, *Full Circle* (1974), p 50
24 Thompson (2010), p 115
25 Diamond, 'Sir John Dill and Winston Churchill: A Clash in Strategy' (2018)
26 *Ibid*
27 Rothwell, *Anthony Eden* (1992), p 250
28 James, *Anthony Eden* (1986), p 623
29 Martin & Hardy, *Dark and Hurrying Days* (1993), pp 63, 71
30 Thompson (2010), p 49; IWM Forrester (Oral history) #27182
31 Coats, *Of Generals and Gardens* (1976), p 65
32 Reid, *Last on the List* (1974), p 111

33 *Ibid*, p 114
34 Forty, *Battle of Crete* (2001), p 16
35 Reid (1974), p 114
36 Simpson (1981), pp 29–30; Ewer, *Forgotten Anzacs* (2016), p 74
37 Hill, *Diggers and Greeks* (2010), p 30
38 Playfair (1954), p 230
39 Simpson (1981), p 70
40 Cruikshank, *Greece 1940–1941* (1976), pp 78–9
41 Hill, pp 35–6; Wavell, 'The British expedition to Greece 1941' (1950)
42 Playfair (1954), pp 339–40; Simpson (1981), pp 54, 59
43 Simpson (1981), p 55
44 Gilbert, *Finest Hour* (1983) pp 1005–6;
45 Martin & Hardy (1993), p 36
46 *Ibid*, p 51; Thompson (2010), p 107
47 Ewer (2016), p 79
48 Gilbert (1983), p 1011
49 Churchill, *The Grand Alliance* (1950), p 60
50 Long, *Greece, Crete and Syria* (1953), p 8; Charlton, *The Thirty-Niners* (1981), p 138
51 Long (1953), p 8
52 Martin & Hardy (1993), p 53; Hetherington, *Blamey* (1954), p 175
53 Martin & Hardy (1993), p 53
54 NAA A5954,528/1, p 220; AWM54 534/2/19; Long (1953), p 18; Charlton (1981), p 143
55 McClymont, *To Greece* (1959), p 99; Singleton-Gates, *General Lord Freyberg VC* (1963), p 117–19; Freyberg, *Bernard Freyberg, VC* (1991), p 238
56 Churchill (1950), p 63; Coats (1976), p 86
57 de Guingand, *Generals at War* (1964), pp 22–4; Lewin (1980), p 94
58 Gilbert (1983), p 1012; Lewin (1980), p 96
59 Cunningham, *A Sailor's Odyssey* (1951), p 315
60 Long (1953), p 9
61 Cunningham (1951), p 315
62 Cruikshank (1976), p 107
63 Wilson, *Eight Years Overseas, 1939–1947*, (1950), p 65
64 Lewin (1980), p 94
65 de Guingand (1964), p 27
66 Cruikshank (1976), pp 106–7
67 *Ibid*, p 107; Thompson (2010), pp 118–19
68 Playfair (1954), p 381
69 NAA A5954, 528/1, p 210; Thompson (2010), p 128
70 Reid (1974), p 127
71 Woodhouse, 'The Aliakmon line: an Anglo–Greek misunderstanding in 1941', *Eight Years Overseas, 1939–1947*, (1985); Playfair (1954), p 382
72 Woodhouse (1985)
73 NAA A5954, 528/1, p 210
74 Gilbert (1983), p 1026; Lewin (1980), p 97
75 Charlton (1981), p 141
76 Gilbert (1983), p 1027; Thompson (2010), p 124

77 Cruikshank (1976), pp 112–13; Gilbert (1983), p 1029; Charlton (1981), pp 142–3
78 NAA A5954, 528/1, p 220; Long (1953), p 17
79 McClymont (1959), p 113
80 Long (1953), p 33
81 de Guingand (1964), p 35
82 Long (1953), p 34; Hill (2010), p 77
83 Rowell (1974), p 67
84 Churchill (1950), p 143; Long (1953), p 25
85 NAA A5954, 528/1, p 153

CHAPTER 3   Too late, too little

1   Long, *Greece, Crete and Syria* (1953) pp 39–40
2   Heckstall-Smith & Baillie-Grohman, *Greek Tragedy* (1961), pp 42–9; Thompson, *Anzac Fury* (2010), pp 150–1
3   Johnstone, *'Dearest Geraldine'* (2003), p 53
4   Griffiths-Marsh, *The Sixpenny Soldier* (1990), pp 159–60
5   *Australians at War* Film Archive, 'William "Bill" Robertson'
6   McClymont, *To Greece* (1959), p 195; Ewer, *Forgotten Anzacs* (2016), p 135
7   Unit History Editorial C'tee, *White Over Green* (1963), p 115
8   *Ibid*, pp 114–15
9   *Ibid*, p 115
10 AWM54, 534/2/32; Hetherington, *The Australian Soldier* (1944), p 57; Horner, *General Vasey's War* (1992), p 94
11 AWM52, 5/13/1; Ewer (2016), p 132
12 AWM52, 8/3/8/14; Bentley, *The Second Eighth* (1984), pp 56–7
13 McClymont (1959), p 205; Ewer (2016), pp 141–2; Horner (1992), p 94
14 AWM52, 1/4/12; Fernside & Clift, *Dougherty* (1979), p 63
15 Unit History Editorial C'tee (1963), p 121
16 Horner (1992), p 118
17 Unit History Editorial C'tee (1963), p 120
18 AWM52, 8/3/8/14
19 Johnstone (2003), p 57
20 Long (1953), p 62; AWM52, 8/3/4/9
21 Unit History Editorial C'tee (1963), p 128
22 Henderson, *RMT* (1954), p 53
23 AWM52, 8/3/4/9; Unit History Editorial C'tee (1963), pp 118–19; Granquist, *A Long Way Home* (2010), p 55; Thompson (2010), p 168
24 Granquist (2010), p 56
25 Unit History Editorial C'tee (1963), p 122
26 Crisp, *The Gods Were Neutral* (1960), p 127; Plowman, *Greece 1941* (2018), p 56
27 Barter, *Far Above Battle* (1994), p 85
28 Long (1953), p 44
29 Givney, *The First at War* (1987), p 142; Hill, *Diggers and Greeks* (2010), p 174
30 Barter (1994), p 88
31 Marshall, *Nulli Secundus Log* (1946) p 43; Barter (1994), p 88
32 Selby, *Dr NX 22* (1985), p 198
33 Hocking, *The Long Carry* (1997), p 59
34 Marshall (1946), p 44

35 Givney (1987), p 143; Thompson (2010), p 169
36 Hill (2010), p 166; Ewer (2016), p 158
37 Cook, personal communication
38 Ross, *23 Battalion* (1959), p 33
39 Begg & Liddle, *For Five Shillings a Day* (2000), p 111
40 Ewer (2016), p 174
41 Pringle & Glue, *20 Battalion and Armoured Regiment* (1957), p 53
42 Ewer (2016), p 168
43 Sinclair, *19 Battalion and Armoured Regiment* (1954), pp 77–83; Thompson (2010),
    pp 171–2
44 Cody, *28 (Maori) Battalion* (1956), pp 61, 66
45 Soutar, *Nga Tama Toa (The Price of Citizenship)* (2008), p 123
46 Kohere, *The Story of a Maori Chief* (1949), p 81; Soutar (2008), p 125
47 AWM52, 8/3/1; Givney (187), pp 146–8
48 Kippenberger, *Infantry Brigadier* (1949), p 28; McLean, *Howard Kippenberger*
    (2008), pp 159–60

CHAPTER 4 The knot tightens

1 AWM54, 253/4/2; Hill, *Diggers and Greeks* (2010), pp 178–9
2 AWM54, 253/4/2; AWM52, 8/2/17/18; Long, *Greece, Crete and Syria* (1953),
   p 103; Ewer, *Forgotten Anzacs* (2016), p 223; Hill (2010), p 179
3 Long (1953), pp 91–2; Hill (2010), pp 101–2
4 Long (1953), p 92; Hill (2010), pp 101–2
5 Johnston, *Anzacs in the Middle East* (2013), p 85
6 McRobbie, 'A Young Lieutenant's Song of the Greek Campaign' (1941); Olson,
   Battalion into Battle (2011), pp 113–14
7 AWM52, 8/2/17/18
8 An officer in charge of a brigade is called 'brigadier' regardless of his actual rank.
   Charrington was a colonel, a lower rank than brigadier.
9 Ewer (2016), p 101
10 Wikipedia, 'Battle of Kleisoura Pass'
11 Crisp, *The Gods were Neutral* (1960), pp 90–1
12 Laffin, *Greece, Crete and Syria* (1989), p 20
13 AWM52, 8/3/11/10
14 Long (1953), p 110; Trigellis-Smith, *All the King's Enemies* (1988), p 94
15 Henderson, *RMT* (1954) p 55
16 Cody, *21 Battalion* (1953), pp 47–8
17 *Ibid*, pp 50–1
18 Cody (1953), pp 57–8
19 *Ibid*, p 61; Long (1953), p 95; McClymont, *To Greece* (1959), p 251
20 Baker, *Paul Cullen* (2005), p 66; Hill (2010), p 191
21 Wick, *Purple Over Green* (1977), pp 100–1
22 Ewer (2016), p 197
23 Uren, *Kiwi Saga* (1944), p 83
24 Xanthaki, 'The Tomb' (1976); Blouchou, personal communication
25 Cody (1953), p 66
26 AWM52, 8/3/2/19
27 Wick (1977), p 96; AWM52, 8/3/2/19

28 Marshall, *Nulli Secundus Log* (1946), p 40; Wick (1977), p 97
29 Barter, *Far Above Battle* (1994), p 91
30 Cody (1953), p 67; McLeod, *Myth and Reality* (1986), p 35; Plowman, *Greece 1941* (2018), p 106
31 Marshall (1946), pp 40, 47; Wick (1977), p 97; Barter (1994), p 91
32 Cody (1953), p 69
33 AWM52, 8/3/2/19; Clift, *The Saga of a Sig* (1972), p 68
34 Long (1953), pp 116–19; Wick (1977), p 98; Ewer (2016), pp 204–5, 209–10; AWM52, 8/2/16/7
35 Long (1953), p 117
36 AWM52, 8/3/2/19
37 Ewer (2016), pp 207–8
38 Barter (1994), p 94
39 Long (1953), pp 120–1; Ewer (2016), pp 210–11
40 Wick (1977), p 99
41 Barter (1994), p 95
42 Uren (1944), pp 90–3
43 Xanthaki (1976)
44 Blouchou, personal communication
45 Givney, *The First at War* (1987), p 480
46 Cremor, *Action Front* (1961), p 99
47 Givney (1987), p 479
48 Rowell, *Full Circle* (1974), p 75
49 Barter (1994), p 97
50 AWM, 3DRL 6398
51 Ewer (2016), pp 225–6
52 AWM54, 535/5/5
53 Clift, *War Dance* (1980), p 149
54 Pringle & Glue, *20 Battalion and Armoured Regiment* (1957), p 57
55 Long (1953), pp 129–30
56 Henderson, *RMT* (1954), p 66
57 Ewer (2016), p 214
58 AWM52, 8/3/2/19
59 Forty, *Battle of Crete* (2001), p 38
60 Cody, *28 (Maori) Battalion* (1956), p 70
61 Monteath, *Battle on 42nd Street* (2019), p 40

CHAPTER 5   Sinking ship

1 Hill, *Diggers and Greeks* (2010), p 98
2 MacDonald, *The Lost Battle* (1993), p 110; Hill (2010), pp 103, 106–7
3 Long, *Greece, Crete and Syria* (1953), p 142; Lehmann, *The Leibstandarte* (1987), pp 230–1; Beevor, *Crete* (1991), p 42; Hill (2010), p 108
4 Gilbert, *Finest Hour* (1983), p 1065
5 Higham, *Diary of a Disaster* (1986), p 224
6 Long (1953), p 112
7 Heckstall-Smith, *Greek Tragedy* (1961), p 78
8 *Ibid*, p 76
9 Horner, *High Command* (1982), p 69; Long (1953), p 143; Hill (2010), pp 114–15

10　Heckstall-Smith (1961), p 77

11　Vial, *The War I Went To* (1995), p 142; Hetherington, *Blamey* (1954), p 157

12　Singleton-Gates, *General Lord Freyberg VC* (1963), p 131

13　Stephanides, *Climax in Crete* (1946), pp 13–14

14　Simpson, *Operation Mercury* (1981), p 106

15　Henderson, *RMT* (1954), p 30

16　Simpson (1981), p 106

17　Ballard, *On Ultra Active Service* (1991), pp 56–8

18　*Ibid*, pp 58–9

19　Long (1953), p 143

20　Burdon, *24 Battalion* (1953), pp 41–2

21　Griffiths-Marsh, *The Sixpenny Soldier* (1990), p 173

22　Olson, *Battalion into Battle* (2011), p 122

23　Long (1953), pp 149, 158; Givney, *The First at War* (1987), p 152

24　Cody, *28 (Maori) Battalion* (1956), pp 71–2

25　Ross, *23 Battalion* (1959), p 52

26　McRobbie – 'Adventure in Greece', (1941a); Olson (2011), p 127; Brune, *We Band of Brothers* (2000), p 83

27　Long (1953), p 156

28　Raggett, *All About Sid* (1991), p 64

29　Puttick, *25 Battalion* (1960), p 60

30　*Ibid*, pp 60–1

31　Begg & Liddle, *For Five Shillings a Day* (2000), pp 121–2

32　Heckstall-Smith (1961), p 87

33　*Ibid*, p 104

34　Heckstall-Smith & Baillie-Grohman, *Greek Tragedy* (1961), p 107

35　*Ibid*, pp 116–19; Thomas, *Crete 1941* (1972), p 77

36　Heckstall-Smith (1961), p 119; Thomas (1972), p 78

37　Henderson, *22 Battalion* (1958), pp 32–3

38　Henderson (1954), p 67

39　Hill (2010), p 186

40　Henderson, *Soldier Country* (1978), p 148; Simpson (1981), p 106

41　Long (1953), p 164; Ebury, *Weary* (2009), p 96

42　Unit History Editorial C'tee, *White Over Green* (1963), p 138

43　Ewer, *Forgotten Anzacs* (2016), p 270

44　Heckstall-Smith (1961), pp 127–31; Singleton-Gates (1963), p 135

45　Thomas (1972), p 81

46　AWM52, 8/3/6/9; Hay, *Nothing Over Us* (1984), p 164

47　Hay (1984), p 168

48　Heckstall-Smith (1961), p 135; Sinclair, *19 Battalion and Armoured Regiment* (1954), p 106; Ewer (2016), pp 272–8; AWM52, 8/2/17/28

49　McLean & McGibbon, *The Penguin Book of New Zealanders at War* (2009), p 287

50　Woollams, *Corinth and All That* (1945), pp 11–20, 35

51　Henderson (1954), p 70

52　Ballard (1991), p 68; Simpson (1981), p 107; Norton, *26 Battalion* (1952), p 60

53　Heckstall-Smith (1961), p 97

54　Prince Paul was King George's brother.

55　Comeau, *Operation Mercury* (1961), p 55

56 Heckstall-Smith (1961), p 146
57 *Ibid*, p 147
58 Cook, personal communication
59 Heckstall-Smith (1961), p 149; Thomas (172), p 89; Clark, *The Fall of Crete* (1962), p 111
60 Thomas (1972), p 90
61 *Ibid*, pp 94–6; Beevor (1991), p 54
62 Thomas (1972), p 97
63 Dawson, *18 Battalion and Armoured Regiment* (1961), p 122
64 Kippenberger, *Infantry Brigadier* (1949), p 42; Pringle & Glue, *20 Battalion and Armoured Regiment* (1957), pp 69–70
65 Pringle & Glue (1957), p 73
66 Gullett, *Not as a Duty Only* (1976), p 59; Hay (1984), p 170
67 Gullett (1976), p 60
68 *Ibid*, pp 60–1
69 Heckstall-Smith (1961), pp 195–6; Thompson, *Anzac Fury* (2010), pp 207–8

CHAPTER 6   Kalamata: defiance and faint hearts

 1 Simpson, *Operation Mercury* (1981), p 107; Long, *Greece, Crete and Syria* (1953), p 165
 2 Hay, *Nothing Over Us* (1984), p 172
 3 Griffiths-Marsh, *The Sixpenny Soldier* (1990), pp 177–8
 4 Long (1953), p 171
 5 *Ibid*, p 172
 6 AWM54, 34/2/32; Vial, *The War I Went To* (1995), p 145
 7 Burns, 'Calamity Bay' (1944); Long (1953), p 174
 8 Hay (1984), p 172
 9 Pringle & Glue, *20 Battalion and Armoured Regiment* (1957), p 76
10 Thomas, *Crete 1941* (1972) p 93
11 Griffiths-Marsh (1990), p 180
12 Lee, *Special Duties* (1946), p 89; Beevor, *Crete* (1991), p 52
13 Lee (1946), p 101; Heckstall-Smith, *Greek Tragedy* (1961), p 199
14 Heckstall-Smith (1961), p 199
15 Lee (1946), pp 101–2; Heckstall-Smith (1961), p 200
16 McClymont, *To Greece* (1959), p 452; Brotherhood of Veterans of the Greek Campaign 1940–1941
17 Heckstall-Smith (1961), p 200; Mentiplay, *A Fighting Quality* (1979), p 41
18 Pringle & Glue (1957), p 78
19 *Ibid*, p 82; McClymont (1959), p 455
20 McClymont (1959), p 454
21 *Ibid*, p 456; Mentiplay (1979), p 41; Thompson, *Anzac Fury* (2010), p 204
22 Pringle & Glue (1957), p 85
23 *Ibid*, p 82
24 *Ibid*, p 79; McClymont (1959), p 457; Mentiplay (1979), p 42
25 Pringle & Glue (1957), p 80
26 McClymont (1959), p 457
27 Pringle & Glue (1957), p 83
28 *Ibid*, p 80

29 *Ibid*, p 81

30 *Ibid*

31 McClymont (1959), p 458; Pringle & Glue (1957), p 83

32 Pringle & Glue (1957), p 83

33 Heckstall-Smith (1961), pp 202–3; Thomas (1972), p 103; Thompson (2010), p 204

34 McClymont (1959), p 459; Heckstall-Smith (1961), p 203

35 Thomas (1972), pp 103–4; Thompson (2010), p 205

36 Thomas (1972), p 105; Thompson (2010), p 206

37 Thomas (1972), p 106

38 Heckstall-Smith (1961), pp 204–5; Thomas (1972), p 106; Thompson (2010), p 206

39 Ward, '"Operation Demon" HMS Hero' (2014)

40 Begg & Liddle, *For Five Shillings a Day* (2000), p 113

41 Pringle & Glue (1957), pp 86–7

42 Heckstall-Smith (1961), p 205; Pringle & Glue (1957), p 84; Brotherhood of Veterans of the Greek Campaign

43 Heckstall-Smith (1961), p 206; Brotherhood of Veterans of the Greek Campaign

44 Heckstall-Smith (1961), pp 212–13; Trigellis-Smith, *All the King's Enemies* (1988), p 102

45 Cunningham, *A Sailor's Odyssey* (1951), p 356

46 Pringle & Glue (1957), p 87

47 Henderson, *RMT* (1954), p 70

48 Wick, *Purple Over Green* (1977), pp 111–12

49 Vial (1995), pp 150–5; AWM52, 8/2/16/7, pp 174–7

50 Pringle & Glue (1957), p 83

51 Long (1953), pp 188–9

52 Bolger & Littlewood, *The Fiery Phoenix* (1983), pp 73–6

53 Harper & Richardson, *In the Face of the Enemy* (2010), pp 210–11

54 Levine, *Captivity, Flight and Survival in World War II* (2000), p 22

CHAPTER 7   Welcome to Suda Bay

1 Le Clerq, Arthur, 'The Wreck of the Nancy Lee', 1932

2 Barrett, *We Were There* (1987), pp 9–10

3 Bolger & Littlewood, *The Fiery Phoenix* (1983), p 78

4 Gordon, *The Embarrassing Australian* (1962), p 69

5 Wick, *Purple Over Green* (1977), p 113

6 Hay, *Nothing Over Us* (1984), p 184

7 Gordon (1962), p 68

8 *Ibid*, p 68

9 *Ibid*, pp 68–9

10 Johnson, *The History of the 2/11th (City of Perth) Australian Infantry Battalion 1939–45* (2000), p 91

11 Cox, *A Tale of Two Battles* (1987), pp 16–17

12 Ewer, *Forgotten Anzacs* (2016), p 299

13 Russell, *There Goes a Man* (1959), p 9

14 Unit History Editorial C'tee, *White Over Green* (1963), p 144

15 Carstairs, *Escape from Crete* (2016), p 29

16 Thompson, *Anzac Fury* (2010), p 214
17 Ballard, *On Ultra Active Service* (1991), pp 65–6
18 Stewart, *The Struggle for Crete, 20 May–1 June 1941* (1966), p 77
19 Beevor, *Crete* (1991), p 28
20 Davin, *Crete* (1953), p 20
21 Long, *Greece, Crete and Syria* (1953), p 205; MacDonald, *The Lost Battle* (1993), pp 122, 144, 152; Freyberg, *Bernard Freyberg VC* (1991), pp 267, 270–1; Stewart (1966), p 72; Thompson (2010), p 229; Lenihan, 'The Battle of Crete 1941: The Poverty of Ultra' (2016), pp 16–17
22 Long (1953), p 207
23 Churchill, *The Grand Alliance* (1950), p 241; MacDonald (1993), p 139
24 Wilson, *Eight Years Overseas, 1939–1947* (1950), p 102; Thompson (2010), pp 227–8
25 Davin (1953), p 40; Thompson (2010), p 228
26 Freyberg (1991), p 267
27 Churchill (1950), p 242
28 Thompson (2010), p 230; MacDonald (1993), p 144; Freyberg (1991), p 268
29 Charlton, *The Thirty-Niners* (1981), p 169
30 Barter, *Far Above Battle* (1994), p 108
31 Churchill (1950), pp 243–4; Freyberg (1991), p 271; Stewart (1966), p 61; Thompson (2010), p 233
32 Long (1953), p 207
33 MacDonald (1993), p 146
34 AWM52, 18/2/19; Hill, *Diggers and Greeks* (2010) pp 281–3
35 Thompson (2010), p 246; Barber & Tonkin-Covill, *Freyberg* (1989), p 18
36 Spyrakis, personal communication
37 Thompson (2010), pp 246–7; Davin (1953), p 37
38 MacDonald (1993), p 150
39 Cremor, *Action Front* (1961), p 125; Clarke, *My War 1939–1945* (1990), p 360
40 Bellair, *Amateur Soldier* (1984), p 62
41 Henderson, *22 Battalion* (1958), p 40
42 AWM52, 6/5/1/13; Ewer (2016), p 301
43 Ewer (2016), p 301
44 Ballard (1991), p 73
45 Long (1953), p 216; Palazzo, *Battle of Crete* (2011), p 21
46 Ewer (2016), p 305
47 Thompson (2010), p 249
48 Barter (1994), p 105
49 Hill (2010), p 285
50 Wick (1977), p 126; Hill (2010), p 285
51 Hill (2010), p 290
52 Begg & Liddle, *For Five Shillings a Day* (2000), p 125
53 Clift, *War Dance* (1980), p 161; Clarke (1990), p 363
54 Stephanides, *Climax in Crete* (1946), p 46
55 Pringle & Glue, *20 Battalion and Armoured Regiment* (1957), p 98; Clift (1980), p 161; Robinson, *Journey to Captivity* (1991), p 81; Bishop, *The Thunder of the Guns* (1998), p 256
56 Olson, *Battalion into Battle* (2011), p 151

57 *Ibid*, p 151; Ryan, *POWs Fraternal* (2011), p 152
58 Archer, *Balkan Journal* (1944), p 227
59 Shulman, *Defeat in the West* (1986), p 69
60 Beevor (1991), pp 75–6
61 Clark, *The Fall of Crete* (1962), p 52; Davin (1953), p 81; Beevor (1991), p 75
62 Thompson (2010), p 238
63 *Ibid*, pp 242–4
64 Bennett, *Intelligence Investigations* (1996), pp 195–6; Keegan, *Intelligence in War* (2003), p 207; Lenihan (2016), p 22
65 Ballard (1991), pp 69–71
66 *Ibid*, pp 71–2; Collie, *Code Breakers* (2017), p 52
67 Keegan (2003), p 198; Lenihan (2016), p 17
68 Keegan (2003), p 192; Bennett, *Ultra and Mediterranean Strategy 1941–1945* (1989), p 54; Lenihan (2016), pp 2–5, 25
69 Laffin, *Greece, Crete and Syria* (1989), pp 60–1
70 AWM 3DRL4052
71 Hutching, *A Unique Sort of Battle* (2001), p 69
72 Ballard (1991), p 75
73 Filer, *Crete, Death from the Skies* (2010), p 57
74 Clark (1962), p 37; Palazzo (2011), p 35
75 Cremor (1961), p 130
76 Stewart (1966), p 109; Comeau, *Operation Mercury* (1961), p 61; MacDonald (1993), p 164
77 Givney, *The First at War* (1987), pp 164–6
78 Clark (1962), pp 3–4
79 Farran, *Winged Dagger* (1948), p 84
80 *Ibid*, p 84
81 Ewer (2016), p 313
82 MacDonald (1993), pp 159–60
83 Freyberg (1991), p 286
84 Stewart (1966), p 89; Beevor (1991), pp 80–2; Thompson (2010), pp 253–4
85 Thompson (2010), p 251

CHAPTER 8   Invasion from above

1 Cox, *A Tale of Two Battles* (1987), p 69
2 Clark, *The Fall of Crete* (1962), p 55
3 *Ibid*, p 59
4 Thomas, *Dare to be Free* (1951), p 7; Stewart, *The Struggle for Crete, 20 May–1 June 1941* (1966), p 151
5 Henderson, *RMT* (1954), p 79
6 Hutching, *A Unique Sort of Battle* (2001), p 59
7 Smith, *New Zealand at War* (1995), p 66
8 Comeau, *Operation Mercury* (1961), p 85
9 von der Heydte, *Daedalus Returned* (1958), p 59
10 Stewart (1966), p 165
11 Mourellos, *The Battle of Crete* (1946), p 85: Yiannikopoulos, *The Greek Forces in the Battle of Crete, May 1941* (2017), p 54
12 Hadjipateras & Fafalios, *Crete 1941* (1991), p 80

13 *Ibid*, p 78
14 MacDonald, *The Lost Battle* (1993), p 177
15 Yiannikopoulos (2017), pp 55–6
16 Stewart (1966), p 156
17 A Field Ambulance station for treatment (dressing or surgery) of casualties brought from the battlefield.
18 Henderson (1954), p 82; Hutching (2001), p 156
19 Henderson (1954), pp 82–3; Hutching (2001), pp 156–7, 192; Thompson, *Anzac Fury* (2010), pp 273–5, 279–81
20 von der Heydte (1958), p 66; Simpson, *Operation Mercury* (1981), p 164
21 Davin, *Crete* (1953), p 156
22 *Ibid*, pp 157–60
23 *Ibid*, pp 165–71; Stewart (1966), p 192: MacDonald (1993), pp 197–8; Palazzo, *Battle of Crete* (2011), pp 102–3
24 Yiannikopoulos (2017), pp 47–8; Beevor, *Crete* (1991), p 127
25 Stewart (1966), p 187
26 Henderson, *22 Battalion* (1958), p 66
27 *Ibid*, p 67
28 *Ibid*, p 67; Spencer, *Battle for Crete* (1963), p 138
29 Simpson (1981), p 174
30 Davin (1953), p 123; Henderson (1958), p 68
31 Henderson (1958), p 65
32 *Ibid*, p 51
33 Comeau (1961), pp 97–8
34 Clark (1962), p 71; MacDonald (1993), p 199
35 Stewart (1966), p 175
36 McLeod, *Myth and Reality* (1986), p 36
37 Cox (1987), p 67
38 Davin (1953), pp 109–10; Beevor (1991), p 126
39 Davin (1953), pp 109–10; Henderson (1958), p 70; Clark (1962), p 72; Beevor (1991), p 126
40 Stewart (1966), p 175
41 Henderson (1958), p 65; Thompson (2010), p 297
42 Henderson (1958), p 71
43 Stewart (1966), p 255; Clark (1962), p 103; Simpson (1981), p 198
44 Cody, *28 (Maori) Battalion* (1956), pp 93–5
45 Henderson (1958), pp 62–3
46 Davin (1953), p 118
47 Henderson (1958), pp 55–6; Davin (1953), p 118; Stewart (1966), pp 245–6; Hutching (2001), p 85
48 Olson, *Battalion into Battle* (2011), p 157
49 Givney, *The First at War* (1987), p 177
50 Hadjipateras & Fafalios (1991), p 112
51 Unit History Editorial C'tee, *White Over Green* (1963), pp 156–7;
52 *Ibid*, p 157
53 *Ibid*, p 159
54 Hadjipateras & Fafalios (1991), p 107
55 Cox (1987), p 79; MacDonald (1993), p 204; Beevor (1991), p 154

56 MacDonald (1993), p 204; Beevor (1991), p 154
57 AWM, PR 02043
58 Long, *Greece, Crete and Syria* (1953), pp 234–5; Johnston, *Anzacs in the Middle East* (2013), p 101
59 Ballard, *On Ultra Active Service* (1991), p 78
60 Long (1953), p 235; MacDonald (1993), p 220
61 Stewart (1966), p 290; MacDonald (1993), p 222; Davin (1953), p 197
62 McLeod (1986), p 37
63 von der Heydte (1958), p 119
64 Sinclair, *19 Battalion and Armoured Regiment* (1954), pp 143–4
65 *Ibid*, p 146
66 Hadjipateras & Fafalios (1991), p 156; Lind, *Flowers of Rethymnon* (1991), p 21; Olson (2011), p 169
67 Beevor (1991), p 143
68 Simpson (1981), pp 227–8
69 Ballard (1991), p 78; Collie, *Code Breakers* (2017), p 53
70 Thomas, *Crete 1941* (1972), pp 137–8
71 Beevor (1991), pp 162–3
72 Smith (1995), p 71
73 Davin (1953), p 216
74 Pringle & Glue, *20 Battalion and Armoured Regiment* (1957), pp 108–9
75 Scott, *Searching for Charlie* (2020), pp 150–2
76 Spencer (1963), p 250; Davin (1953), p 216
77 Monteath, *Battle on 42nd Street* (2019), p 92
78 Farran, *Winged Dagger* (1948), pp 95–6; Long (1953), p 236
79 Clark (1962), p 132
80 Clark (1962), pp 132–3
81 Davin (1953), p 220
82 Clark (1962), p 134; MacDonald (1993), p 224; Simpson (1981), p 220
83 Dyer, *Ma Te Reinga (By Way of Reinga)* (1953), p 73; Stewart (1966), p 299
84 Davin (1953), pp 238–9

CHAPTER 9   Fighting withdrawal

1 Davin, *Crete* (1953), p 263
2 Henderson, *22 Battalion* (1958), p 79
3 Farran, *Winged Dagger* (1948), pp 98–9
4 Clark, *The Fall of Crete* (1962), p 109
5 Thomas, *Crete 1941* (1972), pp 145–6
6 Murphy, 'Escape of the King of Greece' (1953), pp 470–3; Hetherington, *Air-Borne Invasion* (1944), pp 63–8; Hadjipateras & Fafalios, *Crete 1941* (1991), pp 71–6
7 Henderson, *RMT* (1954), p 86
8 Winter, *Expendable* (1989), p 32; Taaffe, *The Gatekeepers of Galatas* (2006), p 19
9 Clark (1962), p 157: Freyberg, *Bernard Freyberg, VC* (1991), p 307
10 Ewer, *Forgotten Anzacs* (2016), p 340
11 Clark (1962), pp 82–3; MacDonald, *The Lost Battle* (1993), pp 176–7; Hadjipateras & Fafalios (1991), p 192
12 Davin (1953), pp 291–2
13 Cox, *A Tale of Two Battles* (1987), pp 88–9

14 *Ibid*, p 89
15 Carstairs, *Escape from Crete* (2016), p 46
16 Kippenberger, *Infantry Brigadier* (1949), p 64
17 Dawson, *18 Battalion and Armoured Regiment* (1961), p 153
18 Kippenberger (1949), p 65
19 Stewart, *The Struggle for Crete, 20 May–1 June 1941* (1966), p 387
20 Henderson (1954), p 90
21 Kippenberger (1949), p 65; McConnell, *Galatas 1941* (2006), p 135
22 Kippenberger (1949), p 65; Davin (1953), p 303
23 Davin (1953), p 312
24 Kippenberger (1949), p 67
25 Davin (1953), p 311; Kay, *27 (Machine Gun) Battalion* (1958), p 109
26 Thomas, *Dare to be Free* (1951), p 21
27 *Ibid*, p 24; Kippenberger (1949), p 67
28 Farran (1948), p 100; MacDonald (1993), p 266
29 Ross, *23 Battalion* (1959), p 80
30 Hutching, *A Unique Sort of Battle* (2001), p 183
31 Hadjipateras & Fafalios (1991), p 186
32 Stewart (1966), p 394
33 MacDonald (1993), p 207
34 Hutching (2001), p 183
35 Long, *Greece, Crete and Syria* (1953), pp 263–4; Givney, *The First at War* (1987), pp 190–3; Thompson, *Anzac Fury* (2010), pp 323–5
36 Lind, *Flowers of Rethymnon* (1991), pp 23–4
37 *Ibid*, p 26
38 Johnson, *The History of the 2/11th (City of Perth) Australian Infantry Battalion 1939–45* (2000), p 101; Brune, *We Band of Brothers* (2000), p 100
39 Hadjipateras & Fafalios (1991), pp 152–4; Givney (1987), p 194
40 Long (1953), p 268; Johnson (2000), pp 103–4
41 Long (1953), p 269; Johnson (2000), p 104
42 Johnstone, *'Dearest Geraldine'* (2003), p 84
43 Unit History Editorial C'tee, *White Over Green* (1963), p 162; Long (1953), p 284
44 Fernside & Clift, *Dougherty* (1979), p 76
45 Long (1953), p 290
46 Davin (1953), p 272; Long (1953), p 287; Spencer, *Battle for Crete* (1963), p 240; MacDonald (1993), p 218
47 Long (1953), p 247; Stewart (1966), p 400; Freyberg (1991), p 308
48 Thompson (2010), pp 351–3; Winton, *Cunningham* (1998), pp 210–11
49 Davin (1953), p 345
50 Beevor, *Crete* (1991), p 199; Davie, *The Diaries of Evelyn Waugh* (1976), p 499; Waugh, *Officers and Gentlemen* (1955), p 162
51 Davie (1976), p 498; Beevor (1991), p 198
52 Davie (1976), p 499; Beevor (1991), p 199; Waugh (1955), pp 166–7
53 Beevor (1991), p 204
54 Davin (1953), p 360
55 Hill, *Diggers and Greeks* (2010), pp 217–18
56 Stewart (1966), pp 440–1; Horner, *General Vasey's War* (1992), p 125
57 AWM, PR 02043

58 Davin (1953), p 362
59 Sinclair, *19 Battalion and Armoured Regiment* (1954), p 161
60 Cody, *21 Battalion* (1953), p 101
61 Monteath, *Battle of 42nd Street* (2019), p 159
62 Gordon, *The Embarrassing Australian* (1962), p 77
63 Davin (1953), p 376
64 Soutar, *Nga Tama Toa (The Price of Citizenship)* (2008), p 148
65 Bolger & Littlewood, *The Fiery Phoenix* (1983), p 90
66 Soutar (2008), p 147
67 *Ibid*, p 148
68 Gordon (1962), p 77
69 McLean & McGibbon, *The Penguin Book of New Zealanders at War* (2009), p 297
70 Gordon (1962), p 78
71 IWM Peck (Oral history) #16667; Thompson (2010), p 356
72 Cody, *28 (Maori) Battalion* (1956), pp 120–1
73 Hutching (2001), p 128

CHAPTER 10 Desperation

1   Long, *Greece, Crete and Syria* (1953), p 254
2   Ballard, *On Ultra Active Service* (1991), p 83
3   *Ibid*, pp 84–6
4   *Australians at War* Film Archive, 'William "Bill" Robertson'
5   Pringle & Glue, *20 Battalion and Armoured Regiment* (1957), p 137
6   Davin, *Crete* (1953), p 383
7   Beevor, *Crete* (1991), p 207
8   A popular song from 1906.
9   Pringle & Glue, p 137: Laffin, *Greece, Crete and Syria* (1989), p 81
10 Henderson, *RMT* (1954), p 57
11 Henderson, *22 Battalion* (1958), p 81
12 Davin (1953), p 381
13 Jager, *Escape from Crete* (2004), p 4
14 Hutching, *A Unique Sort of Battle* (2001), p 150
15 *Ibid*, pp 114–15
16 Robinson, *Journey to Captivity* (1991), p 84
17 Cody, *28 (Maori) Battalion* (1956), p 122: Davin (1953), p 393; Stewart, *The Struggle for Crete, 20 May–1 June 1941* (1966), p 437: MacDonald, *The Lost Battle* (1993), p 277
18 Cody (1956), p 126; Davin (1953), p 395
19 Cody (1956), pp 126–7; Soutar, *Nga Tama Toa (The Price of Citizenship)* (2008), p 151; Davin (1953), p 395
20 Ross, *23 Battalion* (1959), p 86
21 *Ibid*, p 95; Mentiplay, *A Fighting Quality* (1979), pp 42–3
22 Davin (1953), p 388: Cody, *21 Battalion* (1953), p 103
23 Long, *Greece, Crete and Syria* (1953), p 296; Bolger & Littlewood, *The Fiery Phoenix* (1983), p 93; Le Souef, *To War Without a Gun* (1980), p 137
24 Long (1953), p 291
25 Fernside & Clift, *Dougherty* (1979), p 81

26 Johnston, *Anzacs in the Middle East* (2013), p 106: Hill, *Diggers and Greeks* (2010), p 227
27 Long (1953), p 291
28 Unit History Editorial C'tee, *White Over Green* (1963), p 172; Fernside & Clift (1979), p 56; Pratten, *Australian Battalion Commanders in the Second World War* (2009), p 101
29 Unit History Editorial C'tee (1963), p 173
30 Hodgkinson, *Before the Tide Turned* (1944), pp 137–8; Davidson, 'The evacuation of the Heraklion Garrison from Crete, 28–29 May 1941' (2004), p 218; Thompson, *Anzac Fury* (2010), pp 375–6
31 Hodgkinson (1944), p 138; Unit History Editorial C'tee (1963), p 172
32 Ewer, *Forgotten Anzacs* (2016), p 353
33 *Ibid*, pp 353–4
34 Unit History Editorial C'tee (1963), p 175
35 *Ibid*, p 176
36 *Ibid*, pp 176–7; Davidson (2004), p 222
37 Unit History Editorial C'tee (1963), p 176
38 AWM52, 8/3/5/6
39 Hutching (2001), p 176
40 Hadjipateras & Fafalios, *Crete 1941* (1991), p 248
41 Beevor (1991), p 209
42 Jager (2004), pp 11–7
43 Robinson (1991), p 86
44 Stephanides, *Climax in Crete* (1946), p 150
45 Thompson (2010), p 367
46 Stewart (1966), p 455
47 Messenger, Young & Rose, *The Middle East Commandos* (1988), p 89
48 *Ibid*, p 89
49 Davie, *The Diaries of Evelyn Waugh* (1976), p 508; Beevor (1991), p 208; Forty, *Battle of Crete* (2001), p 135
50 Simpson, *Operation Mercury* (1981), p 262
51 Stewart (1966), p 438
52 Stephanides (1946), pp 147–8
53 Bishop, *The Thunder of the Guns* (1998), p 295
54 Stephanides (1946), p 155
55 Thompson (2010), p 369
56 Stephanides (1946), p 158
57 Beevor (1991), p 218
58 Thompson (2010), p 360
59 Givney, *The First at War* (1987), p 200; Hill (2010), p 246
60 Givney (1987), p 203; Long (1953), p 272
61 Givney (1987), p 203; Johnson, *The History of the 2/11th (City of Perth) Australian Infantry Battalion 1939–45* (2000), p 105; Beevor (1991), p 215
62 Givney (1987), p 204
63 *Ibid*, p 204
64 Henderson (1958), p 82
65 *Ibid*, p 82
66 Cody (1956), pp 129–30

67 Bishop (1998), p 306

68 Cox, *A Tale of Two Battles* (1987), p 102

69 Sandford, *Mark of the Lion* (1962), pp 100–1; Laffin (1989), p 100

70 Cody (1956), p 130

71 Simpson (1981), p 272; Hadjipateras & Fafalios (1991), p 256

72 Long (1953), p 302

73 MacDonald (1993), p 288

74 Cunningham, *A Sailor's Odyssey* (1951), pp 387–8; Stewart (1966), pp 464–5; Long (1953), p 363

75 MacDonald (1993), p 291

76 Davie (1976), p 507; Messenger, Young & Rose (1998), p 91

77 Beevor (1991), p 223; Messenger, Young & Rose (1998), p 91; Forty (2001), p 136; Lenihan, 'The fog of Waugh: The Evacuation from Sphakia, Crete, May 1941' (2017), pp 9–10

78 Messenger, Young & Rose (1998), p 92; Forty (2001), p 137

79 Messenger, Young & Rose (1998), p 92

80 Lenihan (2017), p 14

81 Beevor (1991), p 225

82 Bolger & Littlewood (1983), p 93

83 Thompson (2010), p 382

84 Horner, *General Vasey's War* (1992), p 130

85 Hay, *Nothing Over Us* (1984), p 189; Barter, *Far Above Battle* (1994), p 121

86 Gordon, *The Embarrassing Australian* (1962), p 86

87 Long (1953), p 305

CHAPTER 11   Left behind

1 Damer & Frazer, *On the Run* (2006), p 31

2 Barter, *Far Above Battle* (1994), p 115

3 Clarke, *My War, 1939–1945* (1990), p 376

4 Winter, *Free Lodgings* (1993), p 7

5 Utz was actually Bavarian but Walker was not to know that. The regiment was stationed in Salzburg, Austria.

6 Gordon, *The Embarrassing Australian* (1962), p 87

7 Jager, *Escape from Crete* (2004), p 28

8 AWM52, 8/3/7/7

9 Jager (2004), p 31

10 Winter (1993), p 9

11 Jager (2004), p 34

12 Henderson, *RMT* (1954), p 97

13 Gordon (1962), pp 90–1

14 Clarke (1990), pp 377–9; Thompson, *Anzac Fury* (2010), pp 390–5

15 AWM, PR 00178; AWM52, 8/3/7/7, pp 53–4; Macartney, 'An epic of the Escape from Crete' (1941); Clark, *The Fall of Crete* (1962), pp 178–9; Gordon (1962), pp 89–90; Damer & Frazer (2006), pp 35–7

16 Clark (1962), pp 179–80

17 AWM52, 8/3/11; Johnson, *The History of the 2/11th (City of Perth) Australian Infantry Battalion 1939–45* (2000), pp 97, 115–16; Hocking, *The Long Carry* (1997), pp 107–9; Brune, *We Band of Brothers* (2000), pp 113–16

18 AWM54, 535/2/19; Long, *Greece, Crete and Syria* (1953), p 240; Bolger & Littlewood, *The Fiery Phoenix* (1983), p 89; MacDonald, *The Lost Battle* (1993), p 216; Beevor, *Crete* (1991), pp 239–40

19 Sinclair, *19 Battalion and Armoured Regiment* (1954), p 257; Yiannikopoulos, *The Greek Forces in the Battle of Crete, May 1941* (2017), pp 58–9

20 Kiriakopoulos, *The Nazi Occupation of Crete, 1941–1945* (2017), p 34

21 Gordon (1962), p 93; Yiannikopoulos (1995), p 53

22 AWM PR 03098

23 Jager (2004), p 48

24 Lind, *Flowers of Rethymnon* (1991), p 48

25 Jager (2004), pp 58–62

26 *Ibid*, p 89

27 Hadjipateras & Fafalios, *Crete 1941* (1991), p 291

28 Henderson (1954), p 98

29 Clark (1962), pp 192–4

30 Carstairs, *Escape from Crete* (2016), p 155

31 Gordon (1962), pp 93–5

32 Jager (2004), pp 126–7

33 Damer & Frazer (2006), p 209

34 *Ibid*, p 94; Hadjipateras & Fafalios (1991), p 292; Edwards, 'The Geoff Edwards Story in World War 2 in Greece and Crete' (1979)

35 AWM, 3DRL 6898

36 Edwards, *The Road to Prevelly* (1989), pp 45–8

37 Wick, *Purple Over Green* (1977), p 145; Barter (1994), p 134

38 Hadjipateras & Fafalios (1991), p 99

39 Henderson (1954), pp 102–3

40 AWM52, 8/3/11; Brune (2000), pp 117–19; Johnson (2000), pp 97–8

41 Henderson (1954), p 103

42 AWM52, 8/3/11; Brune (2000), pp 119–20

43 Lind (1991), pp 90–2

44 *Ibid*, p 93

45 Edwards (1979)

46 Gordon (1962), pp 97–8

47 *Ibid*, pp 98–9

CHAPTER 12   The war rolls on

1 Henderson, *Soldier Country* (1978), p 96

2 Glenny, *The Balkans* (2012), pp 479–83

3 'Crete and After', *Sydney Morning Herald*, 2/6/1941, p 8

4 *The Times*, London, 3/6/1941, quoted in Hetherington, *Air-Borne Invasion* (1944), p 107

5 'Retreat with Honour', *Evening Post*, Wellington, 2/6/1941, p 6

6 Cremor, *Action Front* (1961), p 84

7 de Guingand, *Generals at War* (1964), p 43

8 Freyberg, *Bernard Freyberg, VC* (1991), pp 314–17

9 *Ibid*, p 318

10 Filer, *Crete, Death from the Skies* (2010), p 133

11   Lenihan, 'The Battle of Crete 1941: The Poverty of Ultra' (2016), p 6
12   McLeod, *Myth and Reality* (1986), p 16
13   Filer (2010), p 147
14   Hetherington (1944), p 107
15   *New Zealand Herald*, 'Remaining 39er shows wounds' (2012)
16   Begg & Liddle, *For Five Shillings a Day* (2000), p 141

BIBLIOGRAPHY

NATIONAL ARCHIVES OF AUSTRALIA

A981, GREEC 11	Greece Island of Crete
A1608, E41/1/3	Greece Part 1
A5954, 528/1	Military Campaign in Greece—March–April 1941
B883	2nd AIF Personnel Dossiers, 1939–1947
MP729/7, 35/421/43	Escapees from Greece and Crete

AUSTRALIAN WAR MEMORIAL, CANBERRA

AWM52, 4/2/3	Royal Australian Artillery, 2/3 Field Regiment (unit diary)
AWM52, 5/13/1	2/1 Field Company, Royal Australian Engineers, April 1941
AWM52, 8/2/16	16 Infantry Brigade
AWM52, 8/2/17/18	17 Infantry Brigade, Reports Greece & Crete
AWM52, 8/2/19	19 Infantry Brigade
AWM52, 8/3/1	2/1 Infantry Battalion (unit diary)
AWM52, 8/3/2	2/2 Infantry Battalion (unit diary)
AWM52, 8/3/3	2/3 Infantry Battalion (unit diary)
AWM52, 8/3/4	2/4 Infantry Battalion (unit diary)
AWM52, 8/3/5	2/5 Infantry Battalion (unit diary)
AWM52, 8/3/6	2/6 Infantry Battalion (unit diary)
AWM52, 8/3/7	2/7 Infantry Battalion (unit diary)
AWM52, 8/3/8	2/8 Infantry Battalion (unit diary)
AWM52, 8/3/11	2/11 Infantry Battalion (unit diary)
AWM52 18/1/5	Deputy Assistant Provost Marshal 6 Division, January–October 1941
AWM52, 18/2/19	6 Division Provost Company, January–August 1941
AWM54, 225/1/11	Correspondence during the Campaign in Greece, May–June 1941
AWM54, 534/2/19	General Statement of Situation in Greece
AWM54, 534/2/27	German Army Documents on the Campaign in Greece (transl., WD Dawson)

AWM54, 534/2/32	Report of Activities in Greece, April '41, by RR Vial
AWM54, 534/5/5	Report by Captain KM Oliphant, 2/3 Field Regiment
AWM54, 534/5/14	Narrative on the Campaign in Greece
AWM54, 535/2/19	German Army Documents on the Campaign in Greece (transl., WD Dawson)
AWM67, 3/338 Pt 2	Personal records, Major-General SF Rowell
AWM2021.22.35	Peck, John D—*Captive in Crete* (unpublished draft, 1950)
3DRL/4052	Negus, Lindsay (Lance Corporal)
3DRL/6398	Hackshaw, Alan (Corporal, 2/11th Bn)
3DRL/6756	Baskin, Jon E D (Chaplain, 2/32nd Bn)
PR85/223	Smith, George Frederick DSO ED, (Lieutenant-Colonel)
PR00178	Walker, Keith & Ian (Major & Lieutenant)
PR00798	Foxwell, William Stephen George MM (Lieutenant)
PR00954	Youman, Lawson (Staff Sergeant)
PR02043	Kelly, Charles Alvin (Private)
PR03134	Blain, Reginald Norman (Lieutenant)
PR03192	Browning, John Fordham (Jack) (Lieutenant)

NATIONAL LIBRARY OF AUSTRALIA, CANBERRA
MS8436   Papers of Chester Wilmot, 1872–1990

AUSTRALIANS AT WAR FILM ARCHIVE
(produced by Mullion Creek Productions for the Australian Defence Force Academy, Canberra, 1999–2004)

Leggett, Arthur	#1413
Robertson, William 'Bill'	#2336
Roy, Frank	#1936
Wortham, Phillip	#94

IMPERIAL WAR MUSEUM, LONDON

Clayton, John William (Oral history)	#12585
Peck, John Desmond (Oral history)	#16667
Forrester, Michael (Oral history)	#27182

BOOKS
Ackland, John & Richard Ackland (eds) (1944), *Word from John: An Australian Soldier's Letters to his Friends*, Cassell & Co, Sydney

Adam-Smith, Patsy (2014), *Australian Prisoners of War*, Five Mile Press, Melbourne

Antill, Peter D (2005), *Crete 1941: Germany's Lightning Airborne Assault*, Osprey, Oxford

Archer, Laird (1944), *Balkan Journal*, WW Norton, New York

'Athenian' (1942), *The Greek Miracle* (transl., David Walker), Chapman & Hall, London

Baker, Kevin (2005), *Paul Cullen, Citizen and Soldier*, Rosenberg, Sydney

Ballard, Geoffrey St Vincent (1991), *On Ultra Active Service: The Story of Australia's Signals Intelligence during World War II*, Spectrum Publications, Melbourne

Barber, Laurie & John Tonkin-Covill (1989), *Freyberg: Churchill's Salamander*, Century Hutchinson, Auckland

Barrett, John (1987), *We Were There: Australian Soldiers of World War II*, Viking, Melbourne

Barter, Margaret (1994), *Far Above Battle: The Experience and Memory of Australian Soldiers in War, 1939–1945*, Allen & Unwin, Sydney

Beevor, Antony (1991), *Crete: The Battle and the Resistance*, John Murray, London

Begg, Richard Campbell & Peter H Liddle (eds) (2000), *For Five Shillings a Day: Anzacs and Allies Fighting in the Second World War*, HarperCollins, London

Beilby, Richard (1977), *Gunner*, Angus & Robertson, London

Bellair, John (1984), *Amateur Soldier: An Australian Machine Gunner's Memories of World War II*, Spectrum Publications, Melbourne

Bennett, Ralph (1989), *Ultra and Mediterranean Strategy 1941–1945*, Hamish Hamilton, London

_____ (1996), *Intelligence Investigations: How Ultra Changed History*, Frank Cass, London

Bentley, Arthur (1984), *The Second Eighth: A History of the 2/8th Australian Infantry Battalion*, 2/8th Battalion Association, Melbourne

Bishop, Les (1998), *The Thunder of the Guns: A History of 2/3 Australian Field Regiment*, 2/3 Australian Field Regiment Association, Sydney

Bolger, WP & JG Littlewood (1983), *The Fiery Phoenix: The Story of the 2/7 Australian Infantry Battalion 1939–1946*, 2/7 Battalion Association, Melbourne

Bowden, Tim (2019), *Larrikins in Khaki: Tales of Irreverence and Courage from World War II Diggers*, Allen & Unwin, Sydney

Brugger, Suzanne (1980), *Australians and Egypt, 1914–1919*, Melbourne University Press, Melbourne

Brune, Peter (2000), *We Band of Brothers: A Biography of Ralph Honner, Soldier and Statesman*, Allen & Unwin, Sydney

Burdon, RM (1953), *24 Battalion*, in *Official History of New Zealand in the Second World War*, War History Branch, NZ Department of Internal Affairs, Wellington

Carlyon, Norman D (1980), *I Remember Blamey*, Macmillan, Melbourne

Carruthers, Bob (2013), *German Paratroops, 1939–45: The Fallschirmjäger*, Pen & Sword Aviation, Barnsley UK

Carstairs, James De Mole (2016), *Escape from Crete: War Diary 1941* (transl., Rosemary Tzanaki) (eds, Michael Sweet & Ian Frazer), Society of Cretan Historical Studies, Heraklion

Cassidy, Barrie (2014), *Private Bill in Love and War*, Melbourne University Press

Charlton, Peter (1981), *The Thirty-Niners*, Macmillan, Melbourne

Churchill, Winston S (1950), *The Grand Alliance*, Cassell, London

Clark, Alan (1962), *The Fall of Crete*, Anthony Blond, London

Clarke, Michael (1990), *My War, 1939–1945*, self-published, Melbourne

Clift, Ken (1972), *The Saga of a Sig: The Wartime Memories of Six Years Service in the Second AIF*, KCD Publications, Sydney

_____ (1980), *War Dance: A Story of the 2/3 Aust. Inf. Battalion A.I.F.*, PM Fowler & 2/3rd Battalion Association, Sydney

Clifton, Brigadier George (1952), *The Happy Hunted*, Cassell & Co, London

Coats, Peter (1976), *Of Generals and Gardens*, Weidenfeld & Nicolson, London

Cody, JF (1953), *21 Battalion*, in *Official History of New Zealand in the Second World War*, War History Branch, NZ Department of Internal Affairs, Wellington

_____ (1956), *28 (Maori) Battalion*, in *Official History of New Zealand in the Second World War*, War History Branch, NZ Department of Internal Affairs, Wellington

Collie, Craig (2017), *Code Breakers: Inside the Shadow World of Signals Intelligence in Australia's Two Bletchley Parks*, Allen & Unwin, Sydney

Connell, John (1964), *Wavell: Scholar and Soldier*, Collins, London

Comeau, MG (1961), *Operation Mercury: An Airman in the Battle of Crete*, Severn House, London

Cooper, Artemis (2012), *Patrick Leigh Fermor: An Adventure*, John Murray, London

Cox, Geoffrey (1987), *A Tale of Two Battles: A Personal Memoir of Crete and the Western Desert 1941*, William Kimber, London

Cremor, W (ed.) (1961), *Action Front: The History of the 2/2nd Australian Field Regiment, Royal Australian Artillery, A.I.F.*, 2nd/2nd Field Regiment Association, Melbourne

Crisp, Robert (1960), *The Gods Were Neutral*, WW Norton & Co, New York

Cruikshank, Charles (1976), *Greece 1940–1941*, Davis-Poynter, London

Cunningham, Viscount of Hyndhope (1951), *A Sailor's Odyssey*, Hutchinson, London

Damer, Sean & Ian Frazer (2006), *On the Run: Anzac Escape and Evasion in Enemy-occupied Crete*, Penguin Books, Auckland

Davie, Michael (ed.) (1976), *The Diaries of Evelyn Waugh*, Weidenfeld & Nicolson, London

Davin, DM (1953), *Crete*, in *Official History of New Zealand in the Second World War*, War History Branch, NZ Department of Internal Affairs, Wellington

Dawson, WD (1961), *18 Battalion and Armoured Regiment*, in *Official History of New Zealand in the Second World War*, War History Branch, NZ Department of Internal Affairs, Wellington

de Guingand, Major-General Sir Francis (1947), *Operation Victory*, Hodder & Stoughton, London

_____ (1964), *Generals at War*, Hodder & Stoughton, London

Dyer, HG (1953), *Ma Te Reinga (By Way of Reinga): The Way of the Maori Soldier*, Arthur H Stockwell Ltd, Ilfracombe, UK

Ebury, Sue (2009), *Weary: King of the River*, Miegunyah Press, Melbourne

Edwards, Geoffrey (1989), *The Road to Prevelly*, self-published, Perth

Elliott, Murray (1987), *Vasili: The Lion of Crete*, Century Hutchinson, Auckland

Ewer, Peter (2016), *Forgotten Anzacs: The Campaign in Greece, 1941*, Scribe, Melbourne

Farran, Roy (1948), *Winged Dagger: Adventures on Special Service*, Collins, London

Fergusson, Bernard (1950), *The Black Watch and the King's Enemies*, Collins, London

Fernside, GH & Ken Clift (1979), *Dougherty: A Great Man Among Men*, Alpha Books, Sydney

Fielding, Xan (1954), *Hide and Seek: The Story of a War-time Agent*, Secker & Warburg, London

Filer, David (2010), *Crete, Death from the Skies: New Zealand's Role in the Loss of Crete*, David Bateman, Auckland

Forty, George (2001), *Battle of Crete*, Ian Allan, Hersham UK

Freyberg, Paul (1991), *Bernard Freyberg, VC: Soldier of Two Nations*, Hodder & Stoughton, London

Gerster, Robin (1987), *Big-noting: The Heroic Theme in Australian War Writing*, Melbourne University Press, Melbourne

Gilbert, Martin (1983), *Finest Hour: Winston Churchill 1939–1941*, Heinemann, London

Givney, EC (ed.) (1987), *The First at War: The Story of the 2/1st Australian Infantry Battalion, 1939–45, The City of Sydney Regiment*, Association of First Infantry Battalions, Sydney

Gordon, Harry (1962), *The Embarrassing Australian: The Story of an Aboriginal Warrior*, Lansdowne Press, Melbourne

Grace, Patricia (2009), *Ned & Katina: A True Love Story*, Penguin Books, Auckland

Granquist, Charles (2010), *A Long Way Home: One POW's story of escape and evasion during World War II*, Big Sky Publishing, Sydney

Greacen, Lavinia (1989), *Chink: A Biography*, Papermac, London

Green, Olwyn (2010), *The Name's Still Charlie: A Biography of Lieutenant-Colonel Charles Green DSO*, Australian Military History Publications, Sydney

Griffiths-Marsh, Roland (1990), *The Sixpenny Soldier*, Angus & Robertson, Sydney

Gullett, Henry ('Jo') (1976), *Not as a Duty Only: An Infantryman's War*, Melbourne University Press, Melbourne

Hadjipateras, Costas N & Maria S Fafalios (1991), *Crete 1941: Eyewitnessed*, Random Century, Auckland

Hancock, Kenneth R (1946), *New Zealand at War*, AH & AW Reed, Wellington

Harper, Glyn (2003), 'Major General Howard Kippenberger: The Education of a Commander', in *Born to Lead?: Portraits of New Zealand Commanders* (Glyn Harper & Joel Hayward, eds), Exisle, Auckland

Harper, Glyn & Joel Hayward (eds) (2003), *Born to Lead?: Portraits of New Zealand Commanders*, Exisle, Auckland

Harper, Glyn & Colin Richardson (2010), *In the Face of the Enemy: The Complete History of the Victoria Cross and New Zealand*, HarperCollins, Sydney

Hay, David (1984), *Nothing Over Us: The Story of the 2/6th Australian Infantry Battalion*, Australian War Memorial, Canberra

Headley, Alex with Megan Hutching (2009), *Fernleaf Cairo*, HarperCollins, Auckland

Heckstall-Smith, Anthony & Vice-Admiral HT Baillie-Grohman (1961), *Greek Tragedy*, Anthony Blond, London

Henderson, Jim (1954), *RMT: Official History of the 4th and 6th Reserve Mechanical Transport Companies, 2 NZEF*, in *Official History of New Zealand in the Second World War*, War History Branch, NZ Department of Internal Affairs, Wellington

_____ (1958), *22 Battalion*, in *Official History of New Zealand in the Second World War*, War History Branch, NZ Department of Internal Affairs, Wellington

_____ (1978), *Soldier Country*, Millwood Press, Wellington

Hetherington, John (1944), *Air-Borne Invasion: The Story of the Battle of Crete*, Angus & Robinson, Sydney

_____ (1944a), *The Australian Soldier: A Portrait*, FH Johnston, Sydney

_____ (1954), *Blamey: A Biography of Field Marshal Sir Thomas Blamey*, FW Cheshire, Melbourne

Higham, Robin (1986), *Diary of a Disaster: British Aid to Greece, 1940–1941*, University Press of Kentucky, Lexington KY

Hill, Maria (2010), *Diggers and Greeks: The Australian Campaigns in Greece and Crete*, UNSW Press, Sydney

Hocking, Philip (1997), *The Long Carry: A History of the 2/1 Australian Machine Gun Battalion 1939–46*, 2/1 Machine Gun Battalion Association, Melbourne

Hodgkinson, Lieutenant-Commander Hugh (1944), *Before the Tide Turned: The Mediterranean Experiences of a British Destroyer Officer in 1941*, George G Harrap, London

Hollingworth, Clare (1942), *There's a German Just Behind Me*, Secker & Warburg, London

Holt, Bob 'Hooker' (1981), *From Ingleburn to Aitape: The Trials and Tribulations of a Four Figure Man*, self-published, Sydney

Horner, David (1982), *High Command: Australia and Allied Strategy, 1939–1945*, Allen & Unwin, London

_____ (1992), *General Vasey's War*, Melbourne University Press, Melbourne

Household, Geoffrey (1958), *Against the Wind*, Michael Joseph, London

Howell, Edward (1981), *Escape to Live*, Grosvenor Books, London

Hunt, Sir David (1966), *A Don at War*, William Kimber, London

Hutching, Megan (ed.) (2001), *A Unique Sort of Battle: New Zealanders Remember Crete*, HarperCollins, Auckland

Iatrides, John O (ed.) (1981), *Greece in the 1940s: A Nation in Crisis*, University Press of New England, Hanover NH

Idriess, Ion L (1945), *Horrie the Wog Dog: With the AIF in Egypt, Greece, Crete and Palestine*, Angus & Robertson, Sydney

Jager, Charles (2004), *Escape from Crete*, Floradale Productions & Sly Ink, Sydney

James, Robert Rhodes (1986), *Anthony Eden*, Weidenfeld & Nicolson, London

Johnson, KT (ed.) (2000), *The History of the 2/11th (City of Perth) Australian Infantry Battalion 1939–45*, John Burridge Military Antiques, Perth

Johnston, Mark (1996), *At the Front Line: Experiences of Australian Soldiers in World War II*, Cambridge University Press, Melbourne

_____ (2013), *Anzacs in the Middle East: Australian Soldiers, Their Allies and the Local People in World War II*, Cambridge University Press, Melbourne

Johnstone, Norman M (2003), *'Dearest Geraldine': Letters from a Soldier*, self-published, Sydney

Kane, Pat (1995), *A Soldier's Story: A Mediterranean Odyssey*, Quality Publications, Wellington

Kay, Robin (1958), *27 (Machine Gun) Battalion*, in *Official History of New Zealand in the Second World War*, War History Branch, NZ Department of Internal Affairs, Wellington

Keegan, John (ed.) (1991), *Churchill's Generals*, Warner Books, London

Keegan, John (2003), *Intelligence in War: Knowledge of the Enemy from Napoleon to Al-Qaeda*, Hutchinson, London

Kershaw, Ian (2007), *Fateful Choices: Ten Decisions that Changed the World, 1940–1941*, Allen Lane, London

King, Michael (1981), *New Zealanders at War*, Heinemann, Auckland

Kippenberger, Major-General Sir Howard (1949), *Infantry Brigadier*, Oxford University Press, London

Kiriakopoulos, GC (1985), *Ten Days to Destiny: The Battle for Crete, 1941*, Franklin Watts, New York

_____ (1995), *The Nazi Occupation of Crete, 1941–1945*, Praegar, Westport CT

Kohere, Reweti T (1949), *The Story of a Maori Chief: Mokena Kohere and his Forbears*, AH & AW Reed, Wellington

Laffin, John (1989), *Greece, Crete and Syria*, Time-Life Books, Sydney

Le Souef, Leslie (1980), *To War Without a Gun*, Artlook, Perth

Lee, Air Vice-Marshal Arthur S Gould (1946), *Special Duties: Reminiscences of a Royal Air Force Officer in the Balkans, Turkey and the Middle East*, Sampson Low, Marston & Co, London

Lehmann, Rudolph (1987), *The Leibstandarte* (transl., Nick Olcott), JJ Fedorowicz Publishing, Winnipeg, Canada

Levine, Alan J (2000), *Captivity, Flight, and Survival in World War II*, Praegar, Westport CT

Lewin, Ronald (1978), *Ultra Goes to War: The Secret Story*, Hutchinson, London
_____ (1980), *The Chief: Field Marshal Lord Wavell, Commander-in-Chief and Viceroy, 1939–1947*, Hutchinson, London
Lind, Lew (1991), *Flowers of Rethymnon: Escape from Crete*, Kangaroo Press, Sydney
Long, Gavin (1953), *Greece, Crete and Syria*, Australian War Memorial, Canberra
MacDonald, Callum (1993), *The Lost Battle: Crete 1941*, Macmillan, London
Mackenzie, William (2000), *The Secret History of S.O.E.: The Special Operations Executive 1940–1945*, St Ermin's Press, London
Marshall, Capt. AJ (ed.) (1946), *Nulli Secundus Log*, The 2/2nd Australian Infantry Battalion, AIF, Sydney
Martin, AW & Patsy Hardy (eds) (1993), *Dark and Hurrying Days: Menzies 1941 Diary*, National Library of Australia, Canberra
Mazower, Mark (1993), *Inside Hitler's Greece: The Experience of Occupation, 1941–44*, Yale University Press, New Haven CT
McClymont, WG (1959), *To Greece*, in *Official History of New Zealand in the Second World War*, War History Branch, NZ Department of Internal Affairs, Wellington
McConnell, Lynn (2006), *Galatas 1941: Courage in Vain*, Reed Publishing, Auckland
McDonald, Neil & Peter Brune (2016), *Valiant for Truth: The Life of Chester Wilmot, War Correspondent*, NewSouth, Sydney
McElwain, Roger (2003), 'Commanding Officers of the Infantry Battalions of 2nd New Zealand Division', in *Born to Lead?: Portraits of New Zealand Commanders* (Glyn Harper & Joel Hayward, eds), Exisle, Auckland
McGibbon, Ian (ed.) (2000), *The Oxford Companion to New Zealand Military History*, Oxford University Press, Auckland
McLean, Denis (2008), *Howard Kippenberger: Dauntless Spirit*, Random House, Auckland
McLean, Gavin & Ian McGibbon with Kynan Gentry (eds) (2009), *The Penguin Book of New Zealanders at War*, Penguin Books, Auckland
McLeod, John (1986), *Myth and Reality: The New Zealand Soldier in World War II*, Heinemann Reid, Auckland
Mentiplay, Cedric (1979), *A Fighting Quality: New Zealanders at War*, AH & AW Reed, Wellington
Messenger, Charles, George Young & Stephen Rose (1988), *The Middle East Commandos*, William Kimber, Wellingborough UK
Monteath, Peter (2019), *Battle on 42nd Street: War in Crete and the Anzacs' Bloody Last Stand*, NewSouth, Sydney
Mott-Radclyffe, Charles (1975), *Foreign Body in the Eye: Memoir of the Foreign Service Old and New*, Leo Cooper, London
Mourellos, Giannēs (1946), *The Battle of Crete (Hē machtē tēs Krētēs)*, Mourmel, Heraklion
Murphy, WE (1966), *2nd New Zealand Divisional Artillery*, in *Official History of New Zealand in the Second World War*, Historical Publications Branch, NZ Department of Internal Affairs, Wellington
Murray, Williamson & Allan R Millett (2000), *A War to be Won: Fighting the Second World War*, Belknap Press of Harvard University Press, Cambridge MA
Norton, Frazer D (1952), *26 Battalion*, in *Official History of New Zealand in the Second World War*, War History Branch, NZ Department of Internal Affairs, Wellington
Ohler, Norman (2016), *Blitzed: Drugs in Nazi Germany* (transl., Shaun Whiteside), Allen Lane, London

Olson, Wes (2011), *Battalion into Battle: The History of the 2/11th Australian Infantry Battalion 1939–1945*, self-published, Perth

Palazzo, Albert (2011), *Battle of Crete*, Army History Unit, Canberra

Palenski, Ron (2013), *Men of Valour: New Zealand and the Battle of Crete*, Hodder Moa, Auckland

Papagos, General Alexander (1949), *The Battle of Greece 1940–1941* (transl., Pat Eliascos), JM Scazikis 'Alpha' Editions, Athens

Papayiannakis, Eleftherios (1998), *Crete—The Great Night: June 1941 – May 1945*, Pitsilos, Athens

Playfair, ISO et al (1954), *History of the Second World War: The Mediterranean and Middle East*, Volume 1, 'The Early Successes Against Italy (to May 1941)', HM Stationery Office, London

_____ (1956), *History of the Second World War: The Mediterranean and Middle East*, Volume 2, 'The Germans Come to the Aid of their Ally, 1941', HM Stationery Office, London

Plowman, Jeffrey (2018), *Greece 1941: The Death Throes of Blitzkrieg*, Pen & Sword Military, Barnsley UK

Pratten, Garth (2009), *Australian Battalion Commanders in the Second World War*, Cambridge University Press, Melbourne

Pringle, DJC & WA Glue (1957), *20 Battalion and Armoured Regiment,* in *Official History of New Zealand in the Second World War*, War History Branch, NZ Department of Internal Affairs, Wellington

Propagandakompanie (ed.) (1942), *From Serbia to Crete: Memoirs of an Army's Campaign in the Great German War of Independence* (*Von Serbien bis Kreta: Erinnerungen vom Feldzug einer Armee im grossen deutschen Freiheitskrieg*), (transl., War History Branch, NZ Department of Internal Affairs, Wellington)

Puttick, Sir Edward (1960), *25 Battalion,* in *Official History of New Zealand in the Second World War*, War History Branch, NZ Department of Internal Affairs, Wellington

Raggett, Sidney George (1991), *All About Sid: The Story of a Gunner in World War II*, self-published, Melbourne

Reid, FJM (1999), *Recollections of Greece, March–April 1941: 1939–1946 2/3 Infantry Battalion A.I.F.*, self-published, Sydney

Reid, Miles (1974), *Last on the List*, New English Library, London

Reid, Richard (2011), *Greece and Crete*, Department of Veterans' Affairs, Canberra

Robinson, Charles (1991), *Journey to Captivity*, Australian War Memorial, Canberra

Robson, LL (1988), 'The Australian Soldier: Formation of a Stereotype' in *Australia: Two Centuries of War & Peace* (M McKernan & M Browne, eds), Australian War Memorial, Canberra

Ross, Angus (1959), *23 Battalion,* in *Official History of New Zealand in the Second World War*, War History Branch, NZ Department of Internal Affairs, Wellington

Rothwell, Victor (1992), *Anthony Eden: A Political Biography 1931–57*, Manchester University Press, New York

Rowell, SF (1974), *Full Circle*, Melbourne University Press, Melbourne

Russell, WB (1959), *There Goes a Man: The Biography of Sir Stanley G Savige*, Longmans, Melbourne

Ryan, Sister M Imelda (1990), *PoWs Fraternal: Diaries of S/Sgt Raymond Ryan; Poems of Pte Lawrence (Bouff) Ryan*, Hawthorn Press, Perth

Sabey, Ian (1947), *Stalag Scrap Book*, FW Cheshire, Melbourne

Sandford, Kenneth (1962), *Mark of the Lion: The Story of Capt. Charles Upham, V.C. and Bar*, Hutchinson, London

Scott, Tom (2020) *Searching for Charlie: In pursuit of the real Charles Upham VC & Bar*, Upstart Press, Auckland

Sebag-Montefiore, Hugh (2000), *Enigma: The Battle for the Code*, John Wiley, London

Selby, CH ('Tom') (1985), *Dr NX 22: Memoirs of an Australian Doctor in Peace and War*, self-published, Melbourne

Semmler, Clement (ed.) (1985), *The War Diaries of Kenneth Slessor*, University of Queensland Press, Brisbane

Shulman, Milton (1986), *Defeat in the West*, Secker & Warburg, London

Simpson, Tony (1981), *Operation Mercury: The Battle for Crete, 1941*, Hodder & Stoughton, London

Sinclair, DW (1954), *19 Battalion and Armoured Regiment*, in *Official History of New Zealand in the Second World War*, War History Branch, NZ Department of Internal Affairs, Wellington

Singleton-Gates, Peter (1963), *General Lord Freyberg VC: An Unofficial Biography*, Michael Joseph, London

Smith, Adele Shelton (ed.) (1944), *The Boys Write Home*, Consolidated Press, Sydney

Smith, Paul (1995), *New Zealand at War*, Hodder Moa Beckett, Auckland

Soutar, Monty (2008), *Nga Tama Toa (The Price of Citizenship): C Company 28 (Maori) Battalion 1939–1945*, David Bateman, Auckland

Speed, Brigadier FW (ed.) (1988), *Esprit de Corps: The history of the Victorian Scottish Regiment and the 5th Infantry Battalion*, Allen & Unwin, Sydney

Spencer, John Hall (1963), *Battle for Crete*, White Lion, London

Stephanides, Theodore (1946), *Climax in Crete*, Faber & Faber, London

Stevens, Major-General WG (1965), *Freyberg V.C.: The Man 1939–1945*, AH & AW Reed, Wellington

Stewart, I McD G (1966), *The Struggle for Crete, 20 May – 1 June 1941: A Story of Lost Opportunity*, Oxford University Press, London

Stuart, Lurline & Josie Arnold (eds) (1987), *Letters Home 1939–1945*, William Collins, Sydney

Taaffe, Brian (2006), *The Gatekeepers of Galatas: The Untold Story*, Sabicas, Melbourne

Terzakis, Angelos (1990), *The Greek Epic, 1940–1941* (transl., David Connolly), Greek Army Press, Athens

Thomas, David A (1972), *Crete 1941: The Battle at Sea*, Andre Deutsch, London

Thomas, WB (1951), *Dare to be Free*, Allan Wingate, London

Thompson, Peter (2010), *Anzac Fury: The Bloody Battle of Crete 1941*, Heinemann, Sydney

Tonkin-Covell, John (2003), 'Lieutenant General Bernard Freyberg: A Necessary Commander?' in *Born to Lead?: Portraits of New Zealand Commanders* (Glyn Harper & Joel Hayward, eds), Exisle, Auckland

Trevor-Roper, HR (ed.) (1965), *Blitzkrieg to Defeat: Hitler's War Directives 1939–1945*, Holt, Rinehart & Winston, New York

Trigellis-Smith, S (1988), *All the King's Enemies: A History of the 2/5th Australian Infantry Battalion*, 2/5 Battalion Association, Melbourne

Turton, EB (1945), *I Lived with Greek Guerrillas*, The Book Depot, Melbourne

Tyquin, Michael (2014), *Greece: February to April 1941*, Army History Unit, Canberra

Tzobanakis, Stella (2010), *Creforce: The Anzacs and the Battle of Crete*, Black Dog, Melbourne

Unit History Editorial Committee (1963), *White Over Green*, Angus & Robertson, Sydney for 2/4th Australian Infantry Battalion Association

Uren, Malcolm (1959), *A Thousand Men at War: The Story of the 2/16th Battalion, AIF*, Heinemann, Melbourne

Uren, Martyn (1944), *Kiwi Saga: Memoirs of a New Zealand Artilleryman*, Collins Bros, Sydney

Vial, RR (1995), *The War I Went To*, self-published, Melbourne

von der Heydte, Baron (1958), *Daedalus Returned: Crete 1941* (transl., W Stanley Moss), Hutchinson, London

Wahlert, Glenn (1999), *The Other Enemy?: Australian Soldiers and the Military Police*, Oxford University Press, Melbourne

Wake, Sir Hereward & WE Deedes (eds) (1949), *Swift and Bold: The Story of the King's Royal Rifles in the Second World War 1939–1945*, Gale & Polden, London

Waugh, Evelyn (1955), *Officers and Gentlemen*, Penguin, London

Wick, Stan (1977), *Purple Over Green: The History of the 2/2 Australian Infantry Battalion 1939–1945*, 2/2 Australian Infantry Association, Sydney

Williams, Tony (ed.) (2000), *Anzacs: Stories from New Zealanders at War*, Hodder Moa Beckett, Auckland

Wilson of Libya, Field-Marshal Lord (1950), *Eight Years Overseas, 1939–1947*, Hutchinson & Co, London

Winter, Peter (1989), *Expendable: The Crete campaign, a front-line view*, Moana Press, Tauranga NZ

_____ (1993), *Free Lodgings: The true story of a Kiwi soldier's amazing bid for freedom*, Reed, Auckland

Winton, John (1998), *Cunningham*, J Murray, London

Woollams, Fred (1945), *Corinth and All That*, AH & AW Reed, Wellington

Wright, Matthew (2005), *Freyberg's War: The Man, the Legend and Reality*, Penguin Books, Auckland

Wright, Matthew (ed.) (2010), *Behind Enemy Lines: Kiwi Freedom Fighters in WWII*, Random House, Auckland

PAPERS, ARTICLES, LETTERS, WEBFILES, etc

4th Hussars unit diary, '4th Hussars in Greece' in *The Queen's Royal Hussars Museum* website, www.facebook.com/permalink.php?id=1087446214620464&story_fbid= 4129099597121762

Admiralty (1960), 'Naval Operations in the Battle of Crete, 20th May–1st June 1941 (Battle Summary No. 4)', in *Naval Staff History: Second World War*, Historical Section, Admiralty, London

Age (2004), Obituary of Arnold Gourevitch, *The Age*, 14 April 2004

Aly, Amira Elhamy (2018), '"Number 10" The secret number of the British troops in Egypt!', *Middle East Observer*, Cairo, 1 May 2018, meobserver.org/?p=16217

Ammentorp, Steen (ed.), *Generals.dk* website, www.generals.dk

Auckland Museum, 'Online Cenotaph' in 'War Memorial/Paenga Hira', *Auckland Museum* website, www.aucklandmuseum.com/war-memorial/online-cenotaph/search

Bathurst, Mark (2005), 'Operation Mercury: The Battle of Crete', *New Zealand Geographic*, 73, May/June 2005, nzgeo.com/stories/crete

Boland, Pat (1979), 'Following in the steps of the 2/7th Battalion in Greece', *Despatch* XV, No 4, pp 76–81, NSW Military Historical Society, Sydney

Bracegirdle, Warwick (1990), 'A Visit to Piraeus, Greece 1941', *Naval Historical Review*, June 1990, Naval Historical Society of Australia, Sydney, www.navyhistory.org.au/a-visit-to-piraeus-greece-1941

Bridgeman-Sutton, David (2007), 'The Birthday Present', in *Pipeline Press*, Waikanae, NZ, www.pipelinepress.com/the-birthday-present

Brotherhood of Veterans of the Greek Campaign 1940–1941, *Greek Veterans* website, ww2greekveterans.com

Brown, Martyn (2015), 'After Crete—Consistency and Contradiction in the Use of the New Zealand Military in Greek Matters', www.academia.edu/13065450/

Burns, Tom (1944), 'Calamity Bay', in *Penguin New Writing*, No 19, pp 9–21

Chrysopoulos, Philip (2022), 'Crete Remembers the Razing of Kandanos by the Nazis', *Greek Reporter*, 3 June 2022, www.greekreporter.com/2022/06/03/crete-remembers-the-razing-of-kandanos-by-the-nazis-on-june-3-1941

Cleveland, Les (1984), 'Soldiers' Songs: The Folklore of the Powerless', *New York Folklore* 11, p 79 (1985) www.faculty.buffalostate.edu/fishlm/folksongs/les01

Clever Digit Media, 'Unit History: King's Royal Rifle Corps' in *Forces War Records*, Clever Digit Media Ltd, UK, www.forces-war-records.co.uk/units/1508/kings-royal-rifle-corps

Cosgrove, Patrick (1992), 'Obituary: Sir Charles Mott-Radclyffe', *The Independent*, London, 8 December 1992

Danchev, Alex (1991), 'The Strange Case of Field Marshal Sir John Dill', *Medical History*, 35, pp 353–7

Davidson, IA (2004), 'The evacuation of the Heraklion Garrison from Crete, 28–29 May 1941', *Journal of the Society for Army Historical Research* 82, 331 (Autumn 2004) pp 210–26

Department of Veterans' Affairs, DVA's Nominal Rolls, Department of Veterans' Affairs, Australia, nominal-rolls.dva.gov.au

Diamond, Jon (2018), 'Sir John Dill and Winston Churchill: A Clash in Strategy', *Warfare History Network*, www.warfarehistorynetwork.com/2018/12/09/sir-john-dill-and-winston-churchill-a-clash-in-strategy

Dorney, Sean & Stuart Dorney, 'John Joseph Kiernan Dorney' in *The Dorney Family History*, pp 49–51, www.dorneyfamilyhistory.net/famtree_web/History_dorney

Dyer, Humphrey (2011), 'Dyer's account of bayonet charge at 42nd Street', 28th Maori Battalion website, www.28maoribattalion.org.nz/node/7033

Edwards, Geoff (1979), 'The Geoff Edwards Story in World War 2 in Greece and Crete', Explore Crete website, www.explorecrete.com/preveli/story

Fontaine, Joëlle (2017), 'How Churchill broke the Greek resistance' *Jacobin*, www.jacobinmag.com/2017/05/greece-world-war-two-winston-churchill-communism

Ford, Peter J (2015), *One Man's Battle*, self-published monograph

Frazer, Ian (2016), 'Crete's Secret Lifeline', in *Neos Kosmos*, www.neoskosmos.com/en/36263/cretes-secret-lifeline

Gerolymou, Dina (2020), 'Like the 300 Spartans, "David's 30" Anzacs fought until they were "smashed to pieces"', on website, *SBS Greek*, www.sbs.com.au/language/english/like-the-300-spartans-david-s-30-anzacs-fought-until-they-were-smashed-into-pieces?fbclid=IwAR3XZUR3Rzr9ZN1ep15-XinRR3oHivylpcHu0_PCxPckdzzZSXsJTYnB1LA

Goldstone, Paul (2000), 'Inglis, Lindsay Merritt' in *Dictionary of New Zealand Biography*, *Te Ara* website, teara.govt.nz/en/biographies/4m22/inglis-lindsay-merritt

Hanable, William S (1998), 'Case Studies in the Use of Land-based Aerial Forces in Maritime Operations, 1939–1990', Air Force History & Museums Program, Washington DC, www.media.defense.gov/2013/Sep/16/2001329865/-1/-1/0/AFD-130916-005

Hill, Maria (2008), 'The Australians in Greece and Crete: a study of an intimate wartime relationship, thesis submitted to the Australian Defence Force Academy, University of New South Wales, Canberra, for degree of Doctor of Philosophy in History

Howie-Willis, Ian (2019), 'The Australian Army's Two "Traditional" Diseases: Gonorrhea and Syphilis—A Military-Medical History During the Twentieth Century', *Journal of Military and Veterans' Health* 27, 1 (January 2019), pp 11–22

Hutching, Megan & Ian McGibbon (2011), 'The North African Campaign' (revised by Gareth Phipps), in *New Zealand History*, NZ Ministry for Culture & Heritage, www.nzhistory.govt.nz/war/the-north-african-campaign

_____ (2020), 'The Battle for Crete' (revised by Gareth Phipps), in *New Zealand History*, NZ Ministry for Culture & Heritage, Wellington, www.nzhistory.govt.nz/war/the-battle-for-crete

Hutching, Megan & Rob Rabel (2014), 'The Italian Campaign' (revised by Matthew Tonks) in *New Zealand History*, NZ Ministry for Culture & Heritage, www.nzhistory.govt.nz/war/the-italian-campaign

Kindell, Don, 'Shorter Convoy Series: Arnold Hague Convoy Database' in *Convoy Web*, www.convoyweb.org.uk/index

King, Josh (2019), 'Half a World Away: New Zealanders in the Middle East during the Second World War', thesis submitted to Victoria University of Wellington for degree of Master of Arts in History

_____ (2020), '"Certainly Getting About the World": New Zealanders' Experience of the Middle East as a Place During the Second World War', *Journal of New Zealand Studies* NS30 (2020), 116–13, doi.org/10.26686/jnzs.v0iNS30.65019

Koenig, Marlene Eilers (2020), 'Joyce Brittain-Jones—a King's companion', in Royal Musings, royalmusingsblogspotcom.blogspot.com/2008/08/joyce-brittain-jones-kings-companion

Kosmidis, Pierre, '"Fix bayonets!"—11 am, Tuesday 27 May, 1941: The ANZACs' charge at "42nd Street"' in WW2 Wrecks.com, www.ww2wrecks.com/portfolio/fix-bayonets-11-am-tuesday-27-may-1941-the-anzacs-charge-at-42nd-street

_____ 'April 1941: Operation Marita and the Greek "Maginot Line" that cost the Germans dearly', in WW2 Wrecks.com, www.ww2wrecks.com/portfolio/April-1941-operation-marita-and-the-greek-maginot-line-that-cost-the-nazi-germans-dearly

Lafazani, Olga, 'Piraeus' in *Grassroots Economics*, University of Barcelona, www.ub.edu/grassrootseconomics/?page-id=24

Lenihan, Denis (2016), 'The Battle of Crete 1941: The Poverty of Ultra', *Academia*, www.academia.edu/22144185/The_Battle_of_Crete_1941_The_Poverty_of_Ultra

_____ (2017), 'The Fog of Waugh: The Evacuation from Sphakia, Crete, May 1941', *Academia*, www.academia.edu/35401967/The_Fog_of_Waugh_The_Evacuation_from_Sphakia_Crete_May_1941

Liddell Hart, Basil (2015), North Africa campaigns: World War II, in *Britannica*, www.britannica.com/event/North-Africa-campaigns/Montgomery-in-the-desert

Lind, Lewis J (1971), 'The Land and Sea Battle for Crete, 1941', Naval Historical Society of Australia, Sydney

Macartney, Lieut. Roy (1941), 'An Epic of the Escape from Crete', *The Argus*, Melbourne, 9 August 1941, *Weekend Magazine*, p 3

Markowitz, Mike (2015), 'The DFS 230 Assault Glider', *Defense Media Network*, Faircount Media Group, Tampa FL, defensemedianetwork.com/stories/classics-dfs-230-assault-glider

McIntyre, W David (1998), 'Macky, Neil Lloyd' in *Dictionary of New Zealand Biography*, *Te Ara* website, teara.govt.nz/en/biographies/4m22/macky-neil-lloyd

McRobbie, Arthur (1941), 'A Young Lieutenant's Song of the Greek Campaign', *Western Mail*, Perth, 24 July 1941, p 19

_____(1941a), 'Adventure in Greece', *Western Mail*, Perth, 31 July 1941, p 26

Mnkande, Stephen (2011), *The Crete Campaign*, academia.edu/6011097/The_Crete_Campaign_by_Stephen_Mnkande

Monteath, Peter (2018), 'SOE in Crete: an alternative model of "special operations"?', *Intelligence and National Security*, 33, 6, pp 839–53

_____ (2019), 'Australians in Crete in World War II', *Modern Greek Studies Australia and New Zealand*, special issue (2019) pp 143–62, www.researchnow-admin.flinders.edu.au/ws/portalfiles/portal/15712017/Monteath_Australians_P2019

Murphy, WE (1953), 'Escape of the King of Greece', Appendix II in *Crete* by DM Davin, War History Branch, NZ Department of Internal Affairs, Wellington

New Zealand Herald (2012), 'Remaining 39er shows wounds', *NZ Herald*, Auckland

'Njaco' (2014), 'This Day in the War in Europe: The Beginning', in *WW2AIRCRAFT.NET*, www.ww2aircraft.net/forum/threads/this-day-in-the-war-in-europe-the-beginning.41546/page-84

'One of the boys' (1940), *A Digger's Diary: Ramblings in Egypt with the First Echelon*, Organ Bros, Wellington

Orton, Alan & Mike Beckett (2013), 'Jiggered about Beyond Belief: Layforce 1941', in *Commando Veterans Archive*, www.commandoveterans.org/files/Layforce

Papathanasiou, Iris (2020), 'The adventures of a nine-year-old boy in the battle of Crete', in *Neos Kosmos*, neoskosmos.com/en/165824/the-adventures-of-a-nine-year-old-boy-in-the-battle-of-crete

Paxton-Love, Maggie (2017), *Alf Carpenter: Second to None*, on website *Paxton Love*, www.paxton-love.com/wp-content/uploads/2021/04/ALF-CARPENTER-BIO-Ch-1-to-7-FOR-COMMENT

Richter, Heinz (2013), 'Operation Mercury, the Invasion of Crete', *Journal of New Zealand Studies*, NS16, pp 147–55

Rudd, Bill (2016), 'Other European "Free Men": Crete', in *Anzac POW Freemen in Europe*, www.aifpow.com/Part-5-Other-European-Free-Men/chapter_5_crete

Russell, Duncan (1982), 'Evacuation of Crete, May–June 1941', *Sabretache*, XXIII, Oct/Dec 1982, pp 8–17; Military Historical Society of Australia

Simos, Andriana (2021), '"The Anzacs had great respect for Greece": Nick Andriotakis details the enduring friendship', *The Greek Herald*, Sydney, 20 April 2021, www.greekherald.com.au/culture/history/anzacs-had-great-respect-greece-nick-andriotakis-details-enduring-relationship

Soutar, Dr Monty (2011), 'Sinking of the Hellas—an Anzac story', in *28th Māori Battalion*, 28maoribattalion.org.nz/photo/sinking-hellas-anzac-story

Sweet, Michael (2015), 'Discovering the real warpaths', *Neos Kosmos*, Melbourne, 31 January 2015

SX1543 (Dudley Coleman) (1941), 'Dasher' in *Active Service with Australia in the Middle East*, Australian War Memorial, Canberra

Vial, Brigadier RR (1985), 'A Month in Greece', *Journal of RUSI Australia*, 8, 1, December 1985, pp 48–60

Ward AL (2014), '"Operation Demon" HMS Hero', in *WW2 People's War*, BBC History, www.bbc.co.uk/history/ww2peopleswar/stories/39/a7379139.shtml

Wavell, Field Marshal Earl (1950), 'The British expedition to Greece 1941', *Army Quarterly*, 59, January 1950, pp 178–85

Woodhouse, Monty (1967), 'I. McD. G. Stewart, The Struggle for Crete: A Story of Lost Opportunity', *Balkan Studies*, 8, 2, pp 471–4, www.ojs.lib.uom.gr/index.php/BalkanStudies/article/view/1136/1155

_____ (1985), 'The Aliakmon line: an Anglo-Greek misunderstanding in 1941', *Balkan Studies*, 26, 1, pp 159–93, www.ojs.lib.uom.gr/index.php/BalkanStudies/article/view/1948

Xanthaki, Vassa Solomou (1976), 'The Tomb' (transl., Prof Byron Raizis & Stella Alexopoulou), photocopied draft extract supplied

Yiannikopoulos, George (2017), *The Greek Forces in the Battle of Crete, May 1941*, www.academia.edu/9523561/The_Greek_Forces_in_the_Battle_of_Crete_May_1941

PERSONAL COMMUNICATIONS

Blouchou, Eleni
Blouchou, Vassiliki
Cook, Les (2/8th Battalion AIF)
Mamalakis, Constantinos
Minas, Fiona
Spyrakis, Yianni 'John'

PHOTOS AND SOURCES

Page	Short Description	Source
1	Docks	AWM 6811
	Convoy	AWM 6779
2	Athens crowds	NLNZ (ATL) DA14134
	Bren carrier	AWM 6841
	Cafe	AWM 8809
3	Italian PoWs	NZETC 24 Bn
	Troop train	NLNZ (ATL) DA8170
	Road gang	AWM 8179
4	Explosion	AWM 134865
	Village traffic	AWM 7825
5	Snowline	AWM P2162.004
	Mountain road	AWM 7630
6	Boy with goat	AWM 7752
	Boys with suitcase	AWM 7793
	Climbing rock track	AWM 7779
7	Children	AWM 7615
	Greeks & donkeys	AWM 7615
	Biscuits	AWM 8180
8	Aliakmon ferry	AWM 7848
	NZers climb track	NZETC 26 Bn
9	German tank	Bundesarchiv
	Convoy	IWM
	Surrender	Bundesarchiv Bild 1011-164-0373-19A
10	Crowded truck	IWM E 2733
	Nurses	AWM 87663
	Camouflage	NLNZ (ATL)

11	Suda disembark	IWM E 2760
	Boil billy	AWM P2053.009
	Suda Bay burns	AWM 7845
12	Two-up	AWM 69830
	Freyberg/Hargest/Andrew	NLNZ (ATL) DA13918
	Paratroops	AWM P433.009
13	Mountain troops boarding	Captured photo
	Maleme airfield	IWM
	Regimental Aid Post	IWM E3435E
14	Well	NLNZ (ATL) DA8185
	Partisans	IWM HU66036
	Awaiting evacuation	NLNZ (ATL) DA10739
	Creforce HQ cave	IWM E 3023E
15	Hulme	Public domain; published Oct 41
	Upham	Wikipedia
	Hinton	NLNZ (ATL) PAColl-5547-008
	Destroyer	ATL DA 10655
	Alexandria wounded	NLNZ (ATL) DA1618
16	PoWs from Sphakia	NLNZ (ATL) DA12646
	Saunders	Public domain
	Jager/Travers	Copyright owner (if any) untraceable
	Execution	Bundesarchiv Bilt 1011-166-0512-39

| Cover | New Zealand troops in the transit area between Canea and Galatos, Crete, upon their arrival from mainland Greece. (Recoloured) | New Zealand Department of Internal Affairs, War History Branch: Photographs relating to World War 1914–1918, World War 1939–1945, occupation of Japan, Korean War, and Malayan Emergency. Ref: DA-01110-F. Alexander Turnbull Library, Wellington, New Zealand. /records/22437209 |

AWM – Australian War Memorial
IWM – Imperial War Museum
NLNZ – National Library of New Zealand
ATL – Alexander Turnbull Library (part of NLNZ, probably all NLNZ are in ATL)

INDEX